Economic Inequality, Neoliberalism, and the
American Community College

Patrick Sullivan

Economic Inequality, Neoliberalism, and the American Community College

Patrick Sullivan
Manchester Community College
Manchester, Connecticut, USA

ISBN 978-3-319-83029-2   ISBN 978-3-319-44284-6   (eBook)
DOI 10.1007/978-3-319-44284-6

© The Editor(s) (if applicable) and The Author(s) 2017
Softcover reprint of the hardcover 1st edition 2017
This work is subject to copyright. All rights are solely and exclusively licensed by the Publisher, whether the whole or part of the material is concerned, specifically the rights of translation, reprinting, reuse of illustrations, recitation, broadcasting, reproduction on microfilms or in any other physical way, and transmission or information storage and retrieval, electronic adaptation, computer software, or by similar or dissimilar methodology now known or hereafter developed.
The use of general descriptive names, registered names, trademarks, service marks, etc. in this publication does not imply, even in the absence of a specific statement, that such names are exempt from the relevant protective laws and regulations and therefore free for general use.
The publisher, the authors and the editors are safe to assume that the advice and information in this book are believed to be true and accurate at the date of publication. Neither the publisher nor the authors or the editors give a warranty, express or implied, with respect to the material contained herein or for any errors or omissions that may have been made. The publisher remains neutral with regard to jurisdictional claims in published maps and institutional affiliations.

Cover image © Design Pics Inc / Alamy Stock Photo
Cover design by Henry Petrides

Printed on acid-free paper

This Palgrave Macmillan imprint is published by Springer Nature
The registered company is Springer International Publishing AG
The registered company address is: Gewerbestrasse 11, 6330 Cham, Switzerland

Permissions

Chapter 29 of this book appeared in a somewhat different form as "Measuring 'Success' at Open Admissions Institutions: Thinking Carefully About This Complex Question." *College English* 70.6 (2008): 618–32. Copyright 2008 by the National Council of Teachers of English. Used with permission.

Portions of Chap. 19 and the Conclusion originally appeared in a somewhat different form as "The Two-Year College Teacher-Scholar-Activist." *Teaching English in the Two-Year College* 42.4 (2015): 227–43. Copyright 2015 by the National Council of Teachers of English. Used with permission.

Chapter 25 originally appeared in a slightly different form as "'Ideas about Human Possibilities': Connecticut's PA 12-40 and Basic Writing in the Era of Neoliberalism." *Journal of Basic Writing* Spring 2015. Copyright 2015. Used with permission.

ma già volgeva il mio disio e 'l velle
sì come rota ch'igualmente è mossa,
l'amor che move il sole e l'altre stelle.

but my desire and will were moved already—
like a wheel revolving uniformly—by
the Love that moves the sun and the other stars.

—Dante, *Paradiso* 33.143–45

*****

*To
Susan,
Bonnie Rose,
Nicholas,
and Marigold Hope*

—*my sun and stars*

American colleges and universities must envision a much larger role for higher education in the national life. They can no longer consider themselves merely the instrument for producing an intellectual elite; they must become the means by which every citizen, youth, and adult is enabled and encouraged to carry his education, formal and informal, as far as his native capacities permit.

This conception is the inevitable consequence of the democratic faith; universal education is indispensable to the full and living realization of the democratic ideal. No society can long remain free unless its members are freemen, and men are not free where ignorance prevails. No more in mind than in body can this Nation or any endure half slave, half free. Education that liberates and ennobles must be made equally available to all. Justice to the individual demands this; the safety and progress of the Nation depend upon it. America cannot afford to let any of its potential human resources go undiscovered and undeveloped.

—The Truman Commission Report, 1947

Acknowledgments

This book is dedicated to Martin Luther King's essential premise articulated so memorably in his Nobel Lecture on December 11, 1964—that a great nation is a compassionate nation:

> The rich nations must use their vast resources of wealth to develop the underdeveloped, school the unschooled, and feed the unfed. Ultimately a great nation is a compassionate nation. No individual or nation can be great if it does not have a concern for "the least of these." Deeply etched in the fiber of our religious tradition is the conviction that men are made in the image of God and that they are souls of infinite metaphysical value, the heirs of a legacy of dignity and worth. If we feel this as a profound moral fact, we cannot be content to see men hungry, to see men victimized with starvation and ill health when we have the means to help them.

There are many ways that individuals can be hungry. If a great nation is a compassionate nation, we cannot be content to have adult Americans living lives without hope or promise. Especially with the disappearance of work that pays a living wage in America (Greenhouse; Kalleberg; Shipler; Weil; Wilson), the community college must play an important role in engaging this essential public work in America today. At its most basic, this work is part of our ongoing national efforts to promote equity and social justice (Ignatieff; Rawls; Sen *Development*; Sen *Idea*).

This book, though humble, was made with great joyfulness and love, and it has benefitted tremendously from the help of many. It is with sincere gratitude that I offer these brief words of thanks to the people who have helped make it possible.

This book would not have been possible without the generous support of my home institution, Manchester Community College, and the sabbatical leave I was granted in the fall of 2015. A significant portion of this book was completed during that time. I am deeply indebted to the college for this time to research and write. I am deeply thankful for the college's enthusiastic support of my work.

My heartfelt thanks to the editorial team at Palgrave Macmillan, especially Mara Berkoff and Milana Vernikova. A special thank you to Palgrave Macmillan for believing in this project and believing in the value of community colleges. I also wish to extend my deep thanks to the anonymous reviewers at Palgrave for the excellent feedback and constructive criticism they provided to me throughout the process of writing and revising this book. Your feedback was invaluable to me.

I am indebted to my colleagues at Manchester Community College, where I have taught now for many years. I would especially like to thank my colleagues in the English Department. You are an inspiration to me every day.

I would also like to thank my close friends and colleagues Andrew Paterna, Gena Glickman, George Ducharme, Pat Beeman, David Nielsen, Duncan Harris, Ed Hogan, Lois Ryan, Steve Straight, David Caldwell, Wanda Haynes, Bettylou Sandy, Lucy Hurston, Brenda St. Peter, Julie and Wes Larkin, Michelle and Jeanne Nickerson, Keri Renner, Mike Bogdanski, Kristin Duethorn, Griz, and David Salisbury.

A special word of gratitude to Dan, Dennis, and Molly—extended family members who I hold close in my heart.

I also wish to extend my heartfelt thanks to my great teachers at Mohegan Community College in Norwich, Connecticut, where this journey began many lifetimes ago, especially Jim Coleman, Jim Wright, and John Perch. A special thank you to John Basinger, my lifelong friend and mentor.

Thank you to my inspiring friends and colleagues in the profession affiliated with The National Council of Teachers of English and The Two-Year College English Association, including Howard Tinberg, Sheridan Blau, Jeff Sommers, Christie Toth, Darin Jensen, Carolyn Calhoon-Dillahunt, Holly Hassel, Joanne Baird Giordano, Cheryl Hogue Smith, Jason Courtmanche, Amanda Greenwell, Jessyka Scoppetta, John Pekins, Mariolina Salvatori, Patricia Donahue, Mark Reynolds, Hope Parisi, Cheryl C. Smith, Kathi Yancey, Muriel Harris, Alfredo Lujan, Ellen Carillo,

John Schilb, Kelly Ritter, Leslie Roberts, Jody Millward, Sterling Warner, Lois Powers, Lawrence McDoniel, Jeffrey Klausman, Frost McLaughlin, Miriam Moore, Yufeng Zhang, Jonathan Alexander, and Christine Vassett.

I would also like to thank my amazing students, especially my English 93 and English 9000 students, who have taught me so much.

I offer my deepest thanks to those I have lost who would have been delighted by this book. These include my mother and father, Barbara and Donald Sullivan. And my lifelong friend and mentor, Victor Kaplan, a writer and professor of English at Eastern Connecticut State University.

And finally I offer my deepest thanks to my wife, Susan, and my children, Bonnie Rose and Nicholas, without whom none of this would have been possible. And to my granddaughter, Marigold Hope, who is a blessing every day.

I am, of course, what time, circumstance, and history have made of me, but I am also, thanks to all of you, much more than that. Words cannot adequately express the debt of gratitude I feel for the many gifts you have given me over these many years.

Contents

1 Introduction — 1

Part I Journeys — 15

2 No Regrets. By Scott Kiley

"I got to my outpost in Afghanistan in January 2011. It was so remote it took us about three weeks of traveling to get to where we needed to be." — 19

3 My Journey. By Julie A. Larkin

"I had to use a camp stove to warm up water to bathe and wash my hair. Many times I had to borrow a flashlight or use candles to study." — 25

4 A New Beginning. By Eddie Rivera

"My father, Eddie Rivera Senior, was born on July 14, 1964, in Santurce, San Juan Puerto Rico. He was the first of eight children, four boys and four girls. Growing up he remembers playing with his brothers and sisters outside along with his childhood friends and watching his favorite superhero crush Wonder Woman on their first black and white television." — 31

5 Everything in Life Has a Cost. By Sarah Brihan

"I was accepted into six different schools at the end of my senior year." 35

6 Survival and Resilience. By Chhan D. Touch, MS, FNP

"I do not remember the exact year of my birth or the zodiacal symbol. My mother died while I was just a young child. This is my story and a legacy of a Killing Fields survivor." 39

7 The Accident of My Career and Academic Life. By Bethany Silver

"The accident of my career and my academic life began with a high school dream that crashed and burned." 59

8 The Path I Didn't Choose. By Michelle Nickerson

"I should not be here today telling you that I have completed this master's degree." 67

9 Head Start. By Mikey Palacios-Baughman

"My entire life I was homeschooled. Before you ask, yes I had friends, no it wasn't difficult to meet people, no I never wanted to go to public school and yes I loved it." 71

10 Sabina's Story. By Sabina Mamedova

"In my difficult childhood, I had been forced to leave two countries, my father was murdered, I was forced to learn several languages, and I experienced many forms of discrimination." 75

11 No Longer Trapped. By Jenn Nguyen

"To my innocent youth, I thank you for falling in love with words. With books. To my rebellious teenage years, I thank you for drowning my sorrows with hopeless remedies. To my immature adulthood, I thank you for the beautiful baby that I absolutely adore." 89

12 Coming in from the Cold. By Tanya Knight

"It was in 2006, while driving to work knowing I was going to be terminated or laid off soon I was struck by a song I heard by T.I. and Rihanna. One line said, 'be grateful for the life you have and not worry about the life you don't have.'" 93

13 Slim Chances. By Anton Pettiford

"I wasn't until my best friend received a 35-year prison sentence that I realized my life was critically weighing in the balance, headed toward destruction in need of serious change." 97

14 Recovery. By Abigail Welles

"I was one of two in a graduating class of 896 to graduate with honors from the Honors College." 101

15 Writing My Way to College. By Ashley Riddlesworth

"The drama of the Hollywood world was consuming, however, and I started to realize that celebrity gossip was just that—gossip." 111

16 Journey. By Yanira Hernandez

"As little girls, my sister and I had lots of fun inside too. We played all sorts of things, but my favorite was playing teacher. I always had to be 'the teacher.'"   123

17 What Do These Student Success Stories Tell Us?   131

Part II Democracy's Unfinished Business   143

18 The Truman Commission Report   145

19 Economic Inequality and Higher Education   153

20 "Socialism Means Slavery"   165

21 Unfreedom   177

22 Opportunity Differentials   195

23 Different Psychological Worlds, Part 1   205

24 Different Psychological Worlds, Part 2   221

25 "Ideas About Human Possibilities": Connecticut's PA 12–40 and Developmental Education in the Era of Neoliberalism   241

Part III The Public Good   273

26 A Brief History of the Public Good   275

27	The Consequences of a Deified Market Model	295
28	Development as Freedom	311
29	Measuring "Success" at Open Admissions Institutions	323
30	Diverted Dreams, Cruel Hoaxes, and Institutional Ineffectiveness: The Community College "Failure" Narrative	341
31	The Developmental Education Crisis	357

Part IV Conclusion 373

| 32 | Conclusion: "To Do" List | 375 |

Bibliography 399

Index 427

About the Author

Patrick Sullivan teaches English at Manchester Community College in Manchester, Connecticut. He has taught a wide range of basic writing, composition, and literature classes, and has written articles for a variety of journals, including *Teaching English in the Two-Year College*, *College English*, *College Composition and Communication*, *The Journal of Basic Writing*, *Academe*, *The Journal of Adolescent and Adult Literacy*, *The Journal of Developmental Education*, *The Community College Journal of Research and Practice*, *Innovative Higher Education*, *The Chronicle of Higher Education*, and *English Journal*.

Sullivan is the editor, with Howard Tinberg, of *What Is "College-Level" Writing?* (2006) and, with Howard Tinberg and Sheridan Blau, of *What Is "College-Level" Writing? Volume 2: Assignments, Readings, and Student Writing Samples* (2010) and *Deep Reading: Teaching Reading in the Writing Classroom* (2017). He is also the author of *A New Writing Classroom: Listening, Motivation, and Habits of Mind* (2014). Sullivan has also edited, with Christie Toth, *Teaching Composition at the Two-Year College: Background Readings* (2016), a book in the Bedford/St. Martin's Professional Resources series. He serves as a member of the Editorial Board of *College Composition and Communication*.

List of Figures

Fig. 19.1	Equity indicator 5a: Distribution by family income quartile of dependent family members, aged 18–24, who attained a bachelor's degree by age 24: 1970–2014 (2016, 60)	158
Fig. 19.2	Accuplacer reading scores and family income for new students who applied for financial aid, Fall 2011, 2012, 2013, 2014, and 2015	159
Fig. 21.1	Stowage of the British slave ship 'Brookes' under the regulated Slave Trade Act of 1788	189
Fig. 24.1	A 1916 leaflet promoting a voter referendum to segregate St. Louis. This referendum was approved	230
Fig. 25.1	My gradebook pages for English 9000, fall 2014	253
Fig. 25.2	The attendance record for my English 9000 class, fall 2014	254
Fig. 26.1	Sharecropper Bud Fields and his family at home. Hale County, Alabama. 1936	279
Fig. 26.2	Cotton pickers, Arkansas, on the Alexander plantation at 6:30 a.m., waiting for the workday to start, 1935	280
Fig. 26.3	Eighteen-year-old mother from Oklahoma, now a California migrant, 1937	281
Fig. 29.1	Graduation rate (within six years) from first institution attended for first-time, full-time bachelor's degree-seeking students at four-year postsecondary institutions, by acceptance rate of institution: Cohort entry year 2007	328
Fig. 31.1	New first-time MCC students: Graduation and transfer status	360
Fig. 31.2	The cover of Complete College America's report, *Remediation: Higher Education's Bridge to Nowhere*. 2012	363

Fig. 31.3	Graduation ceremony at Manchester Community College, May 2016. Approximately 60 percent of the students in this graduating class owe their success to developmental English or math courses. In 2016, 896 students graduated with degrees and certificates	364
Fig. 31.4	Photo from graduation ceremony at Manchester Community College, May 2015. Approximately 60 percent of the students in this graduating class owe their success to developmental English or math courses	365
Fig. 31.5	Photo from graduation ceremony at Manchester Community College, May 2015. Approximately 60 percent of the students in this graduating class owe their success to developmental English or math courses	366
Fig. 31.6	Photo from the graduation ceremony at Manchester Community College, May 2016. Approximately 60 percent of the students in this graduating class owe their success to developmental English or math courses	366
Fig. 31.7	Recent graduates from Pierce College in Woodland Hills, California—one of California's 113 community colleges, May 2015. Approximately 39 percent of the students in this graduating class owe their success to developmental English or math courses	367
Fig. 31.8	Graduation ceremony at Southwestern College in Chula Vista, California—one of California's 113 community colleges, May 2015. Approximately 39 percent of the students in this graduating class owe their success to developmental English or math courses	367
Fig. 31.9	MCC's first graduating class in 1965	368

CHAPTER 1

Introduction

"Education that Liberates and Ennobles"

In 1947, President Truman's Commission on Higher Education issued a landmark report, *Higher Education for American Democracy: A Report of the President's Commission on Higher Education, Volumes I–VI*, one of the most important documents ever produced about education in America. No longer content for colleges to serve as bastions of privilege and wealth, the Commission called for a radical new approach to higher education and the establishment of a national system of community colleges across America. The rationale for this new approach to higher education was articulated with some of the most stirring language ever formulated about the role of higher education in a democracy:

> American colleges and universities must envision a much larger role for higher education in the national life. They can no longer consider themselves merely the instrument for producing an intellectual elite; they must become the means by which every citizen, youth, and adult is enabled and encouraged to carry his education, formal and informal, as far as his native capacities permit.
>
> This conception is the inevitable consequence of the democratic faith; universal education is indispensable to the full and living realization of the democratic ideal. No society can long remain free unless its members are freemen, and men are not free where ignorance prevails. No more in mind than in body can this Nation or any endure half slave, half free. Education

that liberates and ennobles must be made equally available to all. Justice to the individual demands this; the safety and progress of the Nation depend upon it. America cannot afford to let any of its potential human resources go undiscovered and undeveloped. (101)

Sixty-five years into this grand experiment, the community college has become central to America's system of higher education, serving millions of students across the nation. As the authors of a recent Two-Year College English Association document note, community colleges now "enroll the majority of African-American, Latino, and Native American college students in addition to returning adult students, dual-enrolled high school students, multilingual and 'Generation 1.5' students, veterans, and students with disabilities" (Calhoon-Dillahunt, Jensen, Johnson, Tinberg, and Toth). Despite significant and demonstrable success across a broad range of indicators, there remains much confusion and misunderstanding about the community college. This book seeks to address these misunderstandings systematically and methodically.

Following psychologists Edward E. Jones and Richard E. Nisbett's landmark work on perception, I have attempted to explore in this book what we might have to gain by adopting an "actor's perspective" of the community college, rather than an "observer's perspective." In so doing, I seek to move our scholarly conversation beyond a purely statistical model of the community college in order to promote a more qualitative, "student-present" (Bishop 199) understanding of this institution. There is much that we can gain from listening to students themselves as they discuss what the community college and its open door policy has meant to them. Here we will learn about students' goals and family histories, and their ideas about education and democracy. In engaging this important qualitative work, we will be privileging a theory of the community college that seeks to be fundamentally informed, to borrow a phrase from economist Amartya Sen, by the lives that people actually "manage—or do not manage—to live" (*Idea* 18; *Development* 142–145). Following Sen, we will also be formulating a "freedom-centered" understanding of the community college and the nature of the social justice in America that is "very much an agent-oriented view" (*Development* 11). In some ways, following Ellen Langer's work on mindfulness, it appears that we have become "trapped by categories" (11–12) in our understanding of the community college and victims of "acting from a single perspective" (16–18). Our reliance on the statistical model of success developed by residential, selective admissions institutions perpetuates a misunderstanding about the nature of the community college and its place in the American system of higher education. This book seeks to address this misunderstanding directly.

"Student-Present" Research

This book features a unique combination of data and research about community colleges and provides an innovative approach for assessing the value of community colleges in America. This book also provides a counter-narrative to the deficit models of community colleges currently enjoying a renaissance now in our legislatures and in much current scholarship devoted to community colleges. Much of what is currently written about student aspirations and community colleges is misleading and misguided—often the result of a deep unfamiliarity with these institutions and the students they serve.

Part I of this book features a selection of student-authored essays from The Community College Success Stories Project, a research project I began in 2015 to draw attention to the good work being done at America's community colleges. This project features essays at an online website written by community college students about their journeys to and from open admissions institutions. We are currently in the beginning stages of implementing this project, but it is my hope that eventually this website will include essays written by students from across the nation. This project received a Conference on College Composition and Communication (CCCC) Research Initiative Grant in 2016, from my professional organization, the National Council of Teachers of English (NCTE). This project has been established to document and preserve for the reading public the many remarkable life stories that are created every day at our nation's community colleges.

The website is located here:

http://www.communitycollegesuccessstories.org/

The primary goal of The Community College Success Stories Project is very simple: To build an archive of thousands of community college success stories that can be searched and accessed by new community college students looking for inspiration and that can serve as a resource for scholars and researchers seeking qualitative data about students who have attended open admissions institutions.

In some important ways, these stories are all literacy narratives of one sort or another, documenting student achievement across a variety of cultural contexts, academic disciplines, and life trajectories. This project privileges writing by college students themselves and therefore provides a unique, personal, and rare glimpse into the kinds of lives being lived by community college students in America.

We see in these artifacts accounts of college life not often studied by educational researchers. It is my hope that this archive of essays (and the small sample of student essays featured in this book) will help readers develop a more informed, sympathetic, and personal understanding of community colleges and the students who attend them. In so doing, I am attempting to reshape our understanding of the modern community college and tell a more complete story about our ongoing efforts to democratize the system of higher education in America. These stories will add evidence to our ongoing discussion that has not been provided before—students telling their own stories and speaking directly to scholars, researchers, and policymakers about their experiences at open admissions institutions. Here I am drawing on the work of Susanmarie Harrington, Wendy Bishop, and Carole Center, who have called for more scholarship that is, to use Bishop's phrase, "student-present" (199). This book is an attempt to honor that call. Harrington defines this type of research as devoting "serious attention to student voices": "In student-present scholarship, the focus is on how students experience broad curricular trends" (96–97). I also seek to help further Sheryl Fontaine and Susan Hunter's work by helping students "write themselves into the story" we are in the process of creating in America about community colleges. My approach here also seeks to support the work of Nobel Laureate Svetlana Alexievich and her commitment to privileging listening as a form of research and knowledge-making—and from this process, forging a new "genre where human voices speak for themselves," telling stories that "are impossible to imagine or invent" (*Voices from Big Utopia*; see also *Voices from Chernobyl*).

In sharing these stories, I also seek to help document the history of the community college and to capture some of the powerful emotions and uniquely American life stories that pulse beneath the surface of the statistics and graduation rates that have too often been asked to speak for these institutions. In embracing this as an important form of qualitative research, we are privileging the value of listening as a path to wisdom, following Oliver Wendell Holmes, Sr.: "It is the province of knowledge to speak, and it is the privilege of wisdom to listen."

Parts II and III of this book examine the economic model that is driving much of the discussion in higher education today—neoliberalism. There is a great deal to discuss here, including a variety of largely invisible forces that help shape the lives of many community college students. The chapters in this section of the book seek to make visible these powerful and often unacknowledged contingencies. In these chapters, I seek to assess the community college's contributions to promoting equity, social justice, and the public good in America. This has long been a controversial subject, and I seek to engage it carefully, bringing new evidence and a fresh perspective to this long-standing debate in the scholarship devoted to the community college.

I position my work here as a seasoned community college teacher and as a scholar with a deep commitment to the community college and to issues related to social justice. I have taught English at my home institution in Connecticut, an open admissions community college in Manchester, Connecticut, for almost 30 years. I have also devoted a significant portion of this time to teaching developmental reading and writing classes, so I am therefore very familiar with the controversies that have accompanied developmental education over the years.

The need to write this book comes from my dissatisfaction with current scholarly treatments of the community college. To my mind, most academic scholarship devoted to this subject misses what is transformative and revolutionary about this great American institution. In this book, I seek to theorize a more balanced, broadly research-based, progressive understanding of America's community colleges.

This book seeks to build on and advance the work of scholars like Mike Rose (*Back to School*), Marilyn Sternglass (*Time to Know Them*), Mina P. Shaughnessy (*Errors and Expectations: A Guide for the Teacher of Basic Writing*), Nell Ann Pickett ("The Two-Year College as Democracy in Action"), John S. Levin (*Nontraditional Students and Community Colleges: The Conflict of Justice and Neoliberalism*), John S. Levin and Susan T. Kater (*Understanding Community Colleges*), and Edward St. John, Shouping Hu, and Amy S. Fisher (*Breaking Through the Access Barrier: How Academic Capital Formation Can Improve Policy in Higher Education*) who have all championed the community college. My goal is to promote progressive thinking about—and provide scholarly support for progressive legislation designed to strengthen—the American community college.

"Closer to an Ideal Society"

Most essentially, I seek to address in this book matters related to equity, social justice, and economic inequality—key issues now in our national conversation about public higher education. Here I seek to address a key question economist Thomas Piketty asks in *Capital in the Twenty-First Century* related to democracy and the public good: "What public policies and institutions bring us closer to an ideal society?" (574). The community college provides one indisputable, emphatic, and inspiring answer to this question. This book also seeks to address, following Adrianna J. Kezar, Tony C. Chambers, and John C. Burkhardt, "one of the most significant challenges confronting higher education: the shift, and perhaps loss, within some institutions and sectors in the role higher education plays in serving the public good" (xiii). We will be spending a considerable amount of time discussing the many different ways we might theorize the idea of the public good in America.

Drawing on the work of Linda Adler-Kassner, Edward Said, and others, I also seek to challenge the persistent, popular, and often alarmist mainstream "failure" narrative about community colleges. For Adler-Kassner, a writing scholar and teacher, the key variable in much debate about higher education involves "narrative" and the need "to work from different stories" (2). At my college this spring (2016), 896 students graduated with degrees and certificates. Graduates came from 101 towns across Connecticut as well as from ten other states. Graduation ceremonies like this occur every year around the nation at America's 1,108 community colleges. This must certainly be regarded as compelling evidence of the important work being done at "democracy's college," especially when we consider the great diversity of students who enroll at open admissions institutions. It may well be that this failure narrative is fueled and sustained, following Stiglitz and Greenwald, by prior beliefs, confirmatory bias, and perceptions that are not necessarily "consciously constructed" (460). This book will examine how certain kinds of narratives have come to dominate public discourse about higher education and community colleges, and we will seek to examine—and challenge—the highly politicized narrative about community colleges currently enjoying great popularity.

Contemporary academic scholarship devoted to the community college has often focused primarily on extending existing theories within higher education and within particular specializations. This has included a focus on students, finance, student services, organizational strategies, and governance. Unfortunately, this approach has produced a form of rigidity that entrenches certain kinds of perspectives and ideas and leaves fundamental questions and assumptions unexamined. It also perpetuates the failure to adequately account for the many unique features of the open admissions institution. This approach to theorizing the community college has had the effect of privileging long-held assumptions and protecting them from critical examination. As theories become rigid, the ideas they contain become self-evident truths that are perpetuated across generations. This book will examine two such theories in considerable detail—the "cooling out" function of the junior college and the so-called "failure" of developmental education—to show this process at work. As times change and data sets are updated, theorists must periodically and systematically reassess cherished beliefs and long-held views and submit them to careful scrutiny. As theorists studying higher education, we must be committed to periodic regeneration and reconstruction. This book seeks to engage in this kind of regenerative and reconstructive scholarly process, especially as it relates to neoliberal economic theory, applying a market model to higher education, and understanding the public good as it relates to the community college.

Unfortunately, community colleges have been defined in public discourse and by a great deal of academic scholarship primarily in terms of "failure." In fact, a "failure" narrative much like the Puritan jeremiad has developed within this body of scholarship that has been remarkably long-lived and resistant to new data, ideas, and assessment. This community college "failure" tradition continues to be robustly appealing, and it has now spanned over 55 years (and counting). A list of representative works in this tradition might read this way:

1960: Clark, Burton. "The 'Cooling-Out' Function in Higher Education." *American Journal of Sociology* 65.6 (1960): 569–76.
1972. Karabel, Jerome. "Community Colleges and Social Stratification." *Harvard Educational Review* 42.4 (1972): 521–62.
1976. Zwerling, L. Steven. *Second Best: The Crisis of the Community College*. New York, McGraw-Hill, 1976.
1986. Zwerling, L. Steven, ed. *The Community College and Its Critics*. San Francisco: Jossey-Bass, 1986.

1989: Brint, Steven, and Jerome Karabel. *The Diverted Dream: Community Colleges and the Promise of Educational Opportunity in America, 1900–1985.* New York: Oxford UP, 1989.
1991. Dougherty, Kevin. "The Community College at the Crossroads: The Need for Structural Reform." *Harvard Educational Review* 61.3 (1991): 311–37.
1994. Traub, James. *City on a Hill: Testing the American Dream at City College.* New York: Da Capo, 1994.
1995: Rouse, Cecilia Elena. "Democratization or Diversion? The Effect of Community Colleges on Educational Attainment." *Journal of Business & Economic Statistics* 13.2 (1995): 217–224.
2001: Dougherty, Kevin J. *The Contradictory College: The Conflicting Origins, Impacts, and Futures of the Community College.* Albany, SUNY Press, 2001.
2011: Beach, J. M. *Gateway to Opportunity? A History of the Community College in the United States.* Sterling: Stylus, 2011.
2011. Flores, Roy. "False Hope" *Inside Higher Ed*, February 17, 2011.
2012. Complete College America. *Remediation: Higher Education's Bridge to Nowhere.* Washington: Complete College America, 2012.
2014: Scherer, Juliet Lilledahl, and Mirra Leigh Anson. *Community Colleges and the Access Effect: Why Open Admissions Suppresses Achievement.* New York: Palgrave Macmillan, 2014.
2015: Bailey, Thomas R., Shanna Smith Jaggers, and Davis Jenkins. *Redesigning America's Community Colleges: A Clearer Path to Student Success.* Cambridge: Harvard University Press, 2015.

How we judge the value of community colleges will depend in some very important ways on what kinds of benchmarks we establish to measure "success," who sets these benchmarks, and what these benchmarks assume about students attending college. A lot will also depend on the perspective we take and the kind of data we collect and privilege. Using the traditional national benchmark established by selective admissions institutions, it therefore might appear to some observers, as Bailey, Jaggars, and Jenkins note in their recent book, *Redesigning America's Community Colleges* (2015), that community colleges are "poorly designed to facilitate completion of high quality college programs" (13). We will examine what is problematic about this claim and document the many ways this perspective is inaccurate and misleading.

"This Imaginary Universe of Perfect Competition"

Part of my goal is also political—to engage vitally important questions for our democracy about equity, social justice, and the public good and to examine the many ways that the community college helps promote these foundational democratic ideals. Here I will be building on conclusions drawn by Pierre Bourdieu and his essay, "The Forms of Capital." Bourdieu suggests that entrenched social, economic, and cultural contingencies serve to make any simple understanding of success and failure—in the marketplace and in the classroom—highly problematic. These various "forms of capital" help determine one's life chances in very potent ways, and they must be regarded as key variables when we seek to measure student success at community colleges. Bourdieau challenges a key principle of neoliberal economic theory, which supposes a radically free marketplace unencumbered by history or class, and posits instead an economic world heavily determined by accumulated capital and wealth:

> Roulette, which holds out the opportunity of winning a lot of money in a short space of time, and therefore of changing one's social status quasi-instantaneously, and in which the winning of the previous spin of the wheel can be staked and lost at every new spin, gives a fairly accurate image of this imaginary universe of perfect competition or perfect equality of opportunity, a world without inertia, without accumulation, without heredity or acquired properties, in which every moment is perfectly independent of the previous one, every soldier has a marshal's baton in his knapsack, and every prize can be attained, instantaneously, by everyone, so that at each moment anyone can become anything. Capital, which, in its objectified or embodied forms, takes time to accumulate and which, as a potential capacity to produce profits and to reproduce itself in identical or expanded form, contains a tendency to persist in its being, is a force inscribed in the objectivity of things so that everything is not equally possible or impossible. And the structure of the distribution of the different types and subtypes of capital at a given moment in time represents the immanent structure of the social world, i.e., the set of constraints, inscribed in the very reality of that world, which govern its functioning in a durable way, determining the chances of success for practices (81).

This book seeks to help illustrate this claim by carefully documenting the operation of very powerful social factors—including family income, inherited wealth, and social class—that create extreme opportunity differentials for individuals in America. Following Bourdieu, I seek to illustrate that every moment is not "perfectly independent of the previous one," that not "every soldier has a marshal's baton in his knapsack," and that the social world is constructed in a way that not "every prize can be attained, instantaneously, by everyone, so that at each moment anyone can become anything."

This understanding of the social world and the operation of various forms of capital has vitally important implications for those who make decisions about community colleges and developmental education programs. Neoliberal ideas about the public good and the power of the market economy have often been used to simplify these very complex economic realities. As P.L. Thomas has observed, this ascendant neoliberal economic model has, in fact, produced two competing narratives about public education in America:

> "No Excuses" Reformers insist that the source of success and failure lies in each child and each teacher, requiring only the adequate level of effort to rise out of the circumstances not of her/his making. As well, "No Excuses" Reformers remain committed to addressing poverty solely or primarily through education, viewed as an opportunity offered each child and within which ... effort will result in success.
>
> Social Context Reformers have concluded that the source of success and failure lies primarily in the social and political forces that govern our lives. By acknowledging social privilege and inequality, Social Context Reformers are calling for education reform within a larger plan to reform social inequity—such as access to health care, food security, higher employment along with better wages and job security. (qtd. in Porfilio, Gorlewski, Carr, and Thomas 1)

We will be examining the foundational neoliberal thinking that informs these two very different approaches to theorizing the role of higher education in a democracy and seeking to determine if this "no excuses" reform serves the public interest and promotes the public good—or instead serves the interests of the already rich and powerful.

In this book, we will be actively embracing the advice of economist F.A. Hayek himself, one of the founders of neoliberalism. In perhaps his most well-known essay, "The Intellectuals and Socialism" (1949), Hayek advocated for coordinated, focused, and long-term efforts to help shape public opinion about the free market and about neoliberal approaches to public policy. Hayek outlined a strategy that targeted "intellectuals" (journalists, teachers, ministers, lecturers, publicists, radio commentators, writers of fiction, cartoonists, and artists) as a way to effectively transmit ideas to a wider audience. Hayek lived and worked at a time when democracy and freedom itself appeared to be at stake. The same might also be said about us now, although in very different ways. These intellectuals, Hayek suggested, "are the organs which modern society has developed for spreading knowledge and ideas, and it is their convictions and opinions which operate as the sieve through which all new conceptions must pass before they can reach the masses" (225). This neoliberal project, as we will see, is obviously well underway in America and worldwide. In the conclusion of this essay, Hayek champions the "courage to be Utopian" as a key tactical and rhetorical strategy, an approach to activist and public relations work that can provide important guidance for advocates of community colleges as well:

> The main lesson which the true liberal must learn from the success of the socialists is that it was their courage to be Utopian which gained them the support of the intellectuals and therefore an influence on public opinion which is daily making possible what only recently seemed utterly remote. Those who have concerned themselves exclusively with what seemed practicable in the existing state of opinion have constantly found that even this had rapidly become politically impossible as the result of changes in a public opinion which they have done nothing to guide. Unless we can make the philosophic foundations of a free society once more a living intellectual issue, and its implementation a task which challenges the ingenuity and imagination of our liveliest minds, the prospects of freedom are indeed dark. But if we can regain that belief in the power of ideas which was the mark of liberalism at its greatest, the battle is not lost. The intellectual revival of liberalism is already underway in many parts of the world. Will it be in time? (237)

Those who care about social justice must embrace the responsibility to help shape public opinion about the nature of the American community college and the many social and civic benefits of higher education. This work can be informed by the power of our ideals—access, opportunity, and the public good—and by translating our research and scholarship for a new generation of Americans. This book is designed to help move this important work forward.

"A CONTINGENT, DISORGANIZED MULTIPLICITY"

For many scholars and legislators, community colleges exist, to borrow a phrase from Pierre Bourdieu, as "a contingent, disorganized multiplicity, interchangeable and innumerable, existing only statistically" (*Distinction* 468). In this book, I am seeking to move beyond this "contingent, disorganized multiplicity" understanding of community colleges and the students who attend them. As John S. Levin and Susan T. Kater note in their preface to *Understanding Community Colleges*, recent legislative initiatives on the state and national levels

> have preoccupied practitioners and policy-makers and both reflect and reinforce the pattern of research on community colleges that deflects attention from both a comprehensive view of the institution, in general, and an experiential view, in particular. (xii)

The research I present to readers in this book seeks to privilege precisely this comprehensive, experiential view of the community college. My goal here, following Ken Meier, is to demystify the community college and "the discourses surrounding it" (3). Although Meier, following Dougherty (*Contradictory*), Vaughan, and others, suggests that "multiple missions and multiple identities are inherent in the organizational and social design of community colleges" (16), community colleges have a core mission and mandate that transcend these multiple identities: a commitment to equity, social justice, and the public good. In this book, I seek to map the operation of this core identity and social function.

I marshal a great deal of evidence in this book, and I have drawn conclusions from this evidence that I believe are vitally important for our democracy and for the future of higher education in America. I present this work humbly and respectfully, with the knowledge that a book like this must always be imperfect and incomplete. I humbly accept the condition of these limitations. I understand that the conclusions forwarded here deserve to be questioned and discussed, and I submit this work to readers in the interest of furthering dialog about important issues facing our nation and our democracy.

A Note About Audience and Style

The primary audience for this book is the community of scholars who have research interests in higher education and the community college. More broadly, this book is written for anyone with a commitment to equity, access, and social justice. This book is likely to be of interest to anyone who wishes to think in new and progressive ways about a great American institution, the community college.

In terms of style, readers should know that I include a significant number of long quotations from primary and secondary sources throughout this book, and I request the reader's forbearance as we engage this material. This methodology allows me employ an objective and deliberate approach to building a complex argument, which provides readers with the opportunity to see the actual language of key documents for themselves and to assess how ideas are framed and articulated in their original sources. Also, in most every case, nothing I could say in terms of paraphrase or summation could possibly equal the eloquence or majesty of the language I am quoting.

As a writer and scholar, I also seek to engage in conversation *collaboratively* alongside important thinkers and writers. I see this as a way of enacting responsible and principled engagement with important ideas, theories, and writers. This becomes especially important if the material we are discussing is likely to be unfamiliar, as it will be in parts of this book for some readers. We will be examining research and theory from a variety of disciplines, including economics, sociology, psychology, and composition theory. Because we will be building a large, complex argument that takes shape only over many pages and many chapters and which requires that we synthesize material from a variety of disciplines across many decades, it is vitally important to maintain a close working relationship to primary documents. Quotations allow me to do this responsibly and thoughtfully. I thank my readers in advance for their patience and good faith as we begin this journey together.

PART I

Journeys

Introduction

This section of the book features a collection of essays written by community college students about their experiences attending an open admissions institution. The authors here are all current or former students who attended Manchester Community College (MCC), my home institution. Each of these student contributors was invited to describe their journey to and from MCC, discuss what attending a community college has meant to them, and reflect on how this opportunity has affected the trajectory of their lives. Some of the students here were just beginning their college experience at the time this book was being written. Others have graduated, started families, and begun careers.

The idea for this approach to telling the story of the American community college—one story at a time—began at an awards ceremony that I attended on our campus in 2007 to honor outstanding student leaders. As awards were distributed and stories told about individual students, their accomplishments, and their lives, I found myself deeply moved and inspired. I thought, "These are amazing stories. If I could assemble them somehow and share them with a wider audience, they would provide scholars, policy makers, and interested parties with a very powerful, very real first-hand portrait of the community college." One student won an award for her work as president of our campus chapter of Habitat for Humanity. This group had spent many Saturdays that year helping to build houses in Hartford. They also sponsored a week-long trip to New Orleans during the summer to help rebuild houses in New Orleans after hurricane Katrina.

Another student received an award for her work with PRIDE, a student club devoted to supporting and promoting gay, lesbian, bisexual, transgender, questioning, and intersex students on campus and educating members and others on campus about GLBTQI issues. This award recipient worked tirelessly all year long to promote these goals.

Another recipient was a veteran who had served in Iraq and was president of our student government association.

It is my hope that the student-authored essays in this section of the book will help begin to tell a different kind of story about community colleges.

Methodology

In 2007, working with our college president and our dean of students, I assembled a list of students with exceptional community college stories to tell and invited them to contribute to this book. As I moved forward with this work, I realized that in order to provide a truly accurate profile of the community college experience, we would also need to include contributions from students who might appear (at least at first glance) to have equally important but quieter kinds of stories to tell.

Overall, I have tried to assemble a fairly typical representative compilation of stories that taken together and considered cumulatively might begin to reflect the incredible variety of student experience on our campuses. My goal was to begin mapping and documenting some of this variety in all its rich and astonishing detail. I respectfully acknowledge that this portrait of community college students is, of course, incomplete, as any such endeavor like this would have to be. In its diversity, however, these stories can help scholars, legislators, and other interested stakeholders begin working toward a richer, more informed understanding of this important American institution. This section of the book is a good-faith effort to communicate to a wider reading public at least a small part of what is so special and inspiring about open admissions institutions.

Ultimately, I ended up adopting what might be described as a modified Zen approach to constructing the final shape of this section of the book. We invited many students to contribute, and we let this section in some ways assemble itself, based on who responded to our invitation and who was ultimately able to complete an essay for us.

A number of the individuals here are former students of mine, who I invited to contribute because I knew they had important—and perhaps paradigmatic—stories to tell about the community college. I am thankful they have been kind enough to share their experiences with us.

What is perhaps most noteworthy about many of the stories included here is how important just one or two college personnel can be in the life of a student, confirming a key insight from Daniel F. Chambliss and Christopher G. Takacs's research reported in their book *How College Works*. Chambliss and Takacs suggest that it is not so much curriculum or programs but *people* that make the most lasting difference for college students. "People," they suggest, "far more than programs, majors, or classes, are decisive in students' experiences of college" (2014, 163). Following approximately 100 students over the course of eight years, Chambliss and Takacs found this insight repeatedly confirmed: "Time after time, in descriptions of a wide variety of situations, students told us of how encounters with the right person could make a decisive difference in their college careers" (3). Chambliss and Takacs conclude by suggesting that "without the motivating presence of friends, teachers, and mentors even the best-designed, potentially most valuable academic programs will fail" (163). This research finding is emphatically confirmed by the stories included here.

The institutional identify of the modern community college has been shaped by a diverse range of social, cultural, historical, and local factors, as Ken Meier notes in his essay, "Community College Mission in Historical Perspective." This list must also, of course, include progressive ideas about social justice and promoting the public good (Levin *Nontraditional*). Nonetheless, despite these variables, a key component of the institutional identity of the modern community college has been a focus on students and teaching rather than on research—that is to say, providing opportunities for precisely the kind of individualized personal contact and support from teachers and staff that Chambliss and Takacs have discovered is essential to the college experience.

Although I am presenting only a small sample of community college student success stories in this book, it is my hope that the Community College Success Stories Project will generate hundreds of such stories. It is my hope that we will eventually produce enough evidence to demonstrate that any one student success story is not atypical but is, in fact, representative of the many different kinds of life stories that community college students are forging for themselves every day on our campuses.

The stories assembled here tell a very different kind of story about community colleges than most higher education scholars and general readers normally encounter—one that is rich with lived human experience and anchored in particular historical, economic, geographical, political, and cultural moments. It is my hope that these stories will help counteract the surprisingly persistent misunderstandings about community colleges. It is my hope that these stories will also lead readers to a deeper understanding about why community colleges are so important for our democracy, how they impact individual student lives, and how very quietly and humbly, far from the spotlight, they do their important work.

Contributors to this section of the book were free to speak at whatever length they wished to about their journeys to and from MCC. Some of the essays featured here are brief. Others are much longer, often because contributors have a more complex story to tell. I hope readers will embrace this variety as a natural manifestation of the many different lives that community college students lead and the many different kinds of stories they have to tell.

CHAPTER 2

No Regrets

By Scott Kiley

My name is Scott Kiley. I am a 24-year-old veteran and this is my journey to Manchester Community College. I was raised in East Hartford, CT. I have two loving, hardworking parents, Ken & Leanne. My mother has run a daycare in our home all my life and my father works for the Hartford Insurance Company. I have two older sisters. Heather is the oldest who's seven years older than me. Sarah is the middle child who's two years older than me. I participated in many activities growing up. My favorites were soccer and Boy Scouts. I started playing soccer when I was around six years old and played high school. I made the varsity team my sophomore through senior year. I joined the Boy Scouts when I was 12. I continued with that all the way through high school, learning all different types of outdoor skills. Right before my 18th birthday, I achieved my Eagle Scout. For my project, I painted a huge fence at a local church. It took me a few weeks to complete it. It was a lot of tough work and I am very proud of myself for accomplishing that goal. I enjoyed doing many activities with likeminded people, such as shooting, hiking, fishing and camping. We all had the same goal in mind, to become Eagle Scouts, and we helped each other out to get there.

Another important part in my journey is my decision to go to a technical high school instead of a traditional high school. I chose to go to Cheney Tech for the culinary program. I know this was the best decision for me because I was able to get more out of that education than I would have if I went to East Hartford High. At Cheney, I wasn't so great at the academic part of the school but I excelled in culinary. I knew I liked culinary when I realized it just came naturally to me. I liked the hands-on work we did in the kitchens. It was easier for me than reading and writing. I looked forward to the rotations in the kitchen and dreaded being in the classroom. The chefs and teachers at Cheney were and continue to be great role models and mentors for me. Chef Hovas is one of the teachers that really helped me throughout high school. He was my soccer coach and teacher. I'm still in contact with him and the other chefs at Cheney to this day.

During my four years of culinary, I have cooked many different types of dishes. My favorite thing to cook was different kinds of meats on the grill. I love working the grill. It's very hot and fast paced. It's something that came so easily to me. When our class would have a catering project, I would always volunteer to do the meats. By the time we were seniors, we all knew what our strengths and weaknesses were and we used that to our advantage. As teenagers, we fooled around a lot and played practical jokes on each other but we always put our very best into our cooking. My favorite memory in the kitchen was when my class was unsupervised and we decided to take pots and pans to play gladiators. Just my luck, when I jumped off one the counter tops, using a wooden spoon as a sword, in comes all three of my teachers. At first they were mad but in the end it turned out to be a big joke. To this day, I am known as the Gladiator of Cheney Tech.

Another important part of my high school was being a part of the wrestling team. I wrestled the 103-pound weight class every year I was on the team. I was the captain of the wrestling team when I was a junior. I loved everything about wrestling, the fact that you put all your strength and might into a six-minute match. Wrestling helped me get ready for the military. I wasn't able to wrestle my senior year due to a shoulder injury that I received the season before. I wrestled with my injured shoulder against doctor's orders. Working through the pain wasn't fun or easy, but it was something I wasn't going to let stop me from reaching my goals and going to the state finals. In the end, I didn't make it to the state finals and I wasn't able to wrestle my senior year because I made that decision, but I live with no regrets. I got surgery on my shoulder in the beginning of my senior year so it would be healed by the time I graduated to join the Army.

Ever since I could remember, I've always wanted to join the military. I'm not sure why, but I felt like it was something I had to do for myself. With the support of my family and friends, I joined the Army a few months after I graduated. I left for basic training in November 2008 down to Fort

Benning, GA. Basic was an eye-opening experience. It was both mentally and physically tough. I learned a lot about myself. The hardest thing about basic was learning how to deal with a drill sergeant screaming in your face, calling you every name in the book. I am strong willed, and I didn't take anything they said personally and I pushed myself as hard as I could possibly push. After 14 long weeks in basic, I graduated as an infantryman. Immediately after I graduated, I found myself on a long flight to South Korea.

I was stationed in South Korea about 10 miles away from the Demilitarized Zone. The DMZ is the border that separates North Korea and South Korea. We were close to the DMZ, so if North Korea decided to cross it with an army we would be called up and try to slow the forces down. Our forces worked together with the South Koreans to establish a plan to face the enemy. It's a very big responsibility for a 19-year-old kid who's fresh out of high school to handle, to stand and defend against a whole nation's force while our forces regroup. Luckily I didn't have to endure that experience.

I had a few interesting experiences with the Korean culture. I had a Korean friend named Parker who took me to go have dinner with his family. The table that we sat at was close to the ground with no chairs, so we sat Indian style. His family was very nice and formal. His father kept giving me shots of Soju, which is a rice alcohol and very popular in Korea. In Korean culture, it is a sign of respect to never pour your own glass and not refill it until it's empty. I also had the opportunity to try their interesting foods, such as dog and kimchi. Trying dog was a new experience for me and even though it didn't taste bad, it wouldn't be something I would eat on a regular basis. While I was there, my unit did the Manchu Mile. The Manchu Mile is a march done in memory of the 85-mile forced march of the 9th Infantry Regiment during the Chinese "Boxer Rebellion" in 1900. Twice a year, the 2–9 Infantry unit does a 25-mile march. It focuses on a team and unit effort, rather than the individual. When I did the march, it was through a mountain where it was so steep that if you put out your hand, you could touch the ground in front of you. It was a long, tough march but I was very proud of myself once I had completed both.

After my year in Korea, I was stationed at Fort Riley, Kansas. The next year was spent preparing for our deployment to Afghanistan. Our training consisted of six weeks in the desert in California. It was extremely hot and miserable. We were there during the hottest months of the year, June into July. Even though I was scared to go to war, I was confident in my skills as an infantryman. With my brothers by my side, we were ready to leave.

I got to my outpost in Afghanistan in January 2011. It was so remote it took us about three weeks of traveling to get to where we needed to be. My unit, the 1–16th infantry, was chosen to do a trial deployment where we work and live with Special Forces. We were out in the middle of nowhere. We didn't have running water so our bathrooms were Port-a-Potties. Our showers were bottles of water. We were up in the north in the Kondoz province. It was a total of 30 people at our OP, 15 of us and 15 of the SF guys. It was a tough lifestyle living the way we did. Our way of resupply was airdrops. An airdrop is where a plane flies over our drop zone, then drops bundles with parachutes out the back off the plane. We would then go out and recover the bundles as quickly as we could. The Taliban would be able see from miles away that we were out in the open and saw it as an opportunity to attack us and take our supplies. While we were up north, I was in a few firefights but nothing too extreme. After four months into the deployment, I went home on mid-tour for two weeks.

While I was home, it was great to spend time with my family and friends. The first few days my parents had rented a cottage right on the ocean. It was a really peaceful time for me. I was able to sit down and reflect upon what I went through the past four months and realize how lucky I was. After the two short weeks, it was time for me to go back to my brothers in Afghanistan. Traveling back and forth from leave took longer than the actual leave. When I got back, I was told that we had finished our mission at our OP and were moving down south where the fighting was heavier.

I was excited to go somewhere new, but I was also very nervous about going south because I knew that it was going to be a whole new ball game. My platoon got split up into smaller groups while we were in transit. Instead of 15, we went down to 10. I thought it to be kind of ironic that we were going to a more dangerous territory with less men and supplies. Before our deployment, I was promoted to a team leader. I was in charge of three guys. It was a great responsibility leading men into combat. I just didn't have to worry about my life but the lives of others. It added more stress to an already stressful situation. There were a few times when I truly thought that I wasn't going to make it out alive. Luckily, I had my brothers by my side. We came together and helped each other through the tough times. The last three months of the deployment were the toughest because we ran out of food and ammo due to logistical problems. I remember one night I shared one piece of bread with three grown men. In the end, we all made it back home alive, but it definitely made it harder than it had to be. After a long 12 months, we were finally on our way back to the States.

During my deployment I had a lot of time to think about my future and what I wanted to do with my life. I realized the army life wasn't for me, so I decided not to reenlist and to get out when my contract was up. It wasn't an easy decision leaving a steady and secure job. I wanted something more with my life. By leaving such a secure job, I knew that I would have to go to college. My time in Afghanistan made me ready to take on the challenge of college, which I wasn't ready for before.

As I said before, I have no regrets in life. I would make all the same decisions that I had made in my life. I've thought a lot about what I want to do in my life and I've decided that one day I want to become a chef and owner of a restaurant. Manchester Community College was the best way for me to pursue the dream. I feel like MCC cares about their students and helping them reach their full potential more so than other culinary schools.

CHAPTER 3

My Journey

By Julie A. Larkin

I was born the second oldest of nine children. I don't recall having much of a childhood as it seemed as though I was always looking after my younger siblings. I remember growing up in a large, poor, Catholic family with an alcoholic father. Times were more than tough most days and my father was abusive of my mother and us children. Many times I stepped in front of my mother to block my father from hitting her and absorbed the punches myself. He was out of work more than he actually had a job, so life was rough. We moved so many times because my father spent most of our money on drinking. Even though my mother did her best to put money away, there were several times we couldn't pay the rent. There were times when we didn't have anything to eat, had no heat, no electricity and no hot water for baths or showers. I had to use a camp stove to warm up water to bathe and wash my hair. Many times I had to borrow a flashlight or use candles to study by. It was because of my background that I made the life changing decision that I would not live that way once I was an adult and out of that environment.

I excelled throughout my school years, but only because I worked hard and fought for everything I accomplished. My recollection is that I didn't receive a lot of praise or encouragement, but something gave me the strength to persevere.

When I was in the 8th grade, my father told me that I should quit school and get a job, but I ignored the pressure he put on me to do so and continued in school even though there were times I didn't have good clothing and no money for food at lunchtime. I had to walk wherever I went because I didn't always have money for bus fare. When I was about 12 years old, I used to babysit my younger siblings to earn $10 a week and I used that to buy clothes and lunch for school. My summers were never carefree because I was expected to stay home all week and take care of my brothers.

When in high school, I was able to obtain a summer job working in the office at the high school doing secretarial duties, like mimeographing attendance sheets, delivering paperwork to classrooms, etc. In my junior year of high school, I remember working almost 40 hours a week at a pizza place and still going to school full time. Occasionally, I would fall asleep in class, but somehow, I was able to keep my grades up. I ended up graduating high school with a B+ and above average for four years of high school and most of my grades were A's.

In my last year of high school, I worked hard to maneuver through the mountains of paperwork required to apply for student loans and scholarships, but all that work didn't seem to accomplish much, even with the help of a guidance counselor. I found out only after I got married at 18 that I had been awarded a grant to attend Trinity College, which was an all female college in Burlington, VT. Unfortunately, I had to decline the grant, because I had moved over two hours away and couldn't attend the college. I was devastated because I was looking forward to going to college right out of high school. Having no support or other guidance as to how to make things work out, I just gave up and settled into married life the best that I could.

After 27 years of marriage and two children, I ended up leaving my husband because I had gone through life changing surgery for cancer and my outlook on life drastically changed. My husband at the time didn't want our life to change and I did all I could to convince him that I wanted more out of life, to live my life, rather than feel like a machine just going to work, coming home and not accomplishing much.

When my two children finished their college education, I decided that I would like to go to college because I had always wanted to go, but never even tried to after I had to decline the first grant I ever received so many years prior.

I took a giant leap of faith in myself and took the assessment test at MCC in 2004 without any preparation. I did well except for Math, which had never been my favorite subject.

I began taking only two classes, one of which was Adults in Transition with Professor Michael DiRaimo, a class that taught how to study, how to plan for tests and how to write essays. I struggled some with the "new" English class because I was so out of touch with the new terminology and what was expected that I almost dropped out of school. The instructor was an adjunct and was new to teaching at MCC. I asked for assistance a few times, but he didn't seem to want to put in the commitment to helping a student in need. I was at my wit's end and decided to discuss the issue with Professor DiRaimo, before making such an important decision as to drop out. He always gave me encouragement to believe in myself and to stick with it. After the supportive discussion with Professor DiRaimo, I made it my priority to seek assistance from online tutoring and from the Writing Center at MCC. Because of that support, I was able to pull an "A" in English. It took hard work, but I decided that I would do whatever it took to achieve those results. In the end, I gained the confidence that I needed to stay in college.

   About a year or so after my first semester, I enrolled for additional classes and created a plan to take the required "core" studies first, before taking too many electives. I was invited to become a member of Phi Theta Kappa and was excited about the prospect of joining an organization that recognized their members for their academic achievements. Eventually, I began to develop more confidence in myself and my leadership abilities and became the Induction Coordinator for new members. I found out soon thereafter that the chapter needed a V.P. of Finance/Treasurer and I also volunteered for that position. As a result of stepping out of my comfort zone, I continued to experience great personal growth along with my academic growth through the next few years at MCC. I was the President of the Phi Theta Kappa, Alpha Upsilon Alpha chapter at MCC for two years, and also served as an Officer-At-Large and the Vice-President of the chapter. After attending several Leadership conferences, Regional and International Conventions, I stepped even further out of my comfort zone and decided to run for the New England Region President, responsible for several Regional Vice-Presidents and 59 chapters throughout New England. My personal growth, leadership abilities and skills and academic success exploded during that year.

   The year prior to becoming New England Region President of Phi Theta Kappa, I served as MCC's Student Government President and experienced another valuable "transformation" in my life. I became more deeply involved in campus and student activities, established a great rapport with faculty and staff at MCC and developed long-lasting friendships with many of them. It has been quite a long and arduous journey, but one that I would do all over again to become the woman that I am today.

I can attribute my overall academic and personal growth directly to my years at MCC, including the influence I received by becoming an active member of Phi Theta Kappa through the chapter on campus at MCC.

I am the first one in my family to have attended and graduated from college. I am a humble and proud woman and find it difficult to acknowledge my successes. While writing this essay, I began reminiscing about my years at MCC, and was overwhelmed by all that has happened to me along my path to graduation. I am just beginning to recognize the qualities that gave me the courage, the strength and perseverance to accomplish all that I have to this day.

My journey to graduation has been an ongoing, soul-searching progression and I am finally able to see that I am equipped with the tools and insight which have made me so successful over the years.

I have always believed that one has to really want to make a better life for themselves and their family. This involves working hard and earning your successes. Sometimes life has other plans that seem to hold us back, but one should not be defeated by life's obstacles. I believe that I would be in the same situation as my siblings are if I ever stopped striving for a better, well-rounded quality of life; so that's what drives me to keep forging ahead into unknown territory and to continue stepping outside my comfort zone personally and academically. My desire is to continue to be involved in some way at MCC as I wish to "pay it forward." Had it not been for the guidance and support of my professors (especially Professor Michael DiRaimo, Dr. Leonard Dupille) other faculty and staff members at MCC, I would not have become the success I am today. Their influence provided the motivation that I needed to stay in college and complete my degree.

Looking back on my experiences at MCC, I am extremely proud of what I have accomplished. Even though it is great to receive recognition, I don't expect it; but I must acknowledge that academic and personal recognition is part of what gave me the strength to continue and complete my Associates in Science college degree. The following are some of the awards that I earned while at MCC:

- Manchester Community College Community Service Award
- Florence Sheils Leadership Award (Phi Theta Kappa) (two years running)
- Distinguished Chapter President (Phi Theta Kappa) (out of 59 chapter presidents eligible)
- Led my Phi Theta Kappa chapter and earned 12 awards when I was President of the chapter
- Distinguished Regional President (Phi Theta Kappa) (1 of 10 in the nation)
- Achieved GPA for President's List – 8 times
- Achieved GPA for Dean's List – 10 times
- Awarded Academic Excellence in Psychology Award – 2012, having earned A's in all 6 Psychology classes
- The only student to complete all 5 of the Psychology classes offered by Dr. Leonard Dupille
- Coca-Cola All US Academic Team Award – CT – 2011
- Served as Student Government President – 2010–2011
- Served as Student Government Treasurer – 2011–2012
- Received the MCC Student Leader Award – 2011
- Was selected to act as the Alumni Advisor for the Phi Theta Kappa at Manchester Community College as of May 2012 (ongoing)

CHAPTER 4

A New Beginning

By Eddie Rivera

"The path to success is never a straight line."

My father, Eddie Rivera Senior, was born in the mid 1960s in Santurce, San Juan, Puerto Rico. He was the first of eight children four boys and four girls. Growing up he remembered playing with his brothers and sisters outside along with his friends and watching his favorite super hero crush Wonder Woman on their first black and white television. Although he remembers having good times as a child, he also remembers his family's economic hardship throughout those years. He grew up in great poverty. At the age of eight he remembers living in a small cabin my grandfather built behind his mother and father's house.

After Eddie graduated high school he decided to do something that changed his life forever. He ventured out and took a plane to New York City to live with some family members in hope for a new beginning. "I left Puerto Rico because I wanted to break the chain of poverty that ran in my family and I wanted my children in the future to experience a different life than the one I grew up in. Moving to New York was a drastic change for me and I didn't speak English. The city's population was double from Santurce and everything was fast paced. It took me a while to adjust." He had to learn how to take a taxi, subways and trains to get around. "All this was new and exciting at first but after a while I felt homesick and questioned if moving to the city was really worth it." Despite the challenges he was facing, Eddie decided to stay in New York and overcame every obstacle.

His first two years in the city was no easy task. He couldn't speak English so it was hard for him to find a job. "It was hard for me to communicate what I wanted to say to people. Luckily my uncle worked at a pizza shop and I was able to work there. I remember this is where I started to learn English. At first my co-workers mocked me because I spoke funny but I was able to speak fluent English fairly quickly." This was his first job in the United States and he worked there for three years.

A few years went by and Eddie decided to get in contact with his mother and father to see how they were doing. He learned they had migrated from Puerto Rico to Connecticut with his seven brothers and sisters so that they could receive a better education and better opportunities. He then moved to Connecticut to help them get situated and the siblings enrolled in school.

In 2003 Eddie enrolled in a computer technician program. He wanted a career that didn't require much schooling and that provided hands-on training. He graduated in 2005 and started working right away as a computer technician. The training he received at the school changed the course of his life and he was able to provide for his children.

Like my father, I also attended a technical high school. I attended A.I. Prince Technical High School. My trade was Auto Collision repair and during my time there I worked on various projects from student cars to instructors' cars. After I graduated in 2008 my goal was to work at a body shop as a painter so I enrolled in Lincoln Technical Institute in 2008 and graduated in 2009 with a certificate in Auto Collision Repair. That dream quickly faded during my summer internship when I realized I wasn't passionate about working on cars my whole life and saw it more as a hobby.

After the internship I took a year off to see what direction I wanted to go in life. I've always thought of attending college but coming from a single income household I never considered actually attending since it is so expensive. But thanks to a friend I had who attended Manchester Community College I was encouraged to apply and I enrolled in the fall semester of 2010.

My first year in college was challenging. I was working full time as a transport aid at a hospital, which consisted of bringing patients to multiple test centers throughout the hospital in order for them to get any examinations needed so that they could move forward with proper treatment or surgery. Although I found my job rewarding, trying to balance both work and school was hard for me. I had no time to use the resources available through the school for extra help and as a result my grades suffered. The following semester I enrolled in a public speaking course with Professor Sullivan. This course really pushed me out my comfort zone and allowed me to grow as a person since I'm more of an introvert. The course consisted of short speeches along with some research. One day during class the professor said something that stuck with me until this day, "Be the Change You Wish to See in the World." The semester after I took Public Speaking I received straight A's and made the dean's list.

Since I was having difficulty balancing a full work load and school I decided to work part time so I could focus more on my education, and thanks to the MCC Foundation I was awarded scholarships which allowed me to focus more on my school work and less on how I was going to pay for tuition. Ever since I took that step of faith my grades improved tremendously and in the spring of 2015 I graduated from Manchester Community College with an Associate's degree and transferred to Central Connecticut State University as a junior. I am pursuing a Bachelor's in Science in Computer Science with a minor in Management Information Systems.

If you are someone who is looking for a new beginning, community colleges provide you with endless opportunities. Don't be afraid to explore a variety of subjects that interest you, follow your passion, and step out of your comfort zone. If it wasn't for the affordability of community college and the resources they offered, I would've never attended college. I'm grateful for the education provided by community colleges and glad I took a step of faith that ultimately altered my destiny.

CHAPTER 5

Everything in Life Has a Cost

By Sarah Brihan

I am a big believer that everything in life has a cost. Whether the cost is high or it is low, every choice we make has an impact. Our job is to decide what choices are best for us and which choices have the highest benefit with the lowest sacrifice. This means that for every person, choices are different for many different reasons. I know for myself, the benefit of going to community college outweighed any sacrifices involved. For others the cost of losing out on a college experience may be too high to part with, and they choose the path of going to a university to study. In this day and age every 18 year old is going to have to make the choice of going to college or not, and if they chose to go, what route they will take. For myself, community college was the best choice that I could have made for myself, financially, personally, and academically.

    I was accepted into six different schools at the end of my senior year. However, the one school that I truly wanted to go to waitlisted me, and ultimately rejected me. At the same time I had experienced three deaths in my family that were looming over my head as I finished up high school. There were days it was difficult to get out of bed, but I continued to fight my way through the grief, and get myself to class every day. When it came time for me to make my decision of where to go to college, I ultimately felt that I was not in a good emotional place to attend school. Paired with being rejected from that school, I also found myself questioning what I wanted to go to school for, which had previously been fashion. Since this path required me to go to a college with that degree, my choices were limited. I decided that I would take a gap year to heal personally, as well as figure out my passion in life.

It seems that fate, or God, or the universe was looking out for me, because I got a job working at a before and after school program. The program truly changed my life. I had previous experience, in high school, volunteering with children, and I even worked at a children's clothing store for two and a half years prior to my gap year. I had never really thought about working with children, since I had mostly just been around them in passing and short amounts of time. After spending over 30 hours a week with students, I began to fall in love with working with children. For the past two and a half years since I started my job, I can proudly say that I have been happy to go to work every single day. While not every minute of every day is happy, I am happy at my job every single day. I once heard that when you find what you are passionate about in life, it only gets better with age, just like all forms of true love. I have truly found one of the great loves of my life, simply by following my intuition and taking time off to figure out what I wanted to do. By the end of my gap year, I found what I wanted to do. I want to become an elementary school teacher.

My students are the very motivator that has inspired me to get a degree in Elementary Education. I decided that instead of taking out loans to pay for college, I would attend Manchester Community College in order to save money. The cost of living at home and being able to work was a benefit to me towards going to community college. There are many misconceptions surrounding community colleges and their programs. I can remember running into a girl from high school and her asking me, "Do you even have majors at community college?" The answer is yes. We absolutely have majors, interests, minors, internships, and many of the other benefits of regular university at community college. In fact I am in a Pathways to Teaching major. My major is geared to fit an elementary education major at my four-year institution I have chosen. Furthermore, there are many different programs and majors at community college that are fit to transfer into surrounding schools and universities. For me to be able to get the same education as many of my university peers at a low cost the financial benefit was clear.

Academically community college has given me so many gifts. When I started my degree at Manchester Community College in Pathways to Teaching, I began taking classes in childcare and child psychology. For example, in my Early Childhood Education class I learned about the different ways in which children learn. Children of the ages between 5 and 8 typically learn best with tangible objects and with rhymes. Furthermore, I used this knowledge for a project I made. I wrote a children's book that teaches children the alphabet, using rhymes and through bright visually stimulating pictures. I was able to create a book where children can easily learn the alphabet. This educational experience from my community college further transitioned into my work life.

Last year one of my students had profound difficulty in learning to read. My experience in school with learning about how children process information gave me the tools I needed to help out that student. I can remember for a few weeks I would take her out in the hall and help her sound out words. As time went on, I used the skills of picking out books with rhyming and brighter colors to help my student learn to read. The better I became at pinpointing books appropriate for her age, and her interest level, in turn with her reading skills, the better she became at reading. This, while a small impact over time, has helped that child gain self-efficacy and better reading skills. I would not have been able to make such an impact if it were not for my education. My schoolwork has clearly provided me with many tools to help me in my career path and at my job.

Mr. Rogers once said, "Anyone who does anything to help a child in his life is a hero to me." Because of my amazing education that has been provided to me at community college, I have made a significant impact in a child's life. Manchester Community College has given me the opportunity to become a hero for children. The most significant things are sometimes small bursts of help from those who are there to mentor and help you grow. I know for that student, she has helped me grow as much as I have helped her grow. Community college has given me the opportunity to change the lives of children around me, and in turn I have been able to positively impact their lives.

Conversely, many people assume that community college means that there is a sacrifice when it comes to getting the social aspects of college. While I admit there have been times I wish I could have lived on campus or with roommates, for myself, the sacrifice of this has ultimately paid off for me. I have been able to save up money that I am able to make, because I can work and go to school, and travel. I have been able to make wonderful life-long friends at my community college, people who truly are smart and kind. Furthermore, I have gotten some unusual experiences at my age that have made my life as happy as it is. When I started at community college, I took a job as a nanny in the morning, paired with working at the school program. So while I may not get to roll out of bed for my eight AMs, I get to drive a kid to school every morning. I have been a big part of that child's life. I have been able to gain work experience in my field that will separate me from the other applicants at grad school and for teaching jobs. Most importantly, I have gained life experiences, and have been able to build a life around what I find to be important.

To sum it up, my experience at community college has changed my life forever. I am able to get a quality education, at a small cost, and I am able to work and find passion in the everyday life of working with children. I have also been able to learn in an environment which is supportive and one I can grow in. Coming back to school, nonetheless college, after taking time off is terrifying. I have been able to bloom so much at Manchester Community College because of the amazing staff and resources available to me. I have also been able to gain work experience in my field, which will help me as I enter the workforce, and I have been able to create bonds with my students that will last a lifetime. College is truly what one makes of it. College is a highly individual place. You chose your major, you chose your school, you chose when you go to class and you also choose if you're going to show up to those classes. A student who takes the time to go to class, to learn and to study is one that truly gets the college experience. One can go to Yale and never show up to class, and not learn a thing, or a student can hire other people to write their papers, but these are the people that get nothing from college. The people who take the time to be present in college and the learning involved are the people who walk away the richest of all.

CHAPTER 6

Survival and Resilience

By Chhan D. Touch, MS, FNP

I am nervously sitting on the available desk without knowing what to expect. Quickly, I am glancing at my surrounding area and observing various faces and colors of scores of students sitting and smiling among themselves. As far as I can figure out, I am the only Asian student in this class. My heart fills with pride for this moment. Indeed, I am actually feeling excitement, pride, curiosity and nervousness.

Who can blame me for such feelings?

After all, this is my first English as a second language (ESL) class in formal education in the United States. It might seem like a minor thing for most people, but, for me, this moment is far greater than anyone can ever imagine. For years, I have dreamed of this moment when I can safely attend a formal classroom and learn without worrying about the rockets, bombs, hand grenades and bullets or being chased by Thai soldiers. This is my ultimate dream as well as my father's wish for my future. Thus, this is the beginning where I begin my life anew in this wonderful country, the United States of America.

Quietly, a tall, slender and curly-haired English professor with eyeglasses is speaking to the class, but I cannot fully understand what he is talking about as he is speaking too fast. I can only hear two words that I presume to be his name.

One by one, each student is standing up and speaking about his or her backgrounds. Mostly, I cannot understand what they are talking about. Up to now, I have been in the United States for about 12 months.

I am still unsure about my new life and what my future will be. I am still adjusting to my new environment and searching for my future. After a student next to me finishes his speech, I know that it is my turn.

Gingerly, I am nervously getting up and murmuring in my strong accent, "My name is Chhan Touch and I am a Cambodian refugee…"

That was fall semester of 1989 at Manchester Community College (MCC), in Manchester, Connecticut. Despite more than 25 years that have gone by, I can still recollect my first and formal education in American. It was where I began a lifelong journey, from being an ignorant refugee to becoming an educator, from being a survivor of the Killing Fields to becoming a health care provider and from giving up on life to embracing it. Nevertheless, there were several people who made a significant impression in my life, helping and guiding me to face and challenge the unknown world. Those people are always in my mind and memories: Narin and Sokphal Kchao (sister and brother-in-law), Neary Touch (my tough but supportive sister), the D'Avanzos (my foster family), Mrs. Diana Hossain and Mr. Patrick Sullivan (English teachers) and Dr. Arnold (Biology teacher). From my initial education at MCC, I have determined to pursue higher education and to make a difference in people's lives. Physically, I am weak, but I am mentally strong and resilient because I had to survive in the most inhospitable environment.

For more than 18 years, spanning from 1970 to 1989, I lived through the most terrifying and unimaginable nightmares. My childhood was smeared with blood and suffering through the brutal civil wars and labor camps. In my teen and early adulthood, I had to survive the famine, the oppression of a communist government and years of despair in various refugee camps along Cambodian-Thai borders. After arriving in the United States on September 1, 1988, I had to overcome many obstacles to achieve my dreams. Throughout these years, it would have been easier to give up and to let go because the dead would feel no pain or suffering. Yet, I have refused to give up. I have been given an opportunity to live while millions perished. Thus, I have determined to survive and succeed in my new life, new country and new identity. For those curious readers, to understand my life, perseverance, struggle, dedication and success, I invite you to travel with me along the path of life from Cambodia to the United States of America. This is the spirit of a survivor, my story[1] and a legacy of a survivor of the Killing Fields, Cambodia.

My Homeland: Cambodia

The kingdom of Cambodia is located in Southeast Asia, adjacent to Thailand in the west, Vietnam in the east, Laos in the North and gulf of Thailand in the south. Shielding from the brutal and vicious wars engulfing in other parts of the borders, my homeland is a pure paradise for my family and her citizens. Famine is non-existent in a country that is plentifully bestowed by nature's gifts—richly fertilized soils, abundant fish in the water, and wild animals in the untouched jungles. There are plentiful stocks of fish in the gigantic Tonle Sap (Freshwater River), one of the biggest freshwater lakes in the world, connecting from the end of the Mekong River to the deep swamps at the far horizon and extending approximately 233 miles in length. In dry season, the lake is shallow with visible edge on the horizon. In rainy season, it is rapidly swelling into a large, deep, and borderless ocean.

On the higher ground, green foliage and healthy forestry becomes a secured sanctuary for wild animals and beasts. Some jungles, such as the Cardamom Mountains, have never been touched for centuries. There are plentiful stocks of various wild animals in the jungles that have sustained the life of its inhabitants for centuries. Going hunting in the wild jungles, one rarely returns home empty-handed. Commonly, hunters can easily find various kinds of meat to supplement their daily meager diets or simply sell them for cash. The fertile soils along the Mekong River and paddy fields yield abundant vegetation and crops throughout the year.

The Phnom Penh City is rapidly growing and expanding, becoming a major business center and main capital city of Cambodia. The city dwellers, the peasants, and the farmers can comfortably live despite the harsh condition of the tropical climate. Life in the city as well as the countryside is peaceful and comfortable. In the city, most businesses are commonly open late into the night where shoppers are incessantly shopping late into the early morning. In the countryside, famers and peasants can plant and harvest sufficient rice and other products to sustain their livelihood year round. Such appeasement and harmony of nature and inhabitants create a wonderful and peaceful paradise on earth for the Cambodians. In the early 1960s, Cambodia is at her most peaceful time—the golden year. Many European tourists come to nickname Phnom Penh City, the only capital in Cambodia, as the Petite Paris.

My parents own a prosperous jewelry store located in the major business district center of Phnom Penh City. Just as other business owners in the area, we are doing well. Our country is not in war unlike our neighbors and our lives are fantastic. Our future is bright and quite promising.

The Civil Wars (1970–1975)

In early 1960, the struggle for superiority and power between communist and capitalist has brought wars to peaceful Southeast Asia. In Vietnam and Laos, blazing wars have destroyed everything. Before long, despite her attempt to avert the oncoming calamity, the catastrophic wars finally spilled into Cambodia.

On March 18, 1970, with the American support, a coup has been carried out by military marshal, General Lon Nol, in Cambodia. The revered King Norodom Sihanouk was ousted from the throne and the country has instantly fallen into anarchy and imminent civil wars. The monarchy rule that dominated Cambodia for centuries is suddenly ended, being replaced by a new government, Khmer Republic, with American support. Almost overnight, everything has completely changed. It is the ideological war between the Khmer Rouge forces, supported by Chinese communists, against the Khmer Republic, supported by the American capitalistic power.

As the brutal civil wars are raging in the countryside, the beautiful Phnom Penh City with her elegant boulevards and pristine buildings and homes is now packed with frightened refugees from the war zones. They have moved to the city to seek protection, shelter and haven from the bloody wars. They will sleep anywhere and do anything to survive. By the end of war, Phnom Penh City swells up with more than three million people. Nights are no longer safe as violent crimes are mushrooming in every part of the city and are dominating every city dweller's life. Television shows graphic images of war casualties. The captured prisoners were tortured, killed, and decapitated to inspire fear in their enemies. Fear and hatred are permeating into everyone's soul. There are now no safe places anywhere in my beautiful country.

Due to fear, my parents have forbidden us from venturing outside without being escorted. Our business is now cut short, especially at night due to frequent robberies. A heavy reinforced metal door is installed to prevent breaking-in. A security guard is now standing by the door of our business to discourage any unwanted attention. A handgun as well as an automatic rifle are placed within reach at the front desk. It is unsettling to see this precaution.

I am, as well as my other siblings, not allowed to walk to school despite the close proximity. My parents always have someone bring us back and forth from school via our car. School is no longer fun as hours are cut short and everyone always rushes to get from one place to another. Something is drastically wrong in my beautiful world.

By 1973, bombs begin falling in the city. The rebel forces have indiscriminately bombed the city. Schools, markets, hospitals, public places, theatres and government buildings are targeted and bombed. A few weeks earlier, my brother's kindergarten classroom was bombed. Although he was miraculously spared, many of his classmates were not. I can still remember the blood-soaked linoleum floor, slippery and grimly stained with fresh blood. The screams for help and the maimed bodies of the lifeless corpses have permanently imprinted in my memory. Up to present day, as I am talking about that event, I can still smell the sharp odor of fresh blood mixing with internal contents and the smell of death.

Finally, due to bombings, public and private schools have ceased to function as they are deemed unsafe under the current situation. Economic crisis becomes a major issue as prices for foods and other necessary items are skyrocketing. People who can afford to begin leaving the country for other safe havens in Europe or American continents. People who cannot and those who choose to remain in Cambodia, just as my parents, begin praying and hoping that the end of war will be at hand. Yet, unlike our hope and pray, the outcome of war becomes the most horrifying nightmares and destruction of our beloved country.

The Exodus (April 17, 1975)

From the radio, we just learned that our new Republic president, Gen. Lon Nol, his family and entourage are leaving for America. The US embassy as well as other foreign embassies begin packing up and hastily departing. High ranking and important military officers are escaping through their military helicopters or on their route toward Thailand in the western part of Cambodia.

The end is fast approaching and we are cheerful for knowing that this brutal civil war will soon be over. Everyone hopes for peace. Yet, we remain jittery and unsure of what to expect from this soon-to-be new government. Previous reports from various rumors about this new government have painted horrifying images of their practices and governance. Yet, due to our decision, we are hopelessly trapped and we can only wish that we will be spared from the unknown fate that we will find out within the next few weeks.

The day has come. On the first and second days of Khmer New Year (April 14 and 15, 1975), there is no one venturing outside to celebrate this once joyful event. For the last few days, the bombings are getting worse and the fighting is edging closer toward the city. Apparently, it is just a matter of time before the Khmer Republic government will be defeated. The streets and markets that are once normally packed with hasty shoppers for the celebration are completely deserted. The city is now simply a ghost town. Residents are hiding inside their houses in order to avoid accidental rockets and flying bullets.

On the third day of Khmer New Year (April 16, 1975), the situation is worse as the fighting is intensifying. Gathering at the lowest level of our house, we are trying to survive from day to day. April is the hottest season of the year. As the temperature and humidity soar to three digits, and we are trying to keep ourselves cool. Electricity is gone for weeks after the rockets hit the energy department. We are fortunate to have plenty of water in reservoir tank. With some firewood for cooking and kerosene to light our darkest nights, we are wondering how long we have to endure this uncertainty. Although we have a well running generator, gasoline is one of the most scarce and expensive commodities.

On the final day of Khmer New Year (April 17, 1975), something happens. We wake up to the absolute silence except the strong burning scents of gun powders that seem to permanently permeate the stiff air. It is eerily quiet. The loud echoes from the rockets and bombs are gone except some small gun fire in the distance. From the top level of our veranda, I see people running on the street in every direction. Behind them, columns of tanks are rolling lazily into the heart of the Phnom Penh City. Indeed, the war is finally over.

In the late afternoon of the same day, my father tells us to pack some of our clothes and foods for immediate departure. Earlier, just as other city residents, he has been ordered by the victorious soldiers to leave our home and the city for three days to avoid imminent bombings from the American air force. In the early evening, carrying our belongings, we are leaving our home and joining thousands of other frightened evacuees on the way out of the city. The streets are packed with a flood of people that seem to endlessly flow into the streets from every corner. Before long, the darkness is shrouding the entire city, save the sporadic and scattered lights from some vehicles which are barely sufficient for anyone to see. Yet, even without light to guide them, the multitudes are continually moving and pushing forward, like the roaring waves that are angrily pounding and trampling on each other by the command of the strong wind. Glancing from the boulevards, houses are abandoned in dark silhouette as their owners are forced to leave them behind. Along the boulevards, scores of dead bodies begin decomposing in the searing heat, cascading unbearable stench of decayed flesh into the air. From the start, I know that it will be one of the longest nights of my life. This might be one of the dreams that I will never wake up from.

The Labor Camp (04/17/75–01/07/79)

Several weeks after leaving our home and city, we are forced to move further away from the city. Realizing that we will not be permitted to return home after three days, my father has decided to take us to his home village in the countryside. Little do we know what is awaiting us in that place will forever change our lives. Every district has transformed into fenceless labor camps where we are forced to work and die from starvation and execution. We are the innocent who are now the prisoners of war of our new government, known as Khmer Rouge (KR = Khmer Communist) or Democratic Kampuchea (DK).

Cambodia has now entered the Year Zero where everything from the past must be erased. The DK compares Cambodia to a field of grass. In order to create a pure and utopian society, the field must be cut and burned. Comparatively, most people except selected groups are regarded as tainted or "old grass" that need to be cultivated, cut or eliminated. They are destined to be executed whereas selected remnants are allowed to live and to produce the "purely" bred communist population. To implement such doctrine, everything from the past is ordered to be destroyed. School, money, privacy, market, family, movies, music, arts, dance, education and others are abolished. Under current government, Cambodia has now entered Year Zero where modernity is eliminated. Population are forced to manually toil by their human strength in the fields—plowing, raking, working, digging, and building—under the watchful eyes of the merciless guards. It is the dream of purely utopian society of the DK.

Strategically, under the DK regulations, anyone who previously related to the old regime, such as educators, professionals, students and business people, are regarded as tainted by the old influences, are deemed unworthy to trust and are thus ordered to be terminated. Everything, living and non-living, belongs to the DK government. All young children are also under the proxy care of the DK. Family relationships and privacy are forbidden. People are ordered to eat at the common kitchen with other hundred people. Foods are controlled, provided and served by the local villagers. Absolute obedience is a must and there is no contest. Any disobedient will find himself or herself dragged to the fields, tortured, executed and discarded. In the DK, there is only one punishment—death—regardless of the degrees of the offenses. Sometimes, this murdering act is carried out by one of the soldiers or family members of the victims. Failure to carry out this order is not an option and will result in the ultimate punishment.

During that time, my siblings are scattered in every direction by the order of the local village leaders. They are taken separately to various unknown destinations. All of our personal possessions, such as clothes and utensils, are confiscated by the village leaders. Per regulation, each family member is allowed to have only one spoon. Each family is allowed to have only one kettle for water boiling and there is nothing else. Family interaction and privacy are non-existent.

Work is the worst and relentless part of all tasks. A twelve to fifteen hour work shift is common among all age groups. Workers are forced to toil in the fields from early in the morning to midnight with little rest and food. One by one, my friends and relatives begin dying, starting from the smallest to the oldest due to overwork. Commonly, there are two types of death—direct and indirect. Direct—the DK implements mass execution where hundreds and thousands are arrested and murdered. Indirect—many are forced to work without food and rest. They are usually succumbed to death from diseases, overwork and starvation.

The majority of people in my village are directly executed. My brother-in-law was one of those unfortunate people. Later, his only daughter also died from starvation and diseases. I have also suffered from severe malnutrition due to lack of food and overwork, but I am fortunate to survive. Yet, it has taken me more than six months to recuperate from my debilitation. For years, my family has lived in constant fear and despair. From day to day, we count our hours and we pray that we can survive another day. This agonizing is almost unbearable. We are just like fish in a drying pond. Sooner or later, just as a matter of time, our ultimate fate will arrive. Despite this knowledge, we are helpless and we have to wait for our final day to come.

The Liberation (January 7, 1979)

After a brief skirmish with neighboring People's Republic of Vietnam (PRV), the DK is invaded and toppled by the stronger People's Republic of Vietnam (PRV) forces on January 7, 1979. Regardless of political reason behind the invasion, Cambodian survivors are exhilarated for surviving.

In the end, my family has survived from the gruesome death by the Khmer Rouge regime. Yet, the atrocities that are inflicted by the DK have been one of the most destructive holocausts in human history. For less than four years, more than three million of seven million lives of innocent Cambodians are painfully perished. Millions are eternally suffered. A beautiful country, my beloved Cambodia, has been permanently scarred.

After removing the DK government, a Vietnamese-supported government, known as People's Republic of Kampuchea (PRK), has become a legitimate and political body of a new government, under the direct supervision and control of PRV, of the scarred and fragmented Cambodia. Surviving Cambodians now have to survive another dictatorial communist government. My family can only hope that at least this PRK will let us survive despite the fact that severe famine and diseases are now plaguing the entire country. Thousands have died from various diseases and lack of food, especially hundreds and thousands of parentless children.

My family is permitted to return to the Phnom Penh City—a city of ghosts. Yet, our homes and everything are confiscated by the new government. We are not allowed to return to our home. We are again homeless and we are forced to seek shelter someplace else. Fortunately, there are thousands of empty and uninhabited homes in the city of ghosts. The reconstruction of the country is almost impossible as every infrastructure has virtually been destroyed. Cambodia is a country full of old people, young children, helpless women, and disabled people. Internationally, the PRK is regarded as a puppet of the PRV, is ostracized and is not recognized by the international communities except the communist countries in Eastern Europe, Soviet Union, and Cuba. No food or financial support is granted to the starving nation. Cambodia is again at the brink of another human catastrophe. Daily surviving is a struggle that seems to have no end.

Making the matter worse, despite being prosecuted and survived by the DK as other Cambodians, Chinese Cambodians are targeted and persecuted by the PRK. Unfortunately, as Chinese Cambodians, my family has suffered the wrath of the current situation, classifying as the second and unwanted class. Being discriminated and labeled, I found it is getting harder to survive. From day to day, the pressure is intensifying. It soon becomes apparent that Cambodia no longer welcomes people with my skin color. We are now seeking an alternative solution for our current dilemma.

In the western part of Cambodia, at the Cambodian-Thai borders, as the rumors have circulated, international agencies are helping and saving Cambodian refugees who escape from Cambodia to seek shelter and haven from starvation and persecution. Some are even granted the privilege to resettle in another country. We now know what we have to do. Yet, it is the journey of no return. Chances of being killed by landmines, bandits and soldiers in the jungles are proportionally high and we could be those nameless victims, but we have no choice and we no longer have any fear. Either way, we would be killed, but we rather die trying to be free from this cruel fate.

The Escape from Phnom Penh City (5:00 am, July 21, 1984)

In early 1980, my sister Narin[2] has escaped to the refugee camps with her husband and in-laws. We heard that she is now living in America. We too wish to join her.

Days earlier, my three sisters escaped from the city to the border areas in the western part of Cambodia. Fortunately, we are not yet detained and investigated by the secret police in the city. Yet, it is just a matter of time and my luck will run out soon. Secret police have no mercy for the escapees. For now, my youngest brother and I are the last to go. My father has refused to leave as he is too old for such a strenuous and dangerous journey. Grievingly, I know that it will be our last time to see each other alive. In his old age, my father has unselfishly permitted me to leave him and to seek for a better life in someplace else. It has been the most difficult decision that I have ever made.

Five days later (July 21, 1984), after bidding my father farewell, evading and escaping the secret police from Phnom Penh City and along the escape routes, I finally come closer to the border. From the last village to the border camps, I have to walk approximately 40 miles across millions of unexploded landmines and scores of bandits as well as wild animals in the jungles. People who dare to venture into those areas will be on their own, taking all chances and risks. After all, it is jungle law—whoever has the gun will be the master. For the unfortunate escapees, after being robbed, men are summarily executed whereas women will be gang-raped and then have their throats slit. Escapees are fully aware that they could be killed on this journey—either from landmines, bandits or wild animals. Yet, nothing can deter them from trying to get out from Cambodia.

Despite the odds, I have survived. On July 28, 1984, I safely arrived at Nong Chan and then Rithysen refugee camps along the Cambodian-Thai borders, surrounded by thick forests and millions of landmines. Yet, along the route, I was captured and placed in temporary prison where I and others bravely broke out and escaped. In the thick jungles, I crossed miles of abandoned lands and forest with unmarked millions of landmines. I survived gunfire from the bandits and miraculously did not step on landmines in the bushes. Whoever stepped on landmines was left to die in the middle of the jungle. The scream of pain and pleading for mercy fell on deaf ears. None would dare to trek into the minefields to rescue others. For weeks, after crossing minefields, I often wake up in the middle of the night, sweating and trembling with fear. I could have been one of those unfortunate souls.

The good news is that my three sisters who left Phnom Penh City earlier are safe. They have fortunately survived the journey despite countless risks and obstacles. For the moment, we are reunited in the middle of nowhere. Amid millions of landmines, I feel trapped. Worse, I literally am in the middle of a war zone. Once again, I feel that I have come to the end of my rope. Frightened and lacking all hope, I begin to wish that I would die soon so the suffering that I have to endure day and night for these years will be gone. At times like this, I wish to be with my father who has always guarded and protected me in time of need. I am wondering how long I have to endure before I will either step on landmine or be shot by the soldiers or enemies.

My family temporarily lived in Rithysen Camp that was established by the guerrilla groups in 1980. It is the biggest among many refugee camps along the Cambodian-Thai borders. Many escapees have stayed there for several decades, but, for some, it is a stopover from the mainland Cambodia to the borders and then deeper into Thailand. The final destination for all Cambodian refugees who intend to resettle to another country is Khao-I-Dang Camp (KID), located eight miles in Thailand and along the gigantic mountains, which is the only hope for all Cambodian refugees. Only legal refugees in KID are currently accepted by the United Nations High Commissioner of the Refugees (UNHCR) and will be granted permission to immigrate to the third country, such as US, Canada, Japan, and European countries. For other refugees who are living in various camps along the borders are regarded as displaced people. They are not recognized as legal refugees and are not permitted to leave for a third country. Thus, thousands will risk their lives just to enter KID Camp. Unfortunately, KID Camp has stopped accepting any refugee since 1982. No one knows what will happen to people who enter that camp illegally. Yet, no one cares to know that fact. We are only trying to move one step and then think another step. Moreover, the eight miles spanning from

Rithysen Camp to KID Camps are blanketed with landmines and patrolled by Thai soldiers. Thousands of those unfortunate Cambodian refugees who sneaked into Thailand toward KID Camp were captured, raped and gunned down in cold blood by the black uniformed Thai soldiers. On this journey, this is one of the most dangerous journeys.

Yet, we have little choice. Despite Narin has tried to sponsor us directly from Rithysen Camp, her application has been denied as we are regarded as displaced people. Thus, our final destination has to be KID Camp. Dead or alive, I have to risk my life to enter KID Camp for it is the only pathway that will lead me to my ultimate dream, the United States of America. Among my family members, we have discussed and agreed that we will begin our journey sometime by the end of the year. Yet, an unforeseen situation propels us to act sooner. For months, rumors have circulated that the camp will be soon attacked by the massive forces of the Cambodian Armies (PRK) with the support of Vietnamese armies (PRV). Although these types of rumors have surfaced every year, we sense that something serious will probably happen this year. Warily, we have to change our plan. For us, time is running out.

One of my older sisters, Nalie has decided to head toward KID Camp per her husband's insistence. He has been in that camp several months earlier and is now urging her and his three-year-old daughter to come along as something big will certainly happen—will be soon. To avoid attention from Rithysen Camp soldiers, as people are barred from leaving for KID Camp, we have subdivided our family into three groups and will take turns to leave at different days and times. With our meager savings, we find people who agree to lead us to KID camp if the price is right, crossing landmines and deadly military squads. We call them "guides."

On 11/5/1984, Nalie, her daughter and three guides leave Rithysen Camp for KID Camp. Throughout day and night, we keep listening for the sound of gunshots, but there are none. The sounds of gunshots mean that someone is killed. Silence means that no one has been hurt or killed. We rejoice for we believe our loved ones have survived the ordeal. Soon, as we have planned, it will be my turn.

A few days later, on 11/10/1984, my designated group (Nalen, a boy named Mao, three guides and me) begin our secret journey toward KID Camp. No one knows for sure what might happen to us, but we determine to ignore the uncertainties and fears. The last group will consist of my oldest sister, Neary, and my youngest brother, Pouv. Rigidly, we are bidding each other goodbye, daring not to utter any fear or we will have no courage to step into the line of the firing squad.

Despite several close calls, we have somehow managed to survive the night and finally entered KID Camp. After passing through the barbwire fences, I am so terrified of the journey that I have refused to come any closer to the fences until the day that I have to leave KID Camp to a new camp in 1988. On 11/23/1984, Neary and Pouv have also made it safely into KID Camp. They too have a harrowing story to tell us of how they manage to elude the soldiers and arrive at the destination as planned. Just prior to their departure, they were ordered to carry ammunition to the front lines and to carry the injured soldiers back to the camp.

Despite our rejoicing for surviving this journey, our hearts feel heavy for the unfortunate loss of our sister, Nalie. We thought that her group made it through the journey. Unbeknown to us at that time, her group unfortunately ran into Thai border soldiers and they, except her daughter and one of the guides, were shot and killed. Her three years old daughter[3] has miraculously survived the attack and was taken by the surviving guide to her father in the KID Camp.

Several weeks later, on Christmas Day of December 25, 1984, the Rithysen Camp with approximately 50,000 residents is heavily attacked and completely annihilated by the Cambodian forces (PRK) and Vietnamese troops (PRV). Hastily, the camp residents have surged into Thailand and are placed in a temporary holding center, Red Hill site, inside Thai territory. After agreement between Thai royal government and the UN has been reached several weeks later, these refugees are transferred to temporary Bang Pu Camp or Site 7 and finally to a permanent Site II camp where they have resided until the camp was closed on March 3, 1993.

I have always remembered that day as vividly as if it has just happened hours earlier despite the span of time. On that night, standing approximately eight miles away in KID Camp, I saw the red flashes of rockets, bombs and gunfights being exchanged. I could feel the trembling echoes of the falling bombs. Despite it was unlikely that Cambodian and Vietnamese troops would attack an international camp deeper in Thailand, strayed bombs could drop in unintended location. Precautiously, all foreign workers were evacuated and all refugees were abandoned and left to defend for ourselves. That night, I prayed that the fighting would not spill into the KID Camp. More than anything else, thankfully, the rest of my siblings left Rithysen Camp at the nick of time.

The Khao-I-Dang Camp (11/10/1984–04/22/1988)

I used to believe that life in the KID Camp must be much more comfortable than Rithysen Camp as it is managed by the UNHCR. At night, it is normally shrouded with electric bright lights. In contrary, Ritthysen Camp has always been dark and desolated. There are no electric lights, running water, well maintained roads, sewages, or protective fences. At night, kerosene lamps or tree saps are used to lighten the misshaped huts, leaving foul odor in the air. Yet, upon arriving KID camp, I am stunned by the reality.

Lying beside KID Mountains, this rectangular camp is about two miles in length and one mile in width with approximately 30,000 Cambodian refugees. Behind the barbwire fences, there are hundreds of long, dirt-floored and bamboo thatched huts. Each hut accommodates about fifty people. At night, kerosene is used to light the hut. There is no running water or electricity. The water is collected from the water station where each legal resident is given four liters (two gallons) of water daily for cooking, bathing, and drinking.

Along the camp perimeter, Thai soldiers are standing guard to prevent unwanted intruders. They have orders to shoot at sight. Some are patrolling inside the camp day and night, searching and looking for illegal refugees. Firewood, meats, vegetables and other condiments are provided in limited quantity to every legal refugee by the UNHCR. Legal refugees can attend vocational and regular schools. Importantly, they are granted privilege to immigrate to a third country. Unfortunately, new refugees are no longer welcome in KID Camp since 1982. Thus, as an illegal refugee, I have nothing. I cannot even use the latrine without permission from the section leader. I am one of the unwanted refugees. To find shelter, use the latrine, obtain rice and water, and be existed, my family has to pay for everything and bribe the section leader to turn his head away.

Again, just like the Khmer Rouge time, I have lived in constant fear because I do not know when Thai soldiers will appear at the door. Moreover, we have to also please and bribe our neighbors since they can either help or report us to the Thai authority and we will instantly be arrested or worse. Traveling from one section to another is also risky. All legal refugees are required to wear their nametags at all times. These nametags contain their personal information. Without wearing it, one will be instantly arrested and thrown in jail. Thus, I can be arrested at any moment and my chance of getting out to a third country is absolutely zero. I am quite depressed as I am again coming to a dead end.

On February 17, 1985, more than 3,000 heavily armed Thai soldiers with supporting helicopters are sent to search and capture all illegal refugees in the camp. More than 1,000 illegal refugees are arrested. Scores are tortured, injured and killed during the search. Despite my secret double-walls and foxhole, I get caught while hiding on top of the roof of a bamboo building. Yet, while I am being transferred to jail, I have managed to slip away. Fortunately, all my siblings have successfully evaded the capture and are now free. Due to this close call, my fear is now multiplied as I do not know what to expect tomorrow. Yet, during this critical moment, something has happened that changes my life forever.

For weeks, the rumor has circulated that former first lady of the United States, Rosalyn Carter,[4] is going to visit the camp. We believe that she has come to help us, the illegal refugees, to obtain our legal status. We are making banners and posters to welcome and to plead for her support and mercy. On June 5, 1985, she comes, but we are barred from getting any closer. We cannot even raise our banners and posters. Yet, we are not chased away or arrested on that day due to the presence of these foreigners. I hope and pray that this foreign woman will be able to convince the Thai government to grant us permission to reside as legal refugees in KID Camp. So far, no one knows when this status will be again granted to any group of refugees. After her departure, the situation in KID Camp has not been improved, but it is getting worse. The hopeful dream becomes elongating without end. I am not sure whether I can endure this uncertainty any longer.

More than three months have passed by quickly. On the early morning of September 29, 1985, we wake up to the joyous news that the UNHCR and the Thai royal government have agreed to grant the legal status to the illegal refugees. I am joyful, but I do not trust Thai soldiers and camp commander. They are notoriously brutal and violent. It might be just a ploy to lure all illegal refugees to get out from their hiding places and to fall into their traps. After I quietly observe the event, I feel strongly that the announcement is genuine.

Despite the intense heat and ill-treatment from the Thai soldiers, it is still one of the best days of my life as I finally become a legal refugee. It means that we are now safe to live in the camp and my future is more promising. Since the beginning of my journey, my dream of reaching the United States is quite slim to impossible. I have expected to be dead along the way, but I now dare to hope for the impossible dream. Surely, I will make it and reach my dream. On September 29, 1985, I along with other

7,100 illegal refugees in KID Camp become legal, known as Ration Card (RC) recipients.[5] It is the turning point of my life and future. Although the dream is still far-fetched, I have at least completed the second phase of my journey and I am still alive.

The Third Country (04/22/1988–08/31/1988)

To my great disappointment and anxiety, the rumor has circulated that RC group will not be granted permission to resettle in another country. To make the matter worse, on December 4, 1985, the RC group is ordered to be transferred to KID Annex Camp, a new camp adjacent to KID Camp. These two camps are separated by barbwire fences and guarding soldiers. Unlike my previous hopeful dream, the future is suddenly gloomy.

A few years have gone by and my hope begins to wean. It is now approaching the end of 1987 and there is no news or even a tiny rumor. It is one of the most difficult periods of my life and I find it extremely difficult to continue to live in this hopeless dream. Consequently, some of my friends have committed suicide by hanging themselves in the nearby mountains. I do not blame them for their decision. Most have survived five years of civil wars, four years of labor camp, five years of communist occupation in Cambodia and years without hope in the desolate camps. We are nothing but prisoners behind the barbwire fences of this camp. Life has become meaningless and unbearable.

Just as my hope is about to die out, a sudden spark reignites this hope again. On a cold morning in January 1988, I wake up to hear a wonderful news that the RCs are now granted permission by the UNHCR and Thai Task Force 80 (TF 80) to be interviewed for the third country resettlement. The impossible dream will now be fulfilled. More than 7,100 joyful RCs are coming out from their huts, hugging and crying with one another under the cool January wind.

The interview process has quickly begun. After several interviews by a branch of the US embassy at Banthai Samart Camp, Aranyaprathet, Thailand, my family has finally been accepted as refugees to resettle in the United States on March 2, 1988. Before long, my family will be transferred to another camp for training and preparing for our new lives in the country of our host.

Finally, on April 29, 1988, my family with other hundreds of immigrants begin leaving the KID Camp for the Phanat Nikhom Camp where we will stay for a few months, readying ourselves and learning new ways of life in a new world. Four months later, on Wednesday August 31, 1988, my family is finally permitted to leave Thailand for the United States of America. After more than 18 years of living in complete despair, constant fears, nightmares and killings, I have for the first time seen a glimpse of hope. Before long, I will taste new freedom and freedom from fear, tears and blood. I can hardly believe myself that I will be finally free.

The American Dreams (09/01/1988)

My journey has finally come to a conclusion on September 1, 1988 upon my arrival in the United States. Yet, I know that my new life is only the beginning and I still have a very long way to go.

From what I have seen in downtown Miami, Florida, as a beggar is seen picking foods from a trash bin, I know that I am ill-prepared to face this new world. Without language, skills, money or any means to survive, my future perspective is gloomy. Nevertheless, I am a survivor of the most brutal regimes in the world and I am sure that I will survive anywhere. From the start, I know that my only way out of poverty is education. My priority is to go to school where I can begin rebuilding my new life in the United States. Thus, below is the brief information about my academic endeavor.

My Academic Achievement

September of 1988, a few weeks after my arrival in the US, I began studying for GED (General Educational Development) at nighttime and working during daytime. Four months later, I successfully passed the general exam and was awarded GED from North Miami Beach High School. Trying to pursue for higher education, I moved to Vernon, CT, after being invited by Mr. D'Avanzo whom I met in the KID Camp.

By fall 1989, I got accepted to Manchester Community College (MCC), in Manchester, CT. It was the turning point of my life because I was granted the opportunity to learn and prepare for my new life and future.

Eventually, I graduated from MCC in the spring of 1991 and I pursued my study at the University of Connecticut, in Storrs, CT, in the following fall semester. In the spring of 1992, I transferred to Atlantic Union College, South Lancaster, Massachusetts, where I graduated with Associate Degree (AS) and Bachelor Degree (BS) in nursing and minor degrees in biology and psychology in spring of 1994 and 1996, respectively.

In the fall of 1997, I got accepted to nursing graduate school at the University of Massachusetts Lowell (UML), in the family nurse practitioner program. Three years later, I finally obtained my Master Degree of Science in Family Nurse Practitioner (MSN, FNP) in May 2000. I was the first Cambodian American to graduate from the UML with a master's degree in family nurse practitioner.

In the fall 2004, I was accepted to the doctoral program, PhD in nursing, at the University of Massachusetts Lowell. In the fall of 2010, after completion of more than half of the entire curriculum for the PhD program, I decided to switch from the PhD program to DNP (doctor of nursing practice). The tasks are extremely difficult. Yet, whether I could accomplish this dream or not, it is irrelevant as long as I have tried my best. I have given myself an opportunity to challenge the impossible. Whatever the outcome, I will be fine. At least, I have tried.

Personal Insights

For more than 18 years of tribulation, tears, blood and unspeakable horror, I have survived. Looking back, I truly believe that negative experiences are not necessarily bad. By no means do I intend to imply that it is good to be a victim of a heinous crime either. Rather, negative experiences have shaped me into a stronger, more resilient and better human being because I know what it means and what it is like to be treated as a slave and subhuman.

Negative experiences are like a double edged sword. I can use it to improve or destroy my life. If I continue living in the past, I will not be able to move forward. Yet, I have survived the Cambodian tragedies and life in the refugee camps, there is nothing in this world that can stop me from reaching and fulfilling my ultimate goal. I have learned to be positive about life because I am a survivor. In fact, survivors are not weak but strong because they have overcome certain situation when most people cannot.

My siblings (Neary, Narin, Nalen and Pouv) and the D'Avanzo family have helped me to believe in myself. My wife and children are the pillars of hope during my despair and depression. Obviously, many have contributed to my present success. Looking back, despite the ugliness of wars and tragedies in my past, I come to believe that there is still compassion and empathy among mankind.

On academic achievement, I wonder what would have happened to me if I was not given an opportunity to start my education at MCC. As I stepped into that educational institution, that moment has been the turning point of my life. Community college education is perfectly designed for people like me with greater disadvantages. With smaller classes and more attention, I was given opportunities to learn according to my own pace. Through this education, I have been transformed from a lowly refugee to an educator. Rather than being a welfare recipient, I have become a citizen that has contributed to the growing and prosperity of this wonderful country, US.

Epilogue

Again, my daughter is stirring gently as my son is sleeping quietly upstairs. I am holding her closer and tighter. My children have given me so much love and comfort, the magic pills that are healing my wounded soul.

As if she can understand me, Nina is reaching out her arms, even in her sleep, gently circling my neck, murmuring in her sleepy voice, "I love you, *Daddy*."

Looking at her, she is still sleeping and snoring lightly. Holding her tightly in my arms, just as what I had done to my little niece, Srey Vy, in the fateful day of 1984 after I learned about the death of my sister, I am murmuring softly at her ear, "I love you, too, baby girl." I feel greatly satisfying for knowing that somebody has always loved me—even in her sleep!

Then, I feel warm tears are teeming in my eyes again—ready to flow.

Yet, I refuse to cry. Now I have so many reasons to be happy—a lovely family, wonderful children, supportive siblings, loving God, peace, security, and a successful career. Moreover, I have cried enough in my lifetime and I do not wish to cry anymore. Yes, I am not alone anymore. Furthermore, I can no longer continue to reside in the past. I can no longer allow myself to be tortured by the past—something that I cannot alter even an iota. I can no longer allow my future marring by the painful memories. It is time now that I have to live on, releasing myself from the eternal nightmares and self-blame that I am carrying along with me for years. Now, I have love surrounding me. It is time to be appreciative and thankful for all I have.

Slowly and gently, as I am letting go all of the painful past and memories, I feel the new joy surging and rejuvenating in my soul. Only then, I begin to smile…

Notes

1. I prefer to use present tense and present continuous tense in my writing as it would bring forth actual and vivid feeling for the readers.
2. My second older sister who came to the US [from the KID Camp] in early 1980.
3. My niece, Srey Vy, later went to Japan with her father. Her Japanese name is Yuka. We have never seen her again after she left the camp for Japan in 1987.
4. Her visit was reported in "Refugee Child," Rome News-Tribune, June 6, 1985, p. 4, a day later after her visit on Wednesday June 5, 1985.
5. I received RC on 09/29/1985, but that status was eventually changed to RH on 11/27/1985—five months before my group (RC) was granted permission to be interviewed for resettlement in the third country.

CHAPTER 7

The Accident of My Career and Academic Life

By Bethany Silver

The accident of my career and my academic life began with a high school dream that crashed and burned. I can say that now, comfortably perched on the pile of poorly crafted early essays that built themselves gradually into an Associate's degree from Manchester Community College. My first real adult learning happened there. The AS was followed by a BA, MA, and an eventual doctorate.

MCC picked me up where high school left off.

In my sophomore year of high school I discovered the Defense Language Institute in California. I loved languages. After nearly 15 years with my family—a family that had Americanized its already halting Canadian farm French, and two years of Spanish at a local Catholic high school, I knew I wanted to be a translator. I loved chatting away with anyone who spoke even a little bit of another language. I was especially zealous in pig-Latin.

Then high school graduation happened.

The Language school in California was a military school. Imagining a proud heritage of military service, following my father's lead with the Navy, I enlisted in the Marine Corps. Diploma in hand, I set off after my dream on a hot August afternoon. Leaving the air-conditioned cool of Bradley International Airport, I landed in the sticky heat of South Carolina in the middle of the night. In a swamp with only slightly more mosquitos than drill instructors, I took my first unsteady step towards a career.

Parris Island, even with all of the learning experiences a Staff Sergeant can plan, was magnificent. It offered breathtaking sunrises that I showed up for every day—early. There were also poetic moments of enlightenment, if you could find them among the 75 other women in your platoon, assembled for evening inspection in underwear and flipflops.

I struggled. People have told me that I don't look like a Marine. Sometimes you just can't argue with what you are not.

Still in the dark some weeks later, I left basic training, and came home. Dream over. As much as I enjoyed languages, the Marine Corps and I parted ways. We haven't spoken since. I never did learn to speak Marine, my embarrassing accent revealing me as a rank and file civilian.

I came home—to get married, and go to hair dressing school. The only problem with that plan was that I needed someone who wanted to marry me.... and I needed to enroll in beauty school. It was late fall—too late to start school, so ... I found a job waitressing. 18 turned to 19, and a whole winter of waiting gave way to spring. From my small place in the world, I expected that I would begin to figure things out. No school. No plan. No career path. I was so far from any real discovery.

In high school the question of college hadn't come up. When my friends were off visiting universities I was waitressing nights and weekends at Shady Glen restaurant. In high school I was an unremarkable scholar at best, and occasionally a noticeably poor one. During my first year of being a high school graduate I realized that most of my friends had headed off to college. I was ... a failed Marine, living at home with Mom and Dad, miles away from being a translator ... and completely without a plan for the rest of my adult life. My largest dreams could fit in the front pocket of my jeans, along with my car keys, random coins, and the ashes of my military career.

I couldn't know that things were going to change.

I didn't notice it at first, but there was a steady chorus playing in the background of my life. Seeming to come from a distant radio station, I would hear it from a customer at work, the lady at the supermarket. Gradually the chorus crept along at louder and louder decibels until I couldn't **not** hear it any more. It was on the lips of the lady at the convenience store, the librarian at Mary Cheney Library, the people who worked with my mother at the hospital, the guy at the Parkade Book Store who asked me if I qualified for a student discount, and my high school friends who were themselves tucked away into college lives—"Are you going to MCC?" Even my neighbor Judy from across the street, herself an MCC grad, asked me the same question, "Beth, when are you going to register for classes at MCC?"

I didn't know what college was about. I couldn't. My family was surprisingly bereft of college degrees. Not a single one hung from our family tree. My grandparents had succeeded as far as the eighth grade, and were proud of the high school diplomas their children had earned. They worked hard in blue collar jobs and were suspicious of soft-handed intellectuals. My mother earned her RN from a nursing school, and my father had spent a year in a technical electronics program after his discharge from the Navy. No one in my family had ever gone to college.

Near the end of summer in 1987, taking the abundant advice from friends, family, and strangers, I visited Manchester Community College. Before I ever opened the door and went inside, I reassured myself. It wasn't a real school. It was a place where people went when they didn't know what they were doing or where they were going. I estimated it might be a smaller failure than my trip to Parris Island.

I only had evidence of making poor choices.

I opened the door to the Lowe Building and went inside. It was August of 1987. There was a long line of students signing up for classes, all of them older and more experienced than me. Every face clearly said, "I have a plan." Every one of them was smarter than me, but I decided that didn't matter. I fixed my gaze on the floor, claimed the spot behind the last person in line, and joined the shuffling human chain. Like the Marine Corps, I followed the queue and took my entry tests. My counselor taught me that there was a finite list of required classes. She suggested five general courses. I signed up.

The night before classes started I didn't sleep. I didn't know what I wanted, but I did have some very specific examples of what I didn't want. I didn't want to go back to high school. I didn't want to go back to Parris Island. I was afraid of losing the scrap of autonomy I had secreted into my life since graduation. By dawn I resolved to learn to be good at ... maybe ... just one thing.

I would like to say that the college experience came naturally—but that wouldn't be true.

I took a lot of classes that first year, face-planting on a number of assignments. In fact, on one of my very first papers I learned that for my professor, it was "the worst paper" he had ever read. My solution was to re-write. He wasn't much older than me, and I figured he hadn't read a lot of papers. I managed a low C on the third re-submission, eventually squeaking by with a B in the course. By the end of my second semester I was still miles from understanding the big picture of a two-year degree.

Gradually, I came to understand that there was more to the world, and to me, than I imagined when I was in high school.

For example, I was elected vice-president of the student senate when no one ran against me. A month or so into my term I accidentally became the president when the current Student Senate president resigned.

I helped found the travel club and went to Venezuela twice, volunteered to be secretary of the ski club, and was invited to honors dinners and scholarship events at MCC. It seems that MCC found something in me that was capable of more. At about the 50 credit mark, 4 semesters in, deep in some unchartered part of myself, a series of previously hidden doors began to open. I became a real, honest to goodness college student.

I knew that English and Math classes requiring more than 5 pounds of reading intimidated me, as well as Mike DiRaimo's Technical Writing classes. The distress of my peers wrangling massive writing assignments from thin air convinced me to keep my distance. I tried two or three times before successfully completing my math requirements, and took as many French and Spanish classes as were offered. I met a lot of very different people, as young as 17 and as old as 84, and they came from all over the world—Bangladesh, Colombia, Nigeria, Ethiopia, Canada, Peru, Enfield and Hartford.

Some of my favorite classes were with people who had lived through the great depression and could tell their story right alongside the textbook in John Sutherland's history class, or Angelo Messore's political science classes.

My foreign language classes were full of interesting people. In addition to having my own mom in French 101, I met Peg, who, at 84 was polishing her conversational skills with our teacher, Mademoiselle Place.

In French 102 I debated the merits of leadership with a colorful man named Roger. He was calmly certain that leadership began with leading a single person—the self. I had previously thought that leaders required followers, and a lot of them. I've found the truth of Roger's insight valuable to this day. He eventually shared with me that he had AIDS. He was the first person I had met with AIDS, and in the late 80's his prospects didn't look good. Eventually we lost touch, yet his lesson in leadership has kept him in my life ever since.

It was these shining moments, when my mind broke the surface of mundane and entered a shimmering place brilliant with possibilities, that came to define my community of learners .... my college experience of MCC. Many of these moments were discovered in my psychology classes with Dr. Levy, in conversation with President Daube, Dean Meisel, and

Dean Corwin. In retrospect, it was these discussions that grounded me in this school, that created the *community* that a community college offers. The invisible net of personal connections with faculty that really cared, and students whose lives and experiences offered a rich texture of real-ness became the foundation of my community. The staff at MCC, a group of accomplished, reflective, and caring adults, spontaneously gave me the guidance and support I didn't know I needed as a first-generation college student and aspiring adult.

In the process of becoming involved in the life of the college, I became my better self. Guidance from caring, educated professionals like Linda Thomas and Dr. Mudry helped me grow more aware of the raw material I was, as I sharpened my critical thinking and writing skills. Eventually I qualified for an English honors class with Patrick Sullivan. I took it as an elective. I confess, there were more than 5 pounds of required reading, and I read every word.

At the beginning of my third year at MCC the faculty and administration broke the news to me. There were more degrees than what MCC offered.

They wanted to know where I was planning to transfer.

What?

In the counseling center Desiree Petgrave patiently offered rooms stacked with resources and information. Dean Dunnrowicz and Dr. Levy encouraged me to look at UConn, UVA, Rutgers, SUNY, and GW. I could afford to apply to three schools. Offered admission to two, I chose UConn.

I finished MCC an unremarkable scholar with regard to my GPA. I graduated with hundreds of other people in May of 1990. I received no awards, wore no honor garb, and wasn't invited to speak. I didn't lead my class in academic performance, and quietly marched on to a four-year school.

For me, and for the people there in support of me, the lack of special honors didn't matter. I wasn't expecting any personal recognition, and neither was my family. It was our first college graduation. When I left MCC, in my self, there was a larger, more socially conscientious, thoughtful person than the girl who had entered the Lowe building three years earlier. Manchester *Community* College, the community part, had pulled together to ground me in the world, to help me root my mind into the infinite possibility of what there is in the world to learn. In the process of discovering college, MCC had discovered and nurtured me.

I went on to UConn to compete academically with people who had been born to go to college, who planned to go to college their entire lives, whose parents had gone to college, who knew that after college comes ... more college. These people had enormous dreams and planned to use every scrap of knowledge to create a future the world couldn't yet imagine. I surprised myself by learning that I was their equal.

I was a strong writer, I spoke great Spanish and French, and I could navigate the library and computer systems like a pro. My science and math skills were all mine—and I knew some of what I didn't know.

When I finished my BA at UConn, I returned to MCC proudly wearing my new Phi Beta Kappa pin, a real graduate from a real four-year program. I thought I was done. Of course, I had thought I was done after high school, and again when I finished MCC. I didn't see the next step. Dr. Levy, in the kindest way possible, asked me what my plans were for graduate school. It was August. I assured him that while I had finished my BA, only the really smart people went on to graduate school. I was married now, and would go off and join the work world.

I didn't understand the next level of academia. I didn't know that I could bring something significant to graduate school. He asked me, as a favor to him, to take just one class. He explained that it would qualify me to tutor at the learning center at MCC. Just one class. I drew on the inspiring thought of returning to MCC to quiet my fear of failing a graduate course. Together my husband and I found enough money. I signed up.

Somewhere in that first semester of graduate school my professor discovered me. My writing skills—technology skills—a willingness to try, and try and try, and get better. A graduate assistantship found me the next semester, funding my studies over the next eight months. I finished my Master's degree the following December, but by then I had applied for doctoral study. Other graduate assistantships followed, along with adjunct teaching at MCC. I cherished my opportunity to come back and teach part-time. Being a psychology professor was so much more than I had hoped for in my pre-MCC life.

Bill and I celebrated the miracle of our daughter in 1997. We decided a full time job would help us give her more. Just after her first birthday I started working at Hartford Hospital. I conducted outcomes research with neurology patients while analyzing data for breast cancer, kidney failure, diabetes, and asthma. It was a teaching hospital. It taught me many things about life, and death.

Healthcare is hard. Stroke patients did not always recover. Breast cancer is a mean disease. Kidney failure, diabetes, asthma—all these things make being human incredibly challenging. Perfectly healthy people made bad decisions that broke their necks and destroyed their brains.

It became too much.

In those long 18 months I realized that there is a special kind of tenacity required of healthcare workers. My amazing mother has this in spades. Not me. And, as I already admitted, sometimes you just can't argue with what you are not. Nor can you escape what you truly are. I left the hospital, but this time I understood why.

Teaching at MCC and other small roles in a larger academic landscape kept me in bread and water until I finished my PhD in 1999. My degree is in learning—Cognition and Instruction. If anyone ever needed to learn more about the world, and how they might contribute to it, it is me.

My dissertation was completed with the help of 350 volunteer MCC students. At our celebration dinner I shared with my husband that we would be having another child. I was 31, and in a very good place. I had a great husband, the beginnings of a small family, and a good education. And even without a job, I was in a good financial place.

I had managed to escape the college loan debt-avalanche for two reasons: the low tuition at MCC, and UConn graduate assistantships. I also had the generous encouragement of my parents, husband, and large extended family. The 'out-of-pocket' costs of all degrees through the PhD amounted to just under $30,000. When my friends celebrate paying off their college loans I can't help but be quietly thankful for never having that experience.

Once someone has an advanced degree much of the world misunderstands the path to and through a career field. People assume that you were born Dr. So-and-So. They imagine you set your goal and then navigated to your current destination using some pre-programmed career-GPS. It is so rarely the case that a career is a straight line.

My first full-time job out of college was teaching psychology at Naugatuck Valley Community College. UConn recruited me to teach and direct their Professional Development Academy. The Hartford Public Schools discovered me there, and invited me to lead their Technology and Library Media Department. Eventually I found myself in Hartford Public

School's Office of Assessment, a field that captured my imagination and has maintained my interest. During my career I have served as faculty at Central Connecticut State University, and worked for the Capital Region Education Council, before arriving in the Bloomfield Public Schools. The long and winding road that has delivered me to this moment in my life would have been very different without MCC.

Manchester Community College opened doors for me, and within me. I was set on the path to finding myself as a learner. In the process, that first college degree changed the trajectory of my existence.

My MCC degree is a catalyst with long-term effects on the culture of expectations for my life, and the lives of my children, and their children. They already know that after high school comes college, and more college. I would like to think that my example inspired my younger sister to pursue and earn her own doctorate, and my mother to complete her BSN and advance her studies at Emory University.

Most importantly, I would like to think that every person who finds MCC finds a well-lit path to a future that's just a little better, a little brighter, a little more informed and empowering than what they would have created otherwise. For me, I know this is true: The community that is MCC has made all the difference.

CHAPTER 8

The Path I Didn't Choose

By Michelle Nickerson

When asked to share my story about my college experience, I jumped at the chance to do so, as my hope is other community college students will read this and become inspired. As a first generation college student who comes from the "lower class," no one talks to you about college. No one talks to you about it because they do not believe that you will ever go that far. No one in your family talks to you about it because they do not know the answers to the questions you might pose, and sometimes, it can make them feel ashamed for not pursuing an education during a time when it was not nearly as common as it is today. More often than not, we first generation students have to work our way through college as well, and we are working toward something that only some of us believe will happen. I am here to tell you that it will if you keep your eyes on the goal.

When I was in high school, I was considered your "average" student, even with a 3.4 grade point average (GPA), and my guidance counselor never spoke to me about college. I could tell he really did not care. In 11th grade, my English teacher asked me what I thought about community college, as he thought I had potential to go to college. I did not know what a community college was, and so he took the time to gather some materials from Manchester Community College (MCC) and to talk to me about it. I appreciate that conversation every single day. Upon graduating from my high school, I applied to MCC, took the placement test, and ignorantly wandered through the first semester of my college education. I was very fortunate to have made a connection to one person at the school that continued to be a friendly face and offered to talk to me any time.

I did not know anything about advisors, what a bursar is, what financial aid was all about, or how to choose a "major" to decide the rest of my life. After my first semester, I made "Dean's List" and was invited to join the International Honor Society for Two Year Colleges, Phi Theta Kappa. I jumped right in to get involved on campus. It was through that experience that I began building connections to other students who were like me, and to professors who genuinely cared about the students they were teaching. I found a connection where I was able to ask all types of questions about college, what to expect and what I should be doing. Also, I was finally surrounded by people who got me, who believed in me and that I could go farther than MCC. It was through this support network that I found the courage to apply to the University of Connecticut, which has a prestigious reputation in the state. Imagine my surprise when I got in to the only school I had applied to for transfer.

Because I was always told I was "average", I did not see what the hype was about getting into UConn. I did not know that it was a competitive school to get into (especially for Business, which was now my major), and I had no idea what it really took to be accepted at this particular school. I simply applied, and I got in. It wasn't until I was already on campus for a year at UConn, when I learned more about the requirements for the School of Business and how many students are accepted each year. There was a moment of, "Wow, I did this on my own. They accepted me because I am smart and highly motivated." Although I had the academic determination to get into UConn, I did not realize how expensive it would be to be a part of this new environment. I struggled my first semester at this new place, and I really could not afford my books, so I was only able to purchase one.

That first semester, my grade point average dropped drastically and I began questioning what I was doing there. Luckily, before I even started at UConn, I was hired into a brand new student worker position in the Student Activities Office, where I was the connection between student clubs and the university. In this small group of people, I built connections with a few of them and we helped each other navigate the murky waters of our four-year education. In addition, one of the most influential people in my life from MCC offered to help me pay for my books, as he saw what it was doing to my academic performance. You see, I am not someone who fails intentionally. I have grown up having to fight for everything I have gotten, and I do not believe that will ever change. Learning to accept a "hand out" was difficult for me, but looking back I am forever grateful to him. I do not believe I would have gotten as far as I have if that one gesture did not happen.

Working in the Student Activities Office, I learned a lot about the field of Higher Education. It was at that time that I realized, hey, this is what I want to be doing. I want to help college students like me who are struggling for any reasons they may have, and show them that they can succeed, too. My last semester at UConn, I took an "Introduction to Student Affairs" class, and that was it. The deal was done and I finally figured out what I wanted to do with my life. Unfortunately, it took me three years to get into a graduate level program, but boy was I happy the way that turned out!

You see, with my Management BS, I did not want to work for corporate America, and I ended up working retail for a couple of years. I was fortunate for this job, because I had been applying for an entire year everywhere I could, and I was either overqualified or not qualified enough to do what I really wanted (Student Affairs). One day, while I was filling in for our cashier, this woman had gotten in line, and I sparked up a conversation with her. As it turned out, she was the Program Coordinator for the Higher Ed. Program at Central Connecticut State University. After getting to know me for a few minutes, she encouraged me to apply to her program, and that was the beginning of my next journey.

I was accepted into Central's Student Development in Higher Education program, and I am currently making plans to graduate with my Master's Degree this year. These past two years have been some of the best years of my life, and I am so grateful for every experience I have had throughout my educational journey. Every person I have met has shaped my path in some way, shape, or form. Now, I am able to see things from the student perspective and the theoretical perspective, and I am able to apply all of this to my current work—helping college students succeed.

The research I have conducted over the last two years shows us that first generation college students often do not make it this far. We are the largest population of college students but we are the least likely to finish our education. Statistically, I should not be here today telling you that I have completed this Master's Degree. Realistically, I am telling you that if I can, you can too and you will. The road will not be easy, but keep your eye on your goal and you can overcome it all. When you feel like you are about to sink, reach out for assistance. There is no shame in asking for help. Talk to your academic advisors to help you stay in school and to get it done correctly. Do not let finances hold you back, because the only way to get out of your situation is to continue with your education. Get involved on campus to build connections with other students, faculty, and staff. These things will help you succeed and reach your goals. Community college students have something special within them that not everyone does—grit and resiliency. The community college will always hold a special place in my heart, and I will never forget where I started my journey.

CHAPTER 9

Head Start

By Mikey Palacios-Baughman

For me, community college was always the plan. See, I'm the youngest of four. And all three of my siblings attended community college at some point or another. So it was never really in question for me to do the same. A lot of people assume I decided to start at community college because I couldn't start elsewhere. That really could not possibly be further from the truth. If I really wanted to, I could have started out at a four year institution. But honestly, what would be the point? According to The College Board's annual survey of colleges, tuition at a four year institution in 2016 on average costs $32,405, per semester (room and board would be an additional $11,506.) Whereas tuition at a community college in 2016 costs on average $3,435, per semester. If you were on the fence about attending community college, you can go ahead and hop off that fence now.

My entire life I was homeschooled. Before you ask, yes I had friends, no it wasn't difficult to meet people, no I never wanted to go to public school and yes I loved it. Most homeschoolers finish high school faster than those who attend public school. We finish faster simply because we have more one-on-one interaction with our teachers. We also are able to go at our own pace, something that public school kids do not have the luxury of doing. So, around when I started my senior year at high school; I started thinking about taking a community college class. So, in my last semester of high school, I signed up for an English 101 course at a local community college. I found that the work load was very manageable despite simultaneously being in high school. So, after the fall semester of 2015, I was ready to start full-time college. I was 17 when I graduated high school. While still 17, I started full-time at Manchester Community College in Manchester, Connecticut.

Community college is a very normal route for home schoolers to take. Always being in a one-on-one environment makes it difficult for some homeschoolers to acclimate themselves to bigger class sizes. So, because community colleges generally have smaller class sizes, a lot of homeschoolers choose to start there to ease into the process. I was no different. I took one class at a community college while in my senior year at high school. I had just turned 17 at the time I attended this community college class, making me the youngest in the class. I was doing this while still simultaneously doing high school level work. Homeschooling allowed me to balance both at a very competitive level. I received the highest grade in my college class while still doing well in high school work.

Manchester Community College was always the plan to start. But I do plan on eventually transferring elsewhere to finish (at the least) my Bachelor's degree. Community college is amazing because it allows students to demonstrate that they have the abilities necessary to complete college level work. This in turn can lead to scholarship opportunities for transfer students. The price of tuition at four year institutions is crazy. So why not start at a community college, get good grades and then get scholarships to finish your degree? Even if you don't get a scholarship, you will still have saved a great deal of money by going to a community college for two years.

My experience so far has been awesome. Community college has proved to be a very welcoming and inviting place. All the people I've met have been wonderful. My classmates have all been supportive and encouraging. And my professors have all genuinely cared about my success. Many of the professors I've had the pleasure of having, have gone above and beyond what I expected. I've had professors use their personal time to help me and to make sure that I understood what the class was teaching. That is the type of thing that a professor at a larger school would probably be unable to do. With the class sizes being so large at many four year institutions, professors often cannot possibly meet with all the students individually who are having trouble. If a student is having a tough time understanding something in community college, however, the professor can meet with them and help them to understand and grow as a student. Every professor

I've had has been willing to do this for me. I've had professors give me their personal phone numbers in case I had any questions when doing work on my own. That is something that is by no means required of the professors, but they did it anyways because they care about their students.

One of the most frustrating myths I hear about community college is that it is somehow worse than a four year institution. Let me tell you right now, pop-culture gets it wrong. Community college is not full of deadbeats. Community college is not full of professors who don't care about their students. Community college, rather, lives up to its name and is a big community of people supporting each other. I have heard from quite a large number of people that the professors at community college are far *better* than a lot of professors at four year institutions. Every professor I've had the pleasure of having at community college has genuinely cared about my success. Not only that, but every professor I've had has pushed me and encouraged me to be the best I could be. Community college is in many ways *better* than a four year institution. First off, the classes are smaller. This enables you to have more one-on-one interaction with your professors. It also allows your professors to offer more assistance if you are struggling to grasp a topic. If you are in a class with 60 other people, there could be too many questions or concerns to get to them all. But with the smaller classes your questions will almost always be fielded from the professor.

Community college is amazing. It has allowed me to flourish as a student in ways I had never thought possible. Community college has brought out the best student inside of me. I've met amazing, supportive people who genuinely care about my academic success. I've had professors who push me and encourage me to be the best student I can be. Everyone who hopes to go to college should seriously consider community college. You will still receive a quality education, while saving money. Community college was the right plan for me.

CHAPTER 10

Sabina's Story

By Sabina Mamedova

My name is Sabina Mamedova. I am an Ahiskan and Meskhetian Turk; these two terms are synonymous, but the Ahiskan term is Turkish and the Meskhetian term is Russian. Ahiska is a city in the region of southern Georgia where my grandparents and ancestors were born. I was born in Uzbekistan in 1989, which was still part of the Soviet Union. However, I grew up in Russia. I have been living in the United States with my mom and my younger sister and brother for over ten years. We were born Muslim and continue to practice the doctrines of Islam. As a typical college student, no one would know that my life story is part of a major historic event. My family's history is replete with events that were unjust for both Muslims and Turks. Sometimes, it is hard even for me to believe that I have lived through such painful experiences. The story I am about to tell is of real events in the lives of Muslim Turks that resulted from religious and ethnic persecution by the U.S.S.R. and continued by Russia.

The story of the Turkish people needs to be told because it is not common knowledge. In World History classes, most of the attention about World War II focuses on Hitler and the Holocaust. The Holocaust was an unspeakable act of religious and racial persecution against the Jews. I intend to point out that Stalin's secret atrocity toward the Turkish people co-occurred with the Holocaust and other ethnic and religious persecutions. This also deserves attention to ensure such atrocities are not repeated. During the persecution of Muslim Turks, other countries did not know about Stalin's *pogroms* and deportations due to the Soviet government's control over media. Even today few people are aware of the massacre and forced relocation of millions of Eastern European Muslims. My grandparents and my great-grandparents were among the Ahiskan Turks who experienced this brutality. I believe that what happened to my people during and after World War II should become universal knowledge.

The experiences of my grandparents, like those of so many others who suffered during the *pogroms*, were not recorded or published until many years after WWII. Until before 1956, my people were banned from any travel or to find family members who had been transported elsewhere. Now, the descendants of those who experienced this violence, and survivors like myself, are moving into other parts of the world, and we are telling our story. I am telling this story in the hope that it will help put an end to discrimination against people for their ethnic origins or religious beliefs.

To understand the tension between Soviet Russia and its inhabitants who identified themselves as Muslim Turks, it is important to learn how these people came to be there in the first place. According to Aydıngün et al., in the article "Meskhetian Turks," the Ottoman Empire expanded into Georgia between the sixteenth and nineteenth centuries and eventually had control over much of southwest Georgia (3). As the Ottoman Empire conquered Georgia, its people settled there and continued to live there. Georgia later became part of Soviet Russia. Josef Stalin, the leader of Soviet Russia from 1928 until his death in 1953, was responsible for my people's forced relocation and deaths. According to Aydıngün et al., Stalin's excuse for deporting the Ahiskan Turks during World War II was that they were disloyal to Russia and that they had collaborated with the German army. However, collaboration is highly unlikely because the German army was never close enough to the border of the Ahiska region of Georgia (6). As Stalin made plans for the deportation, he had my people lay the railroad tracks that, unbeknownst to them, would be used to relocate them to foreign regions of the U.S.S.R. where acts of genocide would be committed against them.

What follows next is the story my grandparents passed down to me about their experiences during Stalin's secret *pogroms*, and their deportation from Georgia to Uzbekistan in November 1944. In the article "Meskhetian Turks," *pogrom* means organized violence against defenseless people and its use is not restricted to Russian Jews alone, but is also representative of Ahiskan (Meskhetian) Turks. Although my grandparents only ranged in age from two to nine years old at the time, their memories are vivid. They, along with all of the other Turkish residents, were told to prepare for a trip. All they were told was that they would be returning in two or three days and not to bring anything. One of Stalin's plans was to take trainloads of people and throw them into the Caspian Sea. However, among my people, legend has it that the Uzbek leader Usman Yusupov, who was known as a staunch Stalinist but who also hid his Muslim religion in fear of persecution, did not want to see this happen to the Muslim Turks. Instead, he told Stalin that he needed these people to work for him. This request saved thousands of people. Stalin had the remaining thousands of Turks loaded into cattle cars and shipped off to the Uzbekistan, Kazakhstan, and Kyrgyzstan regions of the U.S.S.R. Those who refused to board the cattle cars were sent to Siberia where conditions were even worse. Some escaped to Turkey. In addition to deportations, thousands of Turkish men were drafted into the Soviet army to fight the Nazis. The survivors returned not knowing their families had been deported.

After being on the cattle cars for only a few hours, it became obvious to my grandparents and their parents that they were being forcibly relocated and that they would not be returning to their homeland. The conditions in the cattle cars were brutal. Not only did many people freeze to death, but they also died from starvation and a lack of sanitary facilities. Each car had over one hundred people packed tightly inside. Men, women, and children were put into the same car. Many women died because their bladders burst due to lack of privacy. I cannot imagine how horrible it must have been for them in the cattle cars and I am saddened every time I think of it. During the 30-day journey, the train stopped only to dispose of the dead. Approximately forty thousand people died from hunger, disease, and freezing temperatures because of the deportation (Serjik). According to Aydıngün, et al., "within four years after the deportation, the Meskhetian Turks had lost between 15% and 20% of their total population" (6).

My grandparents and their parents suffered immensely when they were left in Uzbekistan. They were homeless and had to scrounge for food. Some days, they had nothing to eat but soup and tea made from grass. My grandparents were less than ten years old at this time. My paternal grandparents spent most of their years in orphanages because their parents died after arriving in Uzbekistan. They had several siblings who were separated and it was not until years later that the survivors reunited. During their first few years in a new land, many people died from malnutrition and disease. In the wintertime, my people ate old, spoiled vegetables that they were able to dig up in abandoned gardens under the snow. However, this made them sick and caused some of them to die. Countless others died from lack of adequate shelter. Summertime brought a new set of problems, which led to more deaths. The swamps were teeming with poisonous snakes, and many people died after being bitten. There was no relief from the extreme heat and humidity. Others found a place to live on farms that were abandoned during the war. The very young and the elderly were especially susceptible to these hardships.

Communism denied the existence of religion. Therefore, it was forbidden to show any acts of practicing any religion publicly. People were hiding their religions from each other because KGB (Soviet secret police) agents were always reporting any non-compliance. Nothing was easy and Muslim Turks in Uzbekistan faced acts of terror based on religious, ethnic and nationalistic prejudice. Practicing Islam was especially dangerous. I remember my mom telling me that some Uzbeki people told her that there is no God, even though Uzbekistan was supposedly a Muslim country. People were abused if they tried to practice or learn anything about Islam. In fact, my grandparents learned a little bit about how to pray but it was always upsetting for my paternal grandmother that she never fully learned the principals of Islam in her lifetime.

Unfortunately, the persecution of Muslim Turks did not end with the *pogroms*. I was born in 1989, a time when many Uzbeki criminals were not happy with the Turks living on their land. According to the Aydıngün et al., although the primary causes of the *pogrom* are uncertain, "rising nationalism," destitution, and overpopulation contributed to "interethnic tensions" (8). Once again, my people were told that they needed to move elsewhere. However, the Turkish people refused to leave because they felt that this was their home since they had been living there for 45 years. In response to the Turks' refusal to leave, the criminals painted large identifying symbols on the front entrance of Turkish homes so that they knew which homes to pillage. During the persecution, many Turks were killed. Some were burned alive. Young girls were kidnapped and raped. Their way of life was destroyed, yet again. As these events were occurring in the Fergana Valley, rumors were circulating that the same thing was going to happen in the area where my grandparents were living. My people believed that these atrocities were planned by authorities because the resulting unrest could justify expelling the Turks.

The Jewish journalist Boris Yusupov, who had lived in Uzbekistan when my people were experiencing rising nationalism and atrocities, made important new claims. He asserted that in 1989, Moscow-led mafia groups asked leaders of the Ahiskan Turks to collude with them in massacring the

Bukhara Jews. The Ahiskan Turks, who rejected this horrendous proposal, were consequently subject to massacre themselves. He claimed that the lives of thousands of Bukhara Jews were saved because the Ahiskan Turks refusal to comply. He further stated that the goal of these Moscow-led mafias in exterminating the Jews by using Turks, was to get rid of the Jews as well as to later claim that the Turks conducted a genocide—a trap which the Ahiskan Turks did not fall for. He claimed that the Fergana Massacre of 1989 was provoked by KGB-led mafias. Many Ahiskan Turks were killed en masse with women, children and the elderly alike, while thousands were displaced to several different countries. Following these atrocities, thousands of Bukhara Jews fled to Israel. Boris Yusupov is a living witness of these events and was a representative of the TASS agency when he made these outstanding revelations. He said that the Bukhara Jews are indebted to the Ahiskan Turks. (This paragraph is paraphrased from a translation by Enise G. Koc from the TV program "Yorunge" with Seyfullah Turksoy).

In response to this persecution, in 1990 the Soviets offered to provide Ahiskan Turks refuge in Rostov and other regions. I was seven months old when my family moved to the Krasnodar Krai region of the U.S.S.R. but only to find that Turkish people were not welcome there either. The house my grandfather was able to afford in Krasnodar Krai was large but in poor condition. My grandparents, my uncle, and another uncle with his wife and child also lived with us. All of us lived in two bedrooms because it was always cold in the house, and this is how we kept warm during the winter. I remember that my parents brought me to my aunt's house every morning so that she could babysit in order for my parents to be able to work and save money. Whatever money was not spent on food was given to my grandfather to improve the house so we could live in better conditions. Although, over time, the house became a more comfortable place to live, it was at the expense of my parents' hard labor, which also prevented me from getting to see them much.

Although we were far from the brutal evictions of Muslim Turks in Uzbekistan, my family did not escape the similar brutal treatment in Krasnodar Krai. At the age of six, I experienced what no child should. My father worked in the town of Ufa to earn decent money to support our family. A week before his return to home he called us to say he was coming. While we were waiting for him, we made a lot of plans as to how we were going to spend our time with him. Since he was away much of the time, we did not get this opportunity very often. He was always sending us presents. I could not wait to thank him for always making us feel like we were important to him, and that we were loved. Unfortunately, the good news of my dad returning home turned into one of the worst experiences of my life. We were waiting for a phone call from him to tell us that he was on his way home, but instead we received a call from his friend who told us the tragic news that my father was murdered in his apartment by thieves. I remember my mother screaming and crying. As a child, I did not know what to do, but I knew I lost part of me on that day because I was really close to my father. He was, and he still is, my hero. Many people who knew my father have told me that he was the nicest person, and that he never turned anyone down when his help was needed. It is hard for me to understand how such terrible things could happen to such good people like my father.

I often think about losing my father, and I feel empty, especially when I recall the times we were together. I cry every time I remember my father and say, "Where are you, father? I need your help; it is so hard to handle this life without you." I would like to know who did this to him. I would like them to see the family that they left desperate and to make them understand how completely they changed our lives. We will never know whether he was targeted because of his nationality or religion or whether he was just in the wrong place at the wrong time. It is impossible to heal the pain, especially when you lose someone that you have always adored. I am always going to miss him.

Everything changed after my father passed away. We had my grandparents, but we still had to support ourselves. I cannot imagine how my mom felt, knowing she had to raise three children alone. I still feel that if we did not move to Russia, my father may not have died. She was very depressed and therefore visited her parents.

My maternal grandparents stayed in Uzbekistan because they thought that this land was part of them, and they said they wanted to die there. They were willing to face whatever danger was coming. After my father's death in 1996, my mom and my little brother went to visit her parents in Uzbekistan where, by now, the abuse had settled down. When it was time for my mother to come back to Russia, she had problems with her passport. My sister and I were left in Russia with our paternal grandparents. One day, my mother called and asked my grandparents if they could send my sister and me to Uzbekistan because she missed us, and it was hard for her to be there without us. A family member took me to my mom in Uzbekistan, and I started school there when I was six years old. Even though it was an Uzbeki school, they were still using the Russian language after the U.S.S.R. collapsed. We stayed in Uzbekistan for two or three months. Finally, my mom's documents were updated, and we were ready to go back to Russia. My Uzbeki teacher was sad to learn that I would be leaving. Even though I was only there for a few months, she said that I was a very bright student. She even asked my mom if I could stay with my uncle so that I could finish school there.

I continued first grade back in Russia. Since I was very shy and quiet in the new school, my Russian teacher concluded that I did not understand the Russian language. When other teachers came to the class, she would say bad things about me, as if I were not in the room. She often called me slow and scolded me for running out of school supplies. I recall a time when I finished my schoolwork early and put it away. The teacher assumed that I was not doing anything and gave me a hard slap on the knuckles with a ruler. The teacher arranged a meeting with commissioners regarding holding me back in the first grade. As I remember, they questioned me while I was terrified in front of high-ranking people and my mean teacher and my fate was sealed. The mean teacher accomplished her goal, only because she did not like me. She saved most of her anger for the Turkish Muslim students since they were the ones who had no recourse to stop the abuse.

The following year my new teacher really cared for me. She took care of me like I was her own child. I was the smallest kid in my class, and maybe this is why she felt the need to protect me. I shared a desk with another student, which was very common in Russia. My teacher concluded that she could not see me sitting behind that desk, so she made me a desk out of a small table and put me in the front of the class. This made me feel special. Unlike my mean teacher, this one would tell everyone that I was the smartest student in school. This teacher would always wonder aloud about why I stayed back. Later, the mean teacher who held me back heard about how well I was doing, and she wanted me to join her second grade class. I was much more comfortable in my new surroundings and did very well in school because of my nice teacher. She acknowledged that I was a good student and made me feel important.

Life was very difficult as a young child caught by racial and religious discrimination. The Russian school was a reflection of what was going on in society at the time, and Turkish students felt injustices inside the school, just as much as they did outside. At school, Russian and Turkish students were segregated in separate classrooms. The Russian students called us black, stupid Turks and other derogatory names. They were punishing us because of our ethnic and religious background. This was pure racism. By the time I was 12 years old, I was deeply aware of the discrimination against our people. This forced separation caused me a lot of pain. I was losing my desire to study because I felt that none of the instructors really wanted to teach us. We were treated as if we were unintelligent and could not think. Eventually, I stopped studying and doing homework. I was going to school just to spend time with my friends. This is an example of a negative result of discrimination.

Discrimination against Turkish Muslims was everywhere. One day my friends and I were coming from school and stopped at a playground to have fun. A few Russian children, who were only four to seven years old, came over and told us that we could not play on their property and could not use the playground. My friends and I did not want to leave because this was a playground that did not belong only to them. I believed that anybody should be allowed to play there. I knew they did not want us there because we were Turkish, and it would bother them if we stayed on the playground with them. The Russian girls called their parents who came and yelled at us to get out of there. What they were doing was not right so we argued with them, but they still made us leave. While we were walking home, three little girls from the playground followed us and shouted that we were black Turks and needed to go back to our "own country." They were following us until we got to a store where both Russians and Turks shopped. People who were passing by also began to yell at us. Suddenly, they started telling the kids that they were right and that Turks did not belong in Russia. Adults even encouraged the children to hit us and to spit on us. I will never forget that day, or especially the face of one girl who was not even five years old. I was able to see the hatred in her eyes. I could not believe such a young child was capable of despising anyone. She was a little girl who was supposed to be playing with dolls, instead of becoming involved in political and racial issues.

Even though the school environment was not always a good one, my friends made me feel like I was just a regular kid. At home, I had more expected of me because I was the oldest child, and I helped my mom support our family. One of our neighbors helped my mother and offered her a job selling clothes door-to-door. Later she also sold jewelry door-to-door but only to Turkish people. This was hard for my mother because she was very shy. She had always had my father to rely on, but now she had to do this for her children. Of course, when my mom went to work, I was the head of the household because I was the eldest child. I had to take care of my siblings.

My independence and maturity showed at a young age. When I was starting first grade, my mom had some black chiffon fabric to make my school uniform because we could not afford to purchase it. I insisted that I would not wear it unless I designed it myself. She let me design the uniform, which I greatly enjoyed wearing. I think my sassiness as a child was a good predictor of the independent person I would become later in life. The responsibilities I had as a young child helped me become a strong person. Before I was ten years old, I started helping my mom with her job. She usually sold the clothes using an informal credit system because we knew and trusted the people. My job was to go out and collect the money that was owed to us. Sometimes, I would deliver the orders if she had to be elsewhere. Eventually, this became my job. Also, my mom took me to the bazaar whenever we needed anything, and always asked my opinion before she bought things. Even though I was only 12 years old, I was responsible for taking my siblings shopping for school and holiday clothes. We would take public transportation all by ourselves, and I was put in charge of my younger brother and sister.

Unfortunately, for me, things only became more difficult as I grew older. I began doing more to help my mother. My younger sister and I would wash my family's clothes by hand, cook, and clean the house. My family had a big yard, so we planted a large garden. At harvest time, my sister and I would cut, wrap and bag the produce. We carried the heavy bags to the person who sold them for us.

There were many Turkish people living in our village. Wherever I went to the stores, I met other Turkish people. Even for those who could not speak Russian, it was easy to get by because there was always someone who could translate. Perhaps this is why my mother never learned the Russian language. Since she could not speak Russian, I often had to translate for her. This made me confident in anything I had to do for my family.

Around the year 2000, we Ahiskan Turks had been settled in Russia for 11 years, and our population was growing very quickly. This was worrisome to the Cossacks, a nationalist group of Russians who see themselves as "pure" Russians. Continually, the Turkish people were being discriminated against and enduring horrible treatment. In the Krasnodar Krai area, the regional government denied us the right to a residence permit. This resulted in us having no citizenship. According to the article, "Meskhetian Turks," many people did not have access to legal employment or "property ownership" (Aydıngün et al., 9). None of my people had any official papers, so we could not legally own a house or property. We had trouble being treated at the hospital, and all Muslim Turkish children born at that time did not exist officially because they also had no papers. Furthermore, all Muslim Turkish youth were prohibited from attending colleges or universities.

Each year, the tensions between Turks and Russians increased. Alexander Vladimir Tkachev, the governor of our region of Krasnodar Krai, was giving speeches almost every day about how he was planning to relocate us, once again, from Russia. News reports were coming out almost daily stating that the Turkish people were causing trouble. However, these reports were always false. He was telling the Russian residents that if the Turkish people would not move out of Russia, their land would be taken from them. The governor said that we should be removed by our roots, meaning he wanted to remove every Turk from Russia. They were envious of our successes and culture due to our families collaborating in saving money resulting in better housing, etc. The Krasnodar Krai government used xenophobia as a tool to ensure that Russian natives and Ahiskan immigrants were wary of each other.

In the Krasnodar Krai region of Russia, my people were not just persecuted because of their ethnicity, but also because of their religion. In 1992, the war between Russia and Chechnya affected all people in Russia who shared the Muslim religion. It was similar to after 9/11, when some Americans started to say that all Muslims were terrorists. In Russia, my people were not allowed to have a religious community. They were not allowed to have ethnic or religious clubs or organizations. On Fridays, my people would meet in someone's house and pray, but on major religious holidays they prayed outside. I experienced this one time when we had a religious holiday and did not go to school. When we returned to school the next day, the security guard told me and the other Turkish students that we should not have come back. He made derogatory remarks about Muslims. Before this, I felt empathy toward this man because he had a disability and had problems walking. I personally believe that, because of our Islamic background, my people faced atrocities in many places.

Because of persecution by the Russian government, Cossacks and Vladimir Tkachev, in 2002 the Muslim Turks protested their lack of equal rights in Krasnodar Krai by having a hunger strike for ten days. We wanted the government to treat us as equal and not force us to relocate again. Everywhere we lived, we were discriminated against because we were Muslim Turks. Eventually, this began to be publicized by UN human rights leader Alvaro Gil Robles. America became aware of this and offered us asylum. Since we had already been living in Russia for 15 years and were not given any documents or citizenship, we were forced to leave for America.

The last few days in Russia were very emotional since not everyone in my family was moving at the time. Many people in our town came to wish us a good trip and a nice life in our new home and country. At this time, we had everything ready and packed, and then we departed from our family and friends with a tearful goodbye. It was the last time we saw my grandmother in person. We were very nervous about traveling to a foreign country that was to become our new home because we did not know what to expect. My experience of America was only from the movies, but that did not prepare me for the diversity of many different nationalities and religions.

In 2005, over twelve thousand Ahiskan Turks were able to come to the United States as refugees. For my entire family, the plan was that my mom and three children would go first, and my grandparents would follow us at a later date. However, my grandfather and uncles never did come because they were able to purchase extremely expensive documentation that enabled them to stay in Russia. At that time, this did not bother the Russians because they got most of the Turkish people out of Russia and sent them to the United States. I am still saddened by this, and we still miss them very much. In my culture, the head of the family is a very important figure. Since we lost our father, my grandparents would have filled this role. Because it has been difficult for my family to put down permanent roots, we continue to lack stability in our lives.

On September 8, 2005, we landed in Baltimore, Maryland. Our caseworker, who spoke a little Russian, helped us with acquiring proper vaccinations and documentation. As we made our way through Baltimore, we saw so many things that I had never seen in Russia. Culture shock would set in for quite a long time. We were very happy to find that the apartment provided for us came fully furnished. We lived there for four days and my mom felt lonely and depressed because she was away from her family and friends. Although we were happy to be away from the discrimination we faced in Russia, we felt alone and depressed in this new environment.

In the beginning, we questioned if coming to America was the right thing to do, but we knew we did not have any choice but to leave Russia. It was very difficult for my mother to take care of us without knowing the language or customs of America. Even though Catholic Family Services offered to support us for a few months, we were petrified as to how we were going to live. These first few days in a new country were some of the worst days of my life. Eventually, we became so frightened that we began to take it out on each other. We would shout at each other and end up in tears. My mom had the most pressure on her because she was responsible for us. She would lash out at us for the slightest provocation.

After four days in Baltimore, we decided to move to Hartford, Connecticut to be closer to our distant relatives. My mom thought this move would relieve our pressure, but it only got worse. Although Catholic Charities Services offered to help us with our move, the help did not come due to delayed documentation, social security, and other important papers from Baltimore. We would have been homeless if my father's distant relatives did not let us stay in their apartment for a month. My family and I used to go to the Catholic Charities every day when we were trying to get housing. It was a lot of pressure on me as a 16 year old because I was the one who had to apply for everything (documents, housing, bills, etc.).

Things finally got better for me and my family once all our documents were in order from Baltimore and our caseworker was able to help more. My brother started middle school; my sister and I began attending Bulkeley High School in Hartford, Connecticut. At first, the school environment was a little strange because students would react strangely towards my siblings and me being from Russia. Not knowing how to speak English was one of my most challenging experiences ever, and I was very embarrassed that I did not know the language. I did not have enough confidence in myself even to initiate a conversation because I thought I would sound unintelligent and embarrass myself. Even though I have a strong grasp on the English language, I still experience these feelings sometimes because I am reminded of how I was teased in Russia. I think I have those feelings because while I was living in Russia, I was teased even though I knew the Russian language fluently. No matter how much I try, I cannot forget how the Russian students taunted me and said that I made the Russian language sound bad because I was Turkish. Sometimes I experience these same feelings when I speak English.

Living in America has allowed me to feel more comfortable about expressing my ethnic identity as a Turkish woman. I feel lucky that we are able to learn more about Islam because in Russia and other countries where my family has lived, we were not able to learn much about our faith. My Turkish background has not caused any issues in this country.

However, I sometimes see people being against Muslims in America. After 9/11 people tend to be anti-Islam because they assume terrorists are the same as the faithful Muslims. Terrorism is contrary to the Muslim faith. Islam is about submission to God, purity and peace. My religion is the unique thing in my world. I am very proud to be part of Islam. Sometimes I think about these problems such as how Muslims are discriminated against. These are the questions that constantly run through my head: How long are people going to have to face discrimination because of their religious beliefs? Is it ever going to stop?

In my senior year of high school I decided to apply to Manchester Community College (MCC) with my advisor's help. Waiting for the acceptance letter made every day seem like it would never end. I finally received my letter of acceptance a week later. This was a very proud moment in my life. I remember walking around, smiling at everyone and telling them that I was accepted to MCC. The reason I was so happy about this school was that in Russia I never would have imagined myself attending college. I believe that if I were still living in Russia, I would not be able to attend college because of the ways we were discriminated against. Most likely, I would not have been allowed to finish high school because I was Turkish. The violent discrimination continues there today.

At first I was very scared that I would not be comfortable at MCC because I did not know anybody there. I started taking English as a Second Language classes, but I was very nervous that I would not understand the professor. The professor saw that some students were uncomfortable. She told us not to be scared and that everything would be fine. When the teacher asked everyone to introduce themselves, I felt so scared that I thought of excusing myself so I could avoid participating. I stayed long enough to realize that I was not the only one in the class with limited English. So I introduced myself and said a little bit about my background. Everyone thought my story was very interesting, which made me feel more comfortable.

When I finally started taking college-level English classes, I was apprehensive because I thought that I would have difficulty interacting with the teachers and the other students. I am happy to say that this never happened. The professors I spoke with about this concern told me that there is no reason anyone should ever make me feel uncomfortable and this reassurance increased my self-esteem. When my classmates became aware of my concern they told me that they were sad that I felt that way. The students in my acting class really went out of their way to make me feel welcome. The professors and students at MCC showed me a welcome I did not experience often in my previous schools. MCC was a big help during a period of major transition in my life, and I will forever be grateful to everyone I have met here.

After graduating from MCC, I enrolled at Eastern Connecticut State University where I am doing very well majoring in political science and theater. I expect to graduate in May 2017.

Acknowledgments Prof. Diana Hossain, who gave me this opportunity and encouraged and guided me throughout the process of writing this paper. Thank you for choosing me for this project. I would also like to thank the MCC Writing Center tutors. Also, kudos to my personal tutors Anna Natilov and Terrence Hoye, and my friends David Travisano and Salim Caksu for their help.

Works Cited

Aydıngün, Ayşegül. et al. 2006. Meskhetian Turks: An Introduction to their History, Culture and Resettlement Experiences. *Worldrelief.org.* Worldrelief. September. Web. August 2015.

Serjik. 2012. History of Ahiska/Meskhetian Turks. *Shennik Ahiska News Magazine,* September 10. Web. May 2015.

CHAPTER 11

No Longer Trapped

By Jenn Nguyen

I like to think of my life as a creative journey. My story begins with the life I lived and the plot twists that make it seem somewhat more interesting if not heartbreaking. I find it's amazing and brave how much will and strength someone has until you find yourself in the position to be brave and strong. It's not the end of the world when life doesn't go the way you plan it. It's just another beginning. It's another beginning to a magical story and my story … well, it's one hell of a story.

My story begins with a child. A child that was terrified of being at home, even if home was supposed to be the safest place to be. A child that hid under the covers or the bed just to be free of a monster's hands for just one night. A child that ran away into her imagination to escape the reality she was living. A child that drowned herself in schoolwork to keep busy. A child that imagined being in the books she read because those worlds made her happy. A child that was lonely despite the love of her siblings. A child that used to be … me.

Despite my troubled childhood, I excelled in school and fell in love with reading and writing. It was the only place I knew where I could be safe from the monsters surrounding me. To move forward several years, my mom moved our family across the state of Rhode Island and I finally thought that I had found peace. Little did I know, my life was starting to slowly spiral down the drain. The demons that haunted me as a child were coming back and there was nothing I could do to stop it.

I. Was. Trapped.

So I did the only logical thing I could think of, I drowned out my sorrow with drugs. With alcohol. My school attendance and grades were declining. Then, I realized I had hit rock bottom. I made the ultimate decision to just give up and drop out of high school. When my mother found out what I had done, at first she was angry and then the look in her eyes, it had changed. She no longer looked at me like I was a person. She no longer looked at me as her daughter. I'm pretty sure the most devastating part of my life at that moment was the way she saw me. As no one.

My mom gave me an ultimatum when I turned 18. It was either go back to school, get a job and contribute, or get out of the house. I had totally given up on school so I decided to get a job. That's when I began my career in the casino business. When you're 18 years old and making the kind of money you do, you love it and that's exactly how I felt [then]. A couple years later, I made poor choices (young and stupid) and ended up pregnant with my only child. Don't get me wrong, I don't regret having my son one bit but I had a life plan. I had goals and dreams but all of that had to be temporarily set aside. I was a mother and my number one priority was this life I had created.

When I realized I'd been in the casino business for five years (in 2011), I started to think about school again. It's been ten years now (2016) and I had only just received my GED in 2015. What was I doing? What was I thinking? Why would I continue to have a career in a business that continually wears me down? Emotionally and mentally drains me to the point where I want to pull my hair out because I can't take it anymore. It's simple. I was scared. I was scared of failing. I was scared of being a failure because now I had a son that looked up to me. I had to prove to someone other than myself that it is never too late to be who and what you want to be.

After I received my GED, I automatically went and enrolled at Manchester Community College. I was giving myself a chance to grow. To learn. To have a career to love. I was giving myself the chance I chose not to take so many years ago. I mean, what did I have to lose? It was basically now or never for me. Whatever I had inside my head tormenting me, I turned it into motivation. I pushed myself day after day and I was extremely hard on myself. After all, I am my own worst enemy. My journey to college wasn't exactly something that was easy, but I've learned so much about myself personally. Every decision I've made so far has brought me closer and closer to my goals and I don't regret any of them. It doesn't matter that it took me such a long time to get back on track, what matters is that I'm finally moving forward. Moving forward to the life I've always wanted. So, hats off to the ones who didn't believe in me. The ones who always thought I would be a failure. If you could only see me now! Because it's been one hell of a ride!

When I look back on the choices I've made, I know I can say that I've made the right ones. When I was younger, I had always wanted to go to a large, four-year college. I looked at community colleges like they were for people who weren't good enough for a regular college. But that was me then. Now, I can honestly say that going to a community college has helped me grow in more ways than one. Everything that I had judged about it then has completely changed for me now. But what exactly was the most meaningful to me about going to a community college? The support. I know it sounds a bit silly but I received so much support from other students and teachers that it was hard for me to give up, even if I wanted to.

Like I've mentioned before, I would drown myself in schoolwork and books, but this time, it's different. As much as I enjoyed it then, I love it even more now. I don't need excuses to want to learn or to throw myself into different worlds that books offer. I can say that I am doing this for me. Another factor that has helped me on my journey is the English class that I had taken. The words of encouragement from both other students and my professor has built up my confidence in writing, which has always been my strongest suit throughout school. However, throughout the beginning weeks of the course, I found myself dragging and didn't think I could get out of it. As weeks progressed, my writing had developed and had so much more heart in it. A lot of soul. A lot of me. If I never settled my issues (with school choices), I never would've chosen to go to community college. It's shown me patience and kindness and for that, I am grateful. So, I've learned to start with baby steps.

These are the baby steps towards the future I've been dreaming of.

In the moments leading up to now, I never thought it was possible for me to finally live a life where I was able to control my happiness and decisions without the influence of others. To my innocent youth, I thank you for falling in love with words. With books. To my rebellious teenage years, I thank you for drowning my sorrows with hopeless remedies. To my immature adulthood, I thank you for the beautiful baby that I absolutely adore. To the present me, I thank you for never giving up on me and believing in me. To the future me, you did it and I am so incredibly proud of you.

CHAPTER 12

Coming in from the Cold

By Tanya Knight

Putting pen to paper I don't know where to start. I have had so many issues/obstacles that came up in my life that felt deliberately placed to prevent me from my climb. My family all migrated to America in the 1980s, and I was raised solely by my mother. My father chose to remain in Jamaica to focus on himself. My mother never graduated from any school nor did she earn any degree. Once she moved all of her children to America she went to Capital Community College in Hartford to earn her nurse's aide certificate. I knew from very young that education was important but didn't quite understand the magnitude. I didn't see the world as a battle of the strongest. My vision only focused on my immediate surroundings.

I went to public school in Hartford, but I never felt any connection to anything being taught. Something didn't feel right. It's as if I was learning what someone wanted me to learn and not what I should be. I closed myself off. I guess I went into a mental arctic circle. In high school I dropped out after being suspended in my junior year. Sadly, no one in my family really paid attention to see I was lost in my own winter storm. I shut every one and everything off. There was a cry there for help but it was so soft, it went unnoticed. Instead of making excuses for myself I continued to fight my way through the cold dark place I locked myself in. At 19, I became pregnant with my first child, a daughter. I was elated for such a gift, but I didn't want her for myself; I was struck by feelings I couldn't describe. My older sister Nicole enrolled me in Capital Community

College but I resented her for it. She told me I could go while pregnant to "feel better about myself." The person I was at 19 wasn't ready to be a "mother." I promised my unborn child that I would do my best to protect, guide, and keep her warm from my cold storm. Chanelle was born the day after Christmas 1996 and we faced impoverished circumstances day after day. We were homeless for months living day to day. Somehow I was able to keep her smiling. Although I was broken, I knew I needed a change. What change? I couldn't explain at this time in my life. Every week I would go to Walgreens pharmacy and buy books for Chanelle that were educational. I never bought her toys, never glorified material things for her to yearn for.

January 1998, we were staying the weekend at my favorite brother's house with his girlfriend and young son who was just months older than my daughter. He woke me up that Sunday morning and stated he needed to speak to me. Once I was out of my sleepy slump I went to talk to him. He was visibly different, and I never had any clue it was something I did. He stated a parable to me that was confusing, "steal from a thief, makes God laugh." I am very analytical so it took me time to deduce he was calling me a thief. I was thrown off by the accusation, being that I was so prideful of only attaining things on my own. It is in this practice that I place value to things. If I didn't attain it on my own, I do not place any worth to it. Once I figured out what he was saying I went to talk to him for clarification. I went to his room and asked him to talk to me. Being that I loved him more than myself, I never thought that I would offend him by asking what did he mean by the accusation. He became so angry he instantly charged towards me. He tried kicking me but missed me just slightly. I ran down the stairs to where both our one-year-old children were. I figured since the kids and his girlfriend were there he would never continue. I was so confused by this reaction that I wasn't aware that he was now in a dark place of rage.

He ran past me into the kitchen, harvesting what I thought was a coffee mug. I was wrong. It was a loaded gun that he placed in my mouth. Unknown to my brother, I was pregnant again and disappointed I couldn't tell anyone. He held the gun in my mouth while choking me with his other hand for what seemed an eternity and told me to give him a reason to kill me. I could only mutter to him "go ahead and shoot, because you already killed what was left of me." At that time his girlfriend came between us and told him, "if you shoot her you have to shoot me as well." Being that she was pregnant with their second child he put the gun away at her urging. He wasn't satisfied with this I guess so he proceeded to start beating me with whatever was closest. Knowing I was pregnant I bent over to protect my stomach allowing the blows to penetrate just my back. His girlfriend again intervened after what felt like an eternity. She threatened to call the police. I lost the baby needless to say.

I spiraled deeper into my mental winter which continued for years. It was in 2006, while driving to work knowing I was going to be terminated or laid off soon I was struck by a song I heard by T.I. and Rihanna. One line said, "be grateful for the life you have and not worry about the life you don't have." He was right. I faced adversities, grief, loss but I wasn't grateful. I researched how could I make the life I have better. I signed up for classes at the new location for Capital Community College. I must admit, even though my journey started, I still lived in a mental state of the deepest part of the abyss. Even after having my second child Tenille in 2003, I was still missing something. I went to classes, however it was so hard to maintain while trying to provide. I then started to have health issues. I would be in class barely conscious, praying to "just make it." Hospital stays, blood transfusions, surgeries became a way of life. My new norm, I guess. I hated every second of it. But see, I wasn't as grateful as I thought.

I met a man Claude in 2008 (we later married), who challenged me in a way that was quite life changing. He didn't allow me to accept defeat, forced me to acknowledge that I alone hold the key to change. I wanted to break free of this mental slavery. I wanted to make my mother proud of me. I wanted to see her cry as she did at my sister Nicole's graduation from college (the first in our family).

My mother passed away in 2013 after living with Alzheimer's disease for three years. I had my last surgery in April 2015. Even though I would never see tears of joy from my mother's face, my goal became to earn my degree to bring them to her grave hoping to feel the joy from within. As Bob Marley's song stated, I would be "coming in from the cold." I was coming out of my storm. I fought to take classes at Manchester Community College. The laws, "system" or life did not make it easy for me, but I had my own goal. People aren't aware of the war that is going on in today's society. We close ourselves off from seeing what is really true. I started to pay attention to the news to hear every time there is a budget "crisis" (there will always be a crisis) and the first to be affected are educational resources. Why is that? I can only assume that lawmakers deem it necessary to cut the very core of life away from people because the blinders we put on our eyes force us into not paying attention.

True war isn't fighting with guns, knives or any weapon of that matter. It is in our schools. From public schools in the city where children like myself attend every day. I was told by my high school counselor "you will never be more than an employee of McDonald's." Is this what we want of our youth? To be told metaphorically by society let's prepare you from birth to work minimum wage because we feel that it is in your best interest to cut the budget on educating you and pour those funds into smoke screen necessities.

For too long, the winter I lived in was a mental captivity. I wasn't prepared for battle. I am now graduating from Manchester Community College as a solider in training. My weapon of choice is a degree in Bimolecular Science on the path to obtaining a Masters degree in Nursing. I am a solider in the army of my children's and their children's future. All that I have faced in my life, although horrific, it prepared me with battle skills that I pass along to my daughters. I know my voice is not loud enough to make enough noise for change, but I hope that one day people realize that there is more to life than meets the eye. I hope to spread the word that the war we hear of is not the true war we face. I came in from the cold, so many doors closed in my face. However, when one door closed many more were opened. "It is you, you You YOU I'm talking to now" says Bob Marley in his song "Coming in From the Cold."

Having the opportunity to attend and graduate from MCC meant a change that I never thought I deserved. At the end of every semester I would thank each professor and look him or her in the eye holding on to the feeling of completing another class. Although they were unaware of what I was doing, they forever impacted my life in ways I can't describe. I carry the weight of my mother's pain on my shoulders because, as a mother, a woman, a daughter I followed in her footsteps and struggled through life. Attending community college has opened doors that are facilitating me to change and create a new path for my daughters and myself.

CHAPTER 13

Slim Chances

By Anton Pettiford

I made the decision to enroll in community college in the fall of 2009—a decision that would ultimately change my life beyond anything I could ever imagine. Fueled in part by the devastating effects of the 2008 financial crisis, years of my own economic strife and motivated by the mistakes of so many people around me, my journey to higher education was nothing short of non-traditional. Not in the sense of the obstacles I encountered along the way, as that was expected, but because of the odds I overcame in reversing the very statistics that for so long had served as anecdotal evidence of failure for those who—before me—had traveled the same road.

Slim chances I had of ever becoming a success, I was told by those whose very job it was to ensure I had the best chance. Teachers, community members, and friends alike did very little early on to lead me in the right direction. So at a very young age I took it upon myself to guide the ship despite the little experience I had navigating rough waters. To say I was lost at sea is metaphorically understated. A lack of positive role models coupled with an ignorance to acknowledge positive influences resulted in a deep immersion in street culture, and the once slim chance I had of becoming successful was—to no one's fault but my own—slowly diminishing.

At age 15, while others were entering high school and making the necessary strides toward adulthood, I was taking steps backward which ultimately lead to me falling into the hands of law enforcement. However, it wasn't until several years later when my best friend received a 35-year prison sentence that I realized my life was critically weighing in the balance, headed toward destruction in need of serious change. Despite inescapable setbacks and persistent turmoil, I still managed to graduate high school, receiving my diploma from an alternative school where a large majority of students were, for one reason or another, handed lengthy jail sentences of their own. From living a life in which the vastness of my potential—certainly untapped—seemed locked and held down by its own internal forces, community college allowed that potential to roam freely. Though it didn't come easy.

I reluctantly began my college career, lacking the perquisite confidence required for college success, due to an abysmal high school academic record where over a four-year journey in three different schools (expelled from two) I managed to never earn a grade higher than a C. How ironic it is, then, that years later, I, now equipped with a bachelors degree in Criminal Justice, once labeled myself an "at-risk" teen, would be employed as an Instructional Aide at Futures School sharing my experiences and insight with at-risk high school students, hoping one day to hear a story of success similar to the one I share with you, knowing that if I can steer just one student in the right direction my failures were well-invested.

Long ago, community college had planted within me the seed of servant leadership; a seed that began to grow in 2010 my first semester at Manchester Community College and has grown steadily throughout my college career to produce a foundation rooted in support of the many branches of hope on which success blossoms. That year I was welcomed with open arms into an institution whose doors opened up a world of opportunity. I hadn't always envisioned a world in which I could find my place. In community college I began to see things through a different lens. As I gained a newfound respect for the value of learning, my vision became clearer. Educators, whom once were perceived as a barrier to progress, were now sought for direction as I came to understand that they were, in fact, there to clear the road to success of unnecessary obstacles and help lead the way.

With their efforts, I became a trailblazer, building confidence with every step. The once timid strolls through campus halls lead to award ceremonies and deafening applause. Below-average grades which were a regular in high school were no longer acceptable. My name on the President's List was expected at semesters' end. Yet I wanted more. Curiosity carried me beyond a well-respected GPA and into a front row seat at every student club meeting, as I gained an interest in extracurricular activities;

an interest that propelled me to leadership roles with intentions to make a difference in the community. I was eager to pay it forward and help others, as I did at my town's local homeless shelter. From there, I went on to help former addicts sustain sobriety in one of Connecticut's most drug infested neighborhoods. Now, tasked with molding into shape our future generation of servant leaders, I continue to live my life for the lives of others. And just to think a community college made this possible.

My success at MCC is the byproduct of an alliance of dedicated administrators, professors, advisors, mentors, and student leaders, all of whom shared one goal in common: student success. The community college opens access to a quality education to millions. Be it a recent high school grad seeking a cheaper alternative to the ever increasing price of attending state and private universities, working adults seeking flexibility in their education, or in my case, a misled teen who demands more from life than failure, community college makes it possible. Never in a million years did the prospect of becoming the first in my family to receive a college degree cross my mind. That possibility became reality in May 2013 as I proudly crossed the stage at commencement and reinforced future successes as I earned a Bachelor's degree in 2015. I share my story not to boast but to serve as a template to exceeding expectations, to not let life transgressions define who you are as a person. This opportunity gives me a platform to reach those in the trenches, struggling to improve their life's circumstances. There is hope. I found it in a community college.

CHAPTER 14

Recovery

By Abigail Welles

Being a passionate writer, I have always been enthralled by stories, specifically the most enticing part that lay between the beginning and the end. Don't misunderstand me; the beginning and ending to a story are not to be underrated. They mark significant points in a journey. However, the chapters in between these two points are the most vital parts of the story as they provide a string of events—the rising action and the falling action, the successes and the failures—that truly consummates a triumphant tale. My story begins in a high school in East Hartford, Connecticut, and continues on roughly six years later at Manchester Community College in Manchester, Connecticut. My journey is one rife with trials and tribulations, devastation, inspiration, and self-acceptance. Let me give you the skinny on my story.

I am going to address the elephant that shares the space in every room I walk into. I have an eating disorder. I am a recovering anorexic. The key word here is *recovering*, a word inferring that I have weathered the perfect storms and am finally understanding how to keep my balance on rough waters and work my sails. Hold on to that word. I still find it interesting that I found this understanding at a small community college in Manchester, Connecticut.

I completely recognize the oddity that is a stranger being perfectly candid. It's weird, I get it. But I feel that my story is rife with many themes and ideas that are relevant to anyone who identifies as human. To anyone who has ever felt hopeless, helpless, and a bit away from their intended path,

I hope you find inspiration in my story. One of the most important things I learned throughout these past six years is the power of silver linings. Good can come from even the greatest devastations, but sometimes these blessings are delivered in unusual packages. Hold on to this word, as well.

I always struggled with self-esteem. Even in childhood, I recall worrying about my appearance and becoming too aware of words such as *weight, calories,* and *fat*. I spent much time using the world around me as a mirror with which to compare myself to its reflection. The eating disorder gene was even one that was snugly woven into the jeans of most of my family members. Despite these obvious red flags, I never expected to become as sick as I did. It happened seamlessly, as I transitioned into my freshman year of high school. The speed with which my illness took over my life was intense, having entered high school in September and having been admitted into the hospital for severe malnourishment by mid-November. Even now in a healthier state of recovery, I still can't tell you the exact point where my passion for a healthy lifestyle turned into a full-blown addiction to starvation and perfection. Mental illness doesn't give a heads up. It just swings and brings down everything in its path.

One of the most prominent stressors I experienced throughout this time in my life, aside from my eating disorder, was my fight for an education. From the moment my struggle with anorexia began in 2010, the support I received from my high school's administration was nonexistent. In the months leading up to my leaving the physical high school setting completely, I faced verbal harassment from the principal and vice principal of my school. It would be an understatement to say that they simply had no compassion for my illness.

They outwardly called me worthless and told me that I wouldn't amount to anything in my life. They called me a truant for not being able to come to school and threatened to have me arrested. On the days that I did muster up enough courage to walk into the building, the vice principal at the time would chase me down the hall and call me out in front of crowds of students, for reasons as silly as not having my I.D. badge visible. This was where my anxiety disorder began to develop into a clinical diagnosis. I began to suffocate from panic attacks regularly on top of the stress induced by my eating disorder and my falling behind in school. It felt as though they were punishing me for having an illness that was completely beyond my control.

I have always been a fighter, or "stubborn" as many of my teachers referred to this quality as. I am a natural advocator, specifically in situations that I feel are unjust and a violation of human rights. There was only one thing that I cared about more than my need to be *skinny* and that was my education. I recognized the unjust treatment they imparted on me and I refused to allow them to strip me of my right to an education. But even the administration was unwilling to back down without a fight.

Usually students in primary or secondary schools who suffer from an illness that prevents them from physically attending school are entitled to homebound tutoring. However, per my high school's administration, I didn't have an illness. It is difficult encouraging people who are ignorant to mental health to set aside their judgments and put forth the compassion needed to understand such a complex illness. So because of their perception of my situation and unwillingness to learn about its reality, they denied me proper accommodations for my illness. Being a young woman who was as stubborn as the last bit of belly fat I claimed clung to my lower abdomen, that was unacceptable. If they weren't going to teach me, then I would teach myself.

In order to succeed, I spent hours in hospital rooms, textbooks spread out on my bed, determined to teach myself the curriculum and surpass the limited expectations of those around me. My mother would consistently go to my high school every morning to receive new work, bring it to the hospital for me to complete, and bring it back to the high school to be passed in. When I eventually was able to go home, this cycle continued. I was worthy of an education, whether my high school's administration wanted to believe that or not.

Picture a child's toy. A big yellow cube with different shaped holes on the top. It is up to the child to take different shaped blocks and slide them through the hole on the cube that matches the shape. If you did it correctly, the block would slide through the hole easily. No effort on the child's part needed. The issue these administrators found with me was that I was a block that didn't quite fit in these cookie cutter shapes. I had an extra edge that simply didn't allow me to, and this was frustrating to them. I required a different solution than what was implemented for the majority of students if I were to succeed in my education. I was too difficult to deal with, a true truant in their eyes, and therefore I needed to be removed.

Despite actual documented diagnosis, the administration continued to trivialize my situation as being less than other better understood illnesses. Unlike a primarily physical condition, where I could show them an x-ray of a broken bone or a tumor, I could never present them with an x-ray of my brain and exclaim, "See? There it is. There's the eating disorder." Mental health is far too abstract and every case is unique to the individual. There was no concrete proof that convinced them of my tragic situation.

I never returned to school after the November hospitalization. Soon after being discharged, I was readmitted into the hospital in January 2011 for anorexia. Naturally, my education became even more of a challenge as I struggled to balance my physical health, mental health, and my schoolwork. I was psychologically and physically unraveling, and this was certainly disheartening. I had always been an academically gifted student, one who truly cares about her studies and successes, so the fact that I was unable to find a steady balance in my life was discouraging. However, I kept on, as I recognized that giving up on my education would be a mistake.

I continued trying to teach myself the required curriculum throughout my sophomore and junior years. Years after my official diagnosis, the administration still refused to provide me with proper homebound tutoring and academic assistance. Every day I chipped away at my piling workload while balancing hours of doctor appointments and therapy sessions. If I wasn't directly stressing about the process of eating, battling self-deprecating thoughts, and working towards recovery, I was in the library working to keep my studies on track. Realistically, a 16-year-old girl could only teach herself so much of a curriculum designed to be implemented by professional educators. I kept my spirits high, knowing that I was fighting an important and worthy battle, but I was still becoming exhausted.

The stress brought on by the administration and their approach to my education caused my anxiety and depression to consume my life. I entered the hospital once more during the summer before my senior year. I was behind in much of my studies and was beginning to question whether or not I would ever be able to catch up in time for my final year of secondary schooling. The administration recognized this doubtfulness and consistently suggested that dropping out of high school was my best option. I was always a conscientious student, one who welcomed challenges and genuinely enjoyed learning. I never suspected that dropping out would be a plausible option. Broken and exhausted while in the hospital for the third time, I was finally ready to concede.

The administration was relieved to hear that I decided to drop out and willingly compiled the necessary paper work. If only they had that same level of eagerness and efficiency when it came to helping me succeed, maybe dropping out would have never been an option. I vividly recall the smug look and arrogance exuded by my guidance counselor when he revealed there was never any chance that I was going to make it to graduation and staying in school was only going to cause me more stress from false hope. The very people whose job is to help students succeed set me up to fail from day one and it was in that moment that I knew I deserved more than what they were giving me. I cancelled my appointment to drop out of school and for once my stubbornness that I was begrudged for throughout my struggle with both hospitals and the school began to prove itself as my greatest tool in regaining control of my life.

We went to mediation with the school in the beginning of the summer of 2013, where we would put in place an educational plan that would enable me to graduate with my high school diploma. After five hours of deliberation, the administration agreed to allow me to finish my education online. The catch was that I would be stripped of many of the credits I worked to earn during my junior year. There was no explanation for the administration taking away credits I had earned fairly, primarily because the only reason they had was spite. I gracefully accepted their challenge.

I had two full academic years worth of curriculum to finish and they expected me to graduate by August of 2015. My class was set to graduate in June 2014 and I was determined to be a part of that group. When I told my guidance counselor this a few weeks after our mediation, he laughed a boisterous belly laugh and shook his head, clearly amused at my irrational goal. Their mocking lit a flame in me that had died out. I needed to prove them wrong, and prove to myself how worthy of an education I was. I worked tirelessly, every day, from the moment I woke up to the moment I went to sleep. I'm sure you can imagine their surprise when I finished all of my graduation requirements, allowing me to graduate in January 2014, a half year before my class. During this time I also managed to finally make it to a healthy weight. An eating disorder is a lifetime struggle, like any addiction. However, being able to make it to a healthy weight from my lowest weight, which went into the low 60s, was an immense accomplishment. It gave me hope that recovery was possible. I did what I thought was impossible. I beat anorexia and received my high school diploma.

This is where my tale finally meets up with Manchester Community College. A month previous to my completion of high school, I asked my guidance counselor to fill out specific forms required for applying to my dream schools. My request went unanswered for weeks, as the deadlines for schools rapidly approached. On December 26, I officially finished all of my essays for my applications after many hours of editing and rewriting. On December 31, I spent all day in front of my computer with my email open, waiting for a response. On January 1, I spent my time personally calling East Hartford High and the guidance center, desperate to get a response. I still remember the devastation that overwhelmed me as I watched the clock count down the last five minutes of the day, promptly hitting midnight.

On January 2, my guidance councilor finally responded. He decided to refuse to fill out the forms as he strongly believed that I would never make it in a college setting and therefore felt that it was pointless and out of line with my best interests to apply to any of my four-year universities. The very administration who decided time and time again that I was unworthy of receiving any academic assistance throughout my illness also decided that I was unfit and unworthy of receiving a higher education beyond high school. However, nothing about my high school education was conventional, so why did my higher education have to be? I decided to pursue an alternative route and enroll in Manchester Community College.

Unfortunately, community colleges have a stigma attached to them that prevents people from seeing their remarkable qualities. I will openly admit that I fell victim to this stigma when I first attended MCC. I remember walking into my first day of class feeling angry. I was angry at my circumstances. I wanted to be in a four-year university. I missed out on four years of my life due to my struggle with an eating disorder and anxiety. I wanted to begin my new chapter in a spectacular way: living in a dorm on the campus of a significant college and having the time of my life. I convinced myself that community college was for people who weren't intelligent enough to go to a four-year college. Community college was for people who would never amount to anything in their lives. I was wrong.

I was so completely wrong in my judgments of Manchester Community College. My bitterness towards my situation was ultimately preventing me from not only seeing but experiencing the astounding community college that is MCC. Once I was able to come to this realization, my personal and academic growth soared. I received acceptance into the Honors College at MCC, where I had the distinct pleasure to work personally with a mentor during my two years. This provided support that enabled me to build my confidence, and in return my anxiety disorder became less of a debilitating force in my life. I became even more ambitious and willing to take risks, and watched as a multitude of doors opened before me. I became a trained moderator for the National Issues Forum and led a community discussion on mental illness during my first semester at MCC. The girl who suffered from severe panic attacks was now fully embracing the art of public speaking.

During my second semester, I became involved with the student government association at MCC. I wanted to further challenge my anxiety by involving myself in leadership roles that would require public interaction. I was an active student representative and encouraged students to become more involved in their college's campus community. Going into my second year of college, I decided that I was ready to return to what I did for so long during high school: advocating. Education was important to me and is a significant factor that allowed me to become who I am today. I worked tirelessly in high school to graduate because no one was willing to help me. I decided to become an active Vice President of the MCC student government so that I could advocate strongly for students and help them receive the educational experience they want and deserve.

During this time, I also became involved in advocacy for civil and human rights. I helped implement an event called "MCC Unites," which aimed to raise awareness around social inequality and racial injustice in the United States. I worked to shed light on controversial issues and help students have constructive conversations despite differing opinions. I used my oppressive experiences in both the medical and education settings to encourage a collective advocacy for human beings facing injustice.

The educational opportunities that my community college provided enabled personal and academic growth, but I still owe much of my success to the remarkable educators at MCC. They saw potential that I was unable to see and that my high school administration told me for so long didn't exist, and they worked to foster it. I had never experienced such compassion and support and with the administration's deprecating judgments that once resonated within me, I began to see the fallacy in their verdicts pertaining to my character and capabilities. I began to believe in myself, which was a novel feeling. Eventually, I even was able to experience moments where I appreciated and loved myself for who I was and what I could do, which was a tremendous accomplishment as I continued my life-long journey of recovery from my eating disorder. With the compassion and encouragement presented to me by the professors at Manchester Community College, I was not only able to achieve academic success but also was able to begin to understand that my value does not lie in my weight—that the width of my waist will never equate to my worth—and that a significant part of what made me beautiful was my kindness, my empathy towards others, my intelligence, and my admirable determination. MCC allowed me to recognize something that my eating disorder and high school never did: that I was worthy of a proper education and a healthy and happy life.

It is exceedingly easy to be angry. It is easy to be bitter about your less than favorable circumstances and hateful towards those who put you in such circumstances and held you down. I know, because I allowed my bitterness and hatefulness to consume my being and nearly caused me to miss out on a tremendous journey of self-discovery and personal and academic growth. My anger nearly stopped my life. I learned that it is one of the most trying challenges to choose positivity over negativity and love over hate. It can be so psychologically demanding to search for the silver linings of situations that seem nothing but disastrous and hopeless. It is downright grueling to rebuild your life from what felt like rock bottom. But choosing to pull yourself back up after you have been defeated and giving yourself another chance is the most rewarding investment you will ever make. Choosing to forgive yourself for your failures and to look forward from your past is tough but worthwhile. I genuinely do not believe that I would have chosen the path that would enable me to forgive and give myself another chance if I had not made the decision to attend Manchester Community College. MCC was my silver lining. So was my eating disorder.

Recovery is about being in a constant state of movement. Whether you are taking a few steps forward, or a few back, you are consistently working towards self-improvement. That was really the prominent theme during my time at MCC. I had taken seven classes in my final semester, five more than I had taken my first semester. I was an active Vice President of the Student Government and advocated for students in ways that my high school administration failed to do for me. While in this position I also developed a successful weeklong event that brought awareness to social inequality and racial injustice in our country. I interned at the college's radio station and learned how to utilize my voice to communicate positive, constructive messages across media platforms. I was one of two in a graduating class of 896 to graduate with honors from the Honors College at MCC. I will never be an adept mathematician or biologist, but I am excellent at understanding human beings of all demographics and showing them remarkable compassion that uplifts and creates immense impact. I am a drastically different person from the 14-year-old girl 6 years ago, a positive change inspired by every failure and blessing.

This college and its outstanding professors gave me the inspiration to reinvent myself and step out of the box I kept myself locked in. They helped me understand that a college education is not a given. There is no entitlement to higher education, and many who are well deserving of receiving it are unable to because of its immense price. My adversity enabled me to become a student unwilling to be deterred by failure. To recognize that our character is not measured by our obstacles but rather how we cope with adversity and overcome it. To step outside of our comfort zones, push our limits, and even be a little imperfect. To understand that no one else will hand you your education, you must take it for yourself.

Yes, this commuter college is very different from a large four-year university in that there are no dorms and perhaps less funding for large-scale events, but its quality is one to be competed with and I have never once felt that my education was being compromised due to it being a "cheaper" educational option. Furthermore, many see community colleges simply as the path for those who find trouble in affording the larger four-year universities. While this is true, and certainly the low tuition has been beneficial for me, many community colleges such as Manchester Community College act as an outlet for those similar to myself, who perhaps were in need of a second chance and needed a smaller place to begin their new chapter of reinvention. I believe that everything happens for a reason, and I am incredibly blessed to have faced the hardships I have endured as they allowed me to grow stronger and led me to the fine educational institution that is MCC. I am a far cry away from who I was before I began my journey at MCC and I can confidently say that I am incredibly proud of the person that this community college helped me become. I would not change one step in my journey. This college gave me a second chance when no one else would and now I am on a successful track working towards immense dreams that will leave an imprint on this world that is as compassionate and inspiring as the imprint that Manchester Community College and its professors have left on me.

CHAPTER 15

Writing My Way to College

By Ashley Riddlesworth

My name is Ashley Riddlesworth and I am proud to say that I am a graduate of Manchester Community College (Class of 2013!). My experiences at MCC have provided me with skills and knowledge that have greatly impacted my life. They have given me the tools necessary to enhance the talents I entered college with and to graduate having developed new ones I didn't know I could acquire. Attending MCC and learning from my professors at the school helped inspire me to become more and to realize my own potential.

I grew up in Torrington, Connecticut, with my mom and my twin sister. My parents divorced when I was in first grade so it was just the three of us after my father moved away. We'd see him on some weekends, but it was inconsistent. The divorce was not easy for me—I tried to be strong as I got older and understood my parents' split, but it was something I struggled with privately. My mom also struggled, but succeeded. She was a single parent right from the beginning and was sure to provide us with the things that we needed to grow up to be good people: skills, information, the necessary material things, fun, and most importantly: love and support. I can't put into words how much that has always meant to me, and how much it reinforced the importance of family in my life.

Growing up, I was a typical American kid. I loved to play outside and be with my friends, but something that set me apart from most of my peers was my early onset passion for reading. I read all the time and begged to be read to before I could do it myself. I slept with books in my crib. My mom still jokes with friends and family members that I put both of my arms around stacks of books while I slept, and there are pictures to prove it! I collected series that were for my age group and older. Reading was something I did constantly. No matter where I went, I brought books with me. I read in the car, on vacation, in school, during recess, at lunch, and I brought stacks of books with me to Girl Scout camp. In elementary school and in middle school, my best classes were reading and writing. I had pen pals all over the world, wrote in journals, and even kept a journal back and forth with some of my teachers when I was little. I continued to preen my passions all the way through high school, where I continued to excel in my writing courses. When it came to making decisions about my future, continuing my journey into the world of literature was absolute, so college was always something I knew would be a part of it.

My high school experience, however, didn't really make the idea of college seem as attractive as I'd hoped it would be during the years of my childhood. The social stigma and pressure of high school affected me significantly, more privately than what could be perceived publicly. I wasn't the most popular girl in school, but I wasn't ridiculed either. I got very good grades, but I wasn't at the top of my class. I wanted so badly to go to a good college or university, but I could hardly afford to pay for my application fees. I had no idea how I would ever afford tuition to the schools of my choosing. At the time I graduated from high school—class of 2002—things like grants and scholarships weren't as easy to find, apply for, or learn about. The guidance department at my high school was lacking heavily, and my family didn't know the first thing about trying to obtain funding of any kind. The Internet was available, but resources that are offered now weren't nearly as reliable or readily available as they are now. My mom didn't know much about it, and my guidance counselor put almost no effort into helping me, despite my cries for help. For me, it seemed hopeless to ever be able to attend, which was heartbreaking.

During high school and for some years after, I did a lot of work in journalism and created a website—or "webzine"—based on celebrity news, called Backstage Pass. Several of my friends at the time were in acting, so I started with interviews with them to begin publishing online. I began contacting agents and representatives of current actors and musicians and featured interviews with them, along with reviews of concerts and television programs. It wasn't long before I had built a foundation so strong that I was traveling around New England every week, having been invited to concerts, shows, and events all over the east coast. I had a lot of fun and I made a lot of friends in the industry, and it set my life in a completely unexpected direction.

My mom was very supportive of everything I wanted to do with writing and journalism. I was much younger than the agents I was working with thought I was, and I had already created an unpaid career in entertainment before I could even drive! My mother chauffeured me around all of the states surrounding Connecticut, sat in on interviews, hooked up recording systems to my phone line so I could document my conversations for publishing, and shouldered the phone bill when I called out of state every day to talk to bands on tour, actors in L.A. and New York, and even to entertainers out of the country I'd composed hours of questions for. We had a lot of fun together, and the experience taught me a lot about what I loved about what I was doing with my life at the time, which was writing. I thought to pursue an education in journalism, and my resume for it was impressive by the time I applied to my selected colleges. I applied to several schools and was accepted, and while simultaneously trying to decide if I would accept from UConn, Hofstra, and Quinnipiac, I knew in the back of my mind that I would never be able to afford to pay the tuition or be approved for the student loans that I needed to attend those schools. Despite this, I pursued my goals and continued to keep my website up and running.

The drama of the Hollywood world was consuming, however, and I started to realize that celebrity gossip was just that—gossip. Every word I published became a gamble, and the interviews I posted had to be combed through to be sure I wasn't allowing one person to ridicule another. There is so much competition in that world, and the more people I met the more sides I was forced to take depending on the situation and who I was talking to at the time. I was uncomfortable with the confrontation some people I interviewed would create for their rivals, and while most of what I did was light and fun, the pressure to keep everyone happy with what I published became tremendous. When I was faced with my first lawsuit for retracted publication based on what one pop star said about another, I began to reconsider my choice of career paths. I enjoyed the writing part of what I was doing, but I ultimately decided that I didn't want to shoulder the blame for he-said/she-said in the interviews I published. The exposure was incredible: I had millions of visitors every day, but the stress of the best story or the best interview wasn't appealing to me anymore because of the repercussions. I wanted to write, but I learned I enjoyed writing more when it was my own work—fiction—outside of my Hollywood job. The "celebrity politics" I'd been dealing with on a more and more regular basis were becoming too stressful for me to deal with, and I eventually put the site on hiatus and took it down. I had decided to focus more on the type of writing I enjoyed most—the type of writing that wouldn't cause turbulence between people, especially.

Spontaneously, I decided I'd wanted to have some new and different life experience before going to college. This is something that I believe many teens right out of high school can relate to. I wanted to make a change, and though I wanted to go back to school I also sought to take some time off before continuing my education. I moved across the country to see what was out there. For me personally, although it wasn't everything I'd wanted it to be, it was the best decision at the time: personal growth was something that I'd needed. I wanted to find myself, and also figure out what I wanted to do with my life. When I applied to the colleges I'd gotten into, I had showcased skills in journalism. While I was good at it, I realized that type of career wasn't going to make me happy. Before I committed to paying for and attending school again, I needed to have some idea of what I loved enough to spend my life doing. The handful of negative interactions in the world of journalism left a bad taste in my mouth for outright public work, and I knew that wasn't the kind of pressure I wanted to be under all the time, especially when I knew I could hurt people doing it.

I spent some time in Arizona and returned home to Connecticut for a short time afterward. During that time, I'd certified in a program in dog grooming and spent some time working with animals and rescues. I networked in the animal care industry, changed many furry little lives for the better, and helped so many dogs that I lost track. It was unbelievably rewarding, and I enjoyed what I was doing. After two years of grooming in my hometown, I moved down to Florida and helped open up a new salon and to build a business in a new location for the company I'd been working for. Although my passion of reading and writing continued, I didn't have the stability or the resources to commit to continued education to work toward a career just yet. Six months later I transferred back up to Connecticut to be with family.

When I moved home from Florida, I continued to work at my job, but it was becoming more and more obvious that something was missing. Inspired by the desire to make my life more full, I began doing what I'd always wanted to, now that my life was more secure: I started writing my first YA fantasy novel. The more planning I did, the more motivated I became. Prior to my decision, I hadn't ever really been given an opportunity to find *my* calling career-wise, and here it was blossoming before me. The closer I came to the completion of my first book, the more I realized how many more opportunities I'd have if I coupled it with a college education. My passion for writing was my biggest motivator in returning to school. I knew college could improve the skills I already had, and at some point in all of my planning, it occurred to me I was finally ready to go back. I just had to figure out how to do it.

Just as when I left high school, I was unable to think of tuition as being something affordable. I loved what I was doing career-wise in the animal industry and I was making decent money, but again, I realized that I wasn't as passionate about it as I was about literature. I wanted to be better and to gain the support I needed to become a published author, and I knew college was where that would begin. I was excited to be planning solidly for college, finally!! Something that had been a part of my entire life would finally have its time to shine. I made it a goal to figure out how I could attend college and continue to work. I was educated about the means to get to school and armed with the motivation to do it, I just needed to find something I could afford and that could accommodate my busy lifestyle.

Money aside, most colleges I'd applied to and gotten into had course schedules that were not exactly practical for someone in my position: I was already working full time, and cutting my hours was not an option when I had so many bills. I was 25, and I knew what I wanted to do with my life. I knew attending college would help me accomplish every goal I'd set for myself. So, how was I going to take on paying my bills by working full-time, writing full-time, and attending college? With an unpredictable work schedule where I was scheduled on weekends and some nights, the regular routine of basic college was impossible for me. I began to research colleges in my area again for the first time since I'd graduated high school.

I decided that a community college was best suited for my situation. The cost was far more practical. They offered grants, the flexibility of degrees and classes was more than I could have ever imagined, the class sizes were better than reasonable, and the availability of my professors would be close to constant, which is something I valued greatly. Feedback was something I wanted and I knew it wouldn't be as available if I were in a class of hundreds students per course. Community college also came with a vast population of students of all ages, which made me feel welcomed immediately. They offered me an abundance of degree options (including several versions of liberal arts/general studies programs for core courses) and a very, very long list of technical certifications and degrees. Certifications for technical programs are just as coveted as degrees, and community colleges offer many in fields that have countless job opportunities in today's most demanding industries.

With a new target in mind, I began to filter through the community colleges within a reasonable radius from where I lived. There were four or five, and after some quick research, MCC was the college I decided to look at first. I loved its location, for one—it was close to everything, but the campus was absolutely set in its own world. It was the perfect community college for me; it truly gave me the live-on campus feel without actually having to live in a dorm. I applied to MCC in the summer of 2009 with a friend and set up an appointment with a student advisor. One of the first things I was told when I met with my advisor was that I would be able to attend, which took off so much pressure! One of the worst parts about applying for the colleges and universities I'd applied to after high school was waiting to see if I'd even have the opportunity to go. Getting excited about college and starting new classes is hard to do when you're not even sure if they'll accept you, and in applying to a community college the pressure was off. It wasn't as if they would just let their students sleep through classes, but it was an equal opportunity that allowed every person to have a decent chance at an education. I was always a good student in high school, but I automatically had a lot of respect for a school that didn't look only at a student's high school transcript to give them an opportunity at an education and a career. I know plenty of people who slacked throughout high school but ended up being extremely successful in college and in their careers. Colleges like MCC don't require you to be a perfect student since grade school to have a chance at a phenomenal future, and that was exactly the type of supportive atmosphere I'd been looking for.

Entrance testing was required, but I passed it easily, which I did not expect because I'd been out of high school for so long. What I did love about the entrance exam at MCC was that it provides students who might not be ready for their first credited courses to take classes in order to develop the skills they need to achieve good marks in the next entry-levels. Even I wasn't sure I'd be able to "get in" to the classes, and even though I did, it was comforting to know that anyone would be able to attend without having the hindrance of forgotten basics. The resources needed in order to reach goals were there for *every* student so that everyone has an opportunity to change their lives with further education.

When I signed up for my courses, I realized something else that quelled my anxiety: I certainly wasn't the only person attending college who hadn't walked off the stage with their high school diploma only a few months before. The vastness of age amongst students was surprising to me, but it made me feel much more welcome. This was something that was extremely important to me and actually made my experience through every year of school that much better. Attending college could be more relaxed in a social manner, without the feeling of attending high school again on a bigger property with more people. MCC was comfortable immediately for me, and I was no longer worried about where I should be fitting in, because everyone made me feel so relaxed. I wasn't paranoid about being a few years older than the typical college freshman. I had only graduated from high school a few years before, but I was still insecure about going back to continue my education after so many of my high school classmates had the opportunity to attend college the fall after we walked. They were graduating college when I was starting, and that made me feel apprehensive. The feel of the MCC campus made me realize that it wasn't *when* you go back to school that's important—it's making the decision *to* go back that is. Knowing this made it that much more enjoyable to take my classes.

I began with four courses (English, Psych, Sociology, and Philosophy) and waited for the fall approach. Entering school for the first time after seven years of being away was extremely intimidating for me, despite my self-assurance that it would be a good experience based on what I'd learned. I knew the basics, but I didn't know anyone there. I was out of the loop in regard to what school and college were like, and I was afraid of what the professors would expect from me right away. Because I'd never felt very challenged in high school, my biggest fear was that when I began college courses I might not be able to keep up with what was being taught to me. Those feelings were quickly put at ease for me, as my professors worked with my classmates and me. I quickly began accomplishing good grades and a positive beginning to my continued education.

About a year into school I noticed there was something wrong with me, especially when I was working at my job. I could almost never feel my fingers, especially my thumbs, and when I did have sensation it was extremely painful. I made an appointment to see a hand surgeon and he told me what I'd considered the worst news in the world at the time: I had extremely severe carpal tunnel syndrome. I had more than 90% paralysis in both of my thumbs, and the condition was suffocating my hands. My CTS was caused by the constant repetitive nature of my job in grooming animals, and not only would it become worse if I continued, but my doctor also informed me that if I continued with my current career path I could develop problems with my elbows, neck, and spine. He recommended that I set a date for surgery that week, and I panicked. I wouldn't be allowed to work or drive for months. I was depressed, and I thought I'd have to take the semester off from college and put not only my job but also my education on hold because of my injuries. How would I work, and more importantly, how would I continue my classes?

Online courses, of course!! Taking courses online actually changed my life—I didn't have to stop school in spite of a serious injury. I was *thrilled* to be able to take advantage of the online education that MCC provided in such a time of despair for me—I could still go to college, even if I couldn't attend physically or write with a pen. I signed up for four courses that semester and notified my professors of my condition, so they would know I would be having a little trouble typing between surgeries. They were incredibly supportive and understanding, and told me to let them know if I was having any trouble with any particular assignments so they could give me an extension. During such a trying time for me, I was still able to go to college and take steps forward when everything else in my life was forced to be put on pause.

Taking classes with such encouraging teachers and flexible schedules also provided me with the time I needed to work toward my ultimate goal at the time, which was to finish writing my first book. Because of the education my teachers provided me I became better at what I already loved to do. I have since completed the first one and have written two more to completion. My confidence has grown and I have so many projects going it's almost overwhelming (in the best way, of course!). Without the support of my fellow students and the confidence of my teachers, I don't know if I could have achieved such huge accomplishments. My teachers—especially in English—played a huge role in my success as a writer, and continue to do so.

Throughout my time in college, the professors at MCC were incredibly encouraging and gave recognition where I needed it, especially when I didn't even know I deserved it! English and writing were always my passion, and even in my other classes, my teachers personally put a lot of positive emphasis on how well I wrote my papers and how fluidly I was able to explain what I'd learnt through words. This built up my self-esteem and made me all the more confident in my own personal endeavors at home. The encouragement I received to fulfill my own dreams by my teachers was invaluable and made me all the more eager to reach for them.

Some of the most prideful moments of my life were when I'd receive my letters congratulating me on making the Dean's List, especially in my harder semesters with classes that were not my strong suit or when work was particularly trying. Two of my most memorable semesters were when I went through my CTS surgeries, and also my last semester before graduation, when I had to attend class on crutches every week because I'd broken my foot. My teachers were very understanding and supportive and my classmates were always kind and accommodating. I was so happy that my hard work and determination had paid off, and it was extremely rewarding to be personally recognized for it when I received my letters.

I think that it goes without saying that the most incredible gift I was given at MCC was learning to become a better writer and all of the benefits this provided me. The importance of learning how to compose more articulately didn't just make me a better storyteller—it made me a better thinker and a better student for every class. My professors went out of their way to be completely involved and to be sure we understood the material, even in our online classes. They allowed for us to collaborate and discuss in order to understand better. In open class discussion, we were not only taught how to think more honestly and thoroughly, but to understand and respect other classmates' opinions and be open to debate or change. These are the types of skills that are essential in life, especially in the workplace for every individual. Becoming more socially responsible and increasing our capacity for compassion and learning were taught in tandem with the importance of history and literature. It wasn't like being in a lecture hall—we were much more connected, which helped us learn together more memorably.

Before I attended community college myself, I had many misconceptions about the benefits and the educational quality I'd receive from choosing one. I, like many, figured that since ivy league schools, state schools, and all of the colleges and universities in between were far more expensive, that going to a community college wouldn't provide me with the same quality of education or attention that paying $50,000 a year would. I couldn't have been more wrong. The education I received has been invaluable to me, and the recognition and personal attention I received from every professor I had made my college experience that much better.

While you never know what you're going to get from a certain professor when you walk into a classroom, I believe that the quality and the passion of each individual working on a college campus is set by that teacher—not by the name of the institution in which they teach. I consider the distinct devotion and goals given by each of my professors throughout my college experience as unmatched, and more valuable than a special name on top of my diploma. I prefer a smaller student-to-teacher in-classroom ratio because it provides a more thorough and attentive college experience. I believe that all colleges do their best to provide the greatest education possible for their students, but attending a college like MCC is a good opportunity for a student to receive the feedback he or she needs from their professor on a smaller scale. Stadium-set classrooms with a 100–500 students for basic classes provide a less meaningful experience, and in attending a community college like MCC, teachers have more of a chance to give each student the focus they need and deserve in finding a career path that's right for them. Every professor I've ever had at MCC has stressed that this begins when you start college, and that was always very important to me.

I also appreciated that my college wasn't excessively pushy about timely graduation and was more focused on being sure that I moved and studied at a pace that was right for my lifestyle. This created an environment that made it possible for me to get the most out of my college experience without feeling like I was being rushed or falling behind. The professors and staff of MCC were always very helpful, and the leniency of the course load I took each semester was entirely up to me. I was able to have a working adult life while attending college. My education didn't have to be rushed unless I wanted it to be. There were several semesters I could only take two or three classes, and that was totally fine. Whether for time-pressed, financial, or personal reasons, there was no discrimination. I had complete flexibility in completion of my degree. I could take two classes one semester, and four or five the next if I wanted to make up for time lost. MCC gave me the license to continue my education at my own pace, without pressure, and with support of the entire college's staff.

Community colleges like MCC strive to give every student an equal opportunity to receiving a college education. Just like in my personal situation, I was not born into a lot of money, nor did I have the means possible to commit to the exponential bills and student loans that major colleges and universities would have burdened me with. Not only did the opportunities at MCC allow for me to attend in the first place, they also led me to where I wanted to be and become in my life: a college graduate and a successful writer, without the burden of tens of thousands of dollars of debt. After graduating I've been able to celebrate and move on to the next step of being a happy, more successful person with a fantastic education, and without the worry of more financial hardships.

I am proud to say that I graduated from MCC. Since the completion of my degree, I have finished writing several of my own projects and am in the process of self-publishing and gaining representation. During and after my time in school, I've also been given opportunities like this to contribute to projects that allow me to do what I love most. I am so thankful for everything I learned during my time in college, and I encourage prospective students to follow their dreams—because you can reach them! Community college gave me the opportunity to be better at what I love and I wouldn't trade how I got here for anything.

I learned so much about myself by attending MCC. Rigorous study sessions I believed I was incapable of, a surprising newfound appreciation for history and sciences, and the capacity to learn and pass on knowledge and information to everyone in my life. MCC taught me about the rewards of hard work—the importance of thinking critically, character development, and the cultivation of skills in leadership. These things have made me a better worker, a better friend, and a better more educated person. Attending this college gave me the opportunity to learn about my own potential and act on it, and these were things I hadn't known would be attached to my continued education.

MCC changed my life in ways I never imagined college ever could. I had never allowed myself to truly believe that college would ever be a real opportunity for me financially. And while the education a student receives at schools like Princeton or Harvard are incredible and known worldwide, those that attend and strive toward those ivy-league type schools fail to acknowledge the importance and value of an education you receive from a school like the one I was lucky enough to attend. What needs to be understood by every person in our society is that learning at a place like MCC creates the opportunity for students like me to be taught by phenomenal educators who deserve far more recognition than they receive. I was offered such monumental opportunities and I took the ones I wanted and applied them to my life—every student deserves this opportunity, and every person should know the value of the hours put in by the extraordinary people involved in making facilities like this stay alive.

My college provided me with the tools I needed to become a more successful individual at my workplace, and in any future careers or endeavors I choose to pursue. What I learned by taking such an array of courses was not just the content of that particular subject, but the way in which to understand them and how each and every one of them applies to everyday life. Not only have I found great importance in the acquisition of knowledge, I now have the skills to apply the concept of education in my everyday life, making my experiences even more rewarding. MCC didn't just teach me the contents of my courses. My professors prepared me for living in this world, how to analyze situations more thoroughly and how to apply proper and realistic problem-solving to what I encounter.

No matter your age or experience, community colleges can provide you with the means to choose your own career path and accomplish your life's goals. They can fit *any* lifestyle, and I believe that makes the education you obtain there even more valuable—and more attainable! My college did more for me than I ever would have expected. It made me a better thinker, problem-solver, and writer. I am more independent, self-reliant and confident. My degree has helped me move up in my current job and continues to push me more quickly in the advancement of my career goals and dreams. Going to MCC was a fantastic blessing, and the education and experience that I received was tremendous. I am so grateful for every fellow student and every professor I had the opportunity to work with at MCC. My experience there was one I will cherish always and I will take it with me throughout the rest of my life.

Chapter 16

Journey

By Yanira Hernandez

My journey begins in the tiny Caribbean island of Puerto Rico. It is known as the island of enchantment and I'd like to share with you why it is enchanting for me. I was born in the barrio of Santurce. It is located in the capital city of San Juan and near the city of Bayamón where most of my family lives. My mother fled the beautiful island just three months after I was born to get away from my father's cheating ways. I have visited the island several times. For me, even though I was raised in Hartford, every time I return to Puerto Rico, I feel connected like I am at home. While I appreciate the beauty of the changing seasons, and the freshly fallen snow that blanket the woods around my home in Coventry in the winter months, I do not like to be cold. I am in my element in tropical weather. The curved and swaying palm trees, the lush El Yunque rain forest, clear blue ocean waters, and rustic countrysides give me a sense of energy and life that is like no other. The beautiful, historic area of Old San Juan full of colorful buildings, churches, and historic monuments like El Morro Fort, take me back to the rich history of my home of Puerto Rico. This tiny speck of paradise is also one that fills my heart with the joy of salsa music and amazing food. All over the island sounds of native music abound and food spots are readily available. Even the poor remind you that you are on the island as it is not uncommon to be offered a coconut shell with a straw at many street corners—and they sell them to you while you wait for the traffic light while sitting in your car! My dream would be to return to Puerto Rico at least twice a year to enjoy the feeling of "enchantment" that it truly brings to me.

The island where much of my family still lives is home for me. When I was growing up in the South End of Hartford, I regularly asked my mother "Why Connecticut?" Having family already here to help her, was the best answer she had. Now that I am an adult, I very much appreciate my life in Connecticut. There are times I really love it and other times ... well, it's just too cold! My childhood was great! My family was kind of poor, but I didn't know it until I was a teenager. My family was full of love, we rarely went hungry, and I have great memories of a community of families that was united and helped each other out. I had countless friends growing up. My sister and I spent most of the summer months outside. We went swimming in our neighborhood pool at Colt's Park. We roller-skated and rode our bikes around our neighborhood. I played with dirt, and collected ladybugs in jars. On rainy days in the spring, I took great joy squishing the earthworms that came up out of nowhere on the sidewalk. I climbed trees and had a million scrapes and mosquito bites all over my legs and arms. My dark brown curly hair would have auburn highlights in July and my skin became dark-chocolate brown from being in the sun for too long without protection. In the fall, right before it was too cold, I made huge piles of leaves with my friends and we would throw ourselves into them without a care in the world. I loved to get dirty.

As little girls, my sister and I had lots of fun inside too. We played all sorts of things, but my favorite was playing teacher. I always had to be "the teacher." I think it was fun for everybody, but for me it was the best! When were weren't playing as a group, I was ridiculed for walking around my house with an imaginary classroom of students. Yes, I talked to invisible students. Some kids have imaginary friends, I had an imaginary group of students. I wasn't crazy. I just used my imagination, a lot. I must say, I had a fantastic childhood. Other than a few times when we barely had anything to eat, I had no idea we were poor.

My parents tried to work things out, but they eventually split up. While I was growing up, my parents drank alcohol. For me, this was normal because most of my friends' parents drank beer and other liquor. Parties and holidays were the main times I noticed the alcohol, even though my Mom and Dad regularly stocked beer in our refrigerator. When I was about nine, my Mom sent us to live with my uncle temporarily. I later found out she went to a rehabilitation facility for alcoholism. The things I took to be "normal" were talked about in family therapy. I guess they weren't as "normal" as I thought. Then, when I was eleven, my Dad left us after being arrested for what I later found out was a drug-related crime.

He went to Puerto Rico and never came back. Again, this was shocking because I had no idea he was involved with drugs or that he did anything illegal. It wasn't until much later I that I found out that he was involved with heroin. Later, when I was a about fifteen, my mother was basically letting me and my sister do whatever we wanted. Obviously for me, this was not a big deal, since I wanted to be on my own. I wanted freedom and didn't think anything of it. Until one day we had our electricity turned off. Apparently because my Mom was addicted to cocaine and had not paid the electric bill in a while.

I have included these heartbreaking things in my story for good reason. Although it has been several years since I have spoken to my mother, I feel she is truly amazing. She overcame an abusive relationship, alcoholism, and drug addiction. She had the will and determination to get a job and no longer depended on welfare. She showed me what it took to raise a family pretty much on her own and returned to college to earn an associate's degree in the middle of all of it. I remember her going to school in the evenings then staying up late nights studying. My Mom is the strongest person I know.

I never doubted my ability in college because Mom always told me she had a lot of fun in high school. She said she didn't always get the grades I had. I felt that because I had pretty good grades in high school, I would do fine in college. This, unfortunately, was not the case. I was fortunate to get good grades. I did my homework, most of the time, and my C's turned into B's and A's by the time I graduated Bulkeley High School in Hartford. In my junior year, I interviewed and was hired to work part-time at The Hartford Insurance Company and a good GPA was one of the requirements to getting the job. After graduating, I continued to work part-time at the insurance company and attended college full-time at Central Connecticut State University. After about a month, I was completely overwhelmed. Not only was the workload too much, but I felt dumb compared to many other students who participated during classes. I was too shy to ask for help and believed I was doomed to fail even if I did ask for help. Unfortunately, my time in college was short and I failed a number of classes. I felt betrayed in a way because all my teachers and my guidance counselor had me believing I was ready for college. Today, I know it wasn't really anyone's fault. I surely believe I wasn't academically ready, but I also feel I did not have the mindset to push through challenging classes.

I continued to work at The Hartford Insurance Company. I had great success there. I worked hard and over time I was given opportunities to learn more things outside clerical duties. The company sent me to different states to get formal training on some computer skills. I was given a company credit card, they rented cars for me and I stayed at fancy hotels. I moved up by working hard and trying my best to impress my boss. I am extremely grateful for the chances the company offered me to prove that I could learn and carry out more responsibilities. While there, I had two boys of my own and have been able to provide a good home for them. To this day, I still provide support for The Hartford, but my position was outsourced to IBM.

This change to working for IBM happened in 2007. Over time my role has changed quite a bit. A few years ago, I not only felt uneasy about the changes happening, but I also felt that I was in a career I did not choose for myself. It was more a ladder of opportunities that I chose to capitalize on in order to increase my salary. I grew unhappy and realized that I didn't really like my job anymore. I didn't want to keep learning about computers and I wanted to work in a field that I felt my job mattered to people. I wanted to do something that I would be remembered for and made a positive difference to people. In spring of 2012, I matriculated to Manchester Community College.

When I started at Manchester Community College, I decided that instead of letting myself give up at the first sign of difficulty, I was going to try my hardest to overcome it. This time would be different. I signed up for a program for adults who had not been in school for a while like myself. The support this program provided was excellent because they taught me important skills and habits of successful students. They helped decrease my anxiety by introducing me to other adults who were returning and gave us an overview on all the facilities available to help us be successful. During my first semester, Professor Michael DiRaimo was friendly, and easy to talk to. He gave us a refresher on writing, we read about the importance of being college educated and made us aware of how getting involved on campus also would be instrumental to our success as students and professionals. There I learned about the Student Government Association and Phi Theta Kappa Honors Society. I thought it would be hard for me to get involved because I still worked full-time while I attending school in the evenings. I decided that I would try and the next semester I took a small role with the Student Government Association on campus.

My experience with the Student Government Association, I believe, helped me stay committed to finishing my degree. The President at the time was a 19-year-old student. He was enrolled full-time and I quickly realized that in his role, he had a lot of responsibility outside his full course load. He gave me hope for my own kids and I was very impressed. The activities I participated in and the students I met made me feel like a part of the student body. I was convinced that I should continue to stay involved on campus while I was a student.

During one of our campus events, I met some members of Phi Theta Kappa Honors Society and decided to volunteer to help with one of their bake sale fundraisers. Then I started attending meetings and they allowed me to participate in their activities even though I was not an official member of the honors society. There I met Professor Sullivan who taught my online Composition class. He is an advisor for the chapter of Phi Theta Kappa and I was excited to meet him because I had only spoke to him online. To my delight, I was not only invited to join Phi Theta Kappa as an official member, but I was also asked to run for President of the chapter! I was so nervous to take on such a big role. I had many doubts because I felt all the students had so much more skills and knowledge than I did. Thankfully, the advisors and other officers offered their help and I was elected President. I served for two years and it was the most amazing experience while at MCC. During that time I made many friends, received awards, became acquainted with several administrators and learned more than I ever imagined possible.

During my first few semesters at MCC, I had been exposed to so many academic and campus experiences and I still wasn't completely sure what my major would be. I couldn't decide if I should pursue another field in Computer Technology or do something completely different. I wanted to get my core classes done and then decide what I wanted to do. Then, in addition to my role in Phi Theta Kappa, Professor Sullivan asked me to participate in an English class designed to help students who needed help with skills needed to take college level English classes. Again, I wanted to be involved and didn't know how I would do it with everything I already had going on, but I tried. I attended as many classes as I could to help the students. I could not always be there, but I then realized that the students seemed to relate to me as I was also a student. I shared with them how at first I was unsuccessful as a college student and I really hoped they would not give up too fast, like I initially did. Professor Sullivan made the class fun by allowing students to pick books to read for pleasure. He was interested in getting feedback from me and other peer tutors he had in the class. Most of the students saw tremendous growth over the course of the semester.

This college preparation course went through some challenges and improvements. There were some challenges to keep offering this course to future students. The curriculum was also transformed for the better. The second semester I participated in tutoring with Professor Sullivan, I was able to dedicate more time to the class. I took extra time to tutor students outside of normal classroom time and helped the students much more during class time. I then realized that I felt like I did when I was a little girl playing school. On evenings and weekends I spent time thinking about ways to help the students and wondering if they were doing their homework. I hoped they would call me to ask for help with their assignments. I surfed the web on teaching techniques and I couldn't wait to see what they wrote for assignments. I loved it! The classroom was where I belonged. I was both relieved and excited that I figured out what I wanted to do.

My experience with the now titled "English 9000" class gave me a sense of purpose and made me very aware of my own struggle as I transitioned from high school to college a long time ago. I found that the reason I wasn't ready for college was that I, like many of the students in this class, graduated high school without being adequately prepared for college level English classes. The lack of strong reading and writing skills was also critical for me to do well in the rest of my classes, not just English. I now feel that being a great English teacher is much bigger than just changing careers for me. It is more about making a difference that will hopefully better prepare students to not only attend college, but to compete with their peers professionally. I also learned that college can help people discover their passion and realize where they fit in this extremely complex world. While I have a high level respect for people who contribute to society in many ways that don't necessarily require a college degree, I do feel that everyone should have strong reading and writing skills. I made the decision to pursue a degree as an English teacher for middle and high school students.

Today, I am a full-time student at Eastern Connecticut State University. I am pursuing a bachelor's degree in English. I will then start working on my master's degree in Secondary Education and I may even pursue a master's degree in Rhetoric and Composition. I completed my associate's degree in December, 2015. While I was heavily involved on campus at Manchester Community College, I have not been as involved at Eastern. I am still employed full-time at IBM supporting The Hartford Insurance Company. Working full-time while attending college was always something that I thought was for exceptional people. I thought it was only for people who required very little sleep and could function at a higher level than I could ever do. Or, I thought, that if you did that much, your grades would suffer. I will tell you I was completely wrong. My thinking has completely changed as I remembered the challenges my mother faced while pursuing her degree. In the face of all the challenges she had to overcome, she earned A's in her classes. My experience working with Phi Theta Kappa also proved to me that when people have a strong desire to do something, no matter how much they have going on, they will find a way. And yes, that means that sometimes less important things are put on hold. It also means there are nights you don't sleep eight, six or even four hours before getting up doing more work. I found great slow-cooker recipes and taught my son how to do his own laundry. I had to miss some family gatherings and watch my favorite TV shows on Netflix during school vacations. In a nutshell, it is hard, things aren't perfect all the time, but nothing stands in my way of achieving my goal.

Finally, I believe that returning to college was the best choice I ever made. I am grateful that Manchester Community College has programs in place for people of all different walks of life. I came to know so many people, including professors who chose a community college for all sorts of reasons. I often wonder if I had some of the same support when I attended college my first time around if that would have made the difference for me to stick with it. My journey was important for me to be the person I am today. With no regrets and simply a feeling of deep gratitude, I hope that stories of successful community college students like myself inspire others to pursue their dreams.

CHAPTER 17

What Do These Student Success Stories Tell Us?

Transition "as Becoming"

The personal stories featured here suggest the need to theorize a more fluid, less rigid understanding of student transition to higher education. Even this brief glimpse into the dizzying variety of ways that students now transition to higher education and pursue a college credential suggests the need for a more open and accommodating understanding of this important transition point in American lives. A report from ACT about this subject, "The Reality of College Readiness 2013," makes it abundantly clear that traditional ideas about attending college have become outmoded:

> This report is intended to raise awareness of the fact that the path to college success is not a linear one for many students. There are significant numbers of qualified students who move through (or in and out of) multiple postsecondary experiences as they pursue their educational goals.
>
> Consider for a moment the following characteristics of undergraduate students:
>
> - 11% of students simultaneously enrolled in more than one institution.
> - 41% of graduates attended more than one institution.
> - 38% enrolled part time.
> - More than two million students brought college credit with them at the time of first full-time enrollment (dual credit, Advanced Payment, online, or College-level Examination Program).

- 30% delayed enrollment a year or more.
- 25% of undergraduates were over age 25.
- 30% of undergraduates enrolled in an online course.
- 29% of community college students transferred to four-year colleges.
- 14% transferred from four-year to two-year colleges (2).

Research on this subject is only now beginning to reflect these complex conditions. In "Navigating Change: A Typology of Student Transition in Higher Education," Trevor Gale and Stephen Parker directly address these changing demographic complexities. Gale and Parker identify three distinct ways that a student's transition to higher education is theorized in the research literature:

1. **transition as induction,** which is theorized as a "fixed turning point" (739) usually immediately after a student graduates from high school. This type of transition is characterized by "linear, chronological, progressive movement" and "relatively fixed structures and systems" (738). The main focus is on navigating "institutional norms and procedures" (738).
2. **transition as development,** which is theorized primarily in terms of identity development and navigating sociocultural norms and expectations. This type of transition is characterized by linear, "cumulative and non-reversible movement," and "discrete, singular, and consecutive identities" (738). Students move from one personal, academic, or career identity to another.
3. **transition "as becoming," (T3)** which essentially "rejects transition as a useful concept" (734) because "the concept of transition itself does not fully capture the fluidity of our learning or our lives" (743; Quinn 127). This theory of transition embraces "multiple narratives and subjectivities," "zigzag, spiral movement," and "flexible systems" and "fluid (ephemeral) identities" (738).

Gale and Parker note that this third definition of transition, which is newly emerging in higher education scholarship, has the potential to generate "new thinking about transitions in HE [higher education] in socially inclusive ways" (735). It accomplishes this by emphasizing "the complexities of life and the interdependence of 'public issues' and 'private troubles'" (744). As we know, this is a key dynamic for many community college students, as the stories included here suggest.

Gale and Parker characterize T3 as "rhizomatic" and employing "zigzag, spiral movement" (738). This understanding of transition theorizes identity formation as a kind of unpredictable, often provisional, and certainly complex lifelong process. The dynamics of "transition as becoming" are theorized not as stage- or age-dependent. They are also theorized as non-linear. In this model, students navigate "multiple narratives and subjectivities" (738: Table 1)—sometimes on a daily basis (i.e., as parents, employees, sons and daughters, neighbors, students, friends, citizens in a community, etc.)—rather than navigating one "pivotal moment of change" in their late teens from high school to college (739). Gale and Parker's emphasis on the "fluidity" of our learning and our lives provides a framework for understanding the many ways that students now transition to higher education, especially at community colleges. As a philosophy, this approach to transition theorizes personal and academic development as a process that occurs over the course of an individual's entire life span.

Gale and Parker also note that "beliefs about learning and knowing," which dominate higher education "are frequently socially exclusive and require students to adopt identities that do not always follow their life trajectories" (743). Gale and Parker call for a theory of transition that affirms the histories of working-class individuals and others from marginalized and under-represented groups (see also Connell). In an important moment in this essay, Gale and Parker endorse the value of the "transition as becoming" perspective precisely because it acknowledges—and honors—the many different ways that students can transition to and from college. Although Gale and Parker hail from Australia and are concerned primarily with universities, this perspective on transitioning to higher education speaks directly to the experience of students at community colleges in America:

> In short, scholars who approach these matters from a T3 perspective argue that the normative and the universal discourses of transition do not capture the diversity of student lives, their experiences of university or of universities themselves. It is impossible, then, to speak of student transition in HE in the singular, in the same way that 'there is no such thing as *an* identity, or *a* discrete moment of transition' (Quinn 2010, 127; emphasis added). Subjectivity

> and flux better describe the contemporary experience of navigating extended periods of formal education (Smith 2009), multiple career paradigms and life patterns (Cohen and Ainley 2000), and 'the fluid experience of time' (Worth 2009, 1051; see also Bauman 2000) ... T3 researchers argue that the 'failure to prioritize the actual views, experiences, interests and perspectives of young people as they see them' (Miles 2000, 10)—particularly 'the lived reality for disadvantaged young people' (Barry 2005, 108)—has been counterproductive. It has led to an overly 'structural perspective on transitions' (Miles 2000, 10). Certainly, HE 'must have structures and processes ... but ultimately it needs greater openness and flexibility. It should mirror the flux of our being, rather than trying to subjugate it with rigidity' (Quinn 2010, 127). (745–6)

A number of key phrases here speak to the mission and mandate of the community college quite eloquently: "diversity of student lives," "multiple career paradigms and life patterns," and "greater openness and flexibility." Furthermore, in honoring the general "flux of our being," a T3 approach to transition would seem to be ideally suited to promote equity and social justice, especially by acknowledging "multiple career paradigms and life patterns" and "the lived reality for disadvantaged young people." Certainly, the stories included in this section of the book emphatically confirm the need for new ways of thinking about transitioning to higher education in America today.

The Actor and Observer

The stories collected here also suggest that multiple perspectives can help us develop a richer, more accurate, and more informed understanding of community colleges and the students who attend them. Personal stories like these can provide perspectives that data sets like graduation rates and program completion numbers simply can't. Ellen Langer, in her work on mindfulness, warns against the dangers of working from a "single perspective," which can cause us to be "trapped by categories" and produce "automatic" kinds of thinking (11–19). A single perspective can also produce what she calls "premature cognitive commitment," whereby we "accept an impression or a piece of information at face value, with no reason to think critically about it" (22). As Amartya Sen has noted in *The Idea of Justice*, "changing places has been one way to 'see' hidden things in the world" (155). For Sen, one way to see hidden things is to move beyond our "positional confinement" (155). He notes that "the need to transcend the limitations of our positional perspectives is important in moral and political philosophy, and in jurisprudence" (155).

We may also be seeing evidence of a psychological dynamic first postulated by social psychologists in the 1950s and now known as attribution theory. Since that time, a robust and complex body of research has developed around this theory, which documents the many ways that we misread individual human intention and behavior that we observe in others. This research includes causal attribution (Heider 1958), actor-observer difference (Nisbett, Caputo, Legant, and Marecek 1973; Pronin, Lin, and Ross 2002), fundamental attribution error (Skitka, Mullen, Griffin, Hutchinson, and Chamberlin 2002), and correspondence bias (Gilbert and Malone 1995). Generally, this research has found that "When we explain the behavior of others, *we tend to overestimate the role of person factors and overlook the impact of situations.* In fact, the tendency to do so is so common that it is known as the fundamental attribution error (correspondence bias)" (*Principles*).

Daniel T. Gilbert and Patrick S. Malone provide a thoughtful overview of this body of research and the many complexities that attend it:

> Despite the homilies of philosophers, no one has yet found a simple formula for understanding others. The problem, of course, is that a person's inner self is hidden from view. Character, motive, belief, desire, and intention play leading roles in people's construal of others, and yet none of these constructs can actually be observed. As such, people are forced into the difficult business of inferring these intangibles from that which is, in fact, observable: other people's words and deeds. When one infers the invisible from the visible, one risks making a mistake. Three decades of research in social psychology have shown that many of the mistakes people make are of a kind: When people observe behavior, they often conclude that the person who performed the behavior was predisposed to do so—that the person's behavior corresponds to the person's unique dispositions—and they draw such conclusions even when a logical analysis suggests they should not. (21)

Edward E. Jones and Richard E. Nisbett's influential research study from the early 1970s on the nature of perception, "The Actor and the Observer: Divergent Perceptions of the Causes of Behavior," research that contributed in significant ways to our understanding of attribution theory, found that significant differences divided observers of individuals and the actors themselves when they sought to explain behavior. Claude M. Steele used this theory to design a variety of research projects that eventually led him to discover the operation of stereotype threat in the lives of African-American and female college students (and, in fact, in the lives of all of us).

His book, *Whistling Vivaldi: How Stereotypes Affect Us and What We Can Do*, synthesizes a lifetime of work devoted to understanding human motivation and behavior. Jones and Nisbett's work provided Steele with a conceptual framework that helped him to uncover very powerful psychological dynamics at work that had previously been hidden from our view. This kind of fundamental attribution error has proved to be a predictable form of "social blindness," to borrow a famous phrase from Gustav Ichheiser (47), an influential early pioneer of attribution theory. Steele found that observers and researchers had missed an essential component of what was being lived through on a daily basis by African American and female students on college campuses. The same may be true for community college students as well.

Because observers have limited knowledge of the actor's life history, their understanding must necessarily be partial. Jones and Nisbett found that this perception is partial in very specific ways, however. One of their key claims is that observers "attach insufficient weight to the situational determinants of behavior and attribute it, on slim evidence, to a disposition of the actor" (81). This means that observers tend to see characterological traits—ability, motivation, and aspects of personality—and not structural or social variables. The actor typically employs situational determinants and contextual factors to explain behavior—in other words, action is informed as much by situation as it is by character. The observer, Jones and Nesbitt note, is "remarkably inclined to see behavior in dispositional terms" (81). As observers, rather than "humbly regarding our impressions of the world as interpretations of it, we see them as understandings or correct apprehensions of it" (86). Because the "context data" are often very different for an actor and an observer, "these different data prompt differing attributions" (83). Jones and Nisbett frame these differences in terms of relative access to a rich and complex lived history and differences in available information:

> Much of the discrepancy between the perspectives of the observer and actor arises from the difference between the observer's inferred history of everyman and the concrete individualized history of the actor himself. The actor has been exposed to a sequence of experiences that are to a degree unique, but the observer is constrained to work with the blunt conceptual tools of modal or normative experience. (84).

The student stories included in Part I of this book serve an important theoretical function, helping us move beyond the blunt conceptual tools of modal and normative experience and providing access to concrete individualized histories. This qualitative data set dramatically illustrates the role that structural and social variables play in the lives of individual community college students. These narratives also allow us to glimpse contingencies hidden by statistics and raw numbers. In this way, important "context data" and unique lived experience can enter our scholarly dialog and help inform the development of public policy related to community colleges. To borrow a phrase from Claude M. Steele, these stories allow us to move beyond the observer's perspective and embrace a deeper understanding of the "students themselves, their motivations, expectations, self-esteem, cultural orientation; the value they placed on education; their work habits; their academic skills and knowledge; their families' emphasis on school achievement; and so forth" (17).

Different Kinds of Data Sets

We might, therefore, profitably regard these journey narratives as an important kind of data set—one that is very different from the single data point that is relentlessly used to assess community colleges: graduation rates. Graduation rates have become so important to the public understanding of community colleges, in fact, that most other factors or variables are routinely ignored, even though open admissions community colleges are very different types of institutions than residential four-year colleges that select their students by way of a competitive admissions process. The use of graduation rates has become so pervasive, in fact, that some legislators and researchers have proposed the radical step of changing the funding model for community colleges nationwide to one based on performance incentives for colleges that improve their graduation numbers (and punish those that don't). As we will see, this is a dangerous and deeply flawed idea. If we wish to embrace the value of multiple perspectives, then qualitative data sets like the one provided here can play a pivotal role in providing knowledge about the unique nature and mission of the modern community college. This kind of qualitative data set offers insight into the lives of students and their relationship to the community college that numbers simply cannot provide. Our understanding of the community college must be considered incomplete without knowledge of the lived experience of students like these. This is information that is routinely overlooked and disregarded as unimportant in most assessments of the community college.

Freedom Is a Function of the Mind and the Spirit

The student success stories featured in this part of the book also provide compelling evidence of the power of community colleges to transform lives in precisely the way this was imagined in 1947 by The Truman Commission. (Our next chapter will examine this legacy in detail.) None of the students included here have taken a traditional route to college. Each had to forge a unique pathway to higher education. Each also found at a community college a form of liberation.

Abby's story about her personal challenges and an unresponsive high school staff helps us understand that not all students make the transition from high school to college seamlessly or easily. A community college helped ensure that her potential did not go "undiscovered and undeveloped." It's also important to note that it was not just job training or technical skills that Abby took from her college experience. The Truman Commission linked democracy, education, and freedom with the development of "the mind and spirit" as well as "character":

> A free society is necessarily composed of free citizens, and men are not made free solely by the absence of external restraints. Freedom is a function of the mind and the spirit. It flows from strength of character, firmness of conviction, integrity of purpose. It is channeled by knowledge, understanding, and the exercise of discriminating judgment. (9–10)

Abby's summary assessment near the end of her essay suggests that the development of her "mind and spirit" as well as her character has, indeed, been a significant aspect of her community college experience: "I am incredibly proud of the person that this community college helped me become."

Other community college success stories featured here reflect the goal of removing, as the Truman Commission put it, "geographic and economic barriers to educational opportunity" (67). In fact, this may be true for each of our contributors, but it is especially noteworthy for Julie, Chhan, Bethany, Michelle, and Sabina. Taken in aggregate, the journeys these students have taken are a living embodiment of what the Truman Commission had in mind when it urged the nation not to let "any of its potential human resources go undiscovered and undeveloped" (101).

Bethany Silver's story embodies this goal in paradigmatic ways. Bethany describes her journey to a doctorate and a job as an academic as "accidental." She worked as a waitress at a local hamburger shop during high school and then enlisted in the Marines after graduation. After leaving the Marines during basic training, she moved back home with her parents and found everyone in town asking her, "Are you going to Manchester Community College (MCC)?" Eventually, she enrolled. Although she would go on to earn numerous advanced academic degrees, her first months in college were not easy:

> I would like to say that the college experience came naturally—but that wouldn't be true. I took a lot of classes that first year, face-planting on a number of assignments. In fact, on one of my very first papers I learned that for my professor, it was "the worst paper I have ever read."

Many years and many degrees later, Bethany reflects back on her community college experience, echoing a famous line from Robert Frost's poem "The Road Not Taken": "The community that is MCC has made all the difference." Following the Truman Commission, this is certainly teaching and learning invested with public purpose and committed to the full realization of our democratic ideals.

And, of course, the international students who share their stories with us here—Chhan, Sabina, Tanya, and Yanira—tell amazing stories about America and the power of our higher education system to transform the lives of individuals from around the world. Chhan is now a Master of Science and Family Nurse Practitioner and is working as a health care provider in Lowell, Massachusetts, an American city that has one of the largest populations of Cambodians outside of Cambodia. He began his journey in a refugee camp in Cambodia, and most days, he was given only one cup of rice and a rotten banana to eat. He wound up enrolling at a community college in Connecticut to pursue what he calls his "American dream." Sabina, Tanya, and Yanira might also be said to be pursuing their own versions of their American dreams. Both Sabina and Yanira have transferred to Eastern Connecticut State University and are pursuing bachelor's degrees. Tanya has transferred to Central Connecticut State University and is pursuing a bachelor's degree.

As it turns out, a number of these students began their journeys at MCC in developmental courses. As we will see, and contrary to much of what has been written about developmental education, developmental programs are a vital contributor to student success at community colleges.

Overall, these journey narratives suggest the vitality of our democratic ideals and confirm in very powerful ways the role of the community college in promoting the public good and working toward a fuller realization of our most foundational ideas about freedom and opportunity.

"A Single Story Line"

Finally, journalist Rebecca Solnit's essay, "The Mother of All Questions," invites us to consider the dangers of a single story line in shaping public perception. Solnit discusses life choices for women in America in this essay, including her own decision not to have children. As it turns out, she continues to receive an enormous amount of uninvited negative feedback about this decision—from family, friends, and even strangers. As she reflects on this experience—on who she is and why she has made the choices she has—Solnit challenges "one-size-fits-all recipes" (6) that govern the way so many of us think about living "a good life." Although Solnit admits that she has made an unconventional choice, she nonetheless finds herself content. Because she has found herself constantly at odds with "society's recipes for fulfillment" (6), she is in a unique position to understand the nature of these recipes. Following her own course in life, she has made choices based on her love of solitude, her being raised by "unhappy, unkind people" (5) whose mistakes she does not wish to replicate, and her desire to write books, which she acknowledges is "a fairly consuming vocation" (5). Her oppositional stance to mainstream narratives about "success" for women has caused her to reflect deeply about these narratives. What she says about such narratives captures one of the key insights that I wish to make about community college students and community colleges in this book:

> Questions about happiness generally assume that we know what a happy life looks like. Happiness is understood to be a matter of having a great many ducks lined up in a row—spouse, offspring, private property, erotic experiences—even though a millisecond of reflection will bring to mind countless people who have all those things and are still miserable.
>
> We are constantly given one-size-fits-all recipes, but those recipes fail, often and hard. Nevertheless, we are given them again. And again and again. They become prisons and punishments; the prison of the imagination traps many in the prison of a life that is correctly aligned with the recipes and yet is entirely miserable.

> The problem may be a literary one: we are given a single story line about what makes a good life, even though not a few who follow that story line have bad lives. We speak as though there is one good plot with one happy outcome, while the myriad forms a life can take flower—and wither—all around us. (6)

Solnit could easily be talking in her reference to "a single story line" about popular perceptions of attending college in America and the implications for individuals who do not (or are unable to) follow this traditional story line. Community colleges are full of such individuals who, for a variety of complex reasons that we will examine in detail in this book, are not able to devote four years of uninterrupted work at a residential college to earn a bachelor's degree and whose pathway to an academic credential is fraught with real and potential complications. This single story line embodies a set of ideological beliefs that help shape the way we construct our understanding of higher education. This single story line privileges certain kinds of possibilities and narrative trajectories and precludes or devalues others. It is a story line, furthermore, that is hugely dependent on wealth, class position, and financial security. One of my goals in this book is to shed light on the many often invisible ways that class position helps determine academic success. Doing so will require that we confront and challenge many of the unacknowledged hierarchies in American higher education (Hassel and Giordano 2013). Rather than posit a monolithic narrative about college, current conditions appear to require, instead, that we construct a more flexible, multimodal, and multivalent model that is designed to be inclusive, forgiving, and welcoming.

This single story line would be dangerous even if we were to characterize the current educational system as a meritocracy. We would still need to accommodate, following Jerome Bruner, the student who is not "the fast, early, and steady producer" (80). As Bruner suggests in *The Process of Education*, a meritocracy

> implies a system of competition in which students are moved ahead and given further opportunities on the basis of their achievement, with position in later life increasingly and irreversibly determined by earlier school records. Not only later educational opportunities but subsequent job opportunities become increasingly fixed by earlier school performance. The late bloomer, the early rebel, the child from an educationally indifferent home—all of them, in a full-scale meritocracy, become victims of an often senseless irreversibility of decision. (77)

The perils Bruner identifies here are those that the community college is ideally suited to address. The community college student body is full of late bloomers, early rebels, and children from educationally indifferent homes. Theoretical accommodation must be made for this important cohort of learners.

Unfortunately, for many who think and write about higher education in America, there still appears to be a "one-size-fits-all recipe" actively at work shaping their understanding about college. We continue to measure success in higher education following the selective admissions model, which is based on selective admissions and full-time residency. As we will see in Parts II and III, this model is highly problematic when applied to open admissions community colleges and the students who attend them.

Like the narrative Solnit examines in her essay, this single story line about higher education has become a kind of prison. Variations from this norm are often regarded as unfortunate, problematic, or simply as "failure." Jonathan Smith and Kevin Stange's essay for the National Bureau of Economic Research, "A New Measure of College Quality to Study the Effects of College Sector and Peers on Degree Attainment," is only the latest in a long line of scholarship that employs this approach to community colleges: "Students starting at a two-year college are much less likely to graduate with a college degree than similar students who start at a four-year college but the sources of this attainment gap are largely unexplained." We will be attending carefully to this achievement gap in the chapters ahead, seeking to understand why students at open admissions institutions graduate at different rates than students who enroll at selective admissions institutions.

As novelist Chimamanda Ngozi Adichie notes in her TED Talk, "The Danger of a Single Story," the way we create a single story is to show people "as one thing—as only one thing—over and over again. And that is what they become." Single stories are dangerous, Adichie suggests, because one story becomes the *only* story. The consequence of the single story is that it "robs people of dignity. It makes our recognition of our equal humanity difficult. It emphasizes how we are different rather than how we are similar." Community college students are actively at work today pioneering new ways to attend college in America. For a variety of reasons which we will examine in this book, these different academic trajectories have been largely unacknowledged, under-valued, or ignored. This book seeks to affirm the immense value of these many different pathways to higher education and to challenge the single story line that continues to be dominant in public discourse about college in America.

PART II

Democracy's Unfinished Business

CHAPTER 18

The Truman Commission Report

"Education Is the Making of the Future"

In 1946, President Truman appointed a special commission to chart a new course for higher education in America. The document produced by this commission, commonly referred to as the Truman Commission Report (published in 1947 in six volumes), reimagined the role of higher education in American life in profound and enduring ways. It is one of the most historically significant documents ever produced on the subject of higher education. It is also a foundational American document in a larger sense, as it speaks with unprecedented candor and eloquence about the nature of democracy and the ideals of equity and social justice in America. The Truman Commission Report articulates a radically inclusive vision of American democracy in ways that few other documents in our long history have ever done. In so doing, it must take its place among classic statements of our ideals, including The Declaration of Independence, the Constitution, the Gettysburg Address, Lincoln's First Inaugural Address ("The mystic chords of memory, stretching from every battlefield and patriot grave to every living heart and hearthstone all over this broad land, will yet swell the chorus of the Union, when again touched, as surely they will be, by the better angels of our nature"), Lincoln's Second Inaugural Address, and Martin Luther King's "I Have a Dream" speech.

The Truman Commission Report was the product of a unique historical moment—the short-lived years of peace and reflection immediately following the global cataclysm of World War II. The horrors of this war clearly inform the thinking of the commission in profound ways, and a keen awareness of atrocities committed during the war and a renewed optimism about democracy can be sensed on virtually every page of this document. The ancient Greek tragedians believed that suffering begets wisdom, and we may be seeing evidence here of this perhaps essential human dynamic at work—that through suffering, wisdom can be earned. Perhaps the most paradigmatic expression of this ancient Greek idea is voiced by the chorus in Aeschylus's play, *Agamemnon*, the first of three plays in *The Oresteia*, a trilogy exploring violence, justice, and the rule of law (circa 458 BC):

> Zeus, whose will has marked for man
> The sole way where wisdom lies;
> Ordered one eternal plan:
> *Man must suffer to be wise* (lines 177–179/Vellacott translation)

The Truman Commission Report is the product of a brief historical moment when our ideals about democracy and individual human dignity had been illuminated in powerful new ways through the immense suffering occasioned by the war. Often just offstage, but implied on every page, we find the Commission measuring democratic ideals against those of authoritarian forms of government, which during World War II produced unspeakable atrocities, along with cruelty, devastation, and unfreedom on an industrial scale. The Truman Commission is particularly eloquent in its efforts to affirm the value of all human life—especially among historically marginalized populations in American society. This aspect of the report clearly draws much of its rhetorical power and authority from our experience in the war. During World War II, we found ourselves contending with a "master race" that regarded many groups of people as "life unworthy of life" and who therefore, following the logic of this thinking, simply did not have the right to live (Evans 3–105).

In page after page, the Truman Commission Report acknowledges that this is a "decisive moment of human history" (Zook 1947, 6) and an important moment for democracy:

> Education is an institution of every civilized society, but the purposes of education are not the same in all societies. An educational system finds its guiding principles and ultimate goals in the aims and philosophy of the social order in which it functions. The two predominant types of society in

the world today are the democratic and authoritarian, and the social role of education is very different in the two systems. (Zook 1947, 5)

The Commission goes on to suggest that "education is the making of the future" (6) and that the nation has important choices to make:

> Perhaps its [education's] most important role is to serve as an instrument of social transition, and its responsibilities are defined in terms of the kind of civilization society hopes to build. (Zook 1947, 6)

The kind of civilization the commission envisions is predicated on the understanding that democracy is "much more than a set of political processes" (Zook 1947, 11). Instead,

> It formulates and implements a philosophy of human relations. It is a way of life—a way of thinking, feeling, and acting in regard to the associations of men and of groups, one with another. (Zook 1947, 11)

Significantly, the democratic civilization heroically imagined here is one radically free from past prejudice and barriers related to gender, race, and economic inequality. This vision of an America liberated from prejudice was clearly inspired by wartime experiences. Minorities played a large combat role in the war, and although the US Armed Services was officially segregated during World War II, minorities were often thrown together fighting a common enemy alongside their white countrymen. Women left the home during the war and worked in munitions factories, shipyards, and the aircraft industry and served in the Women's Army Corps. Rich and poor also shared common cause during this long ordeal, at home and on the battlefield. This unprecedented, collaborative, nationwide effort certainly helped create experiences for Americans that lead to the Civil Rights Movement and the Women's Rights Movement in the years after the war. This shared national sacrifice also helps explain why the Truman Commission framed their recommendations as forcibly and unambiguously as they did. The commission unequivocally acknowledges that America is still "plagued with inequalities" (Zook 1947, 13) and that "many thousands of our citizens continue to live in poverty, disease, hunger, and ignorance" (Zook 1947, 13). The commission identifies these problems, significantly, as "democracy's unfinished business" (Zook 1947, 12).

"The Full and Living Realization of the Democratic Ideal"

The Truman Commission maintained, furthermore, that "the fundamental concept of democracy is a belief in the inherent worth of the individual, in the dignity and value of human life" (Zook 1947, 11). The commission suggests that higher education must play a central role in promoting these values, and it must no longer be available only to the affluent:

> By allowing the opportunity for higher education to depend so largely on the individual's economic status, we are not only denying to millions of young people the chance in life to which they are entitled; we are also depriving the Nation of a vast amount of potential leadership and potential social competence which it sorely needs. (Zook 1947, 29)

Echoing conclusions that will be confirmed only years later in the Coleman Report, published in 1966, the commission also addresses the crucial links between family income, academic success, and college enrollment that are still reflected today in community college completion rates:

> The old, comfortable idea that "any boy can get a college education who has it in him" simply is not true. Low family income, together with the rising costs of education, constitutes an almost impassable barrier to college education for many young people. For some, in fact, the barrier is raised so early in life that it prevents them from attending high school even when free public high schools exist near their homes. (Zook 1947, 28)

No longer willing to accept higher education's long association with privilege and wealth, the commission envisioned, instead, a much more inclusive, more democratic function for higher education in postwar America. Instead of bastions of privilege, the commission imagined a "much larger role for higher education in the national life" (Zook 1947, 101). Informing this vision is the belief in individual potential and agency—and a commitment to social justice and the public good. To address these many complex challenges that faced the nation both domestically and internationally, the commission urged Americans to "act quickly and boldly" so that it could take on "a responsibility for world leadership that is without parallel in history" (Zook 1947, 101).

The commission's most historic practical recommendation comes with the founding of the modern community college:

> To make sure of its own health and strength a democratic society must provide free and equal access to education for its youth, and at the same time it must recognize their differences in capacity and purpose. Higher education in America should include a variety of institutional forms and educational programs, so that at whatever point any student leaves school, he will be fitted, within the limits of his mental capacity and educational level, for an abundant and productive life as a person, as a worker, and as a citizen. . . .
>
> As one means of achieving the expansion of educational opportunity and the diversification of educational offerings it considers necessary, this Commission recommends that the number of community colleges be increased and that their activities be multiplied. (Zook 1947, 67)

For the Truman Commission, the primary goal of the community college focused on the public good:

> Whatever form the community college takes, its purpose is educational service to the entire community, and this purpose requires of it a variety of functions and programs. It will provide college education for the youth of the community certainly, so as to remove geographic and economic barriers to educational opportunity and discover and develop individual talents at low cost and easy access. But in addition, the community college will serve as an active center of adult education. It will attempt to meet the total post-high school needs of its community. (Zook 1947, 67–8)

Perhaps most significant was the mandate given to community colleges—and the progressive democratic rationale informing this mandate. This is a pivotal moment in our nation's history. In a few immortal sentences, the Truman Commission helped establish the modern community college as an agent for change, liberation, and hope in communities across the nation:

> American colleges and universities must envision a much larger role for higher education in the national life. They can no longer consider themselves merely the instrument for producing an intellectual elite; they must become the means by which every citizen, youth, and adult is enabled and encouraged to carry his education, formal and informal, as far as his native capacities permit.
>
> This conception is the inevitable consequence of the democratic faith; universal education is indispensable to the full and living realization of the democratic ideal. No society can long remain free unless its members are freemen, and men are not free where ignorance prevails. No more in mind

> than in body can this Nation or any endure half slave, half free. Education that liberates and ennobles must be made equally available to all. Justice to the individual demands this; the safety and progress of the Nation depend upon it. America cannot afford to let any of its potential human resources go undiscovered and undeveloped. (Zook 1947, 101)

The most striking moment here may be the commission's mention of slavery and freedom—"No more in mind than in body can this Nation or any endure half slave, half free." This passage appears to be candidly acknowledging—and perhaps also renouncing—our nation's long history of discrimination and exploitation, perhaps with the devastating racial atrocities of World War II freshly in mind. Whatever sources may have inspired the language here, a new course is being set for American higher education that draws inspiration from our most cherished ideals related to equality, democracy, and freedom in all the forms it can take.

It is significant to note that the commission envisioned "social responsibility" and "public purpose" as an essential component of higher education in America. These are ideas that are currently being actively challenged today in a variety of ways:

> To preserve everybody's right to life, liberty, and the pursuit of happiness, then, we need first to become aware of the fact that there is no longer room for isolationism in any successful life, personal or national. No man can live to himself alone, expecting to benefit from social progress without contributing to it.
>
> Nor can any *group* in our society, organized or unorganized, pursue purely private ends and seek to promote its own welfare without regard to the social consequences of its activities. Business, industry, labor, agriculture, medicine, law, engineering, education ... all these modes of association call for the voluntary development of codes of conduct, or the revision of such codes as already exist, to harmonize the special interests of the group with the general welfare.
>
> Toward these ends, higher education must inspire its graduates with high social aims as well as endow them with specialized information and technical skill. Teaching and learning must be invested with public purpose. (Zook 1947, 10–11)

As we will see, this idea of a larger "public purpose" for higher education is now being vigorously contested by some scholars and economists (Becker *Human Capital;* Friedman and Friedman, *Free* 175–188). As it turns out, there is a significant body of research that suggests that wealthy, powerful, and highly organized groups have put special interests before concern with the public good (Mayer; Meek "Somerdale"; Piketty; Putnam; Reich), drawing legitimacy from the same economic thinkers who have challenged the idea of the public good itself by seeking to cast all transactions in a democracy simply as economic exchanges of one form or another. As we will see, there is much that requires careful consideration here.

The short-lived peaceful years immediately following World War II proved to be a very productive time in America, providing our nation with hard-earned clarity and wisdom—and the opportunity to reassess the founding ideals of our democracy and to reflect on long-standing divisions in our country (Kennedy; Carnes *Columbia*; Carnes *Us and Them*). Historian James T. Patterson has called this the era of "grand expectations." Community colleges would come to play a major role in these grand expectations, as America sought to embrace its most foundational principles and, to borrow a phrase from Martin Luther King, set forth to honor the "sacred obligation" of guaranteeing for all of its citizens the unalienable rights of life, liberty, and the pursuit of happiness ("I Have a Dream" 217). The Truman Commission Report helped lay the theoretical foundation for this work, which is still ongoing and which eventually came to include the Civil Rights Movement and the Women's Movement. In its commitment to democratizing America's system of higher education, the Truman Commission challenged long-held assumptions about daily life in America and also confronted pernicious, deeply inscribed patterns of thought and behavior in our nation. In its unequivocal commitment to equality, social justice, and the public good, the Truman Commission set an ambitious agenda for postwar America. Part of the project of this book is to assess our progress toward realizing these ambitious goals—and to recommend adjustments in our public policy, where necessary, so that we can continue making progress toward the full realization of these noble aspirations. Every new community college that was chartered in the years following this report constituted a practical embodiment of these ideals. Each new community college, with its "brick and mortar," literally embodied the inspiring democratic belief in the power of individual human agency and potential voiced in the Truman Report—made real in communities and neighborhoods across America by the presence of these new "community" colleges.

CHAPTER 19

Economic Inequality and Higher Education

EXTRACTIVE VERSUS INCLUSIVE ECONOMIC INSTITUTIONS

The Truman Commission Report initiated a burst of enthusiasm nationwide for expanding access to higher education, and new community colleges began appearing in towns and neighborhoods across America. Before World War II, there were approximately 200 junior and community colleges in the US. Now, there are 1108 (American Association of Community Colleges [AACC] "Fast"). Much of this growth occurred during the 1960s, when 457 new public community colleges were established (AACC "Community"). As we know, the community college has had a long and complex history (Boggs; Meier; Zamani-Gallaher Lester, Bragg, and Hagerdorn), but the foundational center of the modern community college's mission has always focused on opportunity and access. As we have seen, at its birth in 1947, the modern community college was theorized quite deliberately as a way to systematically address "social problems" (Zook 1947, 20–22) and help promote "a fuller realization of democracy" (Zook 1947, 8–14). In many ways, the community college has become an academic and economic equalizer—providing access to higher education and better jobs through open admissions policies and convenient and affordable access. The journey narratives written by community college students featured in Part I of this book suggest the many ways that this equalizing function can be realized at these institutions. Unfortunately, however, data from a wide variety of sources suggest we are experiencing a de facto retreat in America from our commitment to access and affordability in ways that may be compromising the community college mandate and also the health of our democracy.

Despite making great strides forward in the years following the Truman Commission Report, which was accomplished by significant public investment in higher education and a shared sense of common purpose, the last 30 years have been an era of eroding public and governmental support for higher education and gradual disinvestment—on both the state and national levels—in higher education. Our sense of common purpose in relation to the public good, social justice, and higher education has also become dangerously fragmented. Especially in terms of addressing economic inequality, a key concern for the Truman Commission, we appear to have entered an era of regression in relation to access, social justice, and higher education. Community colleges find themselves under attack on a variety of fronts, and some have even argued that it is time to close the community college's open door. If education's "most important role is to serve as an instrument of social transition, and its responsibilities are defined in terms of the kind of civilization society hopes to build" (Zook 1947, 6), we must examine what kind of civilization we are currently building. The available evidence suggests that we have made substantial progress on many fronts but that America continues to be, in the language of the Truman Commission Report, "plagued with inequalities" (Zook 1947, 13).

A robust body of research on economic inequality suggests that we are currently in the process of developing what economists Daron Acemoglu and James Robinson call an "extractive" economy—one designed to "extract incomes and wealth from one subset of society to benefit a different subset" (76). For Acemoglu and Robinson, extractive economic institutions are structurally designed to produce extraordinary wealth for a small group of citizens and hardship and limited economic prospects for everyone else. The key choice, Acemoglu and Robinson suggest, is between "inclusive" institutions, which produce opportunity and prosperity, and "extractive" institutions, which impede economic growth and limit opportunity:

> The central thesis of this book is that economic growth and prosperity are associated with inclusive economic and political institutions, while extractive institutions typically lead to stagnation and poverty. (91)

Although they do not mention community colleges specifically, Acemoglu and Robinson's "inclusive" institutions function precisely the way community colleges do. In a section of the book entitled "Engines of Prosperity," for example, Acemoglu and Robinson observe that "inclusive economic institutions create inclusive markets, which not only give people freedom to pursue the vocations in life that best suit their talents but also provide a level playing field that gives them the opportunity to do so" (76–77). This is language that could easily describe the open admissions community college, an inclusive economic institution that gives people "freedom to pursue the vocations in life that best suit their talents," that "level" the playing field, and that provide "opportunity" to individuals seeking to pursue education and training beyond high school.

In fact, at times, Acemoglu and Robinson sound as if they are quoting from the Truman Commission Report itself when they talk about the importance of "inclusive" institutions and educational opportunity. Here, for example, they are discussing the "low education level of poor countries" (78):

> The price these nations pay for low education of their population and lack of inclusive markets is high. They fail to mobilize their nascent talent. They have many potential Bill Gateses and perhaps one or two Albert Einsteins who are now working as poor, uneducated farmers, being coerced to do what they don't want to do or being drafted into the army, because they never had the opportunity to realize their vocation in life. (78–79)

The economic model Acemoglu and Robinson are theorizing here is not that different than the one the Truman Commission theorized in 1947.

Anthony B. Atkinson (*Inequality: What Can Be Done?*), Joseph E. Stiglitz (*The Price of Inequality: How Today's Divided Society Endangers Our Future*), and Robert B. Reich (*Saving Capitalism: For the Many, Not the Few*) have all written important books on the subject of American economic inequality, and all suggest that economic inequality is a very real threat to our democracy. This perception is widely shared among academics and non-academics alike. Atkinson notes on the first page of his book, for example, that "when the Pew Research Center's Global Attitudes Project asked respondents in 2014 about the 'greatest danger to the world,' it found that in the United States and Europe 'concerns about inequality trump all other dangers'" (1). Stiglitz warns about the danger of America developing a "dual economy"—a term often used to describe economies in developing countries (289). This dual economic structure creates a divided country with a dramatically compromised sense of community—producing, in effect, two distinct societies, the haves and the have-nots, "living side by side, but hardly knowing each other, hardly imagining what life is like for the other" (289). The wealthy in this dual society "live in gated communities, send their children to expensive schools, and have access to first-rate health care" (289). The rest of the population "live in a world marked by insecurity, at best mediocre education, and in effect rationed health care" (289). Perhaps, most significantly, "at the bottom are millions of young people alienated and without hope" (289; 118–45).

Economic Inequality and Higher Education

Issues related to economic inequality have become perhaps even more problematic now than when community colleges first began multiplying in towns and cities across the US after World War II. The data and research here are overwhelming and alarming. Stiglitz summarizes the current state of affairs in a recent White Paper for the Roosevelt Institute (2014) this way:

> Perhaps the most disturbing aspect of America's outsized inequality is the inequality of opportunity. The American Dream is, in reality, a myth. The US has some of the worst inequality across generations (social mobility) among wealthy nations. The life prospects of a young American are more dependent on the income and education of his parents than in other advanced countries.
>
> Given the enormous increase in inequality that has occurred in the US over the past three decades, any measure that harms those at the bottom should also be unacceptable and measures that impose undue burdens on the middle class should receive careful scrutiny. (5)

Stiglitz notes that "it has increasingly been noted that America is becoming a plutocracy—not the land of opportunity that it perhaps once was, and that it likes to think of itself as still being" (23; Reich). Paul Tough has shown that the development of this new American plutocracy has had a profound impact on higher education. He suggests, in fact, that we have come to the point now that "whether a student graduates [from college] or not seems to depend today almost entirely on just one factor—how much money his or her parents make. To put it in blunt terms: Rich kids graduate; poor and working-class kids don't" ("Who" 28). Tough's essay provides a sobering analysis of the massive college "graduation gap" between the haves and the have-nots in America. An imposing body of current research confirms this claim about economic inequality and educational attainment in America.

Sean Reardon, for example, in his essay in *Whither Opportunity?: Rising Inequality, Schools, and Children's Life Chances*, notes that conditions in the US related to education and economic inequality have been growing *worse* in the last 25 years:

> The achievement gap between children from high- and low-income families is roughly 30 to 40 percent larger among children born in 2001 than among those born twenty-five years earlier. In fact, it appears that the income achievement gap has been growing steadily for at least fifty years, though the data are less certain for cohorts of children born before 1970. (93)

Reardon finds that rising income inequality, differential investments in children's cognitive development, and increased segregation by income continue to drive and broaden this achievement gap.

Ellwood and Kane have shown that economic class plays a crucial, long-term role even in how *young children* think about their academic futures:

> If children from poorer families believe they are unlikely to go to school [college] (because of financial constraints), they do not work as hard in school and achieve lower scores and grades, further obscuring the true impact of family income. (301)

A report from the Pell Institute, *Indicators of Higher Education Equity in the United States: 2016 Historical Trend Report* (2016), provides a devastating longitudinal perspective of the relationship between family income and college success. Figure 19.1, drawn from this report, highlights these differences over a 44-year period. Unfortunately, the scope and nature of our class and economic inequality problems remain stubbornly persistent (Delbanco). As Patricia McDonough observed in her 2004 report for the American Council on Education, the US appears to be in a state of regression related to access and opportunity in higher education:

> Widespread evidence exists that the United States is experiencing a *de facto* retreat from its longstanding commitment to providing equal college opportunity and instead is offering an increasingly stratified higher education system.... In 2004, the playing field of education is anything but

level, and the general public has become virtually inured to reports by policy makers, assessment experts, researchers, and journalists about the large and persistent achievement gaps in the K–12 system, especially for low-income students, urban students, and students of color (Barton 2004). In fact, despite four decades of major policy efforts, the college participation gap between low-income and high-income students today is roughly the same as it was in the 1960s. (1)

Much of this research confirms once again what the Truman Commission acknowledged in 1947 and the Coleman Report documented in 1966: the significant relationship between academic success—in all ways that this can be measured, including college completion rates—and family income. Furthermore, two reports from the National Center for Education Statistics suggest that our "achievement gap" numbers in primary and secondary school systems, while narrowing somewhat, also remain significant (*Achievement Gaps: How Black and White Students in Public*

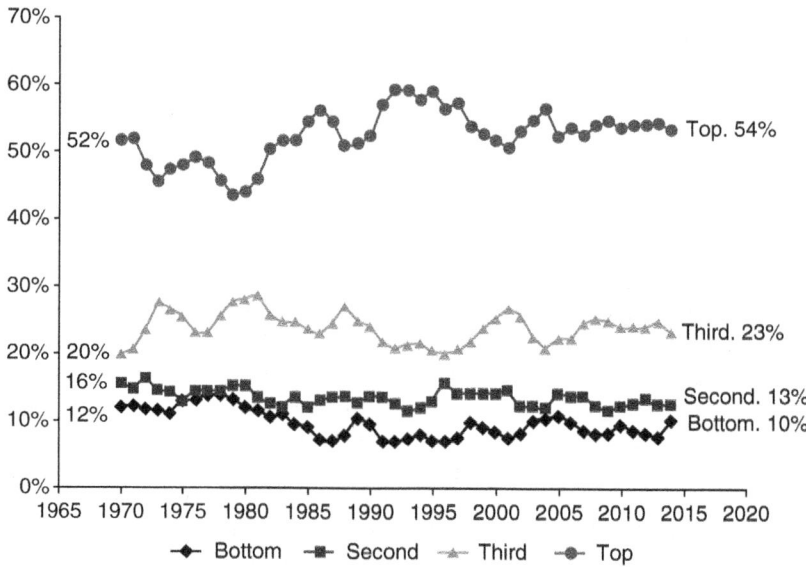

Fig. 19.1 Equity indicator 5a: Distribution by family income quartile of dependent family members, aged 18–24, who attained a bachelor's degree by age 24: 1970–2014 (2016, 60)
(*Source*: Cahalan et al. (2016))

Schools Perform in Mathematics and Reading; Achievement Gaps: How Hispanic and White Students in Public Schools Perform in Mathematics and Reading). Issues related to race and class are obviously at play here, as they almost always are when we talk about education (Brandt 172–86; Massey; Massey and Denton; Rothstein *Class*). To provide just one telling example from my home institution for how this important dynamic can play out in a community college context, reading comprehension scores— indispensible for success at college—track closely at our institution with family income (see Fig. 19.2). These local data show a strong positive relationship between reading scores and family income. This graph helps contextualize general national trends related to family income, academic success, and credential acquisition, and it complicates significantly our understanding of how we might measure "success" at open admissions institutions. These data also show why community college professionals must pay close attention to national conversations about economic inequality and social justice.

Suzannne Mettler in her book, *Degrees of Inequality: How the Politics of Higher Education Sabotaged the American Dream* (2014), sums up the current state of affairs related to income inequality and higher education this way: "In short, our system of higher education contributes, increasingly,

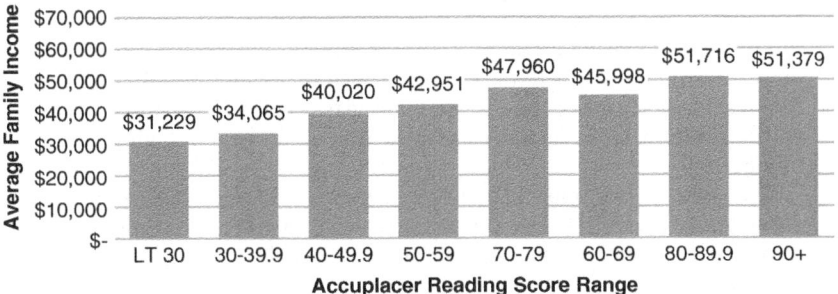

Fig. 19.2 Accuplacer reading scores and family income for new students who applied for financial aid, Fall 2011, 2012, 2013, 2014, and 2015 (*Source*: Manchester Community College Office of Planning, Research, and Assessment)

to rising inequality, as it stratifies Americans by income group rather than providing them with ladders of opportunity" (8). Mettler documents the many ways that our current system of higher education "widens economic inequality and fosters social division" (12). Significantly, one of Mettler's solutions for this problem is to "strengthen community colleges" (194–5).

"POTENTIALLY TERRIFYING"

A number of recent books have illustrated how insidious this regression has become and suggest that this trend has been deepening and worsening in recent years. Elizabeth A. Armstrong and Laura T. Hamilton's book, *Paying for the Party: How College Maintains Inequality*, for example, documents the often invisible ways that privilege perpetuates itself in higher education. Armstrong and Hamilton conclude from their five-year longitudinal study that the way many large state colleges and universities "currently organize the college experience systematically disadvantages all but the most affluent" (3):

> We were initially puzzled by the extent to which the university's organizational arrangements disadvantaged all but the most affluent. After all, public universities were founded with the explicit intent of sponsoring mobility among disadvantaged groups. Through deeper consideration of the history of American higher education, we learned that elite private education was founded to serve the affluent and that the consolidation of local elites has also been one of the missions of public universities. More recently, the tilt to the affluent has intensified, as declines in state funding have chipped away at the mission of public universities. Tuition increases and intensified pursuit of those who pay full tuition ensure that public universities cater to the often less studious segment of the affluent that they can successfully attract. As a result, we see a large and growing mismatch between what many four-your institutions provide and what most Americans seeking higher education need.
>
> The title of the book [*Paying for the Party: How College Maintains Inequality*] reflects the cost of this mismatch. When universities direct resources to attracting and serving affluent, socially oriented students—"paying for the party," if you will—other students and families bear the cost. They place their faith in a system that does not serve them well, and pay the price with a lower-quality education and limited career options. American society also loses, as the potential of students from ordinary means remains unrealized. (xii–xiii)

Armstrong and Hamilton's work provides a rare glimpse inside what some education writers are calling "the country-clubization of the American university" (qtd. in Armstrong and Hamilton 241). The university studied here functions perhaps most essentially, alas, as a "bastion of privilege" and not an "engine of opportunity."

Jenny M. Stuber offers additional insight into this often invisible social process in her study, *Inside the College Gates: How Class and Culture Matter in Higher Education*. Stuber documents "how social class influences the ways in which students navigate the college environment" (3). Her conclusions are similar to those of Armstrong and Hamilton: "The experiential core of college life—the social and extracurricular worlds of higher education—operates as a setting in which social class inequalities manifest and get reproduced" (4). Stuber's work demonstrates how social and cultural capital, along with distinct social-class worldviews of affluent and working-class students, shape their experience of—and success at—college in powerful ways. Stuber's study confirms Pierre Bourdieu and Jean-Claude Passeron's important claim about education promoting inequality and economic stratification. As Stuber notes, "because educational institutions are structured not in class neutral ways, but in ways that reflect the social and cultural presumptions of the dominant classes, students who enter higher education with the social and cultural tools of the dominant classes are likely to have greater success" (164). We can see very clearly here, following Bourdieu and Passeron, that "education plays an important role in aiding and abetting the reproduction of social inequality and social exclusion" (Tzanakis 76).

Claudia Goldin and Lawrence F. Katz note in *The Race between Education and Technology* that "inequality today is as high as it was during the Great Depression" (3). Goldin and Katz chronicle how our historic investment in public colleges and universities has paid rich dividends in terms of quality of life and the production of a skilled and competitive workforce. Goldin and Katz note that America's approach to education was a triumph of "egalitarianism" over elitism:

> This chapter traced the origins of the many virtues of American education—its public provision and public funding, existence of small fiscally independent units, separation of church and state, gender neutrality, openness, and forgiveness. These features can be summed up as egalitarian in nature. The democratic, republican vision of education triumphed over an elitist one in which private schools would exist for some and charity or pauper schools would serve the others. (161)

One key element of this system, for Goldin and Katz, is its "open structure in which youthful transgressions were often forgiven" (129). They show that, beginning in the very first years of our democracy, America developed "a far more open and forgiving system" than "those of other economically advanced nations of the day" (155). This investment in "egalitarianism" paid huge dividends in all sorts of ways. Unfortunately, as Goldin and Katz note, the commanding lead the US enjoyed internationally for many years in terms of educational attainment has slipped considerably, as a host of recent reports suggest (Ripley; Sahlberg; Tough, *How* 148–97; Tucker). This "slowdown in the growth of educational attainment,"

> is the single most important factor increasing educational wage differentials since 1980 and is a major contributor to increased family income inequality. If technology continues to race ahead (and history suggests it will) and educational attainment does not begin to increase rapidly, we are likely to see continued increases in inequality. For many reasons, then, the United States *must* find a way to increase the stock of educated Americans. (325)

Serious words here, for sure. Although Goldin and Katz mention community colleges only briefly (260, 266–7, 279–80), they do note that such institutions serve the important function of bringing college "the closest to the people" (260). The open admissions community college is an institution that, by its very mandate, is designed to be "open and forgiving," that privileges "egalitarianism" over elitism, and that brings college "to the people."

Thomas Piketty's recent, much-heralded economic study, *Capital in the Twenty-First Century*, also has important things to say about economic inequality, class, and higher education. Piketty also suggests that education can counterbalance and offset privilege, inherited wealth, and economic inequality. For Piketty, there couldn't be more at stake:

> The overall conclusion of this study is that a market economy based on private property, if left to itself, contains powerful forces of convergence, associated in particular with the diffusion of knowledge and skills; but it also contains powerful forces of divergence, which are potentially threatening to democratic societies and to the values of social justice on which they are based.
>
> The principal destabilizing force has to do with the fact that the private rate of return on capital, r, can be significantly higher for long periods of time than the rate of growth of income and output, g.

> The inequality $r > g$ implies that wealth accumulated in the past grows more rapidly than output and wages. This inequality expresses a fundamental logical contradiction. The entrepreneur inevitably tends to become a rentier, more and more dominant over those who own nothing but their labor. Once constituted, capital reproduces itself faster than output increases. The past devours the future.
>
> The consequences for the long-term dynamics of the wealth distribution are potentially terrifying, especially when one adds that the return on capital varies directly with the size of the initial stake and that the divergence in the wealth distribution is occurring on a global scale. (571)

The key phrase here, of course, is "potentially terrifying." Although Piketty does not mention community colleges specifically, he might as well be speaking about them when he talks about democratic societies, "the diffusion of knowledge and skills," and improving "the public good." Echoing the language of the Truman Commission report, Piketty links education directly to "the best way to organize society and the most appropriate institutions and policies to achieve a just social order" (31):

- Knowledge and skill diffusion is the key to overall productivity growth as well as the reduction of inequality both within and between countries. (21)
- Over a long period of time, the main force in favor of greater equality has been the diffusion of knowledge and skills. (22)
- It is obvious that lack of adequate investment in training can exclude entire social groups from the benefits of economic growth. (22)

Boiled down to its most essential, Piketty suggests that the most important question here relates to social justice: "What public policies and institutions bring us closer to an ideal society?" (574). The open admissions community college provides one indisputable, emphatic, and inspiring answer to that question.

This conversation about social justice and economic inequality is also linked in important ways to our ongoing discussion of developmental education reform at open admissions institutions (Bailey; Hassel et al.; Hodara, Jaggars, and Karp). As Bailey, Jeong, and Cho note, withdrawal from developmental classes is "still closely related to race and income" (27). This is why recent discussions about altering open admissions policies in some states (Fain; Bailey, Hughes, and Jaggars; Flores; Rose "Remediation") become again most essentially discussions about social justice and the public good, about opportunity and access, and, following the Truman Commission, about "the fundamental concept of democracy" as "a belief in the inherent worth of the individual, in the dignity and value of human life" (11).

The community college was created and mandated to help offset the "immense influence of the family on child development and school achievement" (Haskins and Sawhill 126), and, as we will see, this social dynamic is perhaps even more complex than it may appear even to professionals and researchers in our field. Before we examine these complexities in detail, however, we must carefully assess the economic theory that drives so much public policy debate in higher education and which has become the primary lens through which we understand and evaluate so much in America today, including higher education and community colleges: neoliberalism.

CHAPTER 20

"Socialism Means Slavery"

"The Crisis of Our Times"

Neoliberal economic theory has become ascendant in America in recent decades, and this body of theoretical work has been used to shape public policy in profound ways, especially in the US and Britain, often well beyond areas traditionally associated with economics, including higher education, where neoliberal theory has found a central place. Neoliberal economic theory has informed decades of thinking about higher education—often in ways that have been incremental, subtle, and largely hidden from view. Wendy Brown has called this development a "stealth revolution" in her book on neoliberalism, *Undoing the Demos*. Brown suggests, in fact, that neoliberalism is "quietly undoing basic elements of democracy," including "principles of justice, political cultures, habits of citizenship, practices of rule, and above all, democratic imaginaries" (17). Although this claim may sound hyperbolic, this sense of the danger of neoliberal policies—at least as they are being currently practiced in the US—is now widely shared (Atkinson; Piketty; Reich; Stiglitz *Price*). Neoliberal ideas applied to higher education have also come under sharp attack in recent years (Kezar, Chambers, Burkhardt; Lambert; Nixon; Slaughter and Rhoades).

It is perhaps ironic that such ideas are being described as undemocratic because neoliberalism grew out of formative experiences during

World War II and emerged from a group of thinkers deeply concerned with preserving individual freedom and democratic ideals and forms of government. In fact, much of the foundational work of neoliberalism issues from the same historical period as the Truman Commission Report. Many of the foundational economists who we now associate with neoliberalism—F.A. Hayek, Joseph A. Schumpeter, and Milton Friedman, for example—developed their ideas in response to their experience of World War II, with the goal of saving democracy and capitalism from the dangers of socialism, communism, and fascism. Hayek was born in Austria in 1899, saw firsthand the rise of Nazi Germany, and spent the war years in Britain teaching and writing. Schumpeter was born in Austria in 1883 and also had firsthand experience living in Germany before the war, leaving Europe in 1932 for the US. American Milton Friedman was born in 1912 and was a member of the Mont Pelerin Society (MPS), a highly influential group of economists, historians, philosophers, and public affairs scholars from Europe and the United States who met at Hayek's invitation at Mont Pelerin, Switzerland, after the war. This group met for ten days, from April 1 to April 10, 1947, to discuss "the crisis of our times" (Mont). Like the Truman Commission Report, neoliberalism is informed in essential ways by the many social, political, and economic movements associated with World War II.

"A Living Intellectual Issue"

F.A. Hayek's famous book, *The Road To Serfdom*, perhaps the most essential neoliberal text, began in the early 1930s as a memo to the director of the London School of Economics (LSE), Sir William Beveridge, about the relationship between fascism and capitalism (Caldwell 1). This memo eventually grew into the book we know today, which is deeply informed by Hayek's residency in Britain as a professor at the LSE during the war. Written primarily for a British readership and published in 1944, *The Road To Serfdom* expresses a deep wariness about central control of state functions and champions capitalism, individual liberty, and freedom from government economic control. In his introduction to the book, Hayek states these claims simply and memorably:

> It is necessary now to state the unpalatable truth that it is Germany whose fate we are in some danger of repeating. The danger is not immediate, it is true, and conditions in England and the United States are still so remote

from those witnessed in recent years in Germany as to make it difficult to believe that we are moving in the same direction. Yet, though the road be long, it is one on which it becomes more difficult to turn back as one advances. If in the long run we are the makers of our own fate, in the short run we are the captives of the ideas we have created. Only if we recognize the danger in time can we hope to avert it. (58)

Hayek goes on to say that

> Few are ready to recognize that the rise of fascism and naziism was not a reaction against the socialist trends of the preceding period but a necessary outcome of those tendencies. (59)

Such socialist trends, Hayek believed, always lead to "tyranny" (59). For Hayek, "socialism" is where authoritarian rule and loss of personal freedom always converge. Hayek suggested that democracies were in perilous danger because "if we take the people whose views influence developments, they are now in the democracies in some measure all socialists" (59). Hayek's primary proposition—that centralized control of national economies inevitably leads to loss of freedom and dangerous levels of government control and repressive authority—has certainly been proved correct. Recent socialist experiments in the Soviet Union, Cambodia, China, North Korea, and Cuba, for example, all might be said to have begun as socialist or communist utopias of one sort or another but ultimately devolved into repressive, highly restrictive authoritarian states with greatly limited personal freedom. Whether we can apply Hayek's warnings to democracies, however, as they often are, continues to be contested. And whether we can apply his ideas to public policy related to democratic institutions beyond central economies (like those related to higher education and community colleges, for example) is an important question for us all.

Hayek is also certainly correct when he acknowledges the power of ideas to shape public life, suggesting that we are "captives of the ideas we have created" (*Road* 58). This may be the one point of agreement between Hayek and his famous ideological adversary, John Maynard Keynes, and a moment of significant importance for our discussion here. Keynes famously observed that the ideas of economists exert a very powerful influence indeed:

> The ideas of economists and political philosophers, both when they are right and when they are wrong, are more powerful than is commonly understood.

> Indeed the world is ruled by little else. Practical men, who believe themselves to be quite exempt from any intellectual influences, are usually the slaves of some defunct economist. (383)

This has certainly proved to be the case in all sorts of ways—and it is certainly the case today in higher education, as we will see. In some deeply unfortunate ways, we have become slaves to these ideas and this deified market model.

Hayek also believed in the power of ideas, and he believed with equal passion that it was necessary for those committed to liberty and economic freedom to actively help shape public discourse about these ideas. In his 1949 essay, "The Intellectuals and Socialism," Hayek addressed this issue directly:

> Unless we can make the philosophic foundations of a free society once more a living intellectual issue, and its implementation a task which challenges the ingenuity and imagination of our liveliest minds, the prospects of freedom are indeed dark. But if we can regain that belief in the power of ideas which was the mark of liberalism at its greatest, the battle is not lost. (237)

In this section of the book, I seek to examine two sets of contending and powerful ideas that have been profoundly influential in shaping life in modern America. They each address perhaps the most foundational subject we have in our power to engage as Americans—how to build a strong and healthy democracy. Each also addresses the essential question that Piketty poses so memorably: "What public policies and institutions bring us closer to an ideal society?" (574). One set of ideas has been formulated by neoliberal economists like F.A. Hayek and Milton Friedman. The other set of ideas has been formulated by the Truman Commission and economists like Amartya Sen and Joseph E. Stiglitz. If so much depends on our ongoing "battle of ideas," as Hayek and Keynes both suggest, then there is certainly value in putting these two foundational sets of ideas about America, the public good, and the development of a strong democracy into dialog with one another. We must also keep in mind that when theory is translated into practice, it can be used in ways that would be unrecognizable to the original framers of those theories. As David Harvey notes in his book, *A Brief History of Neoliberalism*,

> there are, as we shall see, enough contradictions in the neoliberal position to render evolving neoliberal practices (vis-à-vis issues such as monopoly power and market failures) unrecognizable in relation to the seeming purity

of neoliberal doctrine. We have to pay careful attention, therefore, to the tension between the theory of neoliberalism and the actual pragmatics of neoliberalization. (21)

This is excellent advice that can help guide us as we move forward with this analysis.

As we assess these two sets of competing ideas, I invite readers to keep in mind three key questions we are asking in this book about community colleges, the public good, and building a strong democracy in America:

- What kind of democratic society do we want to build?
- What are the most appropriate institutions and policies to achieve a just social order?
- What public policies and institutions bring us closer to an ideal society?

As we do this work, let us keep in mind Karl Polanyi's warning in *The Great Transformation* about the dangers of market economists discussing freedom and liberty. Polanyi cautioned that the peril in free market economic theory is that in privileging the idea of freedom, this idea "degenerates into a mere advocacy of free enterprise" (265). This can often translate in practice into "the fullness of freedom for those whose income, leisure and security need no enhancing, and a mere pittance of liberty for the people, who may in vain attempt to make use of their democratic rights to gain shelter from the power of the owners of property" (265).

"Socialism Means Slavery"

A careful examination of Hayek's *The Road to Serfdom* reveals a set of ideas that many individuals familiar with the modern political version of neoliberalism might not recognize. Throughout this book, Hayek is most interested in combatting "central control" of national economies. His discussion of "socialism"—a word that has now gained great currency in American public discourse as a reliable rhetorical pejorative that derives its ideological power from Hayek, Schumpeter, and Friedman and can be used to discredit any government program whatsoever—is limited primarily to central control of national economies. Hayek acknowledges, for example, that "combating general fluctuations of economic activity and the recurrent waves of large-scale unemployment which accompany them" is "one of the gravest and most pressing problems of our time" (148–9). We must remember that at the time Hayek was writing *The Road to Serfdom*, capitalism was believed to be a failed economic system and many countries were experimenting with central control of their economies, with a corresponding catastrophic loss of personal freedom. This occurred in Italy, Germany, Spain, and Russia during this period. Many democracies were also seriously considering—or already practicing—a degree of central control over national economies to combat the economic hardship caused by the Great Depression. These include the US and Franklin D. Roosevelt's (FDR) New Deal (Kennedy; Hiltzik), Britain, and France, which in 1936 elected its first socialist prime minister, Léon Blum, who presided over the Popular Front government until June 1937 (Birnbaum).

Hayek notes with great alarm the growing menace of socialism: "Although we had been warned by some of the greatest political thinkers of the nineteenth century, by Tocqueville and Lord Acton, that socialism means slavery, we have steadily moved in the direction of socialism" (67). In current political discussions about government and public policy in America, Hayek's ideas about "socialism" often get radically simplified and distorted and are frequently used to discredit any kind of governmental action that can be said to inhibit a free market and freedom of choice. These distortions often creep into discussions of higher education as well, as we will see, lending simplified ideological support for applying neoliberal business models in areas of public life that are not national economies and not essentially economic transactions. This has had a devastating effect on educational policy in the last 30 years (Armstrong and Hamilton; Darling-Hammond *Flat*; McMahon *Higher*; Mettler; Ravitch *Reign*; Ripley; Schneider; Tucker; Turner).

Hayek notes that at the historical moment in which he is writing, "socialism has replaced liberalism as the doctrine held by the great majority of progressives" (76). He goes on to say in his ironically titled chapter, "The Great Utopia," that "socialism began increasingly to make use of the promise of a 'new freedom'" (77):

> The subtle change in meaning to which the word "freedom" was subjected in order that this argument should sound plausible is important. To the great apostles of political freedom the word had meant freedom from coercion, freedom from the arbitrary power of other men, release from the ties which left the individual no choice but obedience to the orders of a superior to whom he was attached. The new freedom promised, however, was to be

freedom from necessity, release from the compulsion of the circumstance which inevitably limit the range of choice of all of us, although for some very much more than for others. Before man could truly be free, "the despotism of physical want" had to be broken, the "restraints of the economic system" relaxed. (77)

Hayek suggests that the demand for this new freedom is "only another name for the old demand for an equal distribution of wealth" (78).

"Security Against Severe Physical Privation"

Hayek does not dismiss this idea out of hand, however. He suggests a variety of ways that we might use public policy to address the disparities of income that capitalist systems produce. Hayek identifies a number of government actions that could address these legitimate concerns over income disparities without exerting central control over a national economy. Much of this for Hayek ultimately comes down to two factors—individual choice and luck:

> It is significant that one of the commonest objections to competition is that it is "blind." It is not irrelevant to recall that to the ancients blindness was an attribute of their deity of justice. Although competition and justice may have little else in common, it is as much a commendation of competition as of justice that it is no respecter of persons. That it is impossible to foretell who will be the lucky ones or whom disaster will strike, that rewards and penalties are not shared out according to somebody's views about the merits or demerits of different people but depend on their capacity and their luck, is as important as that, in framing legal rules, we should not be able to predict which particular person will gain and which will lose by their application. And this is nonetheless true, because in competition chance and good luck are often as important as skill and foresight in determining the fate of different people.
>
> The choice open to us is not between a system in which everybody will get what he deserves according to some absolute and universal standard of right, and one where the individual shares are determined partly by accident or good or ill chance, but between a system where it is the will of a few persons that decides who is to get what, and one where it depends at least partly on the ability and enterprise of the people concerned and partly on unforeseeable circumstances. This is no less relevant because in a system of free enterprise chances are not equal, since such a system is necessarily based on private property and (though perhaps not with the same necessity) on inheritance, with the differences in opportunity which these create.

> There is, indeed, a strong case for reducing this inequality of opportunity as far as congenital differences permit and as it is possible to do so without destroying the impersonal character of the process by which everybody has to take his chance and no person's view about what is right and desirable overrules that of others. (134)

Rather than abandoning those whose choices and luck do not lead to success in a free market economy, Hayek suggests that policies can be put in place to assist them. This passage suggests that Hayek, in principle, supports certain kinds of endeavors that address economic inequality and opportunity differential as long as they don't require central control of national economies, as they did in Italy, Germany, Spain, and Russia at the time Hayek was writing.

Hayek develops this point in more detail in his important chapter on "Security and Freedom":

> It will be well to contrast at the outset two kinds of security: the limited one, which can be achieved for all, and which is therefore no privilege but a legitimate object of desire; and absolute security, which in a free society cannot be achieved for all and which ought not to be given as a privilege—except in a few special instances such as that of the judges, where complete independence is of paramount importance. These two kinds of security are, first, security against severe physical privation, the certainty of a given minimum of sustenance for all; and, second, the security of a given standard of life, or of the relative position which one person or group enjoys compared with others; or, as we put it briefly, the security of a minimum income and the security of the particular income a person is thought to deserve. (147–8)

About the first kind of security—"security against severe physical privation"—Hayek has this surprising claim to make:

> There is no reason why in a society which has reached the general level of wealth which ours has attained the first kind of security should not be guaranteed to all without endangering general freedom. (148)

And he restates it here at the end of this chapter:

> There can be no question that adequate security against severe privation, and the reduction of the avoidable causes of misdirected effort and consequent disappointment, will have to be one of the main goals of policy. (156)

It appears that Hayek is suggesting that as long as public policy does not seek to direct and control a national economy, these are goals that can and should be addressed. Hayek's primary point—"that individual freedom cannot be reconciled with the supremacy of one single purpose to which the whole of society must be entirely and permanently subordinated" (213)—does not preclude government intervention in ways that seek to address this kind of privation to promote social justice and the public good. Hayek devotes a considerable portion of *The Constitution of Liberty* (1960), in fact, to describing more precisely how this should—and should not—be accomplished. We will be examining this material in a later chapter. Overall, *balance* emerges as a key guiding principle for Hayek as he seeks to provide security against severe privation while also nurturing a strong free market. Hayek acknowledges that converting this goal into actual public policy will require considerable thoughtfulness and care:

> There are difficult questions about the precise standard which should thus be assured; there is particularly the important question whether those who thus rely on the community should indefinitely enjoy all the same liberties as the rest. An incautious handling of these questions might well cause serious and perhaps even dangerous political problems; but there can be no doubt that some minimum of food, shelter, and clothing, sufficient to preserve health and the capacity to work, can be assured to everybody. (148)

This is an essential question that we will examine as we move forward to assess whether government programs—and which kinds of government programs—can help build a strong democracy and help us move closer to an ideal society. In some significant ways, the modern community college, which was chartered at roughly the same time *The Road to Serfdom* was published, was mandated to help America provide precisely this kind of opportunity and security from privation for its citizens. The community college system in the US was also designed to offset the privileges that attend inherited wealth and the ownership of private property and "the differences in opportunity which these create."

It is perhaps surprising to note that Hayek's comments here are not that dissimilar to Martin Luther King's famous remarks on this same subject 20 years later, delivered in his Nobel Lecture from December 11, 1964, "The Quest for Peace and Justice." Although these two thinkers are generally thought to represent very different ideological positions, they both voice similar concerns about the persistence of privation and the nature of a just society:

> Why should there be hunger and privation in any land, in any city, at any table when man has the resources and the scientific know-how to provide all mankind with the basic necessities of life? Even deserts can be irrigated and top soil can be replaced. We cannot complain of a lack of land, for there are twenty-five million square miles of tillable land, of which we are using less than seven million. We have amazing knowledge of vitamins, nutrition, the chemistry of food, and the versatility of atoms. There is no deficit in human resources; the deficit is in human will. The well-off and the secure have too often become indifferent and oblivious to the poverty and deprivation in their midst. The poor in our countries have been shut out of our minds, and driven from the mainstream of our societies, because we have allowed them to become invisible. Just as nonviolence exposed the ugliness of racial injustice, so must the infection and sickness of poverty be exposed and healed—not only its symptoms but its basic causes. This, too, will be a fierce struggle, but we must not be afraid to pursue the remedy no matter how formidable the task.
>
> The time has come for an all-out world war against poverty. The rich nations must use their vast resources of wealth to develop the underdeveloped, school the unschooled, and feed the unfed. Ultimately a great nation is a compassionate nation. No individual or nation can be great if it does not have a concern for "the least of these." Deeply etched in the fiber of our religious tradition is the conviction that men are made in the image of God and that they are souls of infinite metaphysical value, the heirs of a legacy of dignity and worth. If we feel this as a profound moral fact, we cannot be content to see men hungry, to see men victimized with starvation and ill health when we have the means to help them. The wealthy nations must go all out to bridge the gulf between the rich minority and the poor majority.

Both Hayek and King appear to suggest that a wealthy nation like ours has a moral obligation not to turn its back on the less fortunate. Both suggest that thoughtful public policy can be used as an effective tool to address long-standing and deeply engrained privation. Both also suggest that thoughtful public policy can be used to offset the advantages conferred by inherited wealth and the ownership of private property and "the differences in opportunity which these create." Overall, a careful reading of Hayek suggests that within his work there is certainly room for governmental endeavors that promote social justice and the public good. Hayek clearly appears to believe that such public policy measures can—and perhaps should—be accomplished within a free market system.

CHAPTER 21

Unfreedom

"Dissatisfaction with the Distribution of Income"

Milton Friedman's work is also important to consider in relation to neoliberal economic theory and current public policy discussions in the US related to higher education and community colleges. Friedman was a colleague and associate of Hayek's, and he is an important neoliberal theorist whose work has been widely influential in the US. He shared many of Hayek's views about the dangers of "central control," socialism, and the role of government in a free market economy, although he often articulates these ideas very differently than Hayek. Friedman was Ronald Reagan's favorite economist, and his ideas were instrumental in helping to shape the neoliberal revolution that Reagan and Margaret Thatcher inaugurated in the 1980s in the US and Britain.

Friedman has been perhaps most responsible for translating Hayek's ideas about "central control" of a national economy for a more general audience. As he did this, Friedman developed a remorseless, almost fundamentalist cynicism about government itself, and he has popularized a deeply pessimistic view of government and public policy. Like many who currently employ neoliberal ideas for political purposes, I'm afraid that Friedman also sometimes allows himself to simplify very complex economic, social, cultural, and political conditions (especially in his writing for general audiences) as he defends the power of the market and individual freedom. This is an aspect of public debate about higher education and community colleges that has become problematic in recent years, as we will see.

Overall, like Hayek, Friedman eschews "collectivism," and he has famously suggested that education ("Role") and perhaps even road building should be handled by the private sector ("Why" 5; *Capitalism* 30–1). Friedman was tireless in his condemnation of the "dangers of big government" (*Free* 7; *Capitalism*), and he believed that government worked best when it served as "an umpire, not a participant" (*Free* 4). In "The Power of the Market" chapter of *Free To Choose*, he and his co-author, his wife Rose Friedman, provide a justly famous account of how an ordinary wooden pencil gets created, demonstrating how "cooperation through voluntary exchange" works in the free market (11–13).

His belief in the extraordinary power of the market to create opportunity for individuals, however, leaves him feeling rather fatalistic about economic inequality and those individuals at the bottom rungs of the economic ladder. In *Free to Choose*, he and Rose Friedman engage the question of economic inequality and opportunity differentials much as Hayek does—by focusing on "chance" and "choice":

> The amount of each kind of resource each of us owns is partly the result of chance, partly of choice by ourselves or others. Chance determines our genes and through them affects our physical and mental capacities. Chance determines the kind of family and cultural environment into which we are born and as a result our opportunities to develop our physical and mental capacity. Chance determines also other resources we may inherit from our parents or other benefactors. Chance may destroy or enhance the resources we start with. But choice also plays an important role. Our decisions about how to use our resources, whether to work hard or take it easy, to enter one occupation or another, to engage in one venture or another, to save or spend—these may determine whether we dissipate our resources or improve and add to them. Similar decisions by our parents, by other benefactors, by millions of people who may have no direct connection with us will affect our inheritance.
>
> The price that the market sets on the services of our resources is similarly affected by a bewildering mixture of chance and choice. Frank Sinatra's voice was highly valued in twentieth-century United States. Would it have been highly valued in twentieth-century India, if he had happened to be born and to live there? Skill as a hunter and trapper had a high value in eighteenth- and nineteenth-century America, a much lower value in twentieth-century America. Skill as a baseball player brought much higher returns than skill

as a basketball player in the 1920s; the reverse is true in the 1970s. These are all matters involving chance and choice—in these examples, mostly the choices made by consumers of services that determine the relative market prices of different items. But the price we receive for the services of our resources through the market also depends on our own choices—where we choose to settle, how we choose to use those resources, to whom we choose to sell their services, and so on. (21–2)

Here we see the Friedmans echoing an important idea of Hayek's—"individual responsibility" (*Constitution* "Responsibility and Freedom," 133–147). This focus on personal responsibility has had important ramifications for policy decisions across a wide range of domains, including higher education and even developmental education reform (Hassel, Klausman, Giordano, O'Rourke, Roberts, Sullivan, and Toth; Otte and Mlynarczyk). It has helped produce what might be described as a stoic and perhaps unsympathetic approach toward hardship, need, and privation. In some cases, a focus on personal responsibility has conveniently simplified the many ways that wealth, privilege, and opportunity become stratified in market economies. The Friedmans' comments about this subject in *Free To Choose* are paradigmatic of this approach to inequality:

> In every society, however it is organized, there is always dissatisfaction with the distribution of income. All of us find it hard to understand why we should receive less than others who seem no more deserving—or why we should be receiving more than so many others whose needs seem as great and whose deserts seem no less. The farther fields always look greener—so we blame the existing system. In a command system envy and dissatisfaction are directed at the rulers. In a free market system they are directed at the market. (22)

For Friedman, the way to build a strong democracy is to protect freedoms, have government function as an "umpire" (*Capitalism* 25–7), and create a strong market economy. Although Friedman admits that government should "have the function of relieving misery and distress," he also suggests, following Hayek, that this function must be handled with great care and thoughtfulness:

> Finally; the government would have the function of relieving misery and distress. Our humanitarian sentiments demand that some provision should be made for those who "draw blanks in the lottery of life." Our world has become too complicated and intertwined, and we have become too sensitive, to leave

this function entirely to private charity or local responsibility. It is essential, however, that the performance of this function involve the minimum of interference with the market. There is justification for subsidizing people because they are poor, whether they are farmers or city-dwellers, young or old. There is no justification for subsidizing farmers as farmers rather than because they are poor. There is justification in trying to achieve a minimum income for all; there is no justification for setting a minimum wage and thereby increasing the number of people without income; there is no justification for trying to achieve a minimum consumption of bread separately, meat separately, and so on. ("Neo-Liberalism" 8–9)

Friedman has done perhaps more than anyone to champion the power of the market, to celebrate the power of individual freedom and choice, and to acclaim the opportunity and prosperity produced by capitalism.

"Government Is the Problem"

To these ends, Friedman sometimes allows himself to oversimplify complex situations in order to make dramatic political points, sometimes providing very simple answers to complex problems. Unfortunately, this distorts the nature of these problems, compromises the purpose of public debate, and devalues the role of reasoned discourse and the use of evidence and research in the realm of public policy. A paradigmatic example of this is *Why Government Is the Problem*, a short 18-page pamphlet that is adapted from Friedman's 1991 Wriston Lecture presented in New York City and sponsored by the Manhattan Institute. In the published version of this speech, Friedman contends that most of the major social ills in America—"deteriorating education, lawlessness and crime, homelessness, the collapse of family values, the crisis in medical care" (Executive Summary)—can be traced to ill-advised government policies and practices. Unfortunately, Friedman offers very little evidence or research supporting these claims. He supports his positions, instead, primarily through bold sweeping statements, self-assurance, and a few stirring anecdotal examples. This has become the model for one sort of neoliberal approach to public policy debate in recent years, a dangerous practice because it erodes confidence in the important role of evidence and logical reasoning, and it subverts the necessity for providing the "burden of proof" that is the basis for all legitimate argumentation. Such an approach to public policy degrades and problematizes the role of reasoned discourse in governance and policy debate.

As we know, the title of this book—*Why Government Is the Problem*—has provided proponents of neoliberalism with a blunt, very effective, all-purpose rhetorical tool that can be used to disparage almost any kind of government program or initiative. It draws its ideological power from its links to classic economic theory, but even as a book like Hayek's *The Road To Serfdom* suggests, the relationship between government, economies, and democratic rule is much more complex than government simply being wrong all the time. Also, as David Harvey has shown, neoliberal economists and politicians who embrace this economic model typically support government interventions when they benefit business and capital (including subsidies and tax incentives for capitalist enterprises and the use of public resources for building infrastructures conducive for business ventures) but they routinely do not support government intervention in other instances. So, the neoliberal approach to "central control" is often selective and inconsistent (Harvey 64–86; Brown).

Government's role in supporting educational initiatives has also been called into question by neoliberal theorists on many fronts over the course of many years. Ominously for those of us who care deeply about education in America, Friedman has claimed that "next to the military, education is the largest socialist industry in the United States" ("Why" 2; *Free* 150–88). Friedman also established a key market formulation applied to education—return on investment—that has been deeply influential in the intervening years. "Input has tripled," he writes in *Why Government is the Problem*, but "output is going down" (2). Here we see the "accountability" movement and the neoliberal business model for education being born. As we will see, this business model applied to education has become highly problematic (Darling-Hammond; Ravitch *Reign*; Ripley; Rizga; Russakoff; Tucker).

"The Shame of Slavery Only Excepted"

More serious problems of simplification occur in *Free to Choose*, perhaps Friedman's most important and widely read book. As the title of this book suggests, "freedom" is its central focus, and Milton and Rose Friedman credit freedom with producing a golden economic age in both Great Britain and the US:

> Economic freedom is an essential requisite for political freedom. By enabling people to cooperate with one another without coercion or central direction, it reduces the area over which political power is exercised. In addition, by

dispersing power, the free market provides an offset to whatever concentration of political power may arise. The combination of economic and political *power* in the same hands is a sure recipe for tyranny.

The combination of economic and political *freedom* produced a golden age in both Great Britain and the United States in the nineteenth century. The United States prospered even more than Britain. It started with a clean slate: fewer vestiges of class and status; fewer government restraints; a more fertile field for energy, drive, and innovation; and an empty continent to conquer.

The fecundity of freedom is demonstrated most dramatically and clearly in agriculture. When the Declaration of Independence was enacted, fewer than 3 million persons of European and African origin (i.e., omitting the native Indians) occupied a narrow fringe along the eastern coast. Agriculture was the main economic activity. It took nineteen out of twenty workers to feed the country's inhabitants and provide a surplus for export in exchange for foreign goods. Today it takes fewer than one out of twenty workers to feed the 220 million inhabitants and provide a surplus that makes the United States the largest single exporter of food in the world.

What produced this miracle? Clearly not central direction by government—nations like Russia and its satellites, mainland China, Yugoslavia, and India that today rely on central direction employ from one-quarter to one-half of their workers in agriculture, yet frequently rely on US agriculture to avoid mass starvation. During most of the period of rapid agricultural expansion in the United States the government played a negligible role. Land was made available—but it was land that had been unproductive before. After the middle of the nineteenth century land-grant colleges were established, and they disseminated information and technology through governmentally financed extension services. Unquestionably, however, the main source of the agricultural revolution was private initiative operating in a free market open to all—the shame of slavery only excepted. And the most rapid growth came after slavery was abolished. (2–3)

The key phrase in this passage for our purposes here, included almost as an afterthought, is this: "the shame of slavery only excepted." The "empty continent to conquer" is also problematic in paradigmatic ways, of course, for a number of reasons. The continent was by no means empty, as we know (Brown *Bury*; de las Casas; Said *Culture*). We also know that the capitalist free market in the US in the nineteenth century was not "a free market open to all." Friedman is selectively and cavalierly simplifying a very complex period in our national history. Some of this may be attributable to the traditional antagonism between free market capitalists like Friedman and the interests of labor in all its forms. Some may simply be a function of a now old-fashioned and discredited historical understanding of this period, the institution of slavery, and this "empty" continent. Whatever the case, the many conclusions drawn from this understanding must be called into question. Given Dr. Friedman's many academic achievements and his deep knowledge of economic systems, this might also be an instance of willful blindness and obfuscation. After all, even common sense suggests that the massive institution of slavery which had been an integral part of the US economy for over a century—and over which we fought a bloody Civil War—must have had a significant impact on our economic development. Do we really wish to dismiss almost 100 years of slavery and slave labor by using only part of one sentence, strung on almost as an afterthought? And whatever "shame" Dr. Friedman is willing to acknowledge about the role of slavery in this economic golden age, he and Rose Friedman appear to wish to take back altogether in the next sentence: "And the most rapid growth came after slavery was abolished," suggesting that slavery was just a minor contributor to this economic miracle. In less than two sentences, then, Freidman has swept away almost 100 years of US economic history. Unfortunately, "the combination of economic and political *power* in the same hands" was, indeed, "a sure recipe for tyranny"—but not in the way the Friedmans suggest it does here.

Edward Said is famous for suggesting that "the power to narrate, or to block other narratives from forming and emerging, is very important to culture and imperialism" (*Culture* xiiii) and that may be what we are witnessing here—the formation of a particular, selectively shaped narrative about American economic history and the free market that promotes certain kinds of understandings and values and blocks others from forming or emerging. Said has helped us understand the power of narrative and, perhaps even more importantly, how narratives shape perception in very powerful ways:

> Readers of this book will quickly discover that narrative is crucial to my argument here, my basic point being that stories are at the heart of what explorers and novelists say about strange regions of the world; they also become the method colonized people use to assert their own identity and the existence of their own history. The main battle in imperialism is over land, of course; but when it comes to who owned the land, who had the right to settle and work on it, who kept it going, who won it back, and who now plans its future—these issues were reflected, contested, and even for a time decided in narrative. As one critic has suggested, nations themselves *are* narrations. The power to narrate, or to block other narratives from forming and emerging, is very important to culture and imperialism, and constitutes one of the main connections between them. (*Culture* xii–xiii)

We may be seeing Milton Friedman engaged in precisely this kind of narrative- and nation-building—where certain kinds of ideas about democracy and capitalism are affirmed, shaped, and presented to readers, while less appealing or less convenient aspects of that history are blocked, foreclosed, or dismissed. We must recognize, of course, that market-based economies have brought wealth and prosperity to millions across the globe. But we must also acknowledge other less flattering, less pleasant truths as well so that we don't simplify or distort the historical record. We must also understand that if Dr. Friedman can be wrong about this, he can be wrong about other things as well.

It is deeply ironic that this dismissal comes embedded within a panegyric to freedom ("private initiative operating in a free market open to all") for of course most of the economic miracle that Friedman discusses was achieved on the backs of slaves and then by newly freed slaves after the Civil War, who effectively worked as indentured servants as share-croppers (Foner; Morgan; Wilkerson). This economic miracle was made possible not by freedom—but, to borrow an important phrase from Hayek, by the "unfreedom" of slaves (*Road* 135). This cannot simply be dismissed as a small and insignificant factor, as there were millions of slaves involved, providing the manual labor in the fields that made this economic transformation possible. This is an example of ideology distorting public policy debate in the service of furthering its own interests, regardless of common sense and documented evidence, another hallmark we see in much public policy debate coming from neoliberals today. There is simply no way to formulate a legitimate understanding of the growth of capitalism in America without recourse to slavery and the abundant, uncompensated slave labor it was built upon. It was, in fact, the very opposite of freedom that produced this economic miracle, which makes the title of the Friedmans' book, *Free To Choose*, so deeply problematic—and paradigmatic of a certain kind of neoliberal approach to public policy. "Slave labor" is an ugly term, but that is what it was. As Eugene Genovese notes in *Roll, Jordan, Roll*,

> The slaveholders of the South, unlike those of the Caribbean, increasingly resided on their plantations and by the end of the eighteenth century had become an entrenched regional ruling class. The paternalism encouraged by the close living of masters and slaves was enormously reinforced by the closing of the African slave trade, which compelled masters to pay greater attention to the reproduction of their labor force. Of all the slave societies in the New World, that of the Old South alone maintained a slave force that reproduced itself. Less than 400,000 imported Africans had, by 1860, become an American black population of more than 4,000,000. (5)

To put this as plainly as I can, the economic miracle Friedman praises in *Free to Choose* was created not by an economic system or inspiring ideas about freedom but by those four million slaves, who provided the labor in the fields.

Symbolic Annihilation

There is an imposing body of scholarship on this subject, and this work provides a more nuanced and detailed picture of this period in our history. Unfortunately, it is very clear that it was not capitalism, freedom, or the free market that produced this economic miracle. It was slavery, unfreedom, and systematic brutality practiced by the wealthy and powerful upon millions of the enslaved and powerless. This scholarly work, as Greg Grandin notes, includes Eric Williams's study, *Capitalism and Slavery*, which was published in 1944, the same year as *The Road To Serfdom*, and more recent works that include "The Other Side of Slavery: Black Labor, Cotton, and Textile Industrialization in Great Britain and the United States" (1994) by Ronald Bailey, *The Making of New World Slavery: From the Baroque to the Modern, 1492–1800* (2nd ed, 2010) by Robin Blackburn, and *River of Dark Dreams: Slavery and Empire in the Cotton Kingdom* by Walter Johnson (2013). Grandin, author of *The Empire of Necessity: Slavery, Freedom, and Deception in the New World*, summarizes the current research consensus this way:

> Despite all this scholarly work, each generation—from W.E.B. Du Bois to Robin Blackburn, from Eric Williams to Walter Johnson—seems condemned to have to prove the obvious anew: Slavery created the modern world, and the modern world's divisions (both abstract and concrete) are the product of slavery. Slavery is both the thing that can't be transcended but also what can never be remembered. ("Capitalism")

Two additional works I would like to discuss in this regard are recent and revealing. Edward Baptist's book about this subject, *The Half Has Never Been Told: Slavery and the Making of American Capitalism*, demonstrates that the "true narrative" about American capitalism "has been left out of history" (xxii), thanks in part to individuals like Friedman. As I am attempting to suggest, narrative plays a key role in shaping how we understand the world and what we understand to be possible and impossible. This will be especially important when we move on to discuss community colleges. For many years, Baptist notes, historians treated American slavery as "fundamentally different from the rest of the modern economy and separate from it" (xviii). The traditional historical narrative about this time period was that "slavery and enslaved African Americans had little long-term influence on the rise of the United States during the nineteenth century" (xviii). Obviously, this narrative was—and continues to be—convenient and self-serving for all sorts of reasons. This is part of what Eichstedt and Small have called the "symbolic annihilation" of enslaved people. As Baptist notes,

> From the 1790s to the 1860s, enslavers moved 1 million people from the old slave states to the new. They went from making no cotton to speak of in 1790 to making almost 2 billion pounds of it in 1860. (xxiii)

Baptist demonstrates that "changes that reshaped the entire world began on the auction block where enslaved migrants stood or in the frontier cotton fields where they toiled" (xxiii). Here is how Baptist describes this nineteenth-century economic miracle, a passage that can be usefully paired with the Friedmans' analysis of this same "golden age":

> In the span of a single lifetime after the 1780s, the South grew from a narrow coastal strip of worn-out plantations to a sub-continental empire. Entrepreneurial enslavers moved more than 1 million enslaved people, by force, from the communities that survivors of the slave trade from Africa had built in the South and in the West to vast territories that were seized—also by force—from their Native American inhabitants. From 1783 at the end of the American Revolution to 1861, the number of slaves in the United States increased five times over, and all this expansion produced a powerful nation. For white enslavers were able to force enslaved Africa-American migrants to pick cotton faster and more efficiently that free people. Their practices rapidly transformed the southern states into the dominant force in the global cotton market, and cotton was the world's most widely traded commodity at the time, as it was the key raw material during the first century of the industrial revolution. The returns from cotton monopoly powered the modernization of the rest of the American economy, and by the time of the Civil War, the United States had become the second nation to undergo large-scale industrialization. In fact, slavery's expansion shaped every crucial aspect of the economy and politics of the new nation—not only increasing its power and size, but also, eventually, dividing US politics, differentiating regional identities and interests, and helping to make civil war possible.

> The idea that the commodification and suffering and forced labor of African Americans is what made the United States powerful and rich is not an idea that people necessarily are happy to hear. Yet it is the truth. (xxi–xxii)

Obviously, this is a very different kind of narrative about a momentous epoch in the history of the free market than the one the Friedmans provide. Because slave owners turned slaves' bodies "into commodities with which they changed the financial history of the Western world" (xxvi), Baptist organizes his narrative to draw attention to the destructive physicality of this economic system, using chapter titles like "Feet," "Heads," "Right Hand," "Left Hand," and "Breath." In so doing, he creates a narrative structure that "allowed the story to take as its center point the experience of enslaved African Americans themselves" (xxiv). Baptist also documents the many ways that the "northern economy's industrial sector was built on the backs of enslaved people" (322). Drawing on hundreds of personal narratives, Baptist's book makes a compelling case for his central point: "Understanding something of what it felt like to suffer, and what it cost to endure that suffering, is crucial to understanding the course of US history" (xxv).

"Craving a Nobler, Cleaner Capitalism"

Sven Beckert makes a similar claim about narrative in his Bancroft Prize-winning book, *Empire of Cotton: A Global History*, which is devoted to examining this historic period from a global perspective. Beckert concludes that "Too often, we prefer to erase the realities of slavery, expropriation, and colonialism from the history of capitalism, craving a nobler, cleaner capitalism" (xviii). In effect, Beckert has written a 600-page book about those six words at the end of the Friedmans' sentence—"the shame of slavery only excepted." To provide just one example of how dangerously simplified the Freidmans' version of this history is (regardless of who the intended audience might be), Beckert's book includes 138 pages of notes and citations (449–587).

Beckert concludes that the history of capitalism

> reveals that capitalists and states arose hand in hand, each facilitating the ascendency of the other. It is easy to assume, in our relentlessly branded world, that today's vast corporations exist entirely on their own. Yet such a simplification misses the reality that, historically, capitalists' greatest source of strength was their ability to rely on unusually powerful states—and simultaneously, for much of capitalism's history, the greatest weakness of these same capitalists was that dependence on the state. (440)

This is a far cry from the model that Friedman provides and advocates for throughout his work—a benevolent and powerfully dynamic free market seeking only to be liberated from ill-advised government intervention.

As he discusses what he calls the "empire of cotton," Beckert seeks to offer "a history of capitalism in action" (xv) in which "cotton became the launching pad for the broader Industrial Revolution" (xiv). Studying the history of cotton, he suggests, allows us to see "the origins of the modern world, industrialism, rapid and continuous economic growth, enormous productivity increase, and staggering social inequality" (xiv).

Beckert suggests the economic miracle of the Industrial Revolution was made possible through a variety to forms of violence that he calls "war capitalism":

> Such a thorough and rapid re-creation of the world was possible only because of the emergence of new ways of organizing production, trade, and consumption. Slavery, the expropriation of indigenous peoples, imperial expansion, armed trade, and the assertion of sovereignty over people and land by entrepreneurs were at its core. I call this system *war capitalism*. (xv)

Because of the new ways it brought continents together, "cotton provides the key to understanding the modern world, the great inequalities that characterize it, the long history of globalization, and the ever-changing political economy of capitalism" (xviii). Beckert devotes an entire chapter to the role of slavery in this process, entitled "Slavery Takes Command" (98–135).

On page 93, Beckert provides a diagram of a slave ship, drawn from a period document, "Stowage of the British Slave Ship 'Brookes' Under the Regulated Slave Trade Act of 1788" from the Library of Congress (see Fig. 21.1). One section of the text of this document reads: "Plan shewing the storage of 130 additional slaves round the wings or sides of the lower deck by means of platforms or shelves (in the manner of galleries in a church) The slaves stowed on the shelves and below them have only a height of 2 feet 7 inches between the beams and far less under the beams." This image communicates very powerfully one small part of the human cost of this economic miracle—and what is lost from our understanding of this period in our history when we rely on thinkers whose interest is in providing a nobler, cleaner version of capitalism. If as Hayek claims, "socialism means slavery," I'm afraid it is also historically true that capitalism has also meant slavery as well. Global capitalism has continued to produce slavery even in the US, and this subject is routinely reported

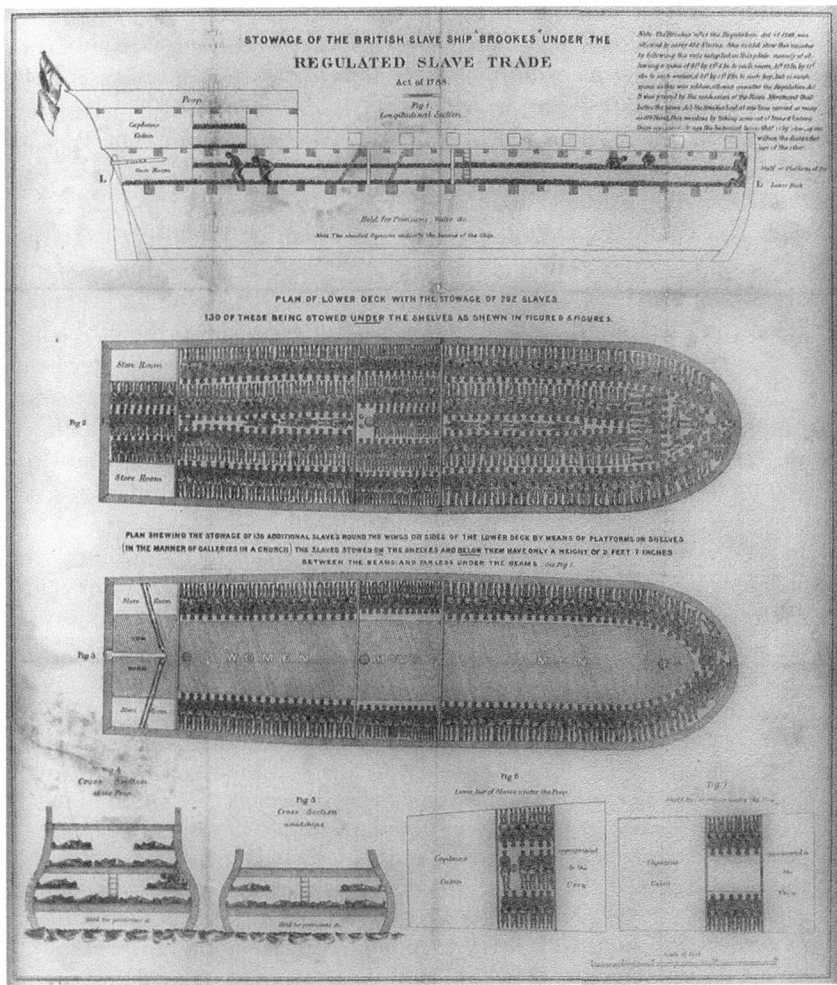

Fig. 21.1 Stowage of the British slave ship 'Brookes' under the regulated Slave Trade Act of 1788
(*Source*: Library of Congress, National Archives and Records Administration. Rare Book and Special Collections Division. http://www.loc.gov/pictures/item/98504459/)

now in the news (Sahadi; United "What"). Nicholas D. Kristof and Sheryl WuDunn have helped document how this affects women globally (*Half the Sky*). Kevin Bales has examined this subject in a series of books, including *Disposable People: New Slavery in the Global Economy*. David Batstone in *Not for Sale: The Return of the Global Slave Trade—and How We Can Fight It* and E. Benjamin Skinner in *A Crime So Monstrous: Face-to-Face with Modern-Day Slavery* have also addressed this issue.

This is a vitally important moment for us, for if Friedman's foundational reading of this period is erroneous or selective, then this casts into doubt all the conclusions he draws from this premise, including his public policy recommendations and his claim that "government is the problem." This does not mean that we still do not have to make careful decisions and choices about the role of government in a democracy and free market economy, as Hayek suggested, but it does mean that we can be liberated from the simplistic formulation that the market is always right and the government is always wrong. It also affirms at least the potential for work that can be done in the name of the public good.

Beckert concludes his book by suggesting that our recognition of "the importance of coercion and violence to the history of capitalism" now "calls into question some of the most ingrained insights into the history of the modern world":

> for example, conceptualizing the nineteenth century, as is so often done, as an age of "bourgeois civilization," in contrast with the twentieth century, which historian Eric Hobsbawm has termed the "age of catastrophe." An assessment such as this can only be derived from a vision of the world that focuses its moral judgments on Europe. Looked at from the perspective of much of Asia, Africa, and the Americas, one can argue just the opposite—that the nineteenth century was an age of barbarity and catastrophe, as slavery and imperialism devastated first one pocket of the globe and then another. It is the twentieth century, by contrast, that saw the weakening of imperial powers and thus allowed more of the word's people to determine their own futures and shake off the shackles of colonial domination. (441)

This is a very different understanding of the "economic miracle" in America than the version the Friedmans provide. Let us return again to Karl Polanyi's warning in *The Great Transformation*—that there is a danger in market economy theory that the idea of freedom "degenerates into a mere advocacy of free enterprise" (265), which translates in practice into "the fullness of freedom for those whose income, leisure and security need no enhancing, and a mere pittance of liberty for the people, who may in vain attempt to make use of their democratic rights to gain shelter from the power of the owners of property" (265). The evidence we have reviewed in this chapter calls into question some of the most foundational understandings of the modern world which inform Friedman's thinking.

"Neoliberalism Has Become Hegemonic as a Mode of Discourse"

All of this may seem very far removed, indeed, from higher education and community colleges, but, unfortunately, it is not. Neoliberal ideas and market models like those espoused by Hayek and Friedman have now moved to the center of the way we understand higher education in America. A business model has introduced an entirely new vocabulary and sociology into our understanding of teaching and learning on college campuses, which include such key market terms as accountability, return on investment, personal responsibility, outcomes assessment, productivity, and efficiency. The University of Chicago economist, Gary S. Becker, in his influential neoliberal study, *Human Capital* (1964; 2nd ed. 1975; 3rd ed. 1993), has even helped challenge the very idea of the public good as it relates to the civic function of higher education. Using a market business model, Becker theorizes higher education as a simple economic transaction. In this scheme, colleges are "multiproduct 'firms'" (208) and private economic gain constitutes "much of the social economic gain" from attending college (211). His book has helped shape the current understanding of higher education and has helped define attending college as "investing in human capital" (xix). As Becker admits in Chapter II: Human Capital Revisited, many readers have criticized his use of the term "human capital" because "they believed it treated people like slaves or machines" (16). Becker's understanding of higher education has been widely embraced and enormously influential in state and federal government agencies and legislatures.

David Harvey, in his book on neoliberalism, has suggested that neoliberalism has now "become hegemonic as a mode of discourse" worldwide:

It has pervasive effects on ways of thought to the point where it has become incorporated into the common-sense way many of us interpret, live in, and understand the world. (3)

This has certainly become the case in higher education. Unfortunately, there are hidden costs to this approach, despite its rhetoric of freedom, productivity, and economic opportunity for all. Systematic disinvestment in public higher education in America in recent years has been driven by neoliberal ideas that challenge the very idea of the public good and that remorselessly emphasize the baleful effects of government activity. A focus on personal choice and personal responsibility—of independent actors pursuing their interests within a free market system—has helped normalize and theoretically validate increasing economic inequality nationwide. It has also helped produce a student debt crisis that has saddled generations of young Americans from poor and middle-class families with debt they will be paying off for decades (Goldrick-Rab). Ideas about labor, efficiency, and cost savings have eviscerated the professoriate, replacing unionized, tenured faculty with disposable, low-wage, part-time labor—adjunct instructors—who are now largely responsible for conducting the sacred work of teaching America's college students. As David Harvey has noted, under neoliberalism, "the figure of 'the disposable worker' emerges as prototypical upon the world stage" (169; Kallenberg). Adjunct faculty have replaced tenure-track positions at an alarming rate:

> Whereas full-time tenured and tenure-track faculty were once the norm, the professoriate is now comprised of mostly non-tenure-track faculty. In 1969, tenured and tenure-track positions made up approximately 78.3 percent of the faculty and non-tenure-track positions comprised about 21.7 percent (Schuster & Finkelstein, 2006). Forty years later, in 2009, these proportions had nearly flipped: tenured and tenure-track faculty had declined to 33.5 percent and 66.5 percent of faculty were ineligible for tenure (AFT Higher Education Data Center, 2009). Of the non-tenure-track positions, 18.8 percent were full-time and 47.7 percent were part-time. (Kezar and Maxey 4)

In addition to the disposable college professor, we may be also seeing the birth of "the disposable student" emerging as well, especially on community college campuses. Chris Mullin has noted in a recent brief for the AACC that "in policy conversations, especially those concerned with policies related to access and choice, there is a silent movement to redirect educational opportunity to 'deserving' students" ("Why" 4). Such a focus, of course, compromises the historic mandate of the community college—and undercuts public policies and public institutions like community colleges that help promote autonomy, self-efficacy (Bandura), and self-authorship (Baxter Magolda).

This neoliberal business model has also led to an extraordinary diminishment of the public and civic functions of higher education. As William Deresiewicz notes in "The Neoliberal Arts: How College Sold Its Soul to the Market," neoliberal economic theory not only has informed funding and policy decisions on the state and federal levels but has also influenced curriculum development and even how students think about college education. Deresiewicz suggests that in higher education, it has come to seem that "only the commercial purpose now survives as a recognized value" (26). The moral, civic, and democratic functions of higher education have been largely lost or eclipsed, he suggests, with our insistent and narrow focus on the market. In the following chapters of this book, we will carefully examine this ubiquitous neoliberal hegemony, especially as it relates to higher education and the community college.

CHAPTER 22

Opportunity Differentials

Neoliberal thinkers celebrate the market economy for the freedom it produces, the equality of opportunity it provides, and the economic growth it generates. They also contend, as Milton Friedman suggests in *Capitalism and Freedom*, that in order for free enterprise and entrepreneurship to flourish, "the scope of government must be limited" (2) and "government power must be dispersed" (3). Personal freedom and an unrestricted free market are held to be paramount, and opportunities are believed to be available to all who want them within a free market economy. Milton and Rose Friedman note in the Introduction to *Free to Choose*, for example, that "the story of the United States is the story of an economic miracle and a political miracle that was made possible by the translation into practice of two sets of ideas" (1). One of these ideas comes from economist Adam Smith and privileges a system of voluntary exchange, "the invisible hand" of the market, and freedom from "external force" and "coercion." (2). The second of these ideas is embodied in the Declaration of Independence and is based on the principle that "every person is entitled to pursue his own values" (2). As we have seen, the Friedmans' claim about this economic miracle is highly problematic.

Neoliberals traditionally stand in opposition to most government activity, maintaining that a strong economy disperses benefits across the entire population. Milton Friedman's *Capitalism and Freedom*, for example, is a book-length expression of these ideas, which theorizes competitive capitalism "as a system of economic freedom and a necessary condition for political freedom" (4). In this view, the market must be made primarily responsible for organizing economic activity. Furthermore, neoliberals also theorize a direct relation between economic freedom and political freedom (Friedman, *Capitalism* 7–21). In theory, all this makes for a compelling argument, but there is a significant body of research that suggests that in practice, the free market does not always expand our freedom, strengthen democratic ideals, or promote prosperity and opportunity for all citizens.

"Unequal Selection"

Pierre Bourdieu's theory of "cultural capital" can help us understand the many ways that opportunity is routinely transmitted across generations in ways that produce significant impediments to upward mobility for those without wealth. Rather than theorizing a relatively level playing field in a free market economy where opportunities are available to all who want them, Bourdieu instead postulates a much more monolithic, impermeable social and economic landscape, where often invisible forms of social and cultural capital are reproduced across various highly stratified cohorts of citizens. Education plays a key role in this process for Bourdieu. His important book, *Reproduction in Education, Society, and Culture*, co-authored with Jean-Claude Passeron, documents "the extremely sophisticated mechanisms by which the school system *contributes* to reproducing the structure of the distribution of cultural capital and, through it, the social structure" (vii). Working against a variety of popular economic theories prevalent in the 1960s—including some which predicted "the demise of class" and "the end of ideology" along with others that celebrated the "extraordinary 'mobility' of American society"(ix)—Bourdieu and Passeron proposed, instead,

> a model of the social mediations and processes which tend, behind the backs of the agents engaged in the school system—teachers, students, and their parents—and often *against their will*, to ensure the transmission of cultural capital across generations and to stamp pre-existing differences in inherited cultural capital with a meritocratic seal of academic consecration by virtue of the special symbolic potency of the *title* (credential). (ix–x)

Bourdieu and Passeron's work demonstrates how educational success and family income track closely together. They conclude, echoing the revelations documented in the Coleman report, that one's "degree of achievement" and "technical proficiency" continue "to stand in very close statistical relationship to social origins, to birth" (x). In societies which "claim to recognize individuals only as equals in right" (x), they suggest that educational systems play a key role in the distribution of capital in all its forms:

> The educational system and its modern nobility only contribute to disguise, and thus legitimize, in a more subtle way the arbitrariness of the distribution of powers and privileges which perpetuates itself through the socially uneven allocation of school titles and degrees. (x)

It should be noted that much of *Reproduction* is devoted to documenting the "painstaking empirical research" and "concrete field descriptions" on which these theoretical propositions are rooted (viii). The modern American community college was designed specifically to address inequalities like this, and in subsequent chapters, we will seek to determine whether the community college offsets and subverts this reproduction process or participates in it, as some have claimed. First, however, I would like to turn our attention to the question of equal opportunity.

In a section of *Reproduction in Education, Society, and Culture* entitled "Unequal Selection and Unequal Selectedness" (72–89), Bourdieu and Passeron discuss the importance of language and "linguistic capital" (72), which is a vitally important consideration for anyone interested in community colleges and open admissions institutions (and developmental education reform as well, of course). Bourdieu and Passeron note that "the influence of linguistic capital, particularly manifest in the first years of schooling when the understanding and use of language are the major points of leverage for teachers' assessments, never ceases to be felt" (73). They note that language acquisition is also largely a function of class position and family resources. They add, moreover, that

> Language is not simply an instrument of communication: it also provides, together with a richer or poorer vocabulary, a more or less complex system of categories, so that the capacity to decipher and manipulate complex structures, whether logical or aesthetic, depends partly on the complexity of the language transmitted by the family. (73)

This is a crucial insight and one that we see playing out in developmental education programs in English and math at community colleges across the nation. As we will see in upcoming chapters, vocabulary acquisition and language development is a key variable for academic success across all disciplines (including math, too, of course) because one's vocabulary and language skills provide much more than an accumulation of discrete word items. Linguistic capital and larger vocabularies provide individuals with more sophisticated ways of engaging problems and enable more complicated kinds of cognition, knowing, and meaning-making. They also provide individuals with a more complex system of categories and the capacity to engage those systems in more productive and meaningful ways. Research conducted by Bourdieu and Passeron, Betty Hart and Todd R. Risley, and others have demonstrated that literacy acquisition is largely a function of family income and class position.

"Time Needed for Acquisition"

In his important essay, "Forms of Capital," Bourdieu demonstrates that the primary way these advantages get passed on and reproduced is "the mediation of the time needed for acquisition" of literacy and technical skills (84). For example, affluent parents of college-age students can provide their children with four years of uninterrupted time to pursue a college degree or credential. This is the traditional, residential college attendance model, which essentially provides students with four, uninterrupted years to devote to earning a degree. The key variable here, of course, is the generous amount of time this academic model provides to students:

> It can immediately be seen that the link between economic and cultural capital is established through the mediation of the time needed for acquisition. Differences in the cultural capital possessed by the family imply differences first in the age at which the work of transmission and accumulation begins—the limiting case being full use of the time biologically available, with the maximum free time being harnessed to maximum cultural capital—and then in the capacity, thus defined, to satisfy the specifically cultural demands of a prolonged process of acquisition. Furthermore, and in correlation with this, the length of time for which a given individual can prolong his acquisition process depends on the length of time for which his family can provide him with the free time, i.e., time free from economic necessity, which is the precondition for the initial accumulation (time which can be evaluated as a handicap to be made up). (84–5)

The vast majority of students attending community colleges find themselves enacting and often actually pioneering a very different, much less generous, and more individually unique and complicated model for attending college and earning a degree. Many students at community colleges juggle an imposing variety of family and personal responsibilities while they attend college, which necessarily complicates and imperils any kind of long-term endeavor like earning a degree. Many community college students are deeply engaged with work responsibilities, families, and their local communities. Statistical profiles like those provided by the National Center for Education Statistics report, *Profiles of Undergraduates in US Post-secondary Education Institutions: 2003–04, With an Analysis of Community College Students*, help tell part of this story (United *Profiles*). But there are other kinds of data sets that have been largely ignored that can provide us with additional kinds of vitally important information and insight. Qualitative data, like the journey narratives included in Part I of this book and the additional journey narratives featured at the Community College Success Stories Project, are an important type of evidence that can help us more accurately understand the lived human experience of this cohort of students. Research data like these bring a deeply human dimension to this scholarly discussion, and they provide an invaluable glimpse into the complex worlds that most community college students live in. Such narratives have the potential to teach us new ways to think about success at community colleges, and they can inspire us to approach with humility and caution any impulse to embrace reductive, categorical, or essentialist conclusions about community colleges and community college students. Unlike four-year residential institutions where students share many commonalities in terms of age, demographics, and living conditions, community colleges enroll students from every possible position along the human life span and from every conceivable kind of circumstance.

For the typical community college student, time is a very precious commodity, indeed. And it is often in very short supply. This becomes a significant variable as we seek to compare success rates across different cohorts of students at different kinds of institutions. Especially when measured against students who are attending school full-time at a residential campus and have four years substantially free from outside work or family responsibilities to complete undergraduate degrees, using a standard "graduation rate" metric is not an effective way to assess these very different cohorts of students and these very different kinds of educational institutions.

"Accumulated History"

As it turns out, Bourdieu's interest in the subject of cultural capital began as he attempted to understand unequal scholastic achievement among children:

> The notion of cultural capital initially presented itself to me, in the course of research, as a theoretical hypothesis which made it possible to explain the unequal scholastic achievement of children originating from the different social classes by relating academic success, i.e., the specific profits which children from the different classes and class fractions can obtain in the academic market, to the distribution of cultural capital between the classes and class fractions. ("Forms" 82)

In his memorable opening paragraph to "The Forms of Capital," Bourdieu suggests that we live a world where there is *not* "perfect equality of opportunity." On the contrary, a variety of very powerful, entrenched, and largely invisible forces are at work to make the playing field quite hierarchical and anything but "equal." Like Piketty, Bourdieu emphasizes the powerful effects of accumulated capital and wealth:

> The social world is accumulated history, and if it is not to be reduced to a discontinuous series of instantaneous mechanical equilibria between agents who are treated as interchangeable particles, one must reintroduce into it the notion of capital and with it, accumulation and all its effects. Capital is accumulated labor (in its materialized form or its 'incorporated,' embodied form) which, when appropriated on a private, i.e., exclusive, basis by agents or groups of agents, enables them to appropriate social energy in the form of reified or living labor. It is a *vis insita*, a force inscribed in objective or subjective structures, but it is also a *lex insita*, the principle underlying the immanent regularities of the social world. It is what makes the games of society—not least, the economic game—something other than simple games of chance offering at every moment the possibility of a miracle. Roulette, which holds out the opportunity of winning a lot of money in a short space of time, and therefore of changing one's social status quasi-instantaneously, and in which the winning of the previous spin of the wheel can be staked and lost at every new spin, gives a fairly accurate image of this imaginary universe of perfect competition or perfect equality of opportunity, a world without inertia, without accumulation, without heredity or acquired properties, in which every moment is perfectly independent of the previous one, every soldier has a marshal's baton in his knapsack, and every prize can be attained, instantaneously, by everyone, so that at each moment anyone can become anything. Capital, which, in its objectified or embodied forms, takes time to accumulate and which, as a potential capacity to produce profits and to reproduce itself in identical or expanded form, contains a tendency to persist in its being, is a force inscribed in the objectivity of things so that everything is not equally possible or impossible. And the structure of the distribution of

the different types and subtypes of capital at a given moment in time represents the immanent structure of the social world, i.e., the set of constraints, inscribed in the very reality of that world, which govern its functioning in a durable way, determining the chances of success for practices. (81)

The modern community college was created with a version of this understanding clearly in mind. The community college as a public institution, in fact, is predicated on the understanding that every moment is not "perfectly independent of the previous one" and that not "every soldier has a marshal's baton in his knapsack." Class position and inherited wealth reduce the chances that "every prize can be attained, instantaneously, by everyone, so that at each moment anyone can become anything." This understanding of the hidden economic dynamics of the social world in which the operation of various forms of inherited capital, privilege, and accumulated wealth help determine success is foundational to an understanding of the community college. As we have seen, the Truman Commission understood this dynamic very well. Given what we know about the rigid, class-based nature of higher education before the advent of the modern community college in the 1960s and 1970s, we can certainly say that the community college has made it possible for more "prizes" to be attained by more people at any given moment than any time previous in the entire history of American higher education. That is a profound and invaluable achievement that strengthens both local communities and our democracy. There is still much work to be done, however, and still many factors related to race, class, and gender at play in higher education today that determine a student's chances of success and that are inadequately understood and accounted for. We will be discussing these in considerable detail in upcoming chapters.

An "Endless Inegalitarian Spiral"

Before we do that, however, let us turn briefly again to consider Thomas Piketty's important work on the nature of capital in free market economies. In many ways, Piketty's conclusions mirror Bourdieu's. What Bourdieu suggests about social capital, Piketty documents using physical capital and private wealth. Because accumulated wealth grows faster than output or wages, the wealthy tend to become "more and more dominant over those who own nothing but their labor" (571). Once constituted, "capital reproduces itself faster than output increases" (571). Piketty estimates the normal growth rates for established national economies like the

US to be about 1–1.5 percent (572): "For countries at the world technological frontier—and thus ultimately for the planet as a whole—there is ample reason to believe that the growth rate will not exceed 1–1.5 percent in the long run, no matter what economic policies are adopted" (572). Piketty estimates that the average return on capital to be between 4 percent and 5 percent. Therefore, it is "likely that r > g [r = private rate of return on capital; g = rate of growth of income and output] will again become the norm in the twenty-first century, as it had been throughout history until the eve of World War I" (572). In the twentieth century, two world wars made it look like this uneven earnings differential had resolved itself more equitably: "it took two world wars to wipe away the past and significantly reduce the return on capital, thereby creating the illusion that the fundamental structural contradiction of capitalism (r > g) had been overcome" (572). This imbalance, Piketty warns, is what explains the current "growth of global inequality of wealth, which is currently increasing at a rate that cannot be sustained in the long run and ought to worry even the most fervent champions of the self-regulated market" (572). Piketty concludes that we cannot rely on only a "vast market predicated on ever purer and more perfect competition" to redress this inequality (573). Instead, Piketty suggests, "if we are to regain control of capitalism, we must bet everything on democracy" (573). This would involve modernizing "any number of social and fiscal policies" (573) to avoid an "endless inegalitarian spiral" (8) and would require significant government intervention, regulation, and progressive public policy. For Piketty, the alternative is what he calls a "globalized patrimonial capitalism" (573), in which economies are directed and controlled by a small number of very wealthy families. This process is already well underway in the US (Duncan and Murnane *Whither Opportunity?*; Mayer; Putnam; Reich; Shipler; Stiglitz *Price of Inequality*).

Piketty views economics as a sub-discipline of the social sciences (573) and suggests that the one thing that sets economics apart from the other social sciences is its "political, normative, and moral purpose" (574). Piketty concludes his book with some thoughts about furthering the interests of "the least well off" (575–7). He suggests—in a key point for our discussion here, both in terms of institutions that move us closer to an ideal society and in terms of free market neoliberalism that came of age after World War II—that the "clash of communism and capitalism sterilized rather than stimulated research on capital and inequality by historians, economists, and even philosophers" (576). In fact, he suggests that "it is long since time to move beyond these old controversies and the historical research they engendered, which to my mind still bears their stamp" (576).

As we seek to move closer to an ideal society, and to move beyond an economic system in which the entrepreneur is becoming "more and more dominant over those who own nothing but their labor" (571), we must think in new ways about opportunity and inequality. The community college is a public institution mandated to engage this work. If we must "bet everything on democracy," then part of this requires us to bet heavily on community colleges. Both Bourdieu and Piketty document how capital is a powerful conservative force, transmitting privilege and power across generations and presenting a kind of closed system to those outside it. Community colleges were designed to help break this old system of privilege and to help provide opportunity for traditionally marginalized populations in America—for "the least well off" among us.

In the next chapters, we will be putting Bourdieu's and Piketty's ideas to the test, examining the many different ways that every moment might not be "perfectly independent of the previous one," that not "every soldier has a marshal's baton in his knapsack," and that the social world is constructed in a way that not "every prize can be attained, instantaneously, by everyone, so that at each moment anyone can become anything." If we are, indeed, "free to choose," as Milton Friedman has famously claimed, the research we will be surveying in the next two chapters shows that not every cohort of individuals is equally free and not every group of individuals has the same choices.

CHAPTER 23

Different Psychological Worlds, Part 1

Although free market economists often acknowledge the role that chance plays in the lives of citizens, as both F.A. Hayek and Milton Friedman do, on balance, they typically spend very little time pursuing the implications of this crucial idea. Such analysis, of course, would necessarily complicate our understanding of the free market and how it does and does not function in a democratic society. It would also necessarily deepen our understanding of the role that a government might be able to play in promoting opportunity, access, and equality for citizens. Because many important and often invisible economic, social, political, and psychological variables are left unexamined, what often emerges is a simplified understanding of the free market and the role of government in nurturing a healthy democracy. Absent from this acknowledgment of chance as a key variable in human life is an understanding of the different psychological worlds produced by luck and chance—and by differentiated access to capital in all of its forms.

This cognitive and psychological dimension of economic theory has been brought into sharp focus in recent years by researchers from a variety of disciplines, and in the next two chapters, we will be examining some of the most important research on this subject. This research provides us with the opportunity to develop a more nuanced, more comprehensive, and more accurate understanding of the free market, especially as it manifests itself in contemporary America today. A key finding here will be a confirmation of Bourdieu's central claim that not every moment in an individual's life is "perfectly independent of the previous one" and that not "every prize can be attained, instantaneously, by everyone, so that at each moment anyone can become anything." There are very powerful, entrenched social, political, and economic forces at work in America today that complicate in profound ways the living realization of a truly free and equal democracy and economic system. Addressing these issues constitutes one very important part of our ongoing work addressing "democracy's unfinished business." Since 1947, the community college has been mandated to help address this unfinished business, and the research reviewed here is work that anyone who seeks to assess the value of community colleges should be familiar with. While we must always acknowledge the importance of agency, personal responsibility, and making good choices as key determinants of an individual's success or failure, we must also acknowledge the largely unseen social, cultural, political, and economic forces that help shape these choices.

An individual American's class position—one's relative wealth and privilege, or one's lack of wealth and privilege—creates uniquely different psychological worlds for individuals. Economic inequality plays a key role here. As the Community College Research Center (2016) has reported,

> An analysis of Education Longitudinal Study (ELS: 2002–06) data shows that 44 percent of low-income students (those with family incomes of less than $25,000 per year) attend community colleges as their first college after high school. In contrast, only 15 percent of high-income students enroll in community colleges initially. Similarly, 38 percent of students whose parents did not graduate from college choose community colleges as their first institution, compared with 20 percent of students whose parents graduated from college.

Margaret Cahalan, Laura Perna, Mika Yamashita, Roman Ruiz, and Khadish Franklin confirm this finding in their report, *Indicators of Higher Education Equity in the United States: 2016 Historical Trend Report*. This report also demonstrates, following landmark conclusions documented in the Coleman Report, that family income continues to predict attainment in higher education and enrollment at two-year colleges. Cahalan, Perna, Yamashita, Ruiz, and Franklin note, for example, that "80 percent of 18- to 24-year-olds from the top family income quartile were enrolled in postsecondary education in 2014, compared with just 45 percent of those in the bottom quartile" (18). In addition, Cahalan, Perna, Yamashita, Ruiz, and Franklin found a direct link between economic scarcity and community college enrollment:

Although characterized as differences in college "choice," "choice" is a misnomer for describing the college destinations of many low-income students. Differences in enrollment patterns by family income reflect the stratification of the financial, academic, and other resources that are required to enroll in different colleges and universities. Students from higher-income families have the resources that enable meaningful choice from among the array of available options nationwide. But, resource constraints and structural failures often limit the "choices" of students from lower-income families to the local or online, non-selective or for-profit postsecondary educational institution (75–76).

Cahalan, Perna, Yamashita, Ruiz, and Franklin document the many ways that rising college costs, along with systematic state and federal disinvestment in higher education and financial aid programs, have made attending college more difficult for poor and middle-class families (see also Goldrick-Rab). These economic factors obviously impact families at the lower end of the economic scale much more significantly than those in upper-income brackets.

As we will see, issues related to class and economic inequality manifest themselves in many surprising and unexpected ways on campuses and in classrooms—and in ways that are not routinely acknowledged in the scholarship devoted to the community college.

Scarcity

We begin our review of this research with Sendhil Mullainathan and Eldar Shafir's work examining the intellectual and emotional effects of "scarcity." Mullainathan and Shafir acknowledge many different types of scarcity that can afflict individuals—involving food, time, companionship, and money—and they use the term "scarcity mindset" to describe the troublesome state of mind created by this condition (19–66). The major focus of their work, however, concerns economic scarcity and poverty. Mullainathan and Shafir theorize scarcity as a kind of intellectual and emotional condition that "changes how we think" (12), compromising cognitive function by using up precious mental "bandwidth" (13). Scarcity, they have found, "affects what we notice, how we weigh our choices, how we deliberate, and ultimately what we decide and how we behave" (12). One product of scarcity is, significantly, "goal inhibition" (31), which makes the pursuit of any kind of long-term goal difficult: "Scarcity creates a powerful goal—dealing with pressing needs—that inhibits other goals and considerations" (31). This is a key finding for those interested in community college students and success rates for long-term goals like degree and program completion.

Mullainathan and Shafir demonstrate how scarcity imposes what they call "a bandwidth tax" on an individual's cognitive capacity, which diminishes "the psychological mechanisms that underlie our ability to solve problems, retain information, engage in logical reasoning, and so on" (47). Mullainathan and Shafir have shown that scarcity impacts both fluid intelligence ("the ability to think and reason abstractly and solve problems independent of any specific learning or experience" [47]) and executive control (our ability to "direct attention, initiate an action, inhibit an intuitive response, or resist an impulse" [53]). They have also found that scarcity reduces functional IQ in clinical tests by a staggering 13 or 14 points (52). It is important to note here that the IQ differentials in these clinical studies were not measured between poor and rich individuals: "Rather, we are comparing how the same person performs under different circumstances. The same person has fewer IQ points when she is preoccupied by scarcity than when she is not. This is key to our story" (32). Applied to poor individuals in real-life settings and in classrooms at community colleges, this means that "Just like the processor that is slowed down by too many applications, the poor here *appear* worse because some of their bandwidth is being used elsewhere" (52).

Speaking about poverty specifically, Mullainathan and Shafir's research revealed that "poverty *itself* taxes the mind" (60). Because poverty reduces fluid intelligence and executive control, "the poor do have lower *effective* capacity than those who are well off. This is not because they are less capable, but rather because part of their mind is captured by scarcity" (60). Using a term borrowed from economics—"bandwidth tax"—they document how scarcity "inhibits our most fundamental capacities" (42). This is a dynamic at play in community college classrooms across the nation, especially in developmental programs among students working many hours each week and coming from families with limited financial resources. A 2017 special report from the Center for Community College Student Engagement, *Making Ends Meet*, provides new information about the alarming level of financial instability among community college students. In the Foreword to this report, Rob Johnstone notes that "this data set provides new connective tissue and insight into students' lives and the ways in which their financial concerns coincide with their academic work and their ability to succeed" (1). Most importantly for our purposes here, the editors conclude that "financial need—however it is measured—correlates with lower educational aspirations" (2). As Ashley A. Smith notes in *Inside Higher Ed*, this report reveals "that nearly half of community college students reported that a lack of finances could cause them to withdraw from their institutions" and that "food, housing and other forms of financial insecurity are a major reason behind students' inability to complete community college" ("Money Woes").

Perhaps even more disturbing is the report from Sara Goldrick-Rab, Jed Richardson, and Anthony Hernandez, *Hungry and Homeless in College: Results from a National Study of Basic Needs Insecurity in Higher Education* (2017). This is largest study of its kind ever conducted about basic needs insecurity among community college students. Goldrick-Rab, Richardson, and Hernandez surveyed 33,000 students in 24 states at 70 community colleges. Their conclusions are sobering, and they help explain why completion rates at community colleges do not match those of four-year, selective admissions institutions. Goldrick-Rab, Richardson, and Hernandez found deep levels of basic needs insecurity in the lives of many community college students:

> We found substantially higher rates of food insecurity among community college students than previously reported, while rates of housing insecurity and homelessness were consistent with prior estimates. Our 2015 report indicated that about half of community college students were food insecure, but this study found that two in three students are food insecure. Both surveys revealed that about half of community college students were housing insecure...
>
> The data presented in this report largely confirm evidence from prior studies, underscoring the need for improvements in policy and practice to support the basic needs security of all undergraduates. Investments in food and housing assistance programs to help community college students complete degrees will yield dividends, helping individuals improve their employment prospects and reducing their need for future support. Such strategies must become priorities of leaders in higher education. (1–2)

Goldrick-Rab, Richardson, and Hernandez also found that "contrary to popular expectations, there appears to be very little geographic variation in hunger and homelessness among community college students. Basic needs insecurity does not seem to be restricted to community colleges in urban areas or to those with high proportions of Pell Grant recipients, and is prevalent in all regions of the country" (1). Anyone who cares about higher education in America must pay careful attention to the conclusions Goldrick-Rab, Richardson, and Hernandez draw from this research, which they provide in the opening sentences of their Executive Summary: "Food and housing insecurity among the nation's community college students threatens their health and wellbeing, along with their academic achievements. Addressing these basic needs is critical to ensuring that more students not only start college, but also have the opportunity to complete degrees" (1).

Mullainathan and Shafir suggest that the cost of this kind of scarcity for individuals is substantial—and often unacknowledged:

> The bandwidth tax changes us in surprising and powerful ways. It is not merely its presence but also its magnitude that is surprising. Psychologists have spent decades documenting the impact of cognitive load on many aspects of behavior. Some of the most important are the behaviors captured in these vignettes [documented in this book]: from distraction and forgetfulness to impulse control. The size of these effects suggests a substantial influence of the bandwidth tax on a full array of behaviors, even those like patience, tolerance, attention, and dedication that usually fall under the umbrella of "personality" or "talent." So much of what we attribute to talent or personality is predicated on cognitive capacity and executive control. (65)

Mullainathan and Shafir suggest that "much of the correlation between income and classroom performance" can be explained by this bandwidth tax (157–163)—mental and physical fatigue, reduction of working memory, and stress caused by scarcity. They suggest that "poverty—the scarcity mindset—causes failure" (155) in the workplace, in the home, and in the classroom. Many of the problems we see in community college classrooms may well be a function of scarcity and the accompanying "failure to follow through, to execute as planned" (169). We will get a chance to test this hypothesis with real students profiled in the final chapter of this section. Scarcity can help produce behaviors that are often puzzling even to seasoned classroom teachers. These include students who do not attend class regularly and are unable to the find time or energy to complete homework and major assignments successfully. The psychology of scarcity predicts that errors like this—not following through, not executing as planned—will be "all too common, perhaps even unavoidable, no matter how motivated the person" (170). In some important ways, students from more affluent families inhabit very different psychological worlds than their less advantaged peers sitting right next to them in classrooms at community colleges.

Paul Tough's recent work on approaches to educating low-income children, which draws on "what we're discovering about brain development, human psychology, and the science of adversity," suggests that an effective new pedagogical approach may now be emerging for this cohort of students ("How" 2016b, 66). This is a development that has significant implications for developmental education reform and community college personnel because it requires a very different kind of classroom approach to teaching than is traditionally used in developmental classes, which often focuses on skill-and-drill instruction (Hern 2011a, b; Rose 2012, 115–142; Hillocks 2002, 1–33). This pedagogy stresses motivation and focuses on what has become known as cooperative learning,

> a pedagogical approach that promotes student engagement in the learning process: less lecture time; fewer repetitive worksheets; more time spent in small groups, solving problems, engaging in discussions, and collaborating on long-term creative projects. (64)

This is a curriculum design that is informed by recent discoveries in science and psychology and is deeply responsive to the psychology of scarcity. It is work that all community college personnel should be familiar with.

32 Million Fewer Words

Another crucial—and until very recently, invisible—variable related to economic inequality and academic achievement is a child's vocabulary. Betty Hart and Todd R. Risley's landmark study, *Meaningful Differences in the Everyday Experience of Young American Children*, published in 1995, documents the way that wealth and class position affect perhaps the most foundational of all academic tools—vocabulary acquisition. Hart and Risley's longitudinal study of 42 American families revealed that children from affluent families develop strikingly more robust vocabularies than children from working-class or poor families. In fact, spoken vocabularies of *children* from professional families were larger than those recorded for the *parents* of families receiving public assistance. Their astonishing finding—that children who grow up in poor families encounter on average 32 million fewer words than children from professional families—obviously has important implications for anyone interested in community colleges and developmental education. Drawing a "linear extrapolation from the averages in the observational data to a 100-hour week (given a 14-hour waking day)," Hart and Risley found that the average child in the professional families [is] provided with 215,000 words of language experience, the average child in a working-class family provided with 125,000, and the average child in a welfare family provided with 62,000 words of language experience. In a 5,200-hour year, the amount would be 11 million words for a child in a professional family, 6 million words for a child in a working-class family, and 3 million words for a child in a welfare family. In 4 years of such experience, an average child in a professional family would have accumulated experience with almost 45 million words, an average child in a working-class family would have accumulated experience with 26 million words, and an average child in a welfare family would have accumulated experience with 13 million words (197–198).

Hart and Risley use phrases like "staggering" (71) and "grave implications" (70) to describe these "massive differences" (70). The implications of this research, of course, are profound and wide-ranging, as Hart and Risley suggest. They note, for example, that vocabulary became for them an effective "dynamic measure of cognitive functioning" (16):

> A vocabulary growth curve provides a direct and continuous measure of a child's intellectual functioning that does not require the hypothetical constructs and statistical assumptions of an IQ test. The growth of the vocabulary in use directly reflects the increasing complexity of the symbols a child learns to manipulate relative to everyday experience. We did not need to infer cognitive growth from monitoring a child's periodic performance on a small set of standardized test items: We could measure learning while it was happening. (16)

This finding confirms Bourdieu and Passeron's claim about "the influence of linguistic capital, particularly manifest in the first years of schooling" (73). A rich and varied vocabulary, as Bourdieu and Passeron point out, allows individuals to "decipher and manipulate complex structures, whether logical or aesthetic" (73)—a key academic skill across all disciplines, of course, as Hart and Risley note. In fact, such massive differences in vocabulary suggest that different cohorts of students inhabit very different cognitive and psychological worlds. If we think especially about college readiness and success in higher education, a rich and varied vocabulary effectively documents familiarity with the world of ideas, abstract thought, and "complex structures" in whatever form they may take. Students in possession of such a vocabulary at a young age have already begun the work of higher learning and preparing for college. While acknowledging that there are many aspects of family life that merit consideration and that help nurture growth, Hart and Risley note that strength of vocabulary may be "most important for the language-based analytic and symbolic competencies upon which advanced education and a global economy depend" (192–3). They also remark on the great value of the "confidence and motivation gained from years of practice and encouragement in manipulating a vocabulary of symbols and using them to solve problems" that professional families provide their children (194).

Another important variable Hart and Risley identified was the cumulative differences between "encouragements" and "discouragements" that children in families from different socioeconomic levels encountered (200). They found that children in professional families received dramatically more encouragements than discouragements (the reverse is true for the poor families they observed), and this encouragement served to provide "affirmative feedback to build the confidence and motivation required for sustained independent effort" (203–204).

A rich, varied vocabulary also equips individuals with the tools to reflect on abstract ideas and pursue sustained trains of thought in ways that will be valued and rewarded in academic settings. As Hart and Risley note, their work predicts the findings of other research on the academic preparation of children for school, which has found, for example, "that in high school many children from families in poverty lack the vocabulary used in more advanced textbooks" (11; Becker 1977). Significantly, vocabulary growth rates were "strongly associated with rates of cognitive growth": "The differences in the size of the children's recorded vocabularies in the two preschool groups were of the same magnitude as the differences in the children's scores on the Peabody Picture Vocabulary Test" (11–12), a standardized instrument to test verbal ability and scholastic aptitude.

In another echo of Bourdieu and Passeron, Hart and Risley found that "the differences in the cultures being transmitted to children through the consistency of what their parents said" (57) to be a significant as well. They found, for example, that educated parents "were transmitting to the next generation an upper-SES [socioeconomic status] culture with its care for politeness and distinctions in status" (58). Bourdieu has written a book on this subject, *Distinction: A Social Critique of the Judgement of Taste*, which examines systems of classification and "the cognitive structures which social agents implement in their practical knowledge of the social world" (468). Bourdieu's book examines the mental structures and symbolic forms that help define and perpetuate class distinctions. Hart and Risley's research may be showing the operation of a similar process at work. Their research suggests, in fact, "the evolution of an increasingly distinct subculture in American society, one in which adults routinely transmit to their offspring the symbolic thinking and confident problem solving that mark the adults' economic activities and that are so difficult for outsiders to acquire in midlife" (204).

Significantly, for those interested in community colleges, Hart and Risley warn that "a trend toward separation into subcultures jeopardizes the upward mobility that has given this nation greatness and presages the tragedy of downward mobility that produces increasing numbers of working poor" (204; Hochschild; Kalleberg; Packer; Vance). For those interested in understanding the real challenges of developmental education, we would do well to consider Hart and Risley's estimate that to "ensure that an average welfare child had a weekly amount of experience equal that of the average child in a working-class family," 41 hours per week of additional out-of-home experience would be required over the course of a number of years (205). Were we to translate this number of hours to developmental reading and writing classes at a community college, students would need to be working, in effect, full time for many *years* in classrooms to offset the advantage enjoyed by children from professional families in terms of vocabulary acquisition. In addition to time on task, such work would have to also focus on "language diversity, affirmative feedback, symbolic emphasis, gentle guidance, and responsiveness" (210). Given the picture that is emerging here, we should be very careful before criticizing modest success rates of developmental education classes nationwide. Impatience with success rates of developmental programs has even bled into public policy, including Connecticut's Public Act 12–40, which by state law limits developmental education to only one developmental course per student. As we will see, this legislation is highly problematic for a number of reasons.

Of course, I don't wish to suggest that growth and development are not possible for students—on the contrary, as a long-time English professor at a community college who has taught basic writing for many decades, I witness academic growth and development every day. Nonetheless, an effective developmental education program must be built around patience, generosity, empathy, and research findings like those we are discussing here. Mullainathan and Shafir suggest that one solution is to build curriculum and programs around multiple points of entry, forgiveness and flexibility and fresh starts (170–1), reducing or assisting with paperwork like financial aid forms (221), and creating "an empathy bridge" between institutions and students from more disadvantaged backgrounds (150). Rather than assuming the problem is "a lack of understanding or of motivation" (169), Mullainathan and Shafir suggest we "design programs structured to be more fault tolerant" (169). Unfortunately, as a nation, we appear to be moving in the opposite direction. The list that Hart and Risley provide for developing more robust vocabularies in young children from financially disadvantaged families—"language diversity, affirmative feedback, symbolic emphasis, gentle guidance, and responsiveness" (210)—would make an excellent pedagogical and philosophical foundation for developmental education programs nationwide.

Parenting Styles

Annette Lareau's study of parenting styles, *Unequal Childhoods: Class, Race, and Family Life*, offers additional insight into the many ways that invisible social forces help determine educational outcomes. Lareau's ethnographic study documents, in fact, the complex process by which social class structures are reproduced and handed down to children by their parents. In many ways, Lareau's work confirms Bourdieu's claims about inequality and social structure. Lareau notes, following Bourdieu, that individuals in a society tend to see unequal social arrangements as "legitimate" and "earned" by individuals (361). They are generally perceived, she suggests, as "resulting from intelligence, talent, effort, and other strategically displayed skills" (361). Lareau's work demonstrates, however, that the situation is much more complex and that individuals in privileged social positions are often "advantaged" in ways that are not the result of intrinsic merit (362). Being careful not to violate "the complexities of family life" and the power of individual agency, Lareau suggests, instead, that "seeing selected aspects of family life as differentiated by social class is simply a better way to understand the reality of American family life" (236). Lareau has found that class position influences "critical aspects of family life," including "time use, language use, and kin ties" (236). Social class, Lareau contends, "does have a powerful impact in shaping the daily rhythms of family life" (8). Her research demonstrates that families in different economic positions clearly share "distinct, life-defining experiences" (8).

Lareau discovered two very different types of parenting styles practiced by families in her study. Middle-class parents practiced what Lareau calls "concerted cultivation." Poor and working-class families practiced what Lareau calls "accomplishment of natural growth" (238–57). These practices, she found, "shape the ways children view themselves in relation to the rest of the world" (4).

The chart included on page 31 of the book—labeled "Typology of Differences in Child Rearing"—provides a convenient, shorthand breakdown of these differences (which are documented in great detail in subsequent chapters). For the child-rearing approach focused on *concerted cultivation*, Lareau found that parents actively fostered and assessed their child's talents, opinions, and skills. The organization of daily life was built around multiple child-leisure activities orchestrated by adults. In such families, language is employed in reasoning and also issuing directives. Parents from these families also allowed children to contest adult statements, which often allowed for extended negotiations between parents and child. Parents also routinely intervened at institutions on behalf of their children, voicing criticisms and engaging in interventions on behalf of their children at institutions (primarily, of course, at school), actively training their child to be advocates for her own interests. Lareau sums up the consequences of this approach to child-reading this way: Children developed an "emerging sense of entitlement" (31).

In the *accomplishment of natural growth* child-rearing approach, practiced by poor and working-class parents, Lareau found that parents allowed their children great freedom to grow and pursue their own interests. The organization of daily life for these families was focused on "hanging out," especially with family and "kin." In terms of language use, Lareau found directives were frequently used, and the questioning or challenging of adults by children was very rare. Generally, children were encouraged to accept and follow the directives of adults. In terms of intervening at institutions, Lareau found that parents from these families depended on and deferred to institutions. They also often expressed a sense of powerlessness and frustration at their inability to intervene effectively for their children. Furthermore, child-rearing practices at home did not always translate effectively to a school context. Lareau sums up the consequences of this approach to child-reading this way: Children developed an "emerging sense of constraint" (31).

Families that Lareau observed using the concerted cultivation approach were often very busy with organized leisure activities and extracurricular events. These activities typically required significant economic resources, of course, resources that most poor and working-class families simply did not have. In one telling example, the Tallinger family, one of the middle-class families Lareau profiles, estimated the cost of their son's extracurricular activities at $4,000 annually (248). Children from middle-class families were also routinely encouraged to interact as equals with adults and authority figures, to shake hands firmly, and look adults and authority figures in the eye (5). It bears repeating that perhaps, not surprisingly, middle-class children in this study "exhibited an emergent version of the *sense of entitlement* characteristic of the middle-class. They acted as though they had a right to pursue their own individual preferences and to actively manage interactions in institutional settings" (6). Significantly, parents of middle-class children navigated the complex world of school much more effectively as advocates for their children than did the parents from poorer families. This is something we see at work at community colleges as well. When poor and first-generation college students struggle, they are much less likely to know how to advocate for themselves than their more advantaged peers. They are also unable to draw on personal or family knowledge about how to navigate the sometimes baffling, complex world of higher education. As Lareau suggests, the concerted cultivation approach to child rearing prepares children to interact in the adult world by training them in "'the rules of the game' that govern interactions with institutional representatives" (6).

Working-class and poor children, in contrast, "despite tremendous economic strain, often have more 'childlike' lives, with autonomy from adults and control over their extended leisure time" (3–4). The accomplishment of natural growth approach to child rearing provides children with a very different and more comparatively carefree childhood experience. This appears to be by design, enacted with the anticipated challenges of economic hardship in adulthood clearly in mind. As Lareau documents, however, having a "childlike" childhood comes at a cost.

Repeatedly throughout the book, Lareau challenges the idea of an "imaginary universe of perfect equality of opportunity." Again and again, she reports that her research reveals an *unlevel* playing field. Here is one such instance among many:

> Public discourse in America typically presents the life accomplishments of a person as the result of her or his individual qualities. Songs like "I Did It My Way," memoirs, television shows, and magazine articles, celebrate the individual. Typically, individual outcomes are connected to individual effort and talent, such as being a "type A" personality, being a hard worker, or showing leadership. These cultural beliefs provide a framework for Americans' views of inequality.
>
> Indeed, Americans are much more comfortable recognizing the power of individual initiative than recognizing the power of social class. Studies show that Americans generally believe that responsibility for their accomplishments rests on their individual efforts. Less than one-fifth see "race, gender, religion, or class as very important for 'getting ahead in life.'" Compared to Europeans, individuals in the United States are much more likely to believe they can improve their standard of living. Put differently, Americans believe in the American dream: "The American dream that we were all raised on is a simple but powerful one—if you work hard and play by the rules, you should

be given a chance to go as far as your God-given ability will take you." This American ideology that each individual is responsible for his or her life outcomes is the expressed belief of the vast majority of Americans, rich and poor.

Yet there is no question that society is stratified. As I show in the next chapter, highly valued resources such as the possession of wealth; having an interesting, well-paying, and complex job; having a good education; and owning a home, are not evenly distributed throughout the society. Moreover, these resources are transferred across generations: One of the best predictors of whether a child will one day graduate from college is whether his or her parents are college graduates. Of course, relations of this sort are not absolute: Perhaps two-thirds of the members of society ultimately reproduce their parents' level of educational attainment, while about one-third take a different path. Still, there is no question that we live in a society characterized by considerable gaps in resources or, put differently, by substantial *inequality*. As I explain in the next chapter, however, reasonable people have disagreed about how best to conceptualize such patterns. They also have disagreed about whether families in different economic positions "share distinct, life-defining experiences." Many insist that there is not a clear, coherent, and sustained experiential pattern. In this book, I demonstrate the existence of a cultural logic of child rearing that tends to differ according to families' social class positions. I see these interweaving practices as coming together in a messy but still recognizable way. In contrast to many, I suggest that social class does have a powerful impact in shaping the daily rhythms of family life. (7–8; see also 233–57; 261–2; 263–311)

Because "access to a good job is now dependent on a college degree," Lareau notes that schools have become a "critical sorting agent for the competitive workforce" (263). Lareau found that "social class provides families with differential resources for complying with school standards" (262). The middle-class parents' interventions, "although often insignificant as individual acts, yielded cumulative advantages" (264). Schools "prioritize and reward particular cultural traits and resources," and "many of these traits are tied to social class standing" (265). A key difference Lareau found sorted by class is language skills, which is a key predictor of academic success (265). Language use will play a crucial role in a child's academic and professional success across her life span for all the obvious reasons. Crucially for our purposes was the focus that middle-class parents gave to the use of language to develop reasoning and negotiating skills (116–20; 190–3; 238–9; 254–5).

Lareau also suggests that the child-rearing practices of the working-class and poor families are built around and a response to, at least in part, a recognition of this *unlevel* playing field. The poor and working-class parents profiled here appear to have a deep appreciation for how hard adulthood is likely to be for their children, and they appear to be attempting to provide their children with some enjoyable childhood years. The difficult challenges of adulthood that await their children appear to be clearly in the mind of many poor and working-class parents, as we see in this passage, which provides perhaps the most succinct (and emotionally powerful) explanation of the sociological and ideological reasoning behind the natural growth approach to parenting, which appears to be tied directly to economic inequality:

> The experiences and concerns that shaped the views of the working-class and poor parents had little in common with those of the middle-class parents. For working-class families, it was the deadening quality of work and the press of economic shortages that defined their experience of adulthood and influenced their vision of childhood. For poor families, it was dependence on public assistance and severe economic shortages that most affected their views about adulthood and childhood. Working-class and poor families had many more worries about basic issues: how to endure food shortages, get children to doctors despite a lack of reliable transportation, purchase clothing, and manage other life necessities. Thinking back over their childhoods, these adults acknowledged periods of hardship but also recalled times without the kinds of worries that troubled them at present. Many appeared to want their own youngsters to spend their time being happy and relaxed. There would be plenty of time for their children to face the burdens of life when they reached adulthood. (249–50)

And those burdens do come. Perhaps the most heartbreaking moment in the second edition of this book (2011) comes when Lareau provides updates for each of the children she studied many years earlier. They are all now well into young adulthood:

> The children of *Unequal Childhoods* have grown up. They are scattered, not only to different cities, but to different positions within our country's system of social stratification. In the five years since I followed up with the study participants, the gaps between them have continued to widen. Garrett Tallinger has recently started a career as an account executive. Alexander Williams is now in medical school. Stacey Marshall has left behind her plan to become a physician and is getting a doctorate in the humanities. Not all of the middle-class youth are professionals: Melanie Handlon is a hair stylist. But in most cases, the educational training of middle-class children has steered them toward spots in the top third of the income distribution. By contrast, none of the working-class and poor youth are employed in the

professional sector. Billy Yanelli is a unionized painter, though he is currently jobless. Wendy Driver is a stay-at-home mom, supported by her husband, who is in the Navy. Harold McAllister is a waiter at a chain restaurant. Tyrec Taylor is looking for work. Katie Brindle, who had moved from cleaning rooms to working at the front desk of a hotel, was laid off with the recession. Her kids are with her ex-husband's parents, and she is now in Florida, working in a nightclub. Some of the working-class and poor youth are content and happy in their lives, but all of them face considerable economic strain. Unlike many youth from middle-class families, their opportunities for advancement are limited.

All parents want the very best for their children. Yet parents do not have the same resources, gifts, or opportunities to give to the children they hold so close to their hearts. As much as the working-class and poor parents loved their children, not one of them was able to set their child firmly on the road to a college degree, the foundation of stable and lucrative employment. These parents were swimming against the tide. Among the girls and boys I studied, crucial pieces of the puzzle were already in place by the time they were ten years old, making it likely that they would end up in situations similar to those of their parents—and most did so. It is not impossible for individuals to significantly change their life position, but it is not common.

In America's meritocratic culture, the idea of a competition implies both fair play and deserved outcomes. The culture suggests that people like Alexander and Garrett study hard in college and are rewarded with good jobs, where they continue to conscientiously apply themselves and, thus, accrue more and bigger rewards. But the fact that many middle-class youth work hard should not blind us to the underlying reality that the system is not fair. It is not neutral. It does not give all children equal opportunities. Not only do schools vary, but in schools and other institutions that sort children into positions in the stratification system, some cultural practices are simply privileged more than others. Our culture's nearly exclusive focus on individual choices renders invisible the key role of institutions. In America, social class backgrounds frame and transform individual actions. The life paths we pursue, thus, are neither equal nor freely chosen. (342–3)

This is a vexing social problem that the modern American community college was designed to address. It is important to note the that poor and working-class parents that Lareau studied "displayed striking levels of pain as they discussed their children's truncated educational careers" (303). One parent was particularly upset over her son's decision to drop out of a community college after just one semester (303). Overall, the poor and working-class parents profiled by Lareau appear to know precisely what is at stake and what the consequences of these truncated educational careers will be.

CHAPTER 24

Different Psychological Worlds, Part 2

NEUROSCIENCE

What Lareau has documented as a sociologist has been confirmed in disturbing ways by neuroscience. A growing number of studies have shown that differences in family background and economic resources appear to affect the development of young children's brains in poor and working-class families in profound ways. This process begins even before birth. A variety of neuroscience researchers have begun to map the differing cognitive capacities created by economic inequality. Cognitive neuroscientist Martha Farah suggests, in fact, that growing up in economically deprived circumstances appears to shape children's brains in ways that also shape their life paths—and also diminishes their chances of ever escaping poverty (Katsnelson 15530). Farah has found, for example, that

> poor children tend to have worse memories than their more affluent peers, in part because of higher levels of stress in poor families. Neuroscience reveals why: One design quirk of the brain is that the hippocampus, a key structure for consolidating memories, happens to be loaded with stress hormone receptors. (Katsnelson 15531)

The emerging picture from neuroscience suggests that the human brain is very responsive to stressful environmental factors and variables, particularly the stress produced by poverty and economic privation. James L. Hanson, Amitabh Chandra, Barbara L. Wolfe, and Seth D. Pollak's research, for example, confirms the link between income and hippocampus development. A recent research study of theirs found that children from lower-income backgrounds had "lower hippocampal gray matter density"—a key variable related to working memory. As we know, working memory is crucial for academic achievement, as it affects a students' ability to focus, remember instructions, and is especially important in math (Klingberg). In fact, Gary W. Evans and Michelle A. Schamberg have found that "childhood poverty is inversely related to working memory in young adults" (6545). Their research documents the operation of neurocognitive or biological mechanisms that "account for income-related deficits in academic achievement" (6545).

Daniel A. Hackman and Martha J. Farah review a variety of recent studies on this subject in which "behavioral, electrophysio-logical and neuroimaging methods have been used to characterize SES [socioeconomic status] disparities in neurocognitive function" and find that socioeconomic status "is an important predictor of neurocognitive performance, particularly of language and executive function, and that SES differences are found in neural processing even when performance levels are equal" (65). Mark M. Kishiyama, W. Thomas Boyce, Amy M. Jimenez, Lee M. Perry, and Robert T. Knight summarize the emerging research findings this way:

> Social inequalities have profound effects on the physical and mental health of children. Children from low socioeconomic status (SES) backgrounds perform below children from higher SES backgrounds on tests of intelligence and academic achievement, and recent findings indicate that low SES (LSES) children are impaired on behavioral measures of prefrontal function. (1106)

It appears that both cognitive capacity and the development of the crucial executive functions of the prefrontal cortex are disrupted by stress and economic hardship. The brain's executive function manages a host of vital academic skills including impulse control, decision-making, encoding and retrieval of memory, verbal fluency, self-monitoring, and planning and prioritizing. Kishiyama, Boyce, Jimenez, Perry, and Knight note that

> children from LSES backgrounds [low socioeconomic status] perform below children from higher SES backgrounds on tests of intelligence, language proficiency, and academic achievement (Bradley & Corwyn, 2002; Duncan, Brooks-Gunn, & Klebanov, 1994). In addition, LSES children are more likely to fail courses, be placed in special education, and drop out of school compared to high SES children (HSES) (McLoyd 1998). (1106)

Even prenatal conditions affect the development of the brain. As Annie Murphy Paul notes in her book, *Origins: How the Nine Months Before Birth Shape the Rest of Our Lives*, "poor children may enter the world already disadvantaged by adversity experienced before birth" (Paul 176; Shonkoff and Phillips). Overall, as Duncan and Murnane have noted,

> Essential properties of most of the brain's architecture are established very early in life by genes and, importantly, early experience. A child's everyday interactions with sights, sounds, and supportive caregivers are important for allowing the brain's wiring to progress appropriately. The brains of children in deprived or traumatic environments often develop differently .... Although it is sometimes possible to remedy problematic early brain development, success in doing so is limited by the shrinking plasticity of the brain as time goes by and the inefficiency with which remediated brain circuitry often operates. ("Introduction" 9)

It is significant to note in this regard that among children "born around 1950, test scores of low-income children lagged behind those of their better-off peers by a little over half a standard deviation, about 60 points on an SAT-type test. Fifty years later, this gap was twice as large" (Duncan and Murnane, "Introduction" 5). As we might expect, this disadvantage associated with economic inequality manifests itself on placement test scores and program and graduation success rates at community colleges.

Early Childhood Caregiving

Early childhood caregiving has also been linked to academic achievement in ways that complement Lareau's research. The research reported in *The Development of the Person: The Minnesota Longitudinal Study of Risk and Adaptation* (Sroufe, Egeland, Carlson, and Collins) has shown that early childhood experiences have an enduring effect on academic achievement well into adulthood. Again, this research reveals the operation of powerful but largely invisible forces shaping individual human lives. This longitudinal study, which was begun in 1975, has now tracked and studied 267 first-time mothers and their children over the entire life-course of these children, from birth into adulthood. Perhaps the most surprising finding produced by this study is the lasting effects of early childhood experiences—especially the care children receive from parents and other caretakers. Many years of research confirm this categorically: "nothing is more important in the development of the child than the care received, including that in the early years" (19).

The Minnesota Longitudinal Study Group found that school success and failure are "hugely influenced by history of care" (21). "Resiliency" in adulthood is also linked closely to childhood caretaking experiences as well (225–229). This research revealed that early childcare, for example, consistently predicted math and reading achievement in later years. L. Alan Sroufe, Byron Egeland, Elizabeth A. Carlson, and W. Andrew Collins explain this remarkable dynamic in relation to "attachment":

> Obviously, connections between early care and later achievement cannot be direct. Having a secure attachment relationship in infancy does not likely change one's "math brain." Rather, we find links through variables such as more regular school attendance, parent involvement with school and schoolwork, and positive child-teacher relationships (Carlson et al., 1999; Jimerson et al. 1999). Regular attendance and ongoing work is required to keep up with math. Such factors probably explain why the correlation between attachment and math achievement is higher than the correlation between attachment and reading comprehension. (187)

Strikingly, Sroufe, Egeland, Carlson, and Collins found that they were able to predict dropping out of high school with "77% accuracy, *using only quality-of-care measures up to age 42 months*" (210; italics in original). The researchers found that early care and early home environment play a pivotal role in a child's long-term development, and this process begins "quite early" and that "psychosocial factors play a critical role" (210; Raby, Roisman, Fraley, and Simpson). Measures of "care, self-esteem, and supportiveness of surrounding context were consistently more powerful than child or maternal IQ in predicting this outcome" (213).

Significantly for our purposes here, this extraordinary longitudinal research study strongly supports a "process" view of human development, rather than a fixed, inborn, "trait" view of human development (227–8; Yates, Egeland, and Stroufe)—one quite similar to Carol Dweck's "growth mindset" formulation, in fact. This means that even IQ itself is "predicted in part by history of care and stimulation in the home" (228)— and is also, crucially, "subject to change in the face of changing support" (228). Functional intelligence appears to be strongly related to such variables as well (228). Even a characteristic like "resilience"—a key trait for these researchers and for anyone interested in understanding success of students at community colleges, especially those in developmental education programs—appears to be learned and adopted as part of a cumulative experiential process:

In the end, we came to view resilience as reflecting developmental process. While it becomes in time a defining feature of some individuals, it is better thought of as the product of the child's experiential history, and ongoing supports and stresses, not as an inherent, immutable characteristic. (227)

Key factors of this developmental process include "measures of care, self-esteem, and supportiveness of surrounding context" (213). In the end, the researchers concede that it is, "on the one hand, discouraging that so many children face so much adversity in the school area; on the other hand, it is encouraging to consider that their problems are not due to inherent limitations" (213). This sentence could serve as a handy shorthand philosophical foundation for developmental education programs at community colleges nationwide. If even characteristics like resilience and functional intelligence are "subject to change in the face of changing support," a well-designed developmental education program can provide such support and the kind of environment that would help nurture these and other qualities.

"Identity Contingencies" and Stereotype Threat

Social psychologists Claude M. Steele and Joshua Aronson first introduced educators to the concept of "stereotype threat"—a destructive form of identity contingency that can subvert academic performance in powerful but largely invisible ways. This form of identity contingency has now been confirmed by hundreds of clinical experiments over many decades by researchers around the world. Stereotype threat, Steele explains in his book on this subject, *Whistling Vivaldi*, springs from "our human powers of intersubjectivity—the fact that as members of society we have a pretty good idea of what other members of our society think about lots of things, including the major groups and identities in society" (5). This means that

> whenever we're in a situation where a bad stereotype about one of our own identities could be applied to us—such as those about being old, poor, rich, or female—we know it. We know what "people could think." We know that anything we do that fits the stereotype could be taken as confirming it. And we know that, for that reason, we could be judged and treated accordingly. (5)

Steele has documented the many ways that these "unrecognized" factors in our lives have contributed "to some of our most vexing personal and societal problems" (11). Again, we find ourselves acknowledging the presence of largely invisible social factors creating different psychological worlds for individuals and affecting educational achievement in powerful ways.

Steele began his professional career in the mid-1980s, attempting to ascertain why African American students at the University of Michigan, while equally prepared to succeed in college as other cohorts of students, consistently struggled academically. For Steele, this was part of a larger, "familiar" problem: "the academic struggles of too many minority students on American college campuses" (17). It seemed to Steele that "something about the social and psychological aspects of their experience [on campus] was likely involved" (20). Mindful of Jones and Nisbett's work on perception, Steele sought to move beyond the "observer's perspective" and to embrace the "actor's perspective" on these campuses—by studying "the students themselves, their motivations, expectations, self-esteem, cultural orientation; the value they placed on education; their work habits; their academic skills and knowledge; their families' emphasis on school achievement; and so forth" (17). As he talked to students, seeking to develop a deeper understanding of their lived experience on campus, he discovered that "they said nothing about expectations, motivation, the value their families placed on education—not even when I pointedly asked them about these things" (18). Instead, they talked mostly about the college environment:

> They talked about being a small social minority. They described needing a space where they weren't made so aware of being a minority. They worried that teaching assistants, fellow students, and even faculty might see their academic abilities as less than those of other students. They described how social life was organized by race, ethnicity, social class. They had few close friends across group lines. They felt that black styles, preferences, and interests were marginalized on campus, sometimes even stigmatized. They noted the small number of black or minority faculty. (19)

Some of Steele's earliest experimental work focused on women and math proficiency, revealing the strong presence of identity threat when women were put in situations where they might confirm the stereotype that they were not as capable as men in math. This stereotype threat—one's gender identity in math-related settings—created significant under-performance among women in clinical experiments. Steele subsequently expanded his research to include Latinos, Native Americans, and African Americans and found that in social situations that threaten an aspect of one's social identity, stereotype threat "impairs performance and other actions by interfering with our thinking" (121). As Jane Elliott famously demonstrated in her classroom exercise segregating brown-eyed and blue-eyed high school students, stigmatized students do poorly academically (Elliott). They don't pay attention. They sit in the back. They don't remember instructions. They are hesitant to respond. They perform poorly when given tests. The same individuals performed differently, however, depending on which group they were placed into and whether they were stigmatized or not. Each of the groups—the brown-eyed and blue-eyed—spent one day in class as part of the stigmatized group and their behavior and academic performance changed dramatically according to which group they were arbitrarily placed into. Elliott's key finding is also a key finding in Steele's research: "the environment, and their status in it, seemed to be an actual component of their ability" (Steele 28).

Steele has discovered that places such as classrooms, college campuses, and sites where standardized tests are administered are "different places for different people" (60). Steele's work thus complicates our understanding of neoliberal ideas about choice, individual freedom, and personal responsibility. Steele notes that in America,

> we stress individuality. We resist seeing ourselves as circumscribed by social identities—our being older, black, white male, religious, politically liberal, and so on. This is probably a good resistance. It pushes us beyond the constraints of identity. Still, our research was revealing a profound importance of social identity: that the contingencies that go with them in specific places at specific times, while often subtle enough to be beneath our awareness, can nonetheless significantly affect things as important as our intellectual functioning. (61)

In the chapter entitled "The Mind on Stereotype Threat: Racing and Overloaded" (114–33), Steele documents through clinical trials the many subtle but often cumulatively significant ways that individuals responding to stereotype threat increase their "cognitive load" (122), reduce their working memory (123), and activate different parts of the brain—heightening activity in the neural region "associated with social and emotional processing (ventral anterior cingulate cortex)" (125).

Much like Mullainathan and Shafir, Steele posits a kind of intellectual, emotional, and psychological stereotype "tax" (127) produced by these stereotypes. This manifests itself in ways that can inhibit academic achievement for young men and women in primary and secondary schools and on college campuses, and it can also exact more cumulative, long-term costs as well: "if people are under threats from stereotypes or other identity contingencies for long periods, they may pay a tax. The persistent extra pressure may undermine their sense of well-being and happiness, as well as contribute to health problems caused by prolonged exposure to the physiological effects of the threat" (127). This is the "mysterious link" (16–43) between identity and intellectual performance that Steele has devoted his career to understanding. Steele concludes by suggesting that all of us are likely to be victims of identity threat at one point or another in our lives: "identity threat of the sort that has been shown to affect the intellectual performance of women and blacks is likely a general phenomenon that, in some form or another, in some situation or another, can affect anyone. There exists no group on earth that is not negatively stereotyped in some way" (88).

Steele also offers advice to educators that should be of value to anyone interested in community colleges, especially in light of the incredible diversity of our student body. Here is how Steele summarizes his lifetime of work:

> Poor college performance has many causes, and the Massey team concluded [in *The Source of the River: The Social Origins of Freshmen at America's Selective Colleges and Universities*] that black and Latino students faced more such "causes" than their white and Asian counterparts. They were less likely to come from a two-parent home; their families were more likely to experience a distracting level of violence and trauma while the student was in college; these students were more likely to come from segregated backgrounds that gave them less access to the cultural knowledge and know-how that go into good college performance; the money they needed for college was a higher percentage of their family income; they were less likely to have gone to a high school with Advanced Placement courses; their precollege friendship networks were less likely to have been focused on college achievement; and so on.
>
> Such findings show how disadvantages tied to race, class, and ethnicity—contingencies of identity, if you will—outside of college, extract a toll on performance in college. These students face "a thousand bites," as Massey put it. Still, like all of the Mellon studies, these studies found that stereotype threat had an undermining effect on college achievement that was in addition to the effect of those other disadvantages. This is a poignant fact. It means that even when black, Latino, and Native American students overcome other disadvantages in trying to gain parity with white and Asian

classmates, they face the further pressure of stereotype and identity threats. Even privileged students from these groups have an extra, identity-related pressure working against their achievement. (158–9)

If stereotype threat can be so debilitating for even economically privileged and very well-prepared African American, Latino, and Native American college students—challenging the sense that they "belong" in college—imagine the many ways these kinds of identity contingencies might affect the performance and overall perseverance of students who do not have that same level of preparation or family support, who may be first-generation college students, and may have a lingering and debilitating sense that they "don't belong" in college.

State and Federal Housing Policies

State and federal housing policies can also be regarded as a significant variable that can affect community college student achievement and create different psychological worlds for different cohorts of students. Richard Rothstein has done important work documenting the many ways that government policies have helped create segregated neighborhoods in America—and the segregated school systems that have developed along with them. Douglas S. Massey, Camille Z. Charles, Garvey F. Lundy, and Mary J. Fischer summarize their research on segregation and its effects on education in their book, *The Source of the River*, this way: whether or not individuals "experienced safe schools and neighborhoods and attended high-quality schools with good teachers and supportive staff depended on whether they grew up under integrated or segregated circumstances" (203). As Linda Darling-Hammond notes in her Foreword to *Surpassing Shanghai: An Agenda for American Education Built on the World's Leading Systems*,

> Both segregation of schools and inequality in funding have increased [in America] over the last two decades, leaving a growing share of African American and Latino students in highly segregated apartheid schools that lack qualified teachers, up-to-date textbooks and materials, libraries, science labs and computers, and safe adequate facilities. (xi)

Rothstein's essay, "The Making of Ferguson," provides a powerful case study of this largely invisible dynamic at work in Ferguson, Missouri, a suburb of St. Louis that erupted into violence in 2014 after a police officer shot and killed Michael Brown, an unarmed black teenager. Rothstein examines the many ways that government policies actively helped shape the neighborhoods in St. Louis and "segregated our metropolitan landscape" nationally (2). Although most of these policies are no longer on the books and "seemingly have been reformed," Rothstein demonstrates that they "still cast a long shadow" over the lives of Americans (4). These policies include racial zoning (see Fig. 24.1 below, drawn from Rothstein's essay), segregated public housing, restrictive real estate covenants (clauses attached to property deeds to prevent African Americans from moving into neighborhoods), subsidization of suburban development for whites only (through, among other things, policies set by the Federal Housing Administration [FHA] for new home mortgages), annexation, spot zoning, expulsive zoning, incorporation, redevelopment (and the use of eminent domain), urban renewal and redevelopment programs, and regulatory

Fig. 24.1 A 1916 leaflet promoting a voter referendum to segregate St. Louis. This referendum was approved
(*Source*: Richard Rothstein, "The Making of Ferguson" (8). Photo reproduced with permission from the Missouri History Museum Library and Research Center)

support of policies in the real estate and financial sectors that promoted segregation (these include blockbusting and racial steering). In 1970, a report completed for the US Commission on Civil Rights identified government agencies themselves as actively fostering segregation:

> Federal programs of housing and urban development not only have failed to eliminate the dual housing market, but have had the effect of perpetuating and promoting it .... HUD has failed to carry out [its] affirmative obligations [to prevent discrimination] and has permitted its programs to be operated in a discriminatory manner in the St. Louis metropolitan area .... As long as HUD continues to condone the discriminatory activities of the local housing and home finance industry—public and private—there is little hope of relief for black families from the existing system of separate and unequal housing conditions. (qtd. in Rothstein 24)

Rothstein's essay chronicles the conversion of towns such as Ferguson into "segregated enclaves" (31). These state and federal policies helped create some of the most intractable social problems at work in America today, which continue to affect academic achievement in grades K-14 among large cohorts of students. In some very real ways, this is an example of "the past devouring the future," to borrow one of Piketty's more ominous phrases about economic inequality (571). As Rothstein suggests,

> Media accounts of how Ferguson became Ferguson have typically explained that when African Americans moved to this suburb (and others like it), "white flight" followed, abandoning the town to African Americans who were trying to escape poor schools in the city. The conventional explanation adds that African Americans moved to a few places like Ferguson, not the suburbs generally, because prejudiced real estate agents steered black homebuyers away from other white suburbs. And in any event, those other suburbs were able to preserve their almost entirely white, upper-middle-class environments by enacting zoning rules that required only expensive single family homes, the thinking goes.
> No doubt, private prejudice and suburbanites' desire for homogenous affluent environments contributed to segregation in St. Louis and other metropolitan areas. But these explanations are too partial, and too conveniently excuse public policy from responsibility. A more powerful cause of metropolitan segregation in St. Louis and nationwide has been the explicit intents of federal, state, and local governments to create racially segregated metropolises. (1)

Rothstein provides a comprehensive review of the history of these government activities, which continue to exert a powerful influence in our lives.

Matthew Desmond's harrowing ethnographic study of poor families in Milwaukee, *Evicted: Poverty and Profit in the American City,* documents the many ways that housing plays a key role in the lives of the poor. It is a complex story, and Desmond makes it clear that affordable housing is a pressing equity and social justice issue in America. "Eviction," he demonstrates, "is a cause, not just a condition, of poverty" (299). Desmond also documents the many ways that

> residential stability begets a kind of psychological stability, which allows people to invest in their home and social relationships. It begets school stability, which increases the chances that children will excel and graduate. And it begets community stability, which encourages neighbors to form strong bonds and take care of their block. (296)

Home, he suggests, is where hope begins (293–313). Desmond makes a compelling case that "public initiatives that provide low-income families with decent housing they can afford are among the most meaningful and effective anti-poverty programs in America" (302). Housing and residential stability obviously affect academic achievement in profound ways. This is another invisible and yet very powerful social variable that comes into play on campuses at community colleges and helps create different psychological worlds for students.

First-Generation College Students

Many first-generation college students also find the college environment intimidating and often baffling, and this often affects their performance and persistence (Mitchell; Chen; Choy). This culture shock can manifest itself in a variety of ways and in various degrees of virulence, from mild discomfort to outright panic and defeat. Navigating this strange new world of higher education often complicates and draws precious energy away from a student's focus on daily responsibilities like completing homework, maintaining momentum on long-term academic projects, and continuing to make satisfactory progress toward earning a degree or a certificate. The language and conventions of college—including how to register or withdraw from a class, what to do when classes are cancelled, why one might wish to meet with an advisor, the availability of additional help at places like a

Writing Center or a Counseling Center, navigating financial aid paperwork and bureaucracy, and even understanding such terms as "GPA" and "office hours"—essentially constitute a new culture that first-generation college students must seek to understand and assimilate into. Strong feelings of anxiety and alienation often accompany this process. Richard Rodriquez and Mike Rose have written eloquently about this subject. Rodriguez's *The Hunger of Memory* and Rose's *Lives on the Boundary* are stirring testimonials about the fraught and complex challenges first-generation students face when they attend college. New college students who have a parent or a sibling who can guide them through this acculturation process have a decided advantage, indeed, over those who do not. Because 36 percent of students who attend community colleges are first-generation college students (AACC "Fast Facts"), those who seek to understand the community college must acknowledge the special challenges faced by first-generation students. Xianglei Chen and C. Dennis Carroll sum things up in their National Center for Education Statistics report on this subject this way:

> Recent research has generated a large body of knowledge about students who are the first members of their families to attend college (referred to as "first-generation students" in this report). The results show that such students are at a distinct disadvantage in gaining access to postsecondary education. Even those who overcome the barriers and do enroll have difficulty remaining enrolled and attaining a degree. (iii)

The research that Chen and Carroll review indicates that first-generation college students are more likely to need remedial help and not persist, bring lower educational expectations with them to college than other cohorts of students (see also Choy), and are more likely to work while in college and live off campus. Perhaps not surprisingly, first-generation students also "did not perform as well as their peers whose parents were college graduates" (vii). Perhaps predictably given these various contingencies that are crucial for our understanding of the community college, first-generation college students are less likely than students with college-educated parents to earn a bachelor's degree:

> The findings from this report indicate that compared with students whose parents attended college, first-generation students consistently remained at a disadvantage after entering postsecondary education: they completed fewer credits, took fewer academic courses, earned lower grades, needed

more remedial assistance, and were more likely to withdraw from or repeat courses they attempted. As a result, the likelihood of attaining a bachelor's degree was lower for first-generation students compared to their peers whose parents attended college. This finding also held after taking into account variables related to degree completion including postsecondary credit production, performance, high school academic preparation, and student background characteristics. Even for students who attended a 4-year institution with the intention of earning a bachelor's degree, first-generation students were less likely to earn a bachelor's degree than were their counterparts whose parents held a bachelor's or higher degree. (ix)

This is another example of the role that largely invisible variables can play in the performance and success of students attending community colleges.

FAMILY RESOURCES AND ACADEMIC SUCCESS

Finally, few data sets confirm the validity of Bourdieu's theories about social capital more powerfully than the continued presence of the economic achievement gap in American education (Rothstein *Class*; United States, *Achievement Gaps: How Black and White Students in Public Schools Perform;* United States, *Achievement Gaps: How Hispanic and White Students in Public Schools Perform*). Since the publication of the Coleman Report in 1966, educators have known that academic success tracks closely with family resources. As Frederick Mosteller and Daniel P. Moynihan suggest, the goal of this committee's work was to go beyond "common sense" solutions and employ "more complex forms of diagnosis" (3) of differences in educational attainment. It is commonly agreed that the findings of this report

> constitute the most powerful empirical critique of the myths (the unquestioned basic assumptions, the socially received beliefs) of American education ever produced. It is the most important source of data on the sociology of American education yet to appear. It was the most complex analysis ever made of educational data in such quantity. (Mosteller and Moynihan 5)

James S. Coleman and his committee tested 570,000 students and consulted with 60,000 teachers and described the facilities of some 4000 schools (Mosteller and Moynihan 5). Ron Haskins and Isabel Sawhill note that this discovery about class and family resources, while initially controversial, has now been widely embraced:

> One of the most famous and widely examined studies in the history of education research, the Coleman Report of 1966, concludes that family background is a more potent influence on school achievement than any measure of the school environment itself, including per pupil expenditures. That conclusion was mightily resisted by the educational establishment, but the basic finding has been replicated so many times that the immense influence of the family on child development and school achievement is now a settled issue, although more recent studies find factors within the school that have impacts on student achievement. (126)

This work and research has, indeed, been updated and reaffirmed, perhaps nowhere more compellingly than in Duncan and Murnane's book, *Whither Opportunity?: Rising Inequality, Schools, and Children's Life Chances* (2011). As the research reported in this volume makes abundantly clear, while we are making some progress related to our race-related achievement gap, our income achievement gap has been growing steadily for many years. As Sean Reardon, one of the contributors to this volume, demonstrates, "the achievement gap between children from high- and low-income families is roughly 30 to 40 percent larger among children born in 2001 than among those born twenty-five years earlier. In fact, it appears that the income achievement gap has been growing steadily for at least fifty years" (93). Reardon notes that rising income inequality, differential investments in children's cognitive development, and increased segregation by income continue to drive and broaden this achievement gap. Reardon concludes his survey of these data with a chilling conclusion: "The combination of these trends creates a feedback mechanism that may decrease intergenerational mobility. As the children of the rich do better in school, and those who do better in school are more likely to become rich, we risk producing an even more unequal and economically polarized society" (111).

Linda Darling-Hammond also finds that a huge "opportunity gap—the accumulated differences in access to key educational resources" is still actively at work in America (*Flat* 28). Darling-Hammond finds that this gap continues to be a function of class and race. In some ways, her book, *The Flat World and Education*, can be read simply as a contemporary updating of the Coleman Report. As Darling-Hammond notes, because we have made some visible progress related to diversity in recent decades, this has lead "many to assume that inequality has been eliminated from the national landscape" (29). Darling-Hammond documents the many ways this is emphatically not the case. Her overall assessment of the condition of American education sounds like it could have been drawn from the Truman Commission Report itself: "While the highest achieving nations are making steep, strategically smart investments in education, the United States is squandering much of its human capital" (25). Darling-Hammond urges Americans "to take the education of poor children as seriously as we take the education of the rich" and "to create systems that *guarantee* all of the elements of educational investment routinely to all children" (279; italics in the original).

Figures of Speech

Free market theorists like Hayek and Friedman champion the "invisible hand" of the market as the primary mechanism that produces opportunity, political freedom, and wealth for individuals. The focus on freedom runs deep in all of this work, and the picture of free market capitalism that emerges from it is of a noble and self-sustaining, self-correcting system that provides opportunity for all and operates best when left free from government intervention. What we see documented in the research reviewed in these two chapters are significant, systemic "unfreedoms" produced by this same system. In some important ways, this is the darker side of the "invisible hand," by which the interests of entrenched power and wealth perpetuate themselves across generations.

It is important to note here, of course, that the figures of speech economists use to characterize economic systems play a crucial role in how we perceive them and how well (or how poorly or incompletely or selectively) we understand how they work. As Donald N. McCloskey notes in his book on this subject, *The Rhetoric of Economics*, "Figures of speech are not mere frills. They think for us" (xvii). As we have seen, a key figure of speech for both Hayek and Friedman is the role that luck and "chance" play in the lives of individuals in a market economy. In some ways, this is an existential acknowledgment of the role of chance and luck in our lives, an idea that has a distinguished literary tradition stretching as far back as the Book of Job and Ecclesiastes and which finds perhaps its greatest expression in Boethius's medieval masterpiece, *The Consolation of Philosophy*. More recently, Nassim Nicholas Taleb has produced two highly regarded, book-length studies of the role of luck and chance in economics: *Fooled by Randomness: The Hidden Role of Chance in Life and in the Markets* and *The Black Swan: The Impact of the Highly Improbable*.

Hayek characterizes the operation of the free market as a combination of chance and choice, and he suggests that "in competition chance and good luck are often as important as skill and foresight in determining the fate of different people" (*Road* 134). Milton and Rose Friedman offer a similar kind of assessment using an identical figure of speech, suggesting that

> Chance determines our genes and through them affects our physical and mental capacities. Chance determines the kind of family and cultural environment into which we are born and as a result our opportunities to develop our physical and mental capacity. Chance determines also other resources we may inherit from our parents or other benefactors. Chance may destroy or enhance the resources we start with. (21–22)

As theorized by Hayek and Friedman, "chance" in a free market economy is produced by independent, random variables that are beyond the control of any individual. Chance is theorized here in very traditional ways—as the equivalent, say, of a flip of a coin, a roll of the dice, or a turn of Fortune's wheel. That is to say absolutely random. Figures of speech can reveal and communicate important insights into complex systems and ideas. They can also be used to obfuscate and hide essential or inconvenient truths. One of the most important and reliable dynamics of a coin flip as a metaphor for "chance," for example, is its absolute unpredictability. No matter how many times one flips a coin, the chances of it coming up heads or tails are always 50 percent, regardless of past history. One is just as likely to be a winner as a loser each time the coin is flipped. Each coin toss is an independent event.

Unfortunately, this does not appear to have ever been the case in free market economies. It is not a system of pure chance and choice in which every moment is independent of every previous moment. As we have seen, and has Thomas Piketty has exhaustively demonstrated, some individuals are much more likely to be winners in this system, and some are much more likely to be losers. In fact, the figure of speech that perhaps best captures what the body of research we have reviewed so far demonstrates is the "stacked deck"—a figure of speech drawn from card-playing whereby the chances of an individual against whom the deck is stacked are much less appealing than 50/50 (Reich xii). The chances of individuals who have the deck stacked in their favor are, of course, much more attractive. Here, we can return again to Bourdeau's seminal critique of neoliberalism's "imaginary universe of perfect competition" and "perfect equality of opportunity":

> It is what makes the games of society—not least, the economic game—something other than simple games of chance offering at every moment the possibility of a miracle. Roulette, which holds out the opportunity of winning a lot of money in a short space of time, and therefore of changing one's social status quasi-instantaneously, and in which the winning of the previous spin of the wheel can be staked and lost at every new spin, gives a fairly accurate image of this imaginary universe of perfect competition or perfect equality of opportunity, a world without inertia, without accumulation, without heredity or acquired properties, in which every moment is perfectly independent of the previous one, every soldier has a marshal's baton in his knapsack, and every prize can be attained, instantaneously, by everyone, so that at each moment anyone can become anything. Capital, which, in its objectified or embodied forms, takes time to accumulate and which, as a potential capacity to produce profits and to reproduce itself in identical or expanded form, contains a tendency to persist in its being, is a force inscribed in the objectivity of things so that everything is not equally possible or impossible. And the structure of the distribution of the different types and subtypes of capital at a given moment in time represents the immanent structure of the social world, i.e., the set of constraints, inscribed in the very reality of that world, which govern its functioning in a durable way, determining the chances of success for practices. ("Forms" 81)

The figure of speech related to "chance" has been a key linchpin for economists like Hayek and Friedman as they have engaged in promoting a nobler, simpler version of the free market to a broad public audience. Unfortunately, this figure of speech does a certain kind of thinking for us, as McCloskey suggests, and also, conveniently and crucially, obviates other kinds of thinking as well. Such a figure of speech actively hinders more complex forms of diagnosis and may actually prevent individuals from even *seeing* certain unsavory and troubling aspects of the free market because they can be dismissed simply and fatalistically as the workings of chance and luck—and beyond human control. There are some aspects of building a strong free market economy and a strong democracy that are, indeed, beyond our control. There are many others, however, that are certainly within our control and that have been—and always will be—responsive to thoughtful public policy.

As much as we may wish to believe otherwise, success in college has always been and perhaps always will be, to a significant degree, a function of class position and family resources. Open admissions institutions and developmental curriculum were created to help combat and offset these kinds of long-standing, structural inequalities. As David

Arendale has noted, developmental courses and other types of learning assistance programs are one of the primary ways we have attempted to address this problem:

> Certain groups of students bring less social capital with them to college—students from low socioeconomic backgrounds, first-generation college students, and historically underrepresented students of color. Learning assistance services, especially developmental courses, are essential for overcoming disadvantaged backgrounds. (2)

It is not just reading, writing, and math skills that we are attempting to address in community college developmental classrooms. We are also attempting to address a whole host of other structural factors—cultural, social, psychological, and economic—that determine success in classrooms.

While we see the power of education to transform lives demonstrated every day on community college campuses, we must also keep in mind the many advantages that family resources confer on the children from affluent families. Students from these families are going to be successful at a greater statistical rate than children from less advantaged families for all the reasons we have documented here. To compare the graduation rates of these different cohorts of students is to perpetuate one of the most compelling and attractive myths about American education—that education is a level playing field and that everyone can succeed if only they can make good choices, work hard, and take responsibility for their own successes and failures. The research that we have surveyed in these chapters suggests, instead, that the actual field conditions in classrooms across America, grades K-14, are much more complicated than that. Good public policy must recognize the imposing complexity of this problem and actively resist quick fixes and simplistic solutions to these complicated conditions. The key lesson here is that we must be very cautious, indeed, as we seek to "untangle the complicated teleology of success or failure in higher education" (Massey, Charles, Lundy, and Fischer 197).

James Coleman's formulation about this subject is one of the most eloquent ever voiced: "the effectiveness of schools in creating equality of educational opportunity lies in making the conditional probabilities of success less conditional" (qtd. in Mosteller and Moynihan 19). This is precisely what the Truman Commission identified as "democracy's unfinished business." The first step in this process must be developing a fuller understanding of the nature and scope of these conditional probabilities.

We have attempted to survey some of the most salient of these in these chapters. In the following chapter, we will examine how these factors come into play in the actual lives of real community college students. Our focus, in fact, will be on a group of students who tested at the lowest levels of Connecticut's community college statewide placement test. For a few perilous months, these students were in jeopardy of being turned away entirely from our open admissions institution.

CHAPTER 25

"Ideas About Human Possibilities": Connecticut's PA 12–40 and Developmental Education in the Era of Neoliberalism

In this chapter, we examine how the many different variables discussed in Chaps. 23 and 24 can come into play in the actual lives of real community college students. In fact, this group of students provides professionals interested in questions related to open access, community colleges, and higher education a unique opportunity to reflect on key questions for our profession and our nation, framed and embodied by very real people with unique life histories. As historian Tony Holt has suggested,

> Stories have power. The power to change things. Thus history is not dead but alive, alive in the sense that our collective memory is what provides the starting points for understanding our contemporary world. Alive also in the sense that through these narratives we make accessible certain ideas about human possibilities and foreclose others. (11)

Had the open door at Connecticut community colleges been closed, these students would have been turned away. Let's meet some of them and hear their stories at this historic moment in the history of higher education—our first cohort of theoretically "undeserving" students.

Connecticut's PA 12–40

In 2012, the State of Connecticut enacted landmark legislation that remade developmental education in our state. This new law, Public Act 12–40, dramatically changed the way remedial education was theorized, designed, and delivered at our community colleges and regional state universities (the University of Connecticut was not affected by this legislation). This legislation drew considerable national attention (Fain; Bailey, Hughes, and Jaggars), and it appears to have inspired similar legislation in Florida, Tennessee, and other states (Crandall and Soares; Hassel, Klausman, Giordano, O'Rourke, Roberts, Sullivan, and Toth; Turk, Nellum, and Soares). Impatient with very modest graduation rates among students who require remedial assistance in English and math, this legislation took the bold step of mandating an accelerated approach to developmental education, requiring all colleges in the system—twelve community colleges and four state universities—to offer a maximum of one semester of remedial work for any student requiring additional preparation for college. Furthermore, colleges were required to offer developmental students who were deemed "likely to succeed in college level work with supplemental support" the opportunity to enroll in a first-year composition class that provided embedded support, following the Peter Adams co-requisite model pioneered at the Community College of Baltimore County (Connecticut 1; Adams, Gearhart, Miller, and Roberts; Cho, Kopko, Jenkins, and Jaggars). As one might expect, there was considerable debate and controversy about this legislation, especially during the two years between the passage of the bill in 2012 and the required implementation date of fall 2014. During the two years given to college personnel before the required implementation date, English teachers at Connecticut's colleges and regional state universities set busily to work researching, designing, and piloting new remedial programs for students. At this moment, we are now four years into this radical experiment of redesigning a state's approach to developmental education by legislative mandate. Because of the complexity of this task and the many unanswered questions about pedagogy that have arisen during this process (some of which go back a long way in the history of basic reading and writing instruction), it appears that developmental curriculum in Connecticut will likely to be a work in progress for many years to come.

One of the most controversial features of this legislative movement was that it appeared to establish a "floor" for matriculation into open admissions institutions in Connecticut—thereby effectively abandoning students who scored below certain cutoff scores (at or below the eighth grade level on our standardized placement test).[1] To many, this meant that we were, in effect, closing the open door at Connecticut community colleges and forsaking both the historic mandate of the Truman Commission and our work addressing "democracy's unfinished business." As we have seen, a significant focus of this mandate was offsetting economic inequality:

The old, comfortable idea that "any boy can get a college education who has it in him" simply is not true. Low family income, together with the rising costs of education, constitutes an almost impassable barrier to college education for many young people. For some, in fact, the barrier is raised so early in life that it prevents them from attending high school even when free public high schools exist near their homes. (Zook 1947, 28)

If "education is the making of the future" (Zook 1947, 6), as the Truman Commission suggested, then

Perhaps its [education's] most important role is to serve as an instrument of social transition, and its responsibilities are defined in terms of the kind of civilization society hopes to build. (Zook 6)

Unfortunately, as Chris Mullin reports in a brief for the American Association of Community Colleges (AACC), "In policy conversations, especially those concerned with policies related to access and choice, there is a silent movement to redirect educational opportunity to 'deserving' students" (4). The initial idea when PA 12–40 was enacted was to remand these underprepared students to regional remediation centers and adult education programs off campus. After considerable debate and much public outcry, this position was softened, and colleges have now been allowed to develop regional "transitional strategies" for such students (Connecticut State). By state law, these strategies must be offered at little or no cost and cannot involve a student's financial aid.

As English teachers in the state of Connecticut got to work responding to PA 12–40, meetings and brainstorming sessions were conducted statewide over the course of two years as we talked about how we might operationalize this new approach to teaching basic reading and writing. During this time, community colleges across the state implemented a variety of transitional strategies courses for our most underprepared students. Some of these strategies relied on existing adult education programs in local towns. Some relied on software programs that focused primarily on the development of reading skills, with the goal of helping students earn better scores on Accuplacer and thus help them test into an approved developmental class. Others, like the one I eventually offered, were more ambitious.

The English department at my home institution, MCC, set forth designing, testing, and implementing a new developmental program over the course of these two years, and as it turned out, I designed the transitional strategies curriculum for our college. This class eventually became English 9000, a "boot camp" course that was provided free of charge and was designed to help students transition into one of our basic reading and writing classes. The development of this course required a great deal of research and discussion, and it occasioned considerable debate among my colleagues in the English department. I offered this class, English 9000, for the first time in the fall of 2014. It was offered free to students. Required textbooks were also purchased for students, funded by a grant to our town's adult education program. The class had an enrollment cap of 20 students, and by the time the course began in late August, it was full. Students who earned a 90 or below on their combined Accuplacer Reading Comprehension and Sentence Skills tests and had taken our challenge essay were advised to register for this class. Each of these students met with a counselor or an advisor to confirm that this was an appropriate placement.

English 9000 was a fascinating course to teach. There were certainly many surprises, and the three of us who taught this class—myself plus two embedded tutors—greatly enjoyed the time we spent with the remarkable group of students in this class. It was a very powerful professional experience for me, bringing a deeply moving human dimension to all sorts of abstract academic questions about opportunity, access, and the ideal of open admissions institutions—even for someone like me, who has taught for many years at a community college and has taught a wide variety of developmental education classes during this time. The students in this class were certainly underprepared for college-level work, but they were also capable of learning—and many did learn enough to move on to one of our two developmental course offerings (which are two versions of the same course: English 93, a traditional three-credit basic reading and writing class and English 96, a six-credit version of English 93, which offers students three additional hours of class time and embedded support). As readers may know, we have all kinds of research now—from neuroscience (Kandel, Schwartz, Jessell, Siegelbaum, and Hudspeth; Doidge; Healy), from studies of IQ and intelligence (Nisbett, Aronson, Blair, Dickens, Flynn, Halpern, and Turkheimer), from psychologists studying the power of social-psychological interventions (Yeager and Walton), from research on how people learn (Bransford, Pellegrino, and Donovan), and from Carol Dweck on "mindsets"—which has shown that intellectual and academic ability is not "fixed." On the contrary, it can be developed under the right conditions. Students who test poorly on placement tests and enroll at community colleges typically bring with them rich and often non-traditional life histories that have helped shape both what they have learned and how they approach the academic enterprise. Much of this has been determined by class position and family resources. This does not mean, however, that students who score weakly on college placement tests can't learn or that their cause is hopeless. Under the right conditions, most students can learn and make progress. The key concern for developmental educators and the legislators who fund these programs, of course, is establishing the right conditions, which must take into account a host of variables—both in and outside of the classroom—that are often actively at work in the lives of very underprepared students.

Curriculum design for developmental courses, which is especially pivotal for students from disadvantaged backgrounds, is a crucial variable here, as Paul Tough and others have suggested (Hassel and Giordano "Blurry"; Hassel and Giordano "First-Year"; Hassel, Klausman, Giordano, O'Rourke, Roberts, Sullivan, and Toth). It is one of the key factors that can help establish the right conditions for students in developmental education classes. There is an emerging consensus in the professional literature on this subject that developmental students need a rich curriculum, full of interesting ideas, engaging readings, and some of the real work of college (Rose, *Back* 115–42; Hern "Unleashing"; Hern "Window"). Both Peter Adams's Accelerated Learning Program and Katie Hern's accelerated curriculum in California—two curricular models that have become central to developmental education reform in recent years—are built around this principle. As Hern notes, too many basic reading and writing classes are "radically disconnected from the core purposes and habits of mind of a college education" ("Unleashing"). Perhaps most importantly, there is "no world of ideas in that classroom," no sense of reading as "a way to join a larger discussion of issues that matter. No opportunity for students to climb into the upper reaches of Bloom's taxonomy, weigh conflicting evidence, and develop their own well-informed viewpoints." A focus on cooperative learning—fewer lectures, less repetitive worksheets, more small group collaborative problem solving and discussion—also appears to be crucial (Tough 2016a, b).

As we develop the next generation of developmental curriculum, we can also be guided by neuroscience and Carol Dweck's research on "mindsets." As readers may know, Dweck's research draws on "the revolutionary discovery that the human brain can change itself" (Doidge xvii). Much like a muscle, we now know that the brain can grow—developing new neural pathways and strengthening existing ones (Bransford, Pellegrino, and Donovan; Kandel, Schwartz, Jessell, Siegelbaum, and Hudspeth). Neural pathways can also decay and atrophy with disuse. These processes occur throughout our lifespan, depending on what we ask our brains to do. Dweck has found that even what students *believe* about intelligence and the human brain shapes how and what they learn ("Brainology"; Dweck *Mindsets*; Blackwell, Trzesniewski, and Dweck). This research is crucial for any understanding of the real potential inherent in developmental education.

I began my English 9000 class by foregrounding this research for my students with a group of readings that included a short essay by Dweck along with an article about neuroscience and brain plasticity. I was seeking to challenge and displace what my students were likely to have believed about themselves and their potential. In general, taken cumulatively, this research by Dweck and others suggests that community colleges shouldn't be turning students away simply because they have very low placement test scores. Instead, following Dweck, we should be theorizing our work as focused on "potential that can be realized through learning" ("Brainology" 1). Sharing this research with my students liberated them from restrictive and outdated understandings of cognitive development and gave them reason to hope and work hard, guided by the latest science and research. This research suggests that "potential" is what open admissions policies, developmental education, and community colleges should continue to be most fundamentally about.

Journeys

So who were these students in English 9000? Where did they come from? And what might we learn from them about developmental education and community colleges? Since this class was among the first transitional strategies classes offered in the state under PA 12–40, we have much to gain from spending a little time getting to know this historic cohort of students. In fact, this group of students provides professionals interested in questions related to open access, community colleges, and higher education a unique opportunity to reflect on key questions for our profession and our nation, framed and embodied by very real people with unique life histories. Had the open door at Connecticut community colleges been closed, these students would have been turned away. Let's meet some of them at this historic moment in the history of higher education—our first cohort of theoretically "undeserving" students.

Inspired by Betsy Bowen and Kathryn Nantz's work with General Education Development (GED) students at an adult literacy center in Bridgeport, Connecticut, I designed and completed an ethnographic study with this cohort of adult education students, conducting semi-structured interviews with most of the students in this class.[2] My goal was to get a fuller understanding of the lives behind the statistics of our most under-prepared developmental students. As it turns out, however, the most compelling data I gathered came not from my interviews but from an essay assignment students completed as part of their coursework for English 9000, which invited them to talk about their family history and document their journey to MCC. I had hoped this assignment would allow students to tell a little bit of their family history and also help position them in positive ways at the college. This assignment was also designed to give students the opportunity to write an essay using multiple paragraphs and get some practice quoting from assigned readings and discussing quotations from this work. The readings for this unit included two chapters from Ken Robinson's book about finding one's direction and passion in life, *The Element: How Finding Your Passion Changes Everything*, and the illustrated children's book *Journey* by Aaron Becker. I wanted to give students in this class something beautiful to look at, and Becker's book also provided a powerful way to frame our "journey" theme for this unit. Students also read a story written by an MCC student, Sabina, about her journey from Russia to America and MCC, which was developed as part of The Community College Success Stories Project and is included in Part I.

The weekend I spent reading these essays was one of the most astonishing I have ever spent as a teacher reading student written work. On a number of occasions, my jaw literally dropped open as I was reading them. Readers should know that we spent two weeks drafting these essays in class, and I spent a good deal of time during these weeks encouraging students to add additional depth and detail to their journey stories. The writing here represents finished, polished work. Of course, these samples don't show what my students can do responding to assigned readings, which we know is crucial for college-level writers (Sullivan "What"). Many of the students in this class were, indeed, eventually able to produce promising work in response to readings because they had become serious about improving their academic skills, they had committed to the process of rereading, revision, and multiple drafts, and they had embraced, following Carol Dweck, the idea that effort is an important part of success and that effort produces learning and growth, especially if the challenge is significant, as it was here.

I invite readers to observe the rich diversity of lived human experience embodied in the excerpts from these essays below and to consider what these stories may have to tell us about the value of community colleges. We may also wish to consider what these excerpts might have to say about us—America, as a nation and a democracy, which has sought to democratize its system of higher education and create opportunities for adult students to attend college regardless of past history. These stories—this data set—communicate important information to us about who our students are and why they might be here. This information is very different than what is communicated by raw numbers like placement test scores or program completion rates. These excerpts tell a very different, much more complex story about "democracy's college" (Pickett)—one that is deeply embedded in global political movements, national and international histories, economic realities for the poor and working class, and gender issues, along with more personal histories, aspirations, and ambitions.

By attending carefully to stories like this—and data sets other than statistics—we help enact Stephanie L. Kershbaum's recommendations about engaging diversity and difference. We can therefore be "*learning with*" our students rather than "*learning about*" them—"and thus always coming-to-know students. As its name implies, coming-to-know is a never-ending process, not a fixed destination; teachers never arrive at a place where they *know* a student" (57). Kershbaum suggests we have much to gain from this kind of orientation:

> Recognizing the contingency of identity and remaining vigilant toward our own orientations to difference is important for us as teachers because our vantage points lead us to see our students in particular ways—some of which can be harmful and damaging. (9)

Kershbaum's work related to how we choose to orient ourselves toward difference is supported by recent work by Trevor Gale and Stephen Parker, who champion theorizing student transition to higher education in socially inclusive ways (735), as we have seen. Furthermore, if we theorize ethnography as "a way of seeing," as Harry F. Wolcott suggests, there may be revealed here conditions and variables normally hidden from view. These humble life stories may well provide important insight for professionals interested in community colleges and developmental education programs.

Here are some of the most powerful and moving moments from my students' journey essays:

Shernette

My name is Shernette Thompson. I was born in Jamaica in a small parish that is called St Mary. I am the baby of the five children. I attended school at age four until age fifteen. I did not get to attend high school because my mother could not afford to pay the fee. She needed us to help to take care of the farm. We had to go to the river to get water to water the vegetables. She planted cabbage, carrots, beans, and corn to bring to the market to sell to provide food for the family. On the land we had cows, chickens, and goats. In the morning we had to get up early to milk the cows before the calves got to their mother. After we get back we would had bring the goats out in the field before the sun get too hot and the grass get shriveled.

Nick

My family is from Van Buren Maine, which is a small town in the northern part of the state. One of the major ways of life is potato farming. My grandfather (PaPere) owned and managed one of these farms for many years. He sold the farm when potato prices fell and my great grandfather was very old and he could not assist with the farm because he had cataracts and became blind.

The family moved into the main part of town and PaPere got a job at the Air Force Base. He would plow the runways for the airplanes in the winter time and in the summer time he was a painting contractor. Eventually he worked year round at the Air Force Base. My other PaPere was a masonry worker. My other Mamere cleaned houses. My grandparents did not have a lot of money. PaPere Boutot grew vegetables and hunted so his family would have food. My Mom and Dad grew up in Van Buren Maine. After high school my Dad joined the military. My Dad was stationed in Germany on a radio relay station; he would relay messages from one site to another. I went to school in Coventry Connecticut. I was able to see in grammar school. I knew how to read and write print. I lost my eyesight in middle school. I had a hard time dealing with it at first I am ok now. I am able to see when it is dark and light outside. I can see when there are lights on in a room. My retina cells died off that is why I became blind.

Octavia

My family is from North Carolina and Puerto Rico. My grandmother from North Carolina. My grandmother's name is Jacqueline Holmes. She was born in the south in 1952. She had work in the fields at an early age of twelve to help the family. She would get up every morning to go to the field to do whatever crop was ready at the time before she went to school. Then after school she had to clean, do homework, cook, and help take care of her siblings. If her parents couldn't go back to the fields to work before it got dark, she would have to go. It was very hard growing up in the south, but her mother always taught that the "the family that prays together stays together." That is true in all walks of life. Besides working in the fields, there was little work for her father to do to make ends meet. He left the family behind and come up north to get a better job. Her mother and other kids where hard during this time. She of praying some nights her mother would go to bed hungry, So that the kids could eat. Finally her father got a job and saved enough money to send for the rest of the family. My grandmother drove the rest of the family to Connecticut, the day after she graduated from school. They were a happy family together once again. My grandmother always said, "There is nothing a person cannot do if they believe in themselves and mostly remember to pray."

Prama

My name is Prama Ro. I was born in a refugee Camp in Thailand in 1996. My parents were born in Burma, which is a country between Thailand and India and below China. In Burma, there are many cultures. My parents were from the Karen group. My family moved to Mae La refugee camp in Thailand because the Burmese soldiers burned down their village and were violent toward the Karen people and they have to running from the Burmese soldiers. At that time, Burmese soldiers didn't care about people. They treated us the Karen like animals. They only wanted to be wealthy and they wanted to keep the power for them. They did not respect the Karen people. They used violence against the people. It took my family about a month to run from the Burmese soldiers. During that month, they had to live in the forest, find their own food and place to sleep.

My family got into the camp in 1984. They had a hard time living in the camp. My family lived there about 25 years. My siblings and I were born in the camp. I grew up in the camp. Life there was hard because we didn't have everything that we wanted. We had little education. To be able to go to school, we had to pay. My parents were lucky because they had jobs when many did not. The house that we lived in was made with bamboo and the roof was covered with leaves. At night, we used candles to read and study. The food, just rice, fish paste, oil, salt and Chile, was rationed every 15 days. Every day we ate the same thing. We carried water to our home in a bucket every afternoon.

We went to school in camp, but we didn't have everything that we needed so the education was poor. The school was also made of bamboo and leaves. We didn't have any power in school and we didn't have computers.

Javan

My journey started in a local town called Manchester it's in Connecticut. It's a small town nice very quiet and relaxing in life. I wanted things that I couldn't have and I would have to work hard for them. Growing up it was a struggle I was raised by my mom and it was only me and my little sister. My father wasn't there for us all the time but he would come around and help out with things. At a young age I would learned different responsibilities and becoming the man of the house. I couldn't believe that I would be in charge of everything like cleaning the house, help my mom out the best way that I can. Everything was a struggle, not having your father around and being able to learn from your mother how to become a young man. Theirs things that your mothers can't always teach but sometimes you have to learn on your own. My mom is a brave woman who was always there for me when things wasn't always good.

Francisco

It begins when I was born in Hartford, CT, September 24, 1995. My parents came to Hartford [from Puerto Rico] to have a better life for me. Their life was crazy before then. They had to help their family in the farm and go to school. One day my grandpa, the father of my dad, was selling pigs next to a store when someone called my father saying that his father got shot. My dad got in the car and rushed to bring his father to the hospital. I don't know the whole story but from that day forward his childhood was hell. He had to quit helping his father out around the house because now grandfather was in a wheelchair. My father was like the man of the house at fourteen years old He was the 3rd oldest of seven children. The rest of them were young so my father had to do all the heavy lifting. He had to wake up at 4 in the morning to feed the pigs, chickens, and then run to the town to buy some bread, rice, and fruit for the family. And then at eighteen, my dad met my mom and they left Puerto Rico to come to Hartford for a better job.

Yadira

This my story, between dealing with my parents splitting up, my brother joining the marines during the new start of war of Afghanistan and Iraq plus my personal school and relationship experience. This is truly a roller coaster of events. Beginning when my mother and father met in Panama City where my father was stationed in the military. My parents were married in 1985 a few months before my brother Junior (family nickname) was born. Then, shortly after, my parents moved to Texas where my dad was stationed for six months. They then moved to Connecticut to raise their family and shortly after that I was born. My parents were an average family living in Hartford. Hartford then wasn't as violent as it is now. Once my parents received great paying jobs, my parents decided to buy a house in East Hartford…

During all this craziness, my big brother junior had joined the marines. It was the hardest thing for me and my mother to adjust to the item of my brother possibly not coming home. This happened during the twin towers when America had announce we have been hit by terrorist and that America will be at war with Afghanistan and Iraq. The thought of my brother not coming home was the worst not only for the simple fact he was my only brother or sibling. During this time my mother and I would wait impatiently for my brother's phone calls and watching the news about the war; in which that was unbearable for the both of us.

***

Another student, who was born and raised in New York and moved to three different parts of the city—Fort Greene, East New York, and Brownsville—lived in a shelter with his family for a number of years and lost a close family member to street violence (a stabbing behind a local corner store near his house). Another student in this class was born in China, met her American husband there, and moved to the US after getting married. Everyone in her family including her mother, father, brother, and grandmother still lives in China. In her journey essay, she acknowledged that leaving her family and friends and moving to a new country continued to be difficult: "A lot of times when I sleep I dream of all the happy times of when I was in China. When I wake up I realize that it wasn't real and it was a dream."

Key Findings

Working on Coursework

Did my students honor the time and resources that were provided to them in this course, which was offered free to them? Very much so. Figures 25.1 and 25.2, from my gradebook pages for this class, suggest that most of the students in English 9000 appear to have been working in good faith to pass this class. This data set suggests that as a group these students valued this opportunity to attend college.

I see little evidence here of tax revenue being wasted. Instead, I see students doing their very best to lift themselves up the academic and economic ladder by their own bootstraps—through hard work, effort, and personal

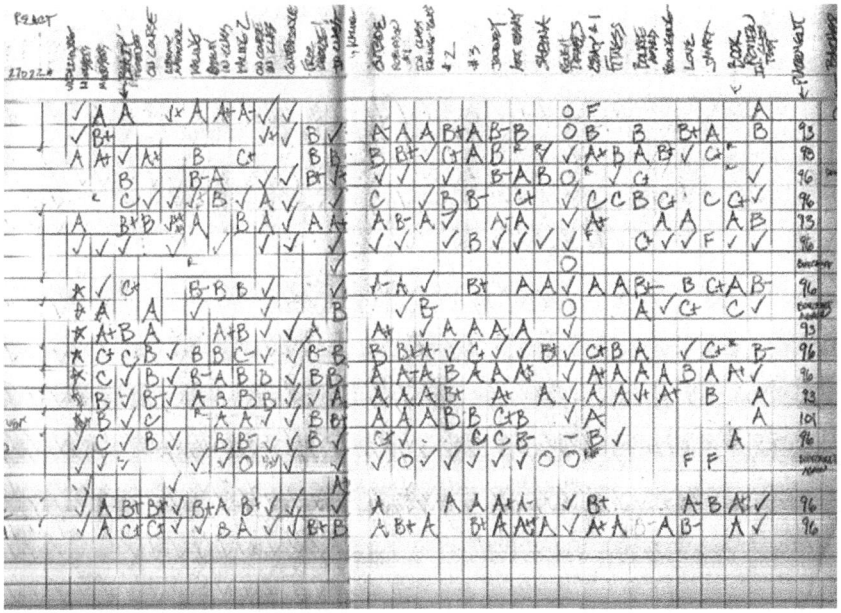

Fig. 25.1 My gradebook pages for English 9000, fall 2014

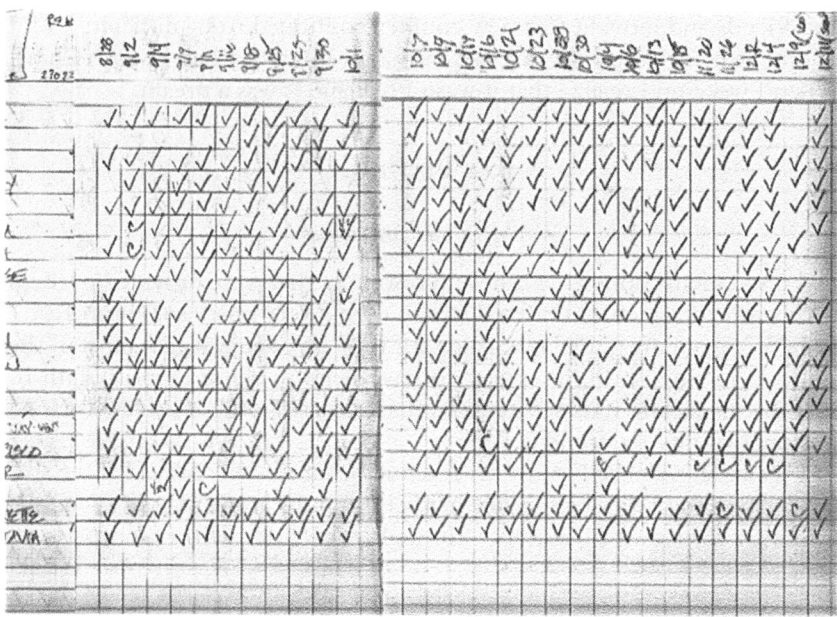

Fig. 25.2 The attendance record for my English 9000 class, fall 2014

responsibility. This is what Haskins and Sawhill call "creating an opportunity society" (1–18; 189–90) by implementing social policies that "reward personal responsibility and enhance mobility" (1). This is precisely what community colleges and developmental education programs are designed to do.

Working Outside of Class

Most of the students in this class had jobs. As we know, this is often the case with students who attend community colleges. What may come as something of a surprise is just how engaged so many of these students were with their jobs and how important the pressure to generate income was for them. This is not something that comes immediately to mind, of course, when we think of a typical college student, and this is part of the narrative about attending college in America that needs to be retheorized and updated. In fact, during the course of the semester, a number of students found it impossible to hold down their jobs and also make it to class and complete their work for school. To give readers a sense of the scope of my students' engagement with work and the kinds of jobs they had while they were in my class, here is a sampling of the data gathered from my interviews related to their working lives:

1. Insurance corporation mailroom/30 hours a week.
2. Retail clothing outlet/22–28 hours a week.
3. Valet parking/40 hours a week.
4. Fast food restaurant/25–30 hours a week.
5. Staff assistant at a church/15–25 hours a week.
6. Driver for a local delivery service/10 hours a week.
7. Cashier at a farmer's market/21 hours a week.
8. Certified nurse's aide/32 hours a week.
9. Retail handler at Goodwill/20 hours a week.
10. Fast food sandwich shop/30 hours a week.

Work was at the center of most of these students' lives. College was something they did *in addition to* devoting a great deal of time and energy each week to work.

Managing Scarcity

On a related note, it also became clear during the course of the semester that many of these students were living on the edge of real financial crisis. As we know, seemingly "minor" events like an illness, reduced hours at work, problems with a vehicle, or other unanticipated events can have catastrophic long-term effects on the ability of less financially advantaged individuals to stay in college and work toward earning an academic credential—a key variable that many discussions about measuring success at community colleges ignore or undervalue. I received a number of e-mails from students in English 9000 during the semester that brought this point home very powerfully. I share one of them here (with the author's permission), to help illustrate the kind of worlds many of these students live in—worlds that are perhaps more precarious than we might imagine:

> From: Brendan
> Sent: Monday, November 03, 2014 3:16 PM
> Hey I am sorry I haven't been going to class I been depress and really been tie up with stuff going on in the family right now my situation is that

> I have no job at all to pay my bills and also helping out my mom out as well so I had to find a job to pay my bills I have no money what so ever I want to finish class but I can't cuz I found a job Monday to Friday 8 am to 4 pm I don't what to do cuz I really don't have a choices about it if next year comes around I wouldn't be able to apply for classes cuz I didn't had the money for it at all I don't if there any way to work it out with you.

This e-mail, composed following the genre conventions of the text message, certainly suggests that this student is much closer to financial and personal hardship than we might normally expect the typical college student to be. I received another e-mail from a female student in this class that was one of the most heartbreaking pieces of correspondence I have ever received from a student. She was the mother of two young children and she was writing to tell me that she had been arrested on charges related to a domestic dispute. It took her longer than expected to post bail, so she had to spend a night in jail. She told me that she was determined to continue with the class but was hesitant to come to campus that week because she had some bruising that hadn't cleared up yet and she felt that would be embarrassing. She asked if arrangements might be made to submit her work another way.

Both of these individuals were among the most dedicated and hardworking students in the class. Both passed English 9000, and both went on to register for classes the following semester. Both of these students have the drive and the ability to be successful college students. It is important to note, however, that going to college for most of these students in this class was a profoundly different experience than the traditional model that students have followed in the past—spending four consecutive years right after high school at college, living on campus, and focusing full time on earning a degree. Much of this difference is due, of course, to economic inequality and vastly different financial situations. Most of these students simply did not have the financial resources to spend four years at college earning a degree. It seems almost cruel to measure the success of these very different cohorts of students with the same simple graduation rates used to assess the effectiveness of other institutions. Because of these challenges, earning a credential or a degree will require extraordinary focus, perseverance, and determination, and also, of course, some degree of luck. Learning about my students' personal situations helped me understand exactly how difficult this journey would be.

Sendhil Mullainathan and Eldar Shafir's work on "scarcity" can help us understand some of the psychological dynamics at play here. As we have seen, Mullainathan and Shafir have found that "scarcity captures the mind" (5–10) in powerfully dangerous ways. Scarcity reduces cognitive capacity, willpower, and patience, creating a shortage of mental "bandwidth" (17) that complicates any task that requires focus, attention, and mental stamina, such as completing a developmental reading and writing course. Scarcity impacts both fluid intelligence ("the ability to think and reason abstractly and solve problems independent of any specific learning or experience" [47]) and executive control (or self-control), and it has reduced functional IQ in clinical tests (52).

We must be very careful employing research like this to make generalizations about cohorts of students, of course, and I can only report what I found in my class. But it certainly appeared that scarcity was a significant factor in the lives of many of my students in English 9000. This scarcity had its greatest impact on their ability to pursue a long-term course of study and complete a degree or a certificate. Most of the students in this class were living much more tenuously than traditional college students who are able to attend a residential college for four years. One English 9000 student, for example, came to class directly from his third-shift job and simply could not stay awake in class. He needed to work full time in order to help his family pay bills (his mother was seriously ill and unable to work). Our program also provided free bus passes for students, and when I announced this to the class, I was quickly able to give away all five of the passes I had available. I had assumed that only one or two students would need them. Taking the bus often added an additional hour each way to my students' days as they traveled to and from campus and to and from work. When the weather permitted, one student rode his bike from Hartford to Manchester to save money, a seven-mile ride each way.

Also, once students moved beyond this free English 9000 course, attending college got a lot more difficult and complicated for many of them. Scarcity played a decisive role here as well. Some deal-breakers involved what less financially strapped families might consider relatively minor amounts of money. One student was frozen out from registering for the spring semester until he paid his outstanding balance from the fall: $502. He had to make a payment plan over the course of a number of months to pay it off. Another student, who did not qualify for financial aid, could not afford the $982 she would have to pay out of pocket for her next English class, our six-credit intensive readiness course, English

96. With tuition costs at open admissions institutions rising, this largely invisible problem related to access and equity is likely to become more pronounced.

Struggling with Reading

In the classroom, the biggest challenge my students faced was with reading, and much of this had to do with the lack of vocabulary acquisition and cognitive development that comes with reading that Betty Hart and Todd R. Risley discovered in their landmark research. My students' struggles with reading, in fact, seemed to emphatically confirm Pierre Bourdieu and Jean-Claude Passeron's key insight about language acquisition and cultural capital:

> language is not simply an instrument of communication: it also provides, together with a richer or poorer vocabulary, a more or less complex system of categories, so that the capacity to decipher and manipulate complex structures, whether logical or aesthetic, depends partly on the complexity of the language transmitted by the family. (73; Bourdieu)

Most of my native speakers had reading scores so low, in fact, that Accuplacer—programmed to branch at a certain threshold for ELL students—began testing them as if they were still in the process of learning English. Here are two samples for two of my native speakers:

1. Accuplacer Reading Comp. 038.0
   LOEP Reading Skills 090.0
2. Accuplacer Reading Comp. 027.0
   LOEP Reading Skills 037.0

Note: LOEP (Levels of English Proficiency) is the ESL Reading Skills test. If a student's raw score is below 40 in Reading Comprehension, the computer-adaptive software branches them into the LOEP test.

As a group, the students in this class found almost everything they were required to read challenging, and most needed considerable discussion and careful supported work with each text we read before understanding it. Reading comprehension was a major challenge all semester long.

One aspect of this problem was that many students in this class were remarkably unconversant with a wide variety of cultural references. A chapter from Mindy Kaling's book, *Is Everyone Hanging Out Without Me?*, proved to be particularly vexing for them. The typical Kaling essay ranges freely across a variety of well-known cultural and pop-cultural reference points, and much of her humor and content is built around these references. Most college-level readers are going to be able to decode this material easily, employing acquired cultural literacy as part of their comprehension strategy. Most of my students were unable to do this—some because they were non-native speakers and did not understand the cultural references and others because they were native speakers who nonetheless were still confused by many of the cultural references that Kaling assumes her audience will understand. Decoding by using contextual cues only got my students so far.

A bigger problem was vocabulary. Contextual clues can be helpful to a degree, but vocabulary is a vitally important variable for reading comprehension. As Catherine E. Snow and Connie Juel note, "We now have reams of studies that show that good and poor readers differ not in the use of context to make better predictions, but in the swift and efficient identification of words" (507; Nation; Perfetti, Landi, and Oakhill). This certainly proved to be the case in this class. My students were often stopped cold because they didn't know a single word ("catastrophe," "conventional," "assumption"). Sometimes, this word was crucial to a passage we were reading. Other times, it was incidental. But the effect was usually the same. One memorable, high-stakes example of this occurred at the end of the semester when students were writing their in-class end-of-the-semester essays (a required element mandated by our program; they took a pre-test at the beginning of the semester and this was their required post-test). Students were given a number of random essay prompts, and two of the best writers in the class were stopped in their tracks by the same prompt because of a word they didn't understand. The prompt began with this sentence: "Americans are bombarded by advertisements every day." Neither of them could figure out what "bombarded" meant. So the prompt looked like this to them: "Americans are _____ by advertisements every day." Understanding the verb in this sentence is crucial to understanding the question that followed. When they raised their hands to ask me for help, I couldn't tell them what the word meant, of course, but I did encourage them to use contextual cues. Significantly, both writers were ultimately unable to make much sense of the question and they each ended up struggling to write a good essay.

Skilled readers and experienced writers would probably be able to write a strong essay in response to this prompt even without knowing that word. They would likely be able to pick up from contextual cues in the rest of that prompt that "bombardment" suggested all sorts of negative things similar to "an intensive and sustained attack by bombs or artillery fire." Strong readers might also have recognized this as a standard, familiar, and much debated academic subject (many textbooks for English classes include chapters that discuss the impact of advertising; others often focus on developing skills for decoding advertisements). This is the kind of question that students in English classes often get asked in junior and senior high school, and it has become a familiar and popular assignment.

What we may be seeing here, in terms of vocabulary development, is another manifestation of scarcity. My ethnographic research revealed that many of these students grew up poor, and as Hart and Risley note, children from poor families often develop a much more limited vocabulary than children who grow up in professional families, encountering on average 32 million fewer words than children from professional families (198). This means that some students in basic writing classes like this one will have heard 32 million fewer words than other students on campus—with corresponding implications for reading comprehension, cultural literacy, and "the capacity to decipher and manipulate complex structures." Given what we know about the crucial link between vocabulary and reading proficiency, many of my English 9000 students will continue to face challenges with reading as they move into the mainstream college-level curriculum. This will be an important and perhaps largely hidden variable as they seek to complete a degree or credential.

In addition to being very poor readers, many of the students in this class also had a very pronounced aversion to reading. On many days, especially at the beginning of the semester, it felt like what I was experiencing was fallout from what Kelly Gallagher has characterized as "readicide"—"the systematic killing of the love of reading, often exacerbated by the inane, mind-numbing practices found in schools" (2; Jolliffe; Smith; Sullivan, *New* 121–45). Readicide is caused, Gallagher suggests, by public policy that values the development of test-takers over the development of lifelong readers (5). For Gallagher, there are some key educational practices that have contributed to this national problem:

> What do teachers and curriculum directors mean by "value" reading? A look at the practice of most schools suggests that when a school "values" reading, what it really means is that the school intensely focuses on raising state-mandated reading test scores—the kind of reading our students will rarely, if ever, do in adulthood. "Valuing reading" is often a euphemism for

preparing students to pass mandated multiple-choice exams, and in dragging students down this path, schools are largely contributing to the development of readicide. (7)

Two recent reports about reading from the National Endowment for the Arts—*Reading at Risk* and *To Read or Not to Read: A Question of National Consequence*—provide disturbing evidence for this claim.

A few bold students were determinedly and almost gleefully demonstrative about this aversion, too, obviously giving voice to years of frustration, disappointment, and hardship ("I hate reading"; "I never read"; "I hate books"). Many claimed never to have completed reading a full book. It seems very clear that we must do a better job of making reading an appealing, enjoyable activity for all students, K-12. Michael W. Smith and Jeffery D. Wilhelm have made this case in two essential books about reading—*Reading Don't Fix No Chevys* and *Reading Unbound*—both of which highlight the importance of student motivation and engagement with reading. Thomas Newkirk also gives eloquent expression to this idea as well: "unless we can persuade students that reading is a form of deep sustained pleasure, they will not choose to read; and because they will not choose to read, they will not develop the skills to make them good readers" (117). Nancie Atwell has championed the importance of reading for pleasure her entire career (*In the Middle*; *Reading*; see also Miller). Important new longitudinal research by Alice Sullivan and Matt Brown—reported in their essay, "Social Inequalities in Cognitive Scores At Age 16: The Role of Reading"—has shown that reading for pleasure provides significant benefits across a variety of academic disciplines (including math) and that "reading is actually linked to increased cognitive progress over time" (37; Wolf). This work confirms the key conclusions by Hart and Risley and Bourdieu and Passeron about the link between reading and the development of a complex system of categories and sophisticated intellectual functions.

Hope Required When Growing Roses in Concrete

How might we best develop a theoretical approach and a curriculum for this cohort of students who are truly unready for college-level work? Rather than turning them away, as some have suggested, as "undeserving," I would like to suggest we adopt a policy built around Jeffrey Duncan-Andrade's idea of "critical hope."

All of my students' stories about coming to college were about hope in one way or another. This is important to keep in mind because in addition to significantly increased public scrutiny of developmental education, the very idea of open admissions at community colleges—a public policy whose most foundational principle is hope—has recently been called into question. Recent essays by Ray Flores and Mike Rose in the online news and opinion website *Inside Higher Ed* provide a paradigmatic example of this ongoing public debate. Flores suggests in his essay, "False Hope," that remedial education has been, by and large, an expensive failure, especially for our most underprepared students: "In summary, students testing into the lowest levels of developmental education have virtually no chance of ever moving beyond remedial work and achieving their educational goals. For those students and their families, developmental education is expensive and demoralizing." Flores suggests that admitting such students is unwise and misguided, an ill-advised use of tax dollars, and "callous at best" because these students "have virtually no chance of becoming college-ready." Of course, narratives about developmental education like this, to borrow a formulation from Tony Holt, make accessible certain ideas about human possibilities and foreclose others (11). Behind this kind of thinking is an economic theory that frames investment in community colleges and developmental education on a business model that privileges return on investment and statistical probabilities and theorizes this investment as a monetary exchange involving durable goods, similar to a business investing in equipment (Becker). P.L. Thomas's observations about neoliberalism and public education in the US are important to keep in mind here:

> "No Excuses" Reformers insist that the source of success and failure lies in each child and each teacher, requiring only the adequate level of effort to rise out of the circumstances not of her/his making. As well, "No Excuses" Reformers remain committed to addressing poverty solely or primarily through education, viewed as an opportunity offered each child and within which ... effort will result in success.
>
> Social Context Reformers have concluded that the source of success and failure lies primarily in the social and political forces that govern our lives. By acknowledging social privilege and inequity, Social Context Reformers are calling for education reform *within* a larger plan to reform social inequity—such as access to health care, food security, higher employment along with better wages and job security. (qtd. in Porfilio, Gorlewski, Carr, and Thomas 1)

A number of recent books have challenged neoliberal economic theory as it has been applied to higher education and have, instead, championed a more progressive, humanistic model, focusing on access and opportunity—and the public good—to address growing concerns about inequality, entrenched power and inherited wealth, and building a strong democracy in America (Brown; Harvey; Kezar, Chambers, Burkhardt). All of this work suggests that we "design for equity," as Marc Tucker recommends in *Surpassing Shanghai: An Agenda for American Education Built on the World's Leading Systems* (2013), a book that examines the world's best ideas about education (213–214).

Hope brought my English 9000 students to our campus, and the dream of a better future is what sustained them through the many challenges they faced during the semester. Instead of sending these students away, we gave them a chance to begin. Most of the students in this class honored that opportunity by working with great diligence and perseverance. As Jeffrey Duncan-Andrade notes in "Note to Educators: Hope Required When Growing Roses in Concrete," there are many different kinds of hope, including many different manifestations of what he calls "false hope." These include "hokey hope," "mythical hope," and "hope deferred." Countering this kind of superficial hope is the complex hope that Duncan-Andrade defines as "critical hope." I would like to see us theorize developmental education as providing precisely this kind of "critical hope":

> On the flipside of these false hopes lies critical hope, which rejects the despair of hopelessness and the false hopes of "cheap American optimism" (West 2008, p. 41). Critical hope demands a committed and active struggle "against the evidence in order to change the deadly tides of wealth inequality, group xenophobia, and personal despair" (West 2004, pp. 296–297). (5)

Duncan-Andrade suggests that this kind of "critical hope" is most essentially about "control of destiny," an "actively present sense of agency to manage the immediate stressors in one's daily life" (4; Sternglass). Community colleges might be said to offer precisely this kind of potential for agency and control of destiny.

Teaching this class was also an inspiring experience for the two tutors who assisted me. One of these individuals, Yanira Hernandez, was an honors student at MCC at the time she was serving as a peer tutor in the class. She worked with me over the course of three semesters (spring 2014, teaching an early version of English 9000, fall 2014, and spring 2015). I was surprised to learn, after being asked by Yanira to complete an Academic Student Assessment form required for a Phi Theta Kappa scholarship application, that working with the students in this class was her "most significant endeavor since attending community college." With Yanira's permission, I share her response to that question:

> My most significant endeavor at Manchester Community College has been the work I did as a tutor for college readiness English classes. For three semesters I spent a great deal of time as an in-class tutor working with students from a variety of backgrounds and abilities. I was exposed to students from different age groups, socioeconomic backgrounds and ethnicities. I also had the great opportunity to work with talented students with developmental and physical challenges. These students displayed a beautiful spirit to overcome challenges I had never seen before. They demonstrated a level of quiet determination for no reward other than their own self-growth.
>
> In this role I was challenged by questions from students and worked with professors to help them learn some key skills to prepare them for college English courses. I also helped students with vital computer skills, time management skills, reading and writing, and helped them gain self-advocacy skills to help them after they complete this course. In this class I coached reluctant students and they gradually gained more confidence throughout the class.
>
> After the first semester I began to realize how important my role as a tutor was. I saw students I worked with becoming involved in school functions. I ran into some of the same students working with the tutors in the Academic Support Center. Walking through campus, students I previously worked with stopped me regularly to tell me how well they were doing. I believe these students, who may not have this opportunity at a four-year institution, are going to make a positive impact in their community. While some of them were learning English as a second language, some of them were veterans and students who graduated high school without the adequate skills to succeed in college. It is critically important for colleges to keep programs like this going to help change the course of life for many that have the determination to improve their lives. When student leaders devote a semester or two to helping their peers, they also learn a great deal from the experience. This experience has stretched my view on what success in college really means. This work as a tutor has made a difference in my life. It has made a positive difference in the students' lives, and it will help our school and our community. I believe that when struggling students get the level of support they need, and see what their hard work can do for them, it helps all of us.

A Great Nation Is a Compassionate Nation

Despite having to overcome a variety of serious academic and nonacademic challenges, many students in this class significantly improved their reading and writing skills by the end of the semester. Some of this was dispositional. As students began to regard reading and writing as more enjoyable and interesting, they worked harder, focused more strategically, and were less likely to give up and stop. This alone made them better readers and writers. Some of it was also practice and modeling, so that they began to get a better sense of how skilled readers and writers worked, what good reading and writing looked like, and what kind of effort is needed to produce strong academic work. Some of it was developing a larger and more effective repertoire of reading and writing strategies. To be sure, each of these students had much more work left to do, and we need to acknowledge this fact even as we celebrate their successes.

As we know, and as the students in this class made abundantly clear, standardized placement tests (or, indeed, any kind of placement protocol, no matter how well intentioned or skillfully designed) can't predict or define potential or what students might be capable of learning or achieving—or what students might be capable of becoming. Placement scores are not destiny. Rather, they provide only a momentary snapshot of a particular skill set, which can always be improved with effort and practice. This becomes especially crucial to keep in mind when such scores are used to determine access to higher education. As Dweck notes, "An assessment at one point in time has little value for understanding someone's ability, let alone their potential to succeed in the future" (*Mindset* 29). Despite these students' limitations and challenges, many did well in this class, earning the right to move forward with their education.

I finished this semester in English 9000 cautiously optimistic about this group of students. Most made substantial progress. Overall, 13 of our initial 20 students graduated from English 9000, and 12 enrolled in one of our basic reading and writing classes in the spring of 2015. Of those who didn't pass, one student decided that college was not for him and indicated that he would not be returning. Two students had trouble attending classes regularly—both because of work obligations. Two other students—each with a significant learning disability—also did not pass English 9000. One of these students repeated English 9000 in the spring and passed. Another student came to college with serious behavioral and maturity issues. This student took a college success class in the spring and passed it with a final grade of "B." Another student was advised to enroll in our ESL curriculum track. All the rest (12 students) moved forward into one of our basic reading and writing courses.

I tracked these students to see how they did in their subsequent English classes in the spring 2015 semester. To my delight, seven of these 12 students (58% of those who took the next English class) passed these courses and within a year had become eligible for our standard first-year college-level English class. If we calculate these numbers using the entire class (20 students), the percentage is 35%. As I reviewed those who didn't pass this subsequent English class, there were a few surprises (students who I expected to do well but didn't) and some that were less surprising (students who moved on but would have had to work very hard to pass).

As a group, the students in this English 9000 were mostly young, hardworking, and full of positive energy and optimism about their futures. Part of their optimism came from us—and the fact that our community college believed in them enough to offer this class and give them a chance to attend college. It would have been a shame to have turned any of them away. Certainly, some of them found out that college, for whatever reason, was not for them, at least at the moment. Many others, though, found themselves fully engaged and were inspired to move forward with their college careers. I see most of the students in this class limited only by the things that limit us all, many of which are beyond our control—how supportive our families are, how much discretionary income we can devote to paying for our college education, how many hours a week we have to work, how much time we can devote to our schoolwork, what kinds of family responsibilities and situations we have, what kinds of support networks we can draw on, what kinds of neighborhood schools we attended, how safe our neighborhoods are, and so on. Given how complex these students' lives are—and how different their situations are from the traditional model of attending college at a residential campus and devoting four years full time to earning a degree—we know for sure, unfortunately, that many challenges await these students that will complicate and imperil their pursuit of a degree or credential.

As I have kept in touch with my students from this class over the last two years, I have seen again and again how precarious many of their situations are and how difficult pursuing a degree is for many of them. Most of this difficulty is driven by limited family resources and economic hardship (Cahalan and Perna; Tough 2014; Wilson). Some of these students have continued on at MCC; others have been delayed or frustrated by various challenges, which have been mostly economic. The key principle we must take away from this study is a profound one, related to equity, agency, and social justice: There is simply no way to predict the course of an individual human life, and educators and state legislatures should not be in this kind of prediction business. We must not let test scores or state legislators decide who gets the chance to attend college. Open admissions policies let individual students decide for themselves, and they are then free to make of this opportunity what they can. In order for this revolutionary policy to remain viable, we are likely going to be called upon to defend it. We must be ready and willing to do so.

As Martin Luther King observed in his Nobel Prize Address,

> Ultimately a great nation is a compassionate nation. No individual or nation can be great if it does not have a concern for "the least of these." Deeply etched in the fiber of our religious tradition is the conviction that men are made in the image of God and that they are souls of infinite metaphysical value, the heirs of a legacy of dignity and worth. If we feel this as a profound moral fact, we cannot be content to see men hungry, to see men victimized with starvation and ill health when we have the means to help them.

There are many ways one can be hungry. If we accept King's premise about compassion, there are few things we do as a society that are more compassionate than offering our citizens—even those who some might consider "the least of these" and perhaps "undeserving"—the opportunity to build better futures for themselves and their families.

Activism

Unfortunately, an ominous and powerful new presence in developmental education has emerged in recent years—the activist, interventionist state legislature. We have clearly entered a new era in which state legislatures feel emboldened to bypass disciplinary expertise and even common sense in order to mandate public policy for developmental curriculum. This is a deeply troubling new development that must be actively resisted. It is impossible not to feel emanating from this kind of legislation both impatience and self-righteousness, and perhaps also a little anger at the slow pace some students take toward proficiency. Such an approach typically dismisses or discounts all the variables we have documented here that make completing coursework and earning a degree difficult for some students.

Where PA 12–40 is informed by disciplinary knowledge and best practices and current innovations in composition studies and developmental education scholarship, the committee that framed this legislation made good choices—mandating multiple measures for placement and embracing an accelerated co-requisite model for developmental curriculum. But the committee appears to have perhaps misread or misunderstood some portions of the research related to the Baltimore acceleration model. Peter Adams and his colleagues do not suggest that every student can be successful in an accelerated program—only that some can, particularly those close to current cut scores who have been underplaced, a common problem produced by standardized tests like Accuplacer (Scott-Clayton and Stacey).

There is also a large dose of what we might call wishful—or even magical—thinking embedded in PA 12–40. This is driven and informed, I'm afraid, by an observer's perspective and a lack of familiarity with basic writers and developmental education. Basic writers in the state of Connecticut are now limited by law to taking only one developmental class. The state legislature has summarily decided that one course is all any student could ever need, and it has decreed, in effect, "by God, that is all they will get." There is a neoliberal economic model at work here suggesting that developmental education itself is the problem, rather than a host of economic, social, and cultural variables that can slow down or stop progress toward completion of a degree for some students. I am hopeful that the research we are examining in this book will help challenge this kind of thinking. As Katherine Mangan notes, "The way policy makers in some states see it, the biggest obstacles preventing students from completing college are the courses that are supposed to help unprepared students catch up" ("Remedial"; Boylan and Goudas; Fain; Goudas and Boylan).

Developmental education reform and legislation like PA 12–40 has focused much-needed attention on students who don't need basic writing classes or who are likely to pass a college-level writing course with additional embedded support in an accelerated curriculum. A related trend that is emerging directly from this reform is that when we remove students who shouldn't have been in basic writing classes to begin with, this changes the makeup of developmental classes significantly. As a consequence, success rates for basic writing courses appear to be falling. This is an issue that has emerged at my home institution and has also become a topic of concern for a national committee of scholars, TYCA's Research Committee, which recently completed a White Paper related to placement reform (Klausman, Roberts, Hassel, Giordano, O'Rourke, Sullivan, and Toth). (I am a member of this committee.) This problem may have always been with us, but the struggles of significantly underprepared students appear to have been hidden by the strong performances of underplaced or misplaced students, who made it seem like these classes were working reasonably well. At a spring English department meeting at my institution in 2015, as we were reporting out and discussing the first full year of implementation of our new developmental curriculum mandated by PA 12–40, this emerged as a key topic of concern. Students in our accelerated courses were doing well, and we appear to have significantly reduced the number of underplaced students in our developmental courses. Unfortunately, our workhorse developmental course, which we now offer in a three- and expanded six-semester-hour format, appears to have significantly lower completion rates. What had worked previously—perhaps because of strong underplaced or misplaced students—no longer appears to work as well. We also face a quandary. By state law, students are only allowed to take one semester of developmental coursework. Are students allowed to repeat this course? What do students do if they don't pass the one developmental class they are allowed to take? At the moment, we don't know the answer to these questions. The law reads as follows:

> Not later than the start of the fall semester of 2014 and for each semester thereafter, no public institution of higher education shall offer any remedial support, including remedial courses, that is not embedded with the corresponding entry level course, as required pursuant to subsection (b) of this section, or offered as part of an intensive college readiness program, except such institution may offer a student a maximum of one semester of remedial support that is not embedded, provided (1) such support is intended to advance such student toward earning a degree, and (2) the program of remedial support is approved by the Board of Regents for Higher Education. (Connecticut 2)

As Hassel, Klausman, Giordano, O'Rourke, Roberts, Sullivan, and Toth note, in this new interventionist era, political concerns often supersede sound educational policy:

> some state legislatures bypass faculty input and appear to engage in political rather than research-based decision making. Florida's changed placement procedures in SB 1720 offer a case in point. By signing the bill into law, the Florida governor mandated what might be considered a version of directed

> self-placement, declaring some students exempt from mandatory placement assessment and giving most students who are assessed as needing developmental instruction multiple remediation options (see "Case Study" above). The law also radically redefines "college ready" by decreeing that a Florida high school diploma for anyone who has been enrolled since the ninth grade earns automatic placement into college-level courses, regardless of other indicators. Finally, Florida is implementing a single placement test with a single cutoff score established by the state board, which ignores differences in student populations in different parts of the state and the varying curricular and institutional programs at different colleges. (233)

In my own state, as I listened to and participated in statewide discussions about implementation of PA 12–40 in the tumultuous months following passage of this legislation, I was alarmed by some of the language I heard being used about underprepared students and the seemingly punitive measures being discussed to deal with them. I spoke with one consultant who was assisting the state with implementation during this process, and he had a similar read on the situation. He said that it appeared to him that some of the framers of this legislation, and some of those who were providing leadership in the initial public discussions of this bill, "simply wanted underprepared students to go away."

The students in my English 9000 class came to our campus, took a battery of placement tests, and formally applied for admission to our institution. Almost all of them came to our college seeking direction, answers, or solutions—seeking different and better futures and lives, and sometimes different and better selves. There is no other place in America where adults can go to pursue this kind of personal transformation and reinvention, which almost always engages the heart as well as the mind. Community colleges provide citizens in our communities with the opportunity to rise above one's past choices, behavior, and history—giving practical embodiment to the proud and noble belief that anything might be possible for any given student. The open admissions policy is an idea that powerfully honors individual student dignity and agency. This is easy to accomplish when students are ready for college. It becomes much more challenging, however, when students are not well prepared and want to attend college anyway. Providing this kind of opportunity for our most underprepared adult learners is difficult and challenging work, but it is where the ideals of the community college—and our democracy—are tested and made most real and vital.

It is not just literacy that we are championing, but an inclusive vision of America and democracy. Following Franklin Roosevelt, let us understand that "the test of our progress is not whether we add more to the abundance of those who have much; it is whether we provide enough for those who have too little" ("Second Inaugural Address"). In this way, we follow Amartya Sen and his insistence that any understanding of justice "cannot be indifferent to the lives that people can actually live" (*Idea* 18), as the research documented here clearly suggests. This is precisely what the Truman Commission had in mind as they candidly assessed, during a time of great national clarity, democracy's unfinished business.

Notes

1. Community colleges in the state of Connecticut currently all use Accuplacer; regional state universities and the University of Connecticut use Scholastic Aptitude Test or ACT scores. PA 12–40 also mandates that all campuses must use "multiple measures" of assessment for placing students.
2. This research received Institutional Review Board's (IRB) review and exemption. About halfway through the semester, when I realized that I would have to document my experience with this extraordinary class, the idea for this project began to take shape. At this time, I told my English 9000 students about the project I had in mind, and I respectfully asked for permission to interview them and use excerpts from their work. Most of the students in the class were eager to participate. I am using their work and their first names with their permission.

PART III

The Public Good

CHAPTER 26

A Brief History of the Public Good

Old Poverty

An important theoretical concept that is being vigorously contested in discussions about higher education in America today is our shared understanding of the public good. In some quarters, the very idea of the public good—independent of economic considerations—is being challenged and dismissed. Furthermore, following the work of economist Gary Becker on human capital, the civic and moral benefits traditionally associated with higher education and a liberal arts education have also been called into question. In the chapters of this section of the book, we will survey the history of this important democratic idea and map its journey into current debates about public policy, higher education, and the community college.

The concept of "the public good" has a long and complex history in America, stretching back hundreds of years to the founding fathers (and founding mothers) and the establishment of our nation. In fact, the first charge made against King George in the Declaration of Independence accuses the monarch of working in ways that subvert the public good:

> The history of the present King of Great Britain is a history of repeated injuries and usurpations, all having in direct object the establishment of an absolute Tyranny over these States. To prove this, let Facts be submitted to a candid world.
>
> He has refused his Assent to Laws, the most wholesome and necessary for the public good.

James Madison's "Federalist Paper No. 10" from 1787—a key document in American history—draws much of its rhetorical power from its appeal to the public good. In this document, Madison discusses ways to protect American citizens from "factions"—"by a faction, I understand a number of citizens, whether amounting to a majority or a minority of the whole, who are united and actuated by some common impulse of passion, or of interest, adversed to the rights of other citizens, or to the permanent and aggregate interests of the community." As Madison seeks to balance the competing demands of the thirteen states with a newly emerging national government, the public good is at the forefront of his concerns: "To secure the public good and private rights against the danger of such a faction, and at the same time to preserve the spirit and the form of popular government, is then the great object to which our inquiries are directed." There are sections of this document examining the roots of "faction" in a democracy that sound as if they could have issued from celebrated European Enlightenment writers like François Duc de La Rochefoucauld and Jonathan Swift, both famous for their candid and unsparing assessment of human nature and the role that passion plays in driving human conduct. Like Rochefoucauld and Swift, Madison grants as much power to "passion," "interests," and "self-love" in human conduct as he does to reason and deliberation. Madison acknowledges this unequivocally: "As long as the reason of man continues fallible, and he is at liberty to exercise it, different opinions will be formed. As long as the connection subsists between his reason and his self-love, his opinions and his passions will have a reciprocal influence on each other; and the former will be objects to which the latter will attach themselves." Like Rochefoucauld and Swift, Madison suggests that men and women do not always behave rationally and are not always naturally inclined to resolve conflicts "with a sole regard to justice and the public good." Furthermore, Madison contends, it is in our nature to seek quarrels wherever we can find them:

> The latent causes of faction are thus sown in the nature of man; and we see them everywhere brought into different degrees of activity, according to the different circumstances of civil society. A zeal for different opinions concerning religion, concerning government, and many other points, as well of speculation as of practice; an attachment to different leaders ambitiously contending for pre-eminence and power; or to persons of other descriptions whose fortunes have been interesting to the human passions, have, in turn, divided mankind into parties, inflamed them with mutual animosity, and rendered them much more disposed to vex and oppress each other than to

co-operate for their common good. So strong is this propensity of mankind to fall into mutual animosities, that where no substantial occasion presents itself, the most frivolous and fanciful distinctions have been sufficient to kindle their unfriendly passions and excite their most violent conflicts. But the most common and durable source of factions has been the various and unequal distribution of property.

For Madison, passion and interests drive human thought and action—and, crucially for Madison and his understanding of the role of government in a democracy, interests are not constrained by reason. As Madison notes in Federalist No. 51: "If men were angels, no government would be necessary." The American government has been explicitly designed to help balance the competing claims of individual passions and interests with "justice and the public good."

We also see Madison developing in Federalist No. 10 one of the first theories of economic inequality in Western thought: "But the most common and durable source of factions has been the various and unequal distribution of property." Crucially for our purposes here, Madison traces the root of most discord in a democracy to the unequal distribution of wealth and the resulting friction, animosity, and conflict that results from this condition, which threatens the public good: "From the protection of different and unequal faculties of acquiring property, the possession of different degrees and kinds of property immediately results; and from the influence of these on the sentiments and views of the respective proprietors, ensues a division of the society into different interests and parties." For Madison, "the regulation of these various and interfering interests forms the principal task of modern legislation, and involves the spirit of party and faction in the necessary and ordinary operations of the government." The establishment of the modern community college could be regarded as one such manifestation of this effort to limit the destructiveness of factions and to address a foundational problem in our democracy—economic inequality. Madison is the first American political thinker (and one of the first in the world, in fact) to acknowledge the important social and political consequences of economic inequality. Almost 250 years later, economic inequality continues to be a key variable in public policy discussions about justice and the public good. It has become central to discussions of higher education and the modern community college as well.

Thomas Jefferson was also keenly interested in the public good, of course, and a passage from his letter to William C. Jarvis in 1820 about the importance of education for promoting the public good has become a foundational touchstone for our understanding of American democracy: "I know no safe depository of the ultimate powers of the society, but the people themselves: and if we think them not enlightened enough to exercise their control with a wholesome discretion, the remedy is not to take it from them, but to inform their discretion by education. This is the true corrective of abuses of constitutional power." And, of course, among the historically significant documents in our tradition that are centrally concerned with the public good, the Truman Commission Report must rank among the most important.

The modern understanding of the public good begins to take form during the Great Depression. Before this global economic crisis, the federal government played a very limited role in the lives of most Americans. In his Address at the College of William and Mary in Williamsburg, Virginia, on May 15, 1926, for example, Calvin Coolidge remarked that "If the Federal Government should go out of existence, the common run of people would not detect the difference in the affairs of their daily life for a considerable length of time. But if the authority of the States were struck down disorder approaching chaos would be upon us within 24 hours." With the advent of the Great Depression, of course, this relationship between the federal government and "the common run of people" changed dramatically. It is perhaps inevitable now—given such comforting historical distance from the lived trauma of the Depression—that the hard edges of this cataclysm have been softened by time and familiarity. When we talk about economic theory today, it is perhaps easy to overlook the depth and scale of the devastation that the Depression brought to America. Photographs from that time help remind us of the deeply moving human dimension of this crisis (see Figs. 26.1, 26.2, and 26.3 from the Farm Security Administration Collection). My father-in-law, who lived through the Depression as a child in Brooklyn, New York, shakes his head gravely as he remembers it. He describes it as a time of grim poverty and privation, when many people went hungry.

One condition that FDR and others in his administration discovered as they began to respond to this crisis was the deeply rooted privation that historian James Patterson has called "old poverty" (38; 40–1). This widespread structural poverty was largely invisible in the US until the Depression. In his book on this subject, *America's Struggle Against Poverty in the Twentieth Century*, Patterson estimates that between 18 and 40 million Americans suffered from this kind of old poverty before the Depression (41), earning less than subsistence income. For many poor

Fig. 26.1 Sharecropper Bud Fields and his family at home. Hale County, Alabama. 1936 (Photographer: Walker Evans.
Source: Library of Congress. http://www.loc.gov/pictures/collection/fsa/item/fsa1998020957/PP/resource/)

Americans, the Great Depression made life only slightly more difficult. Maya Angelou's account of this in *I Know Why the Caged Bird Sings* provides a paradigmatic example of this kind of poverty: "The country had been in the throes of the Depression for two years before the Negroes in Stamps knew it" (41).

Because of the nature of this calamity, many of FDR's policies in response to the Great Depression were necessarily developed improvisationally and experimentally, as David M. Kennedy documents in his book on this period, *Freedom from Fear: The American People in Depression and War, 1929–1945*. FDR's address at Oglethorpe University in Atlanta, Georgia, on May 22, 1932, captures both the extraordinary nature of this crisis and the spirit of FDR's approach to engaging it:

Fig. 26.2 Cotton pickers, Arkansas, on the Alexander plantation at 6:30 a.m., waiting for the workday to start, 1935 (Photographer: Ben Shahn.
Source: Library of Congress. http://www.loc.gov/pictures/collection/fsa/item/fsa1997016144/PP/)

> Do not confuse objectives with methods. When the Nation becomes substantially united in favor of planning the broad objectives of civilization, then true leadership must unite thought behind definite methods.
>
> The country needs and, unless I mistake its temper, the country demands bold, persistent experimentation. It is common sense to take a method and try it: If it fails, admit it frankly and try another. But above all, try something. The millions who are in want will not stand by silently forever while the things to satisfy their needs are within easy reach.

As Kennedy notes, this historic event provided progressive thinkers with an opportunity to address long-standing issues related to poverty and economic inequality in America:

> The "old poor" were among the Depression's most ravaged victims, but it was not the Depression that had impoverished them. They were the "one third of a nation" that Franklin Roosevelt would describe in 1937 as chronically

A BRIEF HISTORY OF THE PUBLIC GOOD

Fig. 26.3 Eighteen-year-old mother from Oklahoma, now a California migrant, 1937 (Photographer: Dorothea Lange.
Source: Library of Congress. http://www.loc.gov/pictures/collection/fsa/item/fsa2000000925/PP/)

> "ill-housed, ill-clad, ill-nourished." By suddenly threatening to push millions of other Americans into their wretched condition, the Depression pried open a narrow window of political opportunity to do something at last on behalf of that long-suffering one-third, and in the process to redefine the very character of America. (168)

This redefinition of the very character of America—and the federal government's role in achieving this transformation—was built around addressing chronic, long-standing economic inequality. FDR's New Deal formulated an important new understanding of the role that the federal government could play in the lives of Americans, focused on a commitment to the public good. In his Second Inaugural Address on January 20, 1937, Roosevelt articulated a vision of the nation that characterized American democracy as necessarily—and perhaps foundationally—committed to the public good:

> I see a great nation, upon a great continent, blessed with a great wealth of natural resources. Its hundred and thirty million people are at peace among themselves; they are making their country a good neighbor among the nations. I see a United States which can demonstrate that, under democratic methods of government, national wealth can be translated into a spreading volume of human comforts hitherto unknown, and the lowest standard of living can be raised far above the level of mere subsistence.
>
> But here is the challenge to our democracy: In this nation I see tens of millions of its citizens—a substantial part of its whole population—who at this very moment are denied the greater part of what the very lowest standards of today call the necessities of life.
>
> I see millions of families trying to live on incomes so meager that the pall of family disaster hangs over them day by day.
>
> I see millions whose daily lives in city and on farm continue under conditions labeled indecent by a so-called polite society half a century ago.
>
> I see millions denied education, recreation, and the opportunity to better their lot and the lot of their children.
>
> I see millions lacking the means to buy the products of farm and factory and by their poverty denying work and productiveness to many other millions.
>
> I see one-third of a nation ill-housed, ill-clad, ill-nourished.
>
> It is not in despair that I paint you that picture. I paint it for you in hope—because the Nation, seeing and understanding the injustice in it, proposes to paint it out. We are determined to make every American citizen the subject of his country's interest and concern; and we will never regard any faithful law-abiding group within our borders as superfluous. The test of our progress is not whether we add more to the abundance of those who have much; it is whether we provide enough for those who have too little.

The key moment in this speech for our discussion here related to the public good and community colleges is this one: "The test of our progress is not whether we add more to the abundance of those who have much; it is whether we provide enough for those who have too little." The modern community college was founded to pursue precisely this admirable goal.

As we know, FDR's vision of an America committed to both government action and the public good produced significant, long-lasting achievements. A brief list of these would certainly have to include the landmark Fair Labor Standards Act of 1938, which helped create safer, more equitable working conditions for all Americans. This bill established child labor laws, along with the minimum wage in America. An anecdote from the campaign trail during the long political battle to get this legislation enacted suggests the nature of the problem FDR was attempting to address. A very large crowd in New Bedford, Massachusetts, was "jammed around my car," FDR recounts, and there was "a girl six or seven feet away who was trying to pass an envelope to me and she was just too far to reach":

> One of the policemen threw her back into the crowd and I said to Gus (*Gennerich*), "Get the note from that girl." He got it and handed it to me and the note said this: "Dear Mr. President: I wish you could do something to help us girls. You are the only recourse we have got left. We have been working in a sewing factory, a garment factory, and up to a few months ago we were getting our minimum pay of $11 a week (I think it was $11 a week) and even the learners were getting $7 or $8 a week. Today the 200 of us girls have been cut down to $4 and $5 and $6 a week. You are the only man that can do anything about it. Please send somebody from Washington up here to restore our minimum wages because we cannot live on $4 or $5 or $6 a week." ("Excerpts")

Letters like this from citizens across America strengthened the President's resolve to address this problem. When asked at a press conference on December 29, 1936, if "something should be done to restore minimum pay and maximum hours," FDR responded in the affirmative: "Something has to be done about the elimination of child labor and long hours and starvation wages" ("Excerpts").

We would also have to include on this list the Social Security Administration, which provides minimum economic security for all Americans. In 2016, nearly 61 million Americans were served by Social Security (Social). The Federal Deposit Insurance Corporation was created by the Banking Act of 1933 and was instituted to preserve and promote "public confidence in the US financial system by insuring deposits in banks and thrift institutions" (Federal). Many family savings accounts were lost during the Depression, as banks failed across the nation. In one year alone, 1930, 1352 banks failed (Kennedy 65), and family savings were lost along with them. None of these safeguards were in place before the Depression. One could plausibly claim that these were all effective government programs that helped promote the public good—and continue to do so, for us all.

Created by the National Industrial Recovery Act of 1933, the Works Progress Administration was another federal program developed during the Depression which produced "1,000 miles of new and rebuilt airport runways, 651,000 miles of highway, 124,000 bridges, 8,000 parks, and 18,000 playgrounds and athletic fields" (Hiltzik 421). In addition, 125,000 public buildings were built or refurbished; 41,300 of these buildings were schools (Hiltzik 421). Much of this infrastructure is still in use today. The Public Works Administration built the Grand Coulee Dam, the Lincoln Tunnel, LaGuardia Airport, the Overseas Highway in Florida linking the Florida Keys to the mainland, and the Triborough Bridge in New York.

We must also remember that we recommit to the ideals of our democracy and to the use of public policy to address the public good every time we vote. We make choices about the use of tax revenue and the programs the government sponsors or initiates, and we can make thoughtful choices in the voting booth about which programs do, indeed, truly serve the public good and which programs inhibit liberty, become coercive in nature, and put us on the road to serfdom. The work of FDR—and the longstanding American embrace of many of the programs initiated during the Depression—suggests that the idea of *balance* is important—where freedom, liberty, and support for a robust free market economy can be enhanced by thoughtful, progressive public policy that promotes the public good. Especially in a wealthy democracy, as Hayek himself has suggested, we have a responsibility to make good choices that benefit not only those who are well off but also those who are ill-housed, ill-clad, and ill-nourished. It could be claimed, to borrow a phrase from Michael Hiltzik, that such public policies seek not "not to dismantle the American capitalist system, but to save it from its own excesses" (426)—especially economic inequality and opportunity differentials. These are chronic, serious, long-standing social problems that the community college was designed to address.

THE CONSTITUTION OF LIBERTY

F.A. Hayek develops a meticulously articulated, richly detailed position on the subject of the public good in his important book, *The Constitution of Liberty*, a volume he conceived of as a kind of companion to *The Road to Serfdom* (Hamowy 6). Overall, Hayek embraces the general principle of the public good and supports a number of government programs devoted to furthering it. He is wary, however, about the prospect of limited governmental activities growing larger and more coercive. As always for Hayek, the key concern in terms of government programs is the distinction between "measures which are and those which are not compatible with a free system" (331). "It is the character," he suggests, "rather than the volume of government activity that is important" (331). One category of government activity that can be engaged in the name of the public good, he concedes, is "those services which are clearly desirable but which will not be provided by competitive enterprise because it would be either impossible or difficult to charge the individual beneficiary for them" (332–333). These include sanitary and health services, construction and maintenance of roads, and efforts "to encourage the advancement of knowledge in certain fields" (333). Other activities include making provisions for "the indigent, unfortunate, and disabled" (374). Hayek also notes that "there is little reason why the government should not also play some role, or even take the initiative, in such areas as social insurance and education, or temporarily subsidize certain experimental developments" (374). The problem "here is not so much the aims as the methods of government action" (374). Perhaps most problematic for Hayek are cases where "instead of administering limited resources put under its control for a specific service, government uses its coercive powers to insure that men are given what some expert thinks they need" (377). Nonetheless, Hayek suggests that "the range and variety of government action that is, at least in principle, reconcilable with a free system is thus considerable" (340).

Hayek also supports the general need for innovative thinking and experimentation in the development of public policy:

> We can probably at no point be certain that we have already found the best arrangements or institutions that will make the market economy work as beneficially as it could. It is true that after the essential conditions of a free system have been established, all further institutional improvements are bound to be slow and gradual. But the continuous growth of wealth and technological knowledge which such a system makes possible will constantly suggest new ways in which government might render services to its citizens and bring such possibilities within the range of the practicable. (340)

What the government can't do, Hayek insists, is "determine the material position of particular people or enforce distributive or 'social' justice" (340). Hayek notes that the "conflict between the idea of freedom and the desire to 'correct' the distribution of incomes so as to make it more 'just' is usually not clearly recognized" (341). For Hayek, a free market economy cannot be required to ensure that "different individuals would receive what someone thought they deserved on moral grounds" (341): "Within the limits set by the rule of law, a great deal can be done to make the market work more effectively and smoothly; but, within these limits, what people now regard as distributive justice can never be achieved" (341). Such a system, "instead of leading to what had been conceived as greater social justice," would "mean a new arbitrary and more inescapable order of rank than ever before" (371). In practice, this would mean the government would "aim at controlling all conditions relevant to a particular individual's prospects and so adjust them to his capacities as to assure him of the same prospects as everybody else" (155). The final third of this book provides a detailed discussion of public policy programs that have created what Hayek calls "the welfare state" (369–383), which endeavors "to manipulate the economy so that the distribution of incomes will be made to conform" to an ideal conception of "social justice" (372). Hayek speaks out against labor unions, progressive taxation plans (he favors a proportional tax schedule because with a progressive scheme, "all incomes above a certain figure are confiscated and those below left untaxed" [440]), housing subsidies and town planning, farm subsidies, and some aspects of social security and education policies. Importantly for our purposes here, Hayek supports limited governmental involvement that promotes education (498–516) and believes that "the case for subsidization of higher education" must rest "not on the benefit it confers on the recipient but on the resulting advantages for the community at large" (505)—a clear recognition of the role that education can play in promoting the public good (and providing a very different rationale than current neoliberal ideas about higher education). Advocates of community colleges can be heartened by Hayek's overall commitment to government policies that promote educational opportunity.

Hayek balances his support for limited government activity designed to promote the public good with a vigorous celebration of "individual responsibility" (133). Hayek devotes an entire chapter to this idea. For Hayek, "liberty and responsibility are inseparable" (133): "Liberty not only means that the individual has both the opportunity and the burden of choice; it also means that he must bear the consequences of his actions and will receive praise or blame for them" (133). Hayek states that "in a free society nobody has a duty to see that a man's talents are properly used" (143) and that "the more a man indulges in the propensity to blame others or circumstances for his failures, the more disgruntled and ineffective he tends to become" (145). Hayek emphasizes that there is a significant difference between helping the truly needy and creating a government that provides a kind of entitlement for every citizen. The danger, for Hayek, is that such an approach to social justice leads individuals to believe that "nothing but circumstances over which they have no control" has "determined their position in life or even their actions (133). Also, "to be constantly reminded of our 'social' responsibilities to all the needy or unfortunate in our community, in our country, or in our world, must have the effect of attenuating our feelings until the distinctions between those responsibilities which call for our action and those which do not disappear" (147).

The balance Hayek strikes here is important—and it is an approach to economic development and social justice that community colleges help promote. Community colleges, and developmental education programs specifically, provide only opportunity—nothing more. Nothing is being given away or guaranteed or offered as a kind of lifetime entitlement. Degrees and certificates must be *earned*, through hard work, focus, determination, often over the course of many years. Offering students the opportunity to attend college or enroll in basic reading, writing, and math courses is simply a way of providing opportunity. As Hayek himself suggests in his chapter on education and research, "Let us by all means endeavor to increase opportunities for all" (510).

The idea of "personal responsibility" has enjoyed great political currency in recent years, and a reductive version of this idea has often been used to challenge open door policies and developmental education programs. After all, the thinking goes, why should taxpayers pay twice to educate the same student, once in high school and again in developmental programs (Arendale 20). Shouldn't students be required to take responsibility for their own choices and prospects? One answer, of course—as we have attempted to document here—is that some individuals start life with better choices than others and are thus responsible in much different ways for their success. Another answer is that adults often think differently than they did when they were teenagers in high school and thus can find seriousness of purpose and new career interests once they are out of school and actively engaged with adult life. This is an understanding of transition to higher education that provides theoretical accommodation for personal adult growth, agency, and change—for second chances, fresh starts, and developing maturity and sense of purpose. For all sorts of reasons, some individuals do not (or cannot) discover this sense of purpose until they have left high school. Community colleges and developmental education programs have been designed, at least in part, to help offset these conditional probabilities of success in ways that ultimately benefit us all. The open admissions institution is ideally suited to provide these kinds of fresh starts and second chances (and first chances, too, of course)—to first-time college students but also to individual citizens who find themselves needing to make a change in their career, improve their prospects, or pursue a different course in life. The community college also opens up opportunities for the late bloomer, the early rebel, and the child from an educationally indifferent home (Bruner 77). That we offer these opportunities speaks to the strength of our democracy and our belief in the potential for lifelong learning, growth, and personal transformation.

"'The Common Good' Is a Meaningless Concept"

Other neoliberal thinkers are more categorical and dismissive in their thinking about the public good. Ayn Rand, for example, is perhaps paradigmatic in this regard. She is among the most absolutist of thinkers in theorizing the relationship between government and its citizens. In *Capitalism: The Unknown Ideal*, Rand dismisses the very idea of the common good. She links pursuit of the common good directly to a favorite target of Hayek's—tyranny:

> Every social system is based, explicitly or implicitly, on some theory of ethics. The tribal notion of "the common good" has served as the moral justification of most social systems—and of all tyrannies—in history. The degree of a society's enslavement or freedom corresponded to the degree to which that tribal slogan was invoked or ignored.
>
> "The common good" (or "the public interest") is an undefined and undefinable concept: there is no such entity as "the tribe" or "the public"; the tribe (or the public or society) is only a number of individual men. Nothing can be good for the tribe as such; "good" and "value" pertain *only* to a living organism—to an individual living organism—not to a disembodied aggregate of relationships.
>
> "The common good" is a meaningless concept, unless taken literally, in which case its only possible meaning is: the sum of the good of *all* the individual men involved. But in that case, the concept is meaningless as a moral criterion: it leaves open the question of what *is* the good of individual men and how does one determine it?

It is not, however, in its literal meaning that that concept is generally used. It is accepted precisely for its elastic, undefinable, mystical character which serves, not as a moral guide, but as an escape from morality. Since the good is not applicable to the disembodied, it becomes a moral blank check for those who attempt to embody it. (20–1)

Rand's formulation here draws on nineteenth-century Romantic literary theory about the heroic individual, radically free from history, politics, ideology, and economics, operating in a pure public sphere of freedom and opportunity (Abrams). Such an individual is unencumbered by history, class, race, gender, or politics. Rand posits here an ahistorical and apolitical understanding of the individual's position in society, one that is predicated exclusively on the individual's determination, will, and personal character strengths. Such an understanding of the individual has a long and distinguished history in the West. For free market economists, such a formulation also functions to help unlink government policy from individual human suffering and hardship. As such, opportunity differentials become primarily the responsibility of the individual—not of the economic system, the society, or the presence or absence of government policies that seek to promote the public good. Such a conception of radical freedom for the individual, however, simplifies or elides much of what we know about the complex nature of living in the world and the role that governments play in making market economies possible. In *Saving Capitalism: For the Many, Not the Few*, Robert B. Reich has urged us to acknowledge that "there can be no 'free market' without government" (4):

A market—any market—requires that government make and enforce the rules of the game. In most modern democracies, such rules emanate from legislatures, administrative agencies, and courts. Government doesn't "intrude" on the "free market." It creates the free market. (5)

As Reich suggests, citizens in a democracy must always be vigilant about who sets the rules of this economic system, what logic is used to change these rules, and whose interests these rules serve:

Few ideas have more profoundly poisoned the minds of more people than the notion of a "free market" existing somewhere in the universe, into which the government "intrudes." In this view, whatever inequality or insecurity the market generates is assumed to be the natural and inevitable consequence of impersonal "market forces."... The "free market" is a myth that prevents us from examining these rule changes and asking whom they serve. The myth is therefore highly useful to those who do not wish such an examination to be undertaken. (3, 6)

As V.G. Kiernan has suggested, "an economic system, like a nation or a religion, lives not by bread alone, but by beliefs, visions, daydreams as well, and these may be no less vital to it for being erroneous" (114). Rand's idea here may well be one of these daydreams—but it is a powerful and dangerous one nonetheless.

What Is an Individual?

All individuals in America benefit from programs that have been established to promote the public good. In fact, one might accurately describe these programs and policies as a "disembodied aggregate of relationships" that make life better for us all—and help create and nurture who we are, what we are able to achieve, and what is both possible and impossible for us to imagine. The government, for example, has devoted considerable resources to ensuring public safety. These offices include local police departments and fire departments, the state police, and the FBI and Homeland Security. We get to work on roads and other transit systems that we have built together as part of our shared commitment to the public good. This includes our national highway system. The Department of Motor Vehicles helps ensure the safety of roads, vehicles, and drivers. The Federal Aviation Administration and the Transportation Security Administration ensures safety at airports and in the skies. The Army, Navy, Air Force, and Coast Guard serve to protect our nation in an increasingly dangerous world. We all benefit from the security they provide.

Many other government programs actively promote the public good and make life better for us all. We have all been educated by a national school system established for the public good. Those of us who have attended state colleges and universities, like my two children, have had their lives enhanced incalculably by the opportunity to earn a college degree at an affordable state university. The two colleges my children attended, the University of Connecticut and the University of Massachusetts, began as land-grant institutions established by the Morrill Acts of 1862 and 1890 to promote the public good. Financial aid programs and loan opportunities established by the government helped make earning a degree possible for my children. The G.I. Bill—enacted with the "desire to avoid the missteps following World War I, when discharged Veterans got little more than a $60 allowance and a train ticket home" (US Department of Veterans Affairs)—provides educational opportunities for our veterans, including my father. The Civil Rights Act of 1964, the Voting Rights Act, and the establishment of the Equal Employment Opportunity Commission addressed long-standing inequalities in America—and made the country a better place for us all. The Clean Air Act—legislation that Milton Friedman did not support, claiming that "private enterprise finds that it is not profitable to pollute" ("Why" 6; Hochschild)—has made the air cleaner and the environment less polluted for us all. Americans, thus, "breathe less pollution and face lower risks of premature death and other serious health effects" (United States Environmental). The Clear Air Act has removed tons of aggregate emissions of six common pollutants from our air—particulates, ground-level ozone, lead, carbon monoxide, sulfur oxides, and nitrogen oxides. In fact, the US Environmental Protection Agency summarizes the cumulative benefits of its work this way:

> emissions reductions have led to dramatic improvements in the quality of the air that we breathe. Between 1990 and 2015, national concentrations of air pollutants improved 85 percent for lead, 84 percent for carbon monoxide, 67 percent for sulfur dioxide (1-hour), 60 percent for nitrogen dioxide (annual), and 3 percent for ozone. Fine particle concentrations (24-hour) improved 37 percent and coarse particle concentrations (24-hour) improved 69 percent between 2000, when trends data begins for fine particles, and 2015.

A recent environmental report about air quality in China, a nation which has embraced the free market and until recently virtually ignored environmental concerns, estimates that air pollution is now killing approximately 4000 people a day in China, accounting for approximately 17 percent of all deaths in that country, primarily, it appears, from burning coal ("Air"; Rohde and Muller.). Chinese journalist Chai Jing's landmark documentary, *Under the Dome*, released in 2015, documents the extent of this devastating pollution in chilling, exhaustive detail (the running time is 143 minutes). *Under the Dome* was viewed 200 million times within days of being broadcast (Jun).

The Food and Drug Administration protects our food, and the public sanitation infrastructure protects our health with water treatment plants, sewer systems, and trash disposal facilities and licensing. The US government has also invested heavily in medical research and alternative energy.

This support of research and development helps drive innovation and market competitiveness (Gates). In fact, Greg Satell, in a recent essay in *Forbes*, identified a number of government programs that have been principal drivers of innovation. These include the Defense Advanced Research Projects Agency, which began as the Manhattan Project in 1958 and "has been a mainstay of technological development, funding development of the Internet, GPS and even Apple's Siri, just to name a few." Also included are the Small Business Innovation Research programs, which helps "young, innovative businesses get started"; In-Q-Tel, a government-funded venture capital program "that invests in startup companies focused on cutting edge technology such as big data analytics and quantum computing"; and the National Institutes of Health (NIH). Satell is especially effusive about this government organization:

> The impact of the NIH cannot be overstated. Researchers there have discovered vaccines for infectious diseases and innovative new treatments. A Congressional study found that as many as 60% of important drugs would not have been discovered without NIH support and that economic returns range from 25% to 40%.
>
> It also funded the Human Genome Project, a $3.6 billion undertaking that has not only revolutionized medical science, but whose economic benefits have been estimated to be nearly $800 billion as of 2011 and will likely multiply many times in the future.

Finally, the Earned Income Tax Credit program provides subsidies for low-income working families, helping to relieve poverty and suffering among poor, working Americans.

Overall, it does not appear that this government investment in the common good looks anything like Rand's hyperbolic "escape from morality." And there is more that we might say here, if space allowed. In fact, it could plausibly be suggested, instead, that these programs (and others like them) help liberate individuals from the unfreedoms of privation, ignorance, racism, unsafe neighborhoods, unhealthy environments, and low ceilings of possibility. Surely, Rand's distaste for language and policy related to the common good derives at least in part from her early traumatic experiences in Russia with the revolution in 1917 and the state-sponsored socialism of the Soviet Union that developed soon after—and the suffering that followed for her family and for many citizens in that nation. Much like Hayek, Rand is working intellectually against a Soviet model of state-sponsored "socialism," which produced suffering and violence on an industrial scale. Rand was also deeply enamored by Hollywood, which appears to have shaped both her conception of America as a young girl in Russia (Mallon) and perhaps also her understanding of the power of narrative and the utility of a certain kind of populist rhetoric.

Nonetheless, as we think about American democracy and the public good, the evidence that we have examined so far suggests that we may be closer not to Rand's formulation but to Martin Luther King's understanding of an American society defined by individuals linked in profound ways to one another. He theorized the nature of this relationship perhaps most eloquently in "Letter from Birmingham Jail": "We are caught in an inescapable network of mutuality, tied in a single garment of destiny." The individual and the public good, in this view, become bound together in powerful, essential ways. Perhaps, in fact, as Edward W. Said has suggested, it may be that "we can no longer say with absolute confidence where individuality ends and the public realm begins" (*Humanism* 42). The individual becomes, in this view, a sovereign constituent upon which a wide variety of different relationships and sources of power converge and intersect. The individual is embedded in a complex, overlapping network of relationships, histories, and contingencies. What affects the public good, in this understanding of the individual, affects us all. This view challenges Rand's conception of the individual as radically independent and self-sufficient, unencumbered by history, culture, family, or economic systems and conditions.

CHAPTER 27

The Consequences of a Deified Market Model

"Merchants of Ideas"

If we embrace the idea that in a healthy democracy, there is a place for thoughtful public policy that seeks to further the public good, we can turn our attention now to higher education. Much debate on this issue in recent years has been framed by neoliberal thinking about the "value added" by higher education to individual human capital (Chambers and Gopaul; Marginson). For neoliberals, as Adrianna J. Kezar notes, "the common or public good emerges from a focus on protection of individual rights and freedoms," "the accumulation of private goods," "the trend toward greater individualism and a move away from community involvement," the "privatization and corporatization of public services," and the general "commercialization and marketization of public life" (24). Public policy is most usefully employed in this model to redefine "the public good as private advancement and economic attainment rather than long-standing missions of social development, social justice, and democratic engagement" (Kezar 24). This shift in policy has occasioned a dramatic reformulation of the nature of the public good and the role of higher education in America. Much of the theoretical emphasis of this discussion has focused on the private returns of higher education for individual citizens. Gary Becker's landmark book, *Human Capital*, which provides the foundational theory for much of this thinking, theorizes education essentially as a business transaction, whereby students make personal investments in their own accumulation of human capital, much the way a business might invest in equipment. The very idea of the public good, in fact, following Hayek, Friedman, Rand, and Becker, has come under sustained attack by some scholars and by many state legislators and politicians. These circumstances have generated a number of important scholarly books and articles about higher education and the public good in recent years. Some of this work seeks primarily to document this change, while other work seeks to actively resist and reframe this understanding of the public good. Virtually all of the scholars contributing to this discussion acknowledge the urgent need for vigorous public debate about this important issue.

This body of work offers readers a wide range of potential responses to this neoliberal understanding of higher education and the public good. For example, in *Academic Capitalism and the New Economy*, Sheila Slaughter and Gary Rhoades provide an informational and historical overview of what they call the "academic capitalist knowledge/learning regime" (309). Knowledge in the neoliberal theoretical framework becomes, they suggest, a new kind of "raw material" (17), much like tin or iron ore. Although Slaughter and Rhoades suggest that this new understanding of higher education "could be resisted" (1), their focus is primarily descriptive. Matthew T. Lambert, in *Privatization and the Public Good: Public Universities in the Balance*, adopts a kind of realpolitik approach, suggesting that public policy informed by neoliberal ideas that question the value of the public good has perhaps been inevitable, given shrinking state resources nationwide and long-term concerns about the loss of jobs in America. Lambert suggests that public institutions will likely have to adopt some form of privatization in order to survive, including the establishment of private partnerships and alternate, non-governmental revenue streams, increased tuition costs, and perhaps reduced access. Wendy Brown is perhaps the most activist in her approach to this debate, suggesting, in *Undoing the Demos: Neoliberalism's Stealth Revolution*, that "neoliberalism, a peculiar form of reason that configures all aspects of existence in economic terms, is quietly undoing basic elements of democracy" (17). Brown submits, in fact, that "democracy is being replaced by plutocracy—rule by and for the rich" (17). Brown advocates active resistance to neoliberal values, ideas, and public policy. Since this body of work examines how economic and philosophical ideas are translated into state budgets, master plans, and funding for higher education, it is important for us to examine this work closely. Neoliberal ideas about the public good have framed recent discussions about community colleges, student success, and the public good on our campuses in powerful ways.

As we think about the politics of this debate, let us pay special attention to the foundational ideas driving this discussion and the legislation that follows from these ideas. Here, we would be embracing both Hayek and Keynes in acknowledging *the power of ideas* to frame public perception and therefore to shape public policy. As Joseph Stiglitz notes,

> One of the most effective ways of influencing public opinion is to capture politicians. After all, politicians are merchants of ideas. (Persuading politicians to adopt one's perspectives and perceptions has a double advantage: not only do they sell ideas to the public; they translate the ideas into legislation and regulation.) For the most part, politicians don't originate ideas; rather, they take those emanating from academia and from public intellectuals, and from within governments and from nongovernmental organizations (NGOs). (*Price* 161)

A great deal depends, then, on ideas "emanating from academia and from public intellectuals."

"Factories for Producing Private Status Goods"

A good place to begin this discussion is with Simon Marginson, who has noted with alarm in his essay, "Higher Education and Public Good," that US higher education is currently in danger of standing for "nothing more, nothing deeper or more collective, no greater public good, that the aggregation of self-interest" (412). This new understanding of the function of higher education in a democracy, he notes, draws from business models and neoliberal thinking about the supreme value of marketplace competition. Marginson labels this approach to higher education "methodological individualism":

> For the methodological individualist the collective or social character of higher education institutions is nothing more or less than the mathematical sum of the private benefits that they provide. There are no common or relational benefits of higher education that condition, precede or succeed those private individual benefits and extend beyond their sum. If such a premise is adopted, and corresponding policies are implemented, there is every danger the collective benefits of higher education could be so weakened over time as to decisively wither any argument for the common funding of higher education institutions to secure such joint objectives. (413)

Marginson recommends that if colleges and universities wish to be more than "factories for producing private status goods" (414), they must articulate "a foundational public purpose—one that is more than a marketing slogan; and one grounded in more than the survival of the university for its own sake, or the survival of students or knowledge or learning for their own sakes" (413). Marginson provides a wide-ranging analysis of the many ways higher education might articulate and frame such a public purpose, but his most foundational recommendation has to do with equity—a key public purpose for community colleges:

> Competition is better at creating private goods than public goods. Smith never argued the invisible hand of the market created an optimal society. His point was that it created another common good, economic prosperity. This had to be modified by factoring in sociability and justice. Hence *The Theory of Moral Sentiments* (1759) explained the affective ties between persons and *The Wealth of Nations*' (1776) advocated state intervention in education, though confining the argument for state support to schooling rather than universities. Arguably, advocates of equity in higher education spend too much energy trying to create the chimera of a fair competition over private goods. It is the competitive order itself that should be tackled, particularly the way status differentials in higher education undermine the commons. The neighbourhood becomes fairer in higher education when the main game is not winner-take-all and, instead, is the production of shared and collective benefits. (424-425)

The community college embodies precisely this impulse toward equity and "shared and collective benefits." Marginson's suggestion that the influence of status differentials in higher education is undermining the commons certainly appears to be borne out by the research we have surveyed regarding economic inequality. This is a problem, he suggests, that we must continue to address with resourcefulness and determination. Marginson appears generally optimistic about the value of resistance and the possibility of forging a more progressive, more "global" understanding of the public good (430–1; Deresiewicz).

"A Moral and Social Crisis"

Jon Nixon's book, *Higher Education and the Public Good*, was written in the aftermath of the Great Recession of 2008—an economic crisis that Nixon identifies "not only as an economic crisis but also as a moral and social crisis" as well (ix). The Great Recession, he contends, "seriously threatened the social cohesion of supposedly advanced states that had hitherto been seen as relatively stable and settled" and "it challenged the market-driven consumerism of the years prior to the economic downturn" (ix). The recession also "highlighted the chronic decline of the public good as both an idea and an ideal" (ix). Given what appears to be historical validation by the recession, Nixon attempts to reimagine the public good "for the changed social, civic, and global circumstances of the twenty-first century" (ix). Perhaps Nixon's most urgent and overarching claim is that "individualism is part of the problem, not part of the solution and that whatever solution is to be found will begin with the rediscovery of shared responsibility" (1). This shared responsibility, he believes, must be built around "a common commitment to social justice and equity" (1). For Nixon, as for us, this is "partly a question of how higher education itself can become more inclusive and open; partly a question of how higher education can assist in the formation of an educated and sophisticated citizenry open to divergence and plurality; and partly a matter of how universities envisage their purpose within civil society" (47).

Higher education thus becomes for Nixon "an essential element within the participative and democratic culture of any vital civil society" (124). Perhaps Nixon's most inspiring claim about higher education—and one that will likely ring true to supporters of the community college—is that "higher education exists to show ordinary people how extraordinary they can be" (125). By engaging this essential democratic work, higher education can help promote the vitally important social qualities of "mutual recognition and mutual understanding" (125). Nixon advocates for an activist approach to challenging neoliberal ideas and also acknowledges that academics have "huge tasks ahead" (134). These include "the intellectual task of defining the ends and purposes of higher education, the imaginative task of reorienting higher education for the needs and aspirations of future generations, and the practical task of ensuring that higher education works at the systems level, the level of institutional structure, and the levels of curriculum and pedagogy" (134). The greatest challenge facing higher education, he believes, "is to re-locate itself at the centre of civic society as an open and permeable space of learning" (134). Like Marginson, Nixon is optimistic about our ability to engage this challenge and achieve progressive public policy related to the public good and higher education.

"If You Know One State, Then You Know One State"

Matthew T. Lambert, in *Privatization and the Public Good: Public Universities in the Balance,* articulates a more accommodating position than either Marginson or Nixon, perhaps (at least in part) because his research included a large number of field interviews with politicians and legislators. In fact, Lambert's book offers a fascinating insider's glimpse into the pragmatic, nuts-and-bolts contemporary workings of higher education public policy development, funding realities, and public policy issues. Dwindling tax revenues are obviously driving many of the changes toward privatization that Lambert documents in this book—but so is "the deliberate attempt to restructure higher education as a market" (117). Lambert employs a case study approach to examine the effects of privatization in three flagship university systems—in Virginia, North Carolina, and California—and he interviews a large number of state legislators and government leaders along with college personnel. It is rare in higher education scholarship to hear directly from legislators themselves, and what Lambert reports from these conversations makes for absorbing reading. One legislator Lambert interviewed, for example, laments the difficult choices he is forced to make as he and his colleagues apportion declining state resources: "I didn't come to [the capitol] to cut budgets, but that's all we can do today. You can't be visionary and forward-thinking when the stare is bleeding, and right now [this state] is close to life-support" (25).

Certainly, reduced tax revenue is a key factor driving public policy decisions in the educational systems that Lambert studies. Another crucial variable, however, is the power of ideas to shape public opinion and public policy. Significantly, Lambert found that each state he studied had its own unique history and foundational ideology. The ideas informing these histories helped guide the legislative approach to higher education in each of these states. In some powerful and surprising ways, Lambert's book affirms Hayek's seminal understanding about "the power of ideas" to shape public policy ("Intellectuals" 237). The local nature of legislation related to higher education is one of Lambert's most important findings. As one of the individuals he interviews puts it, "If you know one state, then you know one state" (23)—suggesting that the politics of higher education is, in some essential ways, always local. Virginia, for example, has a long history of providing only modest state support for higher education, even though the University of Virginia was founded by Thomas Jefferson and was established to embody Jefferson's ideals about the public good. Nonetheless, as former Virginia Secretary of Finance John Bennett told Lambert, Virginia has always been committed to keeping tax burdens low and providing only limited funding for public initiatives: "Virginia is a low-tax, low-spending state. This limits the state funding that is available for higher education" (141). Teresa Sullivan, the President of the University of Virginia when Lambert interviewed her, provided a telling anecdote suggesting how deep this tradition goes:

> In Carr's Hill [the President's House at UVA] there is an original letter by Thomas Jefferson framed under glass, written in 1825, the year before he died, complaining to a friend about how little money the general assembly gives to support the University of Virginia. I think the reason that that letter is there is so that every president understands this is not a new problem. It is not an issue of twenty years ago. The Commonwealth of Virginia has always been relatively reluctant to support public spending really on just about anything (142).

Lambert documents the many ways this plays out in relation to current thinking about public policy, the public good, and higher education in Virginia.

North Carolina, on the other hand, has a very different tradition and history. The North Carolina State constitution, in fact, includes a unique provision that has been an important touchstone throughout the state's history: "The General Assembly shall provide that the benefits of The University of North Carolina and other public institutions of higher education, as far as practicable, be extended to the people of the State free of expense" (155). Lambert reports that many legislators he talked to "describe support for higher education as being in the state's DNA" (156). One North Carolina senator described the tradition this way:

> We used to talk about being the valley of humility between the two mountains of conceit, Virginia and South Carolina, in the land of the aristocracies. This was a farming state, a poor state of immigrants, and so to latch on to something like the university was significantly important to help pull ourselves up. I will say to you that there is not a more significant institution than [UNC] Chapel Hill in pulling the state up. (158)

North Carolina has worked to keep tuition low, historically given priority to in-state students, and consistently understood the state's colleges and universities as "a hearth and home for the state's struggling youth" (159). The University of North Carolina system has managed to do this "even while other states experienced wandering public missions and faltering state support" (162).

The case of California is also instructive. California also has a long history of championing higher education, and Article IX of the California Constitution makes a direct link between the value of education and the public good:

> A general diffusion of knowledge and intelligence being essential to the preservation of the rights and liberties of the people, the Legislature shall encourage by all suitable means the promotion of intellectual, scientific, moral, and agricultural improvement. (qtd. In Lambert 191)

As Lambert notes, "'The California Idea' had its roots in the Progressive era—the idea was that higher education was no longer a privilege, but a right for every citizen" (187). California was the first state to pass community college legislation in the 1920s (187) and after World War II, formulated a Master Plan for higher education that was approved in 1960 (187–8). "The true genius of the Master Plan," Patrick Callahan, former Executive Director of the California Higher Education Policy Center, tells Lambert, "was that California was the first state and really the first government entity anywhere in the world to promise access to higher education to any adult who could benefit from it. That sounds kind of tame now, but no one had ever done that before" (188). California's Master Plan provided a powerful set of ideas that drove public policy in California for many years, producing a world-class higher education system devoted to access and opportunity.

Unfortunately, California also has a referendum system built into its constitution, which means that voters can "propose laws that can be voted on directly by the electorate, essentially bypassing the legislature" (189). What is unique about California is that a number of these referendums ended up producing new laws that had negative consequences for higher education. Proposition 13 was passed in 1989, and this legislation dramatically restructured the tax base in California. Proposition 98 was passed in 1988, requiring that "a minimum percentage of the state budget be spent on K-12 education" (197). The Three Strikes Law, Proposition 184, was passed in 1994 and required increased funding for the criminal justice system. Lambert documents the various ways these referendums had the "unintended consequence" of reducing discretionary funds in the state coffers and therefore requiring reduced government support for higher education across the state (189–219). Unfortunately, Lambert concludes, the lack of a Master Plan and the absence of overarching ideas are currently determining public policy in California: "The state truly doesn't seem to have a clear agenda for what it wants to accomplish today" in terms of higher education (205).

These case studies provide important lessons about "powerful ideas" shaping public policy. Lambert has shown that ideas drive legislation, perhaps even more than fiscal crises do. This is promising news for those who care about community colleges and the ideas of equity and social justice. Lambert concludes his book by calling for a "renewed conversation" about these issues (282): "My research suggests that the country needs a spirited public dialogue, at both the state and federal levels, about the role of higher education" (284). Certainly, this is essential advice, and community college personnel should help lead this conversation.

A "Stealth Revolution"

Wendy Brown's volume is perhaps the most alarming of the recent books about neoliberalism and higher education. As her title suggests, Brown sees neoliberal ideology threatening the very foundation of democracy itself. This "cultural shift," she suggests, has been subtle but insidious, focusing not on "measures of educational quality" but on "metrics oriented entirely to return on investment (ROI) and centered on what kind of job placement and income enhancement student investors may expect from any given institution" (23). President Obama's 2013 proposed college rating system, now significantly modified, was originally designed to measure precisely—and primarily—these outcomes (Toth, Sullivan and Calhoon-Dillahunt). The market, Brown warns, has become "generalized as a form of reason" (67), replacing more humanistic ways of producing knowledge and determining value in the world. Such an approach also displaces traditional moral and civic aspects of a liberal arts education. This kind of "economization of the political" diminishes, she suggests, "the meaning of citizenship itself" (210). Under neoliberalism, Brown suggests, citizens themselves have been transformed into "human capital" and higher education into "human capital development" (176). In such an ideological framework, the very idea of the public good is fatally compromised:

> *Public goods* of any kind are increasingly difficult to speak of or secure. The market metrics contouring every dimension of human conduct and institutions make it daily more difficult to explain why universities, libraries, parks and natural reserves, city services and elementary schools, even roads and sidewalks, are or should be publicly accessible and publicly provisioned. Why should the public fund and administer them? Why should everyone have free access to them? Why shouldn't their cost be borne only by those who "consume" them? (176)

Brown concludes by urging academics to fashion an alternative "road out" of the neoliberal state (220) that is "humane, free, sustainable, and above all, modestly under human control" (221). She warns us of the dangers of "ceding all power to craft the future to markets" (221) and insists that markets don't always know best: "In letting markets decide our present and future, neoliberalism wholly abandons the project of individual or collective mastery of existence" (221). She characterizes the global triumph of neoliberalism as a "stealth revolution," and she urges academics to actively counter this revolution and its deep "antihumanism" (222) not with despair or surrender but with concerted and sustained political action (220–22).

Poor Information

Finally, and perhaps most significantly for our purposes here, is economist Walter W. McMahon's book on this subject, *Higher Learning, Greater Good: The Private and Social Benefits of Higher Education*. McMahon's primary claim is quite simple: "the greater good" created by higher education has been largely unacknowledged and enormously undervalued in policy discussions in America is recent years. His book provides an exhaustive review of the evidence and research that supports this claim. McMahon also addresses these questions as an economist, suggesting that "where there is poor information, private markets fail, and the result is economic inefficiency" (13). Unfortunately, McMahon finds all kinds of "poor information" at play in current discussions about higher education related to the public good.

McMahon suggests that Americans generally have a solid understanding only of the most visible, most self-evident benefits of higher education. This knowledge is usually limited to the contribution that a college education makes to improved salary and earnings. Most Americans are much less aware of the many private benefits that derive from higher education beyond such earnings, what he calls non-market social and private benefits (13). For example, "most students do not know how much more each year of college will contribute to their longevity, to their health, and to their happiness and quality of life" (13). These benefits are "poorly understood and therefor probably significantly underestimated" (13; 118–80). The "lack of specific knowledge about these social benefits is another source of market failure likely to lead to underinvestment" (14).

The non-market private benefits of higher education that McMahon documents are extensive, and they may be surprising even to those who know higher education well. They include better overall health ("The evidence is overwhelming that each additional year spent in college contributes to increasingly better health and, in due course, to greater longevity" [133]), improved longevity and mortality rates, better child health and infant mortality rates ("The research indicates that this does not depend on having specific courses in health fields, only on having more years of formal education" [138]), child education ("Education is a dynamic process within families and within societies over generations" [139]), happiness (this is a complex subject with many variables; college education appears to contribute to the acquisition of some of these variables including income, employment, friendships and social capital, health, and personal freedom and peace [143–7]), improved efficiency in household management ("There are a number of ways that those with a college education use their time and knowledge to make better choices" [147]), and lifelong learning ("An extremely important effect of higher education is the extent to which it facilitates lifelong learning …. [This] is vital in a globalizing economy where visions must shift to the world, and where the living and working environments are changing rapidly due to technology, trade, travel, and better communication" [149]). These non-market private benefits are often unacknowledged in most discussions about public policy related to higher education. McMahon's work articulates and disaggregates the many largely invisible and long-lasting benefits of college education that pay off—and that deliver significant returns on investment—across generations.

McMahon also documents the many social benefits of higher education, what economists call "externalities"—that is, "benefits that spill over to others, including future generations, that are beyond the private benefits of higher education to the individual" (181). McMahon contends that "the proportion of the total benefits of education that are externalities is the best guide to how far the trend toward privatization in the financing of education should go for achieving optimum efficiency" (181). Discussion of these benefits, alas, has been largely absent from recent public policy discussions of higher education and thus constitute another manifestation of poor information leading to market failure. One "key basis" (181) for determining an appropriate level of public support for higher education, McMahon suggests, must be "equity" (181): "This involves the desire to provide for equality of educational opportunity or even something beyond that, such as John Rawls's justice, by providing access to higher education to able students from poor families" (181). Obviously, this is something community colleges have been mandated to do, as McMahon consistently and appreciatively acknowledges (32; 67–8; 213; 283; 300).

Measuring these social benefits is a complex process that has not always been conducted skillfully (182–201), and McMahon works his way through this complex body of research and the various theoretical models used to assess data related to social benefits very carefully. Ultimately, he identifies a whole range of public benefits that spill over to other members of society:

- **intergenerational effects**: "Human capital production is also not subject to diminishing returns over generations. This is an important point that permits increasing education and knowledge to continue to serve as an engine of per capita economic growth perpetually." (189–90)
- **behaviors and attitudes that contribute to democracy, human rights, and civil rights**, including "a less unquestioning acceptance of authority, a desire to participate in public service, and informed participation in the voting process" (203) and more tolerance of other races (209).
- **reduction of income inequality**: "Higher education in the United States and Canada tends to reduce income inequality" (213).
- **reduction of crime rates**: "One additional year of school lowers the subsequent probability of incarceration for white men by 0.1 percentage point, and for black men by 0.37 percentage point" (219).
- **lower welfare, medical, and prison costs for states:** Each additional year of college "eases the state budget squeeze from public assistance, Medicaid, public health, and other welfare costs" (220).
- **a cleaner environment**: "There is now some direct evidence from worldwide data about the effects of expansion of higher education on the environment" (222).

- **social capital and happiness**: "Happiness is a private benefit of higher education, as we saw in Chapter 4, but it also is a social benefit that has some externality elements that spill over to benefit others and contribute to social cohesion and hence to social capital" (223).
- **and the dissemination of new knowledge**: "What is probably the largest and most important social benefit of higher education is the benefit to the broader society from the dissemination of new knowledge" (224).

Many of us benefit in profound ways from the education of others, and this has been a largely ignored aspect of the public good that derives from higher education. As McMahon notes,

> The indirect effects from education have often been estimated, but their feedback on the growth process generally has been ignored. One result of not ignoring these feedbacks is that a portion of the money earnings of current graduates and a portion of current growth both are the result of education externalities from the education of others. (194)

Another vitally important aspect of this understanding of the public good generated by higher education is the value of research generated by college and university graduates. McMahon makes this point very dramatically:

> It is universally recognized by economists that externalities from research are very important since research results are disseminated widely and discoveries can benefit generations still unborn. For example, the value to the economy and the society of the education of just one genius such as John Bardeen, who won two Nobel Prizes in Physics for inventing the transistor that became the foundation for the computer revolution, surely is sufficient to equal the cost of the education of millions worldwide. Marshall (1927, p. 216) said "all that is spent during many years of opening the means of higher education to the masses would be well paid for if it called out just one more Newton, or Darwin, or Shakespeare, or Beethoven." (194)

McMahon then takes the extraordinary measure of providing a monetary estimate of these non-market public goods social benefits—which he values at "$27,726 per year, almost equal to the average increment to male and female earnings after completing a bachelor's" (254). McMahon also calculates the rate of return for all levels of higher education on investment of tax dollars (Table 5.5; 250), which he has updated in a new article in the *Journal of Education Finance* (2015) entitled "Financing Education for the Public Good: A New Strategy." He now calculates that the total return on investment of an associate's degree is 43 percent ("Financing" 432). Therefore, investment in education, he concludes, "pays for itself in advancing development over again in the form of development each 2½ or 3 years depending on the level of education" ("Financing" 432). For McMahon, this is clear evidence of substantial underinvestment in higher education by states, as well as evidence of how short-sighted state and federal cutbacks to higher education are.

McMahon summarizes his findings very simply: "if there is poor information available to the average citizen and politicians about the value of non-market private and social benefits of higher education, then poor investment decisions and policy decisions will result" (2). Unfortunately, he finds that this is precisely what has happened. "Investment in higher education," he concludes, "is significantly below optimum" (252). He closes his analysis with an ominous warning: "The evidence mounts that higher education's service to the public good is seriously at risk" (329).

Again, we return to the question of balance as we seek to strengthen freedom and economic opportunity and also promote the public good. As McMahon suggests, economic efficiency "requires a balance in the degree of privatization that is optimal. Some is essential, but carried too far the interests of the greater good and future generations can be in jeopardy" (12). McMahon is especially concerned about "degree completion rates by students from poor families," which are "falling at the same time that access by these students is diminishing" (215). Declining public support per student has created "a very troubling policy issue, restricted access" (56). Higher net tuition costs created by neoliberal policies, coupled with falling real family income, "restricts access of minorities and students from low- and low-middle-income families the most" (56). Lack of a comprehensive plan for nurturing sustainable, long-term economic growth and simply cutting taxes, McMahon suggests, often becomes problematic:

> The financing problem is that higher education is not seen by political leaders as "the" solution. Tax cuts are another solution often advocated. They clearly stimulate private demand and are very helpful to a cyclical recovery. But their supply side effects on human and physical capital formation, which are important to longer-term productivity growth, are much more controversial among economists. Localized tax breaks to attract firms to one locality are another solution frequently employed. But these have a very localized

focus since they attract firms away from some other locality and therefore cancel out nationwide. They also can subsidize inefficiency and special interests, which is not conducive to longer-term productivity growth. Tax cutting that stimulates local demand can be confused with longer-term investment that raises productivity (including the investment in human capital) and is crucial to long-term sustainable growth. (33).

In the penultimate chapter of the book, McMahon proposes a variety of options for moving forward, including increasing college enrollment rates by 20 percent (301–5) and embracing a more ambitious "universal entitlement approach," which would provide a college education to all high school graduates, modeled on the G.I. Bill (305). There is already some discussion of this idea with proposals to make the first two years of community college free. Tennessee has recently enacted one such program, "Tennessee Promise," which appears to be quite successful, judging from early, statewide assessment of this program (Smith). Beginning with the class of 2015, Tennessee Promise offers two years of community or technical college tuition-free to Tennessee high school graduates. This is "a last-dollar scholarship," meaning it covers college costs not met by Pell, HOPE, or TSAA (Drive "Tennessee"). This endeavor is sponsored by the state's Drive to 55 Alliance, an "alliance of private sector partners, leaders and non-profits working together in support of the state's Drive to 55 initiative to equip 55 percent of Tennesseans with a college degree or certificate by 2025" ("Alliance"). Another key factor in this program is required mentoring and community service:

> While removing the financial burden is key, a critical component of Tennessee Promise is the individual guidance each participant will receive from a mentor who will assist the student as he or she navigates the college admissions process. This is accomplished primarily via mandatory meetings that students must attend in order to remain eligible for the program. In addition, Tennessee Promise participants must complete eight hours of community service per term enrolled, as well as maintain satisfactory academic progress (2.0 GPA) at their institution. (Tennessee "About")

This program, like President Obama's America's College Promise proposal, which also proposed that qualifying students can receive "the first two years of community college free" (Fain "Two"), is precisely the kind of investment in public higher education and community colleges that McMahon advocates.

Overall, McMahon's work provides vitally important long-term perspective and data—that is often overlooked if we are not thinking longitudinally—regarding the deep and enduring value of public investment in higher education and community colleges. McMahon positions community colleges at the center of his recommendations for promoting access and opportunity in American higher education.

All of the work we have reviewed here shares a number of features: concern about neoliberal ideas subverting traditional understandings of the public good; worry about the broad mandate of higher education being reduced simply to job placement and workforce training; alarm at the loss of the civic and moral dimension of higher education; and a sense that access, opportunity, and democratic ideals are being actively subverted by an exclusive focus on certain kinds of marketplace considerations. All of this work also calls for strong public action on the part of citizens and academics who support a more progressive understanding of the public good and the role that higher education can play in moving us closer to an ideal society.

CHAPTER 28

Development as Freedom

REIGN OF ERROR

If we look at what privatization and neoliberal ideas have produced in the public school sector, we see increasing evidence of dysfunction and—I'm afraid there is no other word for this—disaster. Diane Ravitch's *Reign of Error: The Hoax of the Privatization Movement and the Danger to America's Public Schools* and Dale Russakoff's *The Prize: Who's in Charge of America's Schools?* are two recent books that document the effects of market values and business practices on other sectors of the American educational system. For Ravitch, as for us, a key variable has become the power of "narrative":

> Public education is not broken. It is not failing or declining. The diagnosis is wrong, and the solutions of the corporate reformers are wrong. Our urban schools are in trouble because of concentrated poverty and racial segregation. But public education as such is not "broken." Public education is in a crisis only so far as society is and only so far as this new narrative of crisis has destabilized it. The solutions proposed by the self-proclaimed reformers have not worked as promised. They have failed even by their own most highly valued measure, which is test scores. At the same time, the reformers' solutions have had a destructive impact on education as whole. (4)

In her chapter on neoliberal thinking applied to education, "Privatization of Public Education Is Wrong," Ravitch excoriates the "pitiless regime of testing" (303) that has been foisted on the nation's young learners in the interest of, as business leaders often say, "measuring what we treasure" (303).

Ravitch asks, though, "Can anyone honestly say that a test score in reading or math is what they 'treasure' more than anything else?" (303–4). What she says about a business model applied to education bears directly on the mandate of the community college:

> The free market works well in producing goods and services, but it produces extreme inequality, and it has a high rate of failure. That is not how we want our schools to work. The core principle of American public education is supposed to be equality of educational opportunity, not a race to the top or a free market of choices with winners and losers. (304)

Both Ravitch and Russakoff agree that neoliberal ideas applied to education are deeply problematic. One educator cited in Russakoff's harrowing book about privatization and the Newark school system identifies this as the "school failure industry" (71), with consultants often commanding $1,000 a day (71). A similar industry appears to have developed around community colleges as well, as we will see.

Journalist Kristina Rizga's book, *Mission High: One School, How Experts Tried to Fail It, and the Students and Teachers Who Made It Triumph*, takes us inside this process and provides an insider's perspective on the current state of the accountability and school reform movement. Rizga embedded herself in one of our nation's "failing" schools—Mission High School in San Francisco—for four years (2010–2014), and the results of this qualitative research study are significant. Rizga's book is rich with the voices and experiences of students and teachers, as they struggle to learn and succeed despite ill-advised reform requirements and protocols. Rizga's conclusions follow Ravitch and Russakoff's: "The more time I spent in classrooms, the more I began to realize that most remedies that politicians and education reform experts were promoting as solutions for fixing schools were wrong" (ix). For Rizga, "America's business-inspired obsession with prioritizing 'metrics' in a complex world that deals with the development of individual minds has become the primary cause of mediocrity in American schools" (xiii; 241–252). A number of other recent books support this claim, including Linda Darling-Hammond's *The Flat World and Education: How America's Commitment to Equity Will Determine Our Future*, Amanda Ripley's *The Smartest Kids in the World: And How They Got That Way*, Marc S. Tucker's *Surpassing Shanghai: An Agenda for American Education Built on the World's Leading Systems*, Pasi Sahlberg's *Finnish Lessons 2.0: What Can the World Learn from Educational Change in Finland?*, and Paul Tough's *Helping Children Succeed: What Works and Why*.

Development as Freedom

Perhaps rather than turning to Hayek, Friedman, Rand, Becker, and other neoliberal thinkers, we can turn to more contemporary economists for guidance in formulating a balanced approach to theorizing the value of higher education and the public good within a market economy. Economist Amartya Sen has done important work on this subject and on the more general question of social justice itself (*Idea*). In his book, *Development as Freedom*, Sen advocates for activist public policy that promotes a variety of individual freedoms through initiatives designed to promote the public good. "In the context of developing countries in general," Sen emphasizes, "the need for public policy initiatives in creating social opportunities is crucially important" (143). This need, Sen stresses, is equally important in more prosperous nations as well. Development, in this view, consists not just in supporting a market economy but also, crucially, removing "various types of unfreedoms that leave people with little choice and little opportunity of exercising their reasoned agency" (xii). Our understanding of development should not be limited, Sen suggests, only to the growth of a nation's gross national product or the rise in personal incomes (3). Development must also be valued for what it provides in terms of freedoms—and this can be understood as "the principal ends of development" (5). In this regard, Sen is proposing a rather different understanding of freedom and liberty than Hayek, Friedman, and Rand. Sen frames his ideas about freedom and development historically in relation to the shifting fortunes—and changing theoretical valuation—of the free market economy and the economists who champion it, which are both currently enjoying a dominant role in public policy debate. In his acknowledgment of the great benefits the free market has produced, Sen appears to be tipping his hat to both Hayek and Friedman:

> There was a time—not very long ago—when every young economist "knew" in what respect the market systems had serious limitations: all the textbooks repeated the same list of "defects." The intellectual rejection of the market mechanism often led to radical proposals for altogether different methods of organizing the world (sometimes involving a powerful bureaucracy and unimagined fiscal burdens), without serious examination of the possibility that the proposed alternatives might involve even bigger failures than the markets were expected to produce. There was, often enough, rather little interest in the new and additional problems that the alternative arrangements may create.

> The intellectual climate has changed quite dramatically over the last few decades, and the tables are now turned. The virtues of the market mechanism are now standardly assumed to be so pervasive that qualifications seem unimportant. Any pointer to the defects of the market mechanism appears to be, in the present mood, strangely old-fashioned and contrary to contemporary culture (like playing an old 78 rpm record with music from the 1920s). (111)

Sen acknowledges the many benefits of the free market, lauding its impressive powers to generate income and opportunity, even as he suggests ways that we might improve our thinking about both the free market and the public good. He suggests that we must judge "the market mechanism comprehensively in terms of all its roles and effects, including those in generating economic growth and, under many circumstances, even economic equity" (7). He stresses the importance of evaluating weaknesses as well, however:

> We must also examine, on the other side, the persistence of deprivations among segments of the community that happen to remain excluded from the benefits of the market-oriented society, and the general judgments, including criticisms, that people may have of lifestyles and values associated with the culture of markets. In seeing development as freedom, the arguments on different sides have to be appropriately considered and assessed. It is hard to think that any process of substantial development can do without very extensive use of markets, but that does not preclude the role of social support, public regulation, or statecraft when they can enrich—rather than impoverish—human lives. (7)

This is a key moment for us here as we discuss the free market and public policy related to the community college. Sen is theorizing an approach to democracy and nurturing freedom that "does not preclude the role of social support, public regulation, or statecraft when they can enrich—rather than impoverish—human lives." Sen suggests that we chart a kind of philosophical "middle path"—modeled on traditional wisdom from India—between the current political climate "in which the virtues of the market mechanism are now standardly assumed to be so pervasive that qualifications seems unimportant" (111) and developing policy that addresses flaws or blind spots in this system:

Today's prejudices (in favor of the pure market mechanism) certainly need to be carefully investigated and, I would argue, partly rejected. But we have to avoid resurrecting yesterday's follies that refused to see the merits of—indeed even the inescapable need for—markets. We have to scrutinize and decide what parts make sense in the respective perspectives. My illustrious countryman Gautama Buddha may have been too predisposed to see the universal need for "the middle path" (though he did not get around to discussing the market mechanism in particular), but there is something to be learned from his speeches on nonextremeism delivered 2,500 years ago. (112)

Unthinking and uncritical acceptance of any ideology—so that it becomes effectively beyond criticism—is its own form of tyranny, stifling the vital and essential process of good-faith public debate in a democracy.

Sen documents in this book the variety of "unfreedoms" that exist around the world, including poverty (especially in India and sub-Saharan Africa), famine, women's agency, forced labor and slavery involving both children and adults, limited educational opportunities, and the absence of basic human rights. All of these unfreedoms, Sen suggests, can be addressed using the power of the market and the power of progressive public policy. Significantly, Sen defines poverty much the way some of the researchers we have discussed here define it and much the way the Truman Commission defined it in 1947—not simply in economic terms but as a form of "capability deprivation" (87–110). In this view, "poverty must be seen as the deprivation of basic capabilities rather than merely as lowness of incomes, which is the standard criterion of identification of poverty" (87). Sen's focus on removing various types of unfreedoms, acknowledging the role of public policy to enrich lives, and privileging human agency are precisely the values embodied by the modern community college. In many ways, community colleges are devoted to precisely the principle that Sen advocates here—"development as freedom." The market provides certain kinds of freedoms, of course, and institutions and public policy provides others. As Sen suggests,

> Individuals live and operate in a world of institutions. Our opportunities and prospects depend crucially on what institutions exist and how they function. Not only do institutions contribute to our freedoms, their roles can be sensibly evaluated in the light of their contributions to our freedom. To see development as freedom provides a perspective in which institutional assessment can systematically occur. (142)

In these terms, then, an essential question for us is this one: What contributions to our freedoms have community colleges provided?

A Learning Society

Joseph E. Stiglitz and Bruce C. Greenwald also advocate for a progressive approach to balancing support for higher education with building a vibrant free market economy. In *Creating a Learning Society: A New Approach to Growth, Development, and Social Progress*, Stiglitz and Greenwald propose an economic model founded on knowledge acquisition and learning. At the center of this model is the belief that knowledge drives innovation and growth. Stiglitz and Greenwald document the many ways that public policy, government action, and institutions can help nurture "inclusive growth" (467) by promoting learning. Stiglitz and Greenwald demonstrate that "learning touches every aspect of a modern dynamic economy" (21), and they challenge neoliberal ideas about the role of government in spurring economic growth:

> If learning, and R & D more generally, is at the center of the success of an economy, and if there is no presumption that markets are efficient in making decisions which affect the pace of learning (or R & D), then longstanding presumptions against government intervention are simply wrong. (20)

Obviously, this proposal to put learning at the center of our economic policy—and employing the acquisition of knowledge to address inequality—speaks directly to the mission of the community college. In fact, there are passages in this book that sound as if they could have been taken from the Truman Commission Report. Here, for example, Stiglitz and Greenwald discuss "inclusive" democracy, market failure, and inequality in ways reminiscent of passages we examined earlier from the Truman Commission Report:

> Our argument for why inclusive growth is so important goes beyond the standard one that it is a waste of a country's most valuable resource, its human talent, to fail to ensure that everyone lives up to his or her abilities. Rather, it is based on political economy, on an analysis of how inequality affects political processes in ways that are adverse to long-term learning and growth and inclusive democracy. (468)

Stiglitz and Greenwald maintain that "government needs to play an important role in any economy, correcting pervasive market failures, but especially in the 'creative economy,' e.g., financing basic research and providing high-quality education" (468). As it is theorized here, this new economic model requires thoughtful public policy and active governmental involvement designed to help promote learning and knowledge acquisition. Readers may be interested to know that this focus on "learning" is also supported by other economists as well, including Claudia Goldin and Lawrence F. Katz (*The Race between Education and Technology*), whose work we have already discussed, and Robert J. Gordon. In *The Rise and Fall of American Growth: The US Standard of Living since the Civil War*, Gordon summarizes over six hundred pages of analysis this way: "Educational issues represent the most fruitful direction for policies to enhance productivity growth" (643–4).

Stiglitz and Greenwald also address growing concern about neoliberal economic policies and *laissez faire* capitalism, suggesting that a strong social safety network helps spur innovation and risk by making such risk effectively less perilous (141–2; 468). Stiglitz and Greenwald also link systematic government disinvestment in policies that promote the public good, including education, with rising levels of inequality. As we have seen, state and federal governments support a whole range of activities designed to promote the public good, and these programs, Stiglitz and Greenwald suggest, help promote social stability and economic growth. These are programs that benefit us all in a variety of ways:

> Many in the United States are concerned that the country has embarked on an adverse dynamic, moving it toward an equilibrium in which there will be greater inequality and, as a consequence, toward a less dynamic economy and society. As social protections erode and public investments weaken, including in education, inequality increases. The rich turn to private education, private parks, private health insurance, etc., even though public provision might be far more efficient. Rather than working to improve the efficiency of the public sector, those who seek to limit the scope of government work to tear down the public sector, to undermine its credibility, knowing that if they succeed, then there will be a broader consensus for limiting the role of government and thus limiting the extent to which the government can engage in redistributive activities, *even if in so doing, the government is limited in its ability to engage in collective wealth enhancement*. As this happens, inequalities increase, confidence in public provision erodes, and the state takes on a less important role. It is problematic to gauge whether, in the end, even those at the top benefit; but what is not questionable is that the vast majority in the society lose out. (469; italics in original)

Stiglitz and Greenwald also suggest that it makes sound business sense for wealthy Americans to favor a limited government and to challenge the idea of the public good. What appears to be benign in theory (support for the free market) can often become much less benign in practice:

> While ostensibly conservative high-income individuals may claim that they are only trying to prevent such redistributions, a more careful look at the policies they advocate often reveals that they entail redistributions toward themselves; at the very least, they entail ensuring that the government does not ask them to contribute too much for the support of the public good and that it does not curtail their activities exploiting the poor and extracting for themselves a disproportionate share of public assets. (468–9)

A key focus for Stiglitz and Greenwald is how we might build a better, more vibrant, more equitable democracy. They link democratic ideals directly to education:

> Democratic ideals question authority. When America's Declaration of Independence said, *All men are created equal*, it didn't mean that they were of equal physical or mental capacities, but of equal rights, including the right to put forth their ideas into a competitive marketplace of ideas.
>
> But it is exactly that same frame of mind which is so essential for creating a dynamic, learning economy and society. Democracy and an open society are intrinsically interlinked with a learning economy and society. A more open society generates more ideas, a flow of "mutations," which provides not only excitement but the possibility of dynamic evolution, rather than stasis. (466)

To this end, Stiglitz and Greenwald suggest that the shaping of "public opinion" that Hayek defines as crucial in "The Intellectuals and Socialism" is a key variable.

Like Hayek, Stiglitz and Greenwald acknowledge the necessity of addressing public "mindsets" as a prerequisite for any kind of successful public policy development:

> Much of this book, for instance, has focused on policies that change sectoral composition in ways that would promote learning. But at the root of success is changing mindsets (see Stiglitz 1998c). Change has to be viewed as both possible and desirable, and there has to be an understanding that underneath change is *learning*. (457)

Stiglitz and Greenwald devote an entire chapter to this important subject, discussing "societal rigidities," "collective beliefs," and the different ways that "learning mindsets can be created" (459; 457–72). They offer here a kind of sociology of knowledge formation and meaning-making. There are many impediments that actively work against any kind of new idea, including the power of prior beliefs to shape the understanding of new information: "Individuals' perceptions—how they receive and process information—are affected by individuals' prior beliefs" (459). This kind of processing often produces what researchers call "confirmatory bias" (459; Lord, Ross, and Lepper; Darley and Gross), which is very different than the traditional model economists use, "predicated on 'rational expectations,' where it is assumed that individuals process all information fully and rationally" (459–60). They also note that "cognitive frames which shape perceptions are largely socially determined" (460) and, crucially, "not necessarily consciously constructed" (460). They also acknowledge research documenting that "beliefs also affect what is perceived" and that "biases—at every stage of the formation of beliefs—shape perception" (461). Widely held beliefs also "affect *collective* actions," thus further limiting opportunities for change and growth (461; italics in original). All of this information is vitally important for those of us who wish to embrace change and set a new course for higher education in America that promotes equity and social justice.

Stiglitz and Greenwald are also interested in examining the ways that "socially dysfunctional beliefs and policies" (462) persist and reproduce. The 2008 recession serves as a kind of test case for them, dramatically demonstrating how "those wedded to the notion that markets are always efficient and stable perceived the crisis markedly differently from those who are more skeptical of these perspectives" (462). Such individuals "sought to blame government" and "held that view in the face of overwhelming evidence to the contrary" (462). They warn that "because belief systems affect the equilibrium, e.g. by shaping perceptions, elites have a strong incentive to influence people's beliefs" (465). Stiglitz and Greenwald note that standard economic models are based on rational expectations in which "cognitive frames play no role" (465). They conclude by suggesting that understanding the role of cognitive beliefs and narrative frames must be an integral part of any economic theory:

> If beliefs have the profound effects that we have suggested they do, and if at times they change, and at others they do not, then a central part of understanding societal evolution is understanding the dynamics of these changes in beliefs—and the circumstance under which rigidities might arise. (465)

Although we currently appear to be experiencing a sustained period of rigidity in relation to neoliberal ideas about economic development, an important body of scholarship has recently emerged, which we have reviewed here, suggesting new ways that we might theorize economic growth and its relation to freedom, democracy, and economic equality.

A New Mont Pelerin Society

The evidence we have reviewed thus far emphatically supports a change of direction in terms of how we think about democracy, American higher education, and the public good. The Mont Pelerin Society (MPS) and the neoliberal movement that grew out of it have done important work over the years for democracy, but these ideas have clearly run their course. We now have ample evidence to assess the contributions of neoliberalism to American society, and we have longitudinal data as well, so that we can see the effects of neoliberalism, deregulation, and privatization across a significant expanse of time as they have played out not in theory but in the real world over the course of decades. Certainly, neoliberal thinking warned us against the considerable dangers of central control over a national economy, and these warnings helped us make thoughtful choices about how to move forward after World War II and engage the many national and economic challenges that emerged after the war. When neoliberal ideas have been applied to areas of public policy not related to the central control of a national economy, however, the results have been much less benign. Inequality is at historic levels in America. Trust in the power of public policy to improve lives has dangerously eroded. Privatization and deregulation have turned out to amass power in the hands of the already rich and powerful. It may be time to draw inspiration and guidance from a new generation of economists and higher education scholars. Were we to follow this path, we could theorize a new, more progressive Mont Pelerin Society built on the work of Piketty, Bourdieu, Acemoglu and Robinson, Reich, Sen, Stiglitz and Greenwald, Goldin and Katz, Gordon, McMahon, the Truman Commission, and the work of Martin Luther King and educators like Mina Shaughnessy, Nell Ann Pickett, and Marilyn Sternglass. This is an approach to development and public policy that would actively seek to make thoughtful, research-based decisions about the use of legislation and tax revenue to promote the public good. It is an approach that would define development as freedom, inequality as anti-democratic and dangerous to our safety and sovereignty, and learning as the key driver of economic prosperity, national security, and social justice. Understanding that in the long run, nothing will improve the security and vitality of our democracy more than spreading access to higher education as broadly as we can, community colleges would play a key role in this new approach to building a strong and vibrant democracy.

We may appear to have ranged very far afield from the student success stories we began this book with and the stories told by my English 9000 students about their lives and journeys to MCC, but those stories were made possible by progressive thinking and public policy that deliberately sought to promote the public good. This public policy sought to address long-standing issues of economic inequality and was also designed to promote equity and social justice. There are millions of other community college success stories just like those featured in this book—undocumented and perhaps invisible but nonetheless lived and realized. If we regard these stories as perhaps typical of what the community college is able to offer to individual citizens and to our democracy, we can draw inspiration from the fact that they been made possible by the power of ideas, the courage to be utopian, and progressive public policy. Many others just like them, yet to be realized, wait to be written.

CHAPTER 29

Measuring "Success" at Open Admissions Institutions

A Dark and Troubling Mystery

Now that we have examined some of the larger questions at play in current discussions of public policy and higher education in America as they relate to the public good—questions that affect community colleges in profound ways—let us turn our attention now to a concern involving community colleges themselves that has been puzzling and troublesome for many years. It is a question essential to our understanding of the community college and the public good. In examining this concern, we will be scrutinizing a variety of stubbornly entrenched perspectives that have left fundamental questions about community colleges largely unexamined. As theories become rigid, the ideas they contain often become self-evident truths that resist fresh evidence and revaluation and thus can be perpetuated across generations. In this chapter, we will look at one such self-evident truth directly—the so-called "cooling out" function of the junior college.

Graduation rates continue to be used as the standard benchmark for success at most institutions of higher learning, including community colleges, even by those who should know that the use of such a marker of success at open admissions institutions is highly problematic. Using this benchmark for community colleges becomes particularly troublesome when it is used in comparison with graduation rates at selective admissions institutions. These two kinds of institutions are very different in terms of mission and mandate, and this practice necessarily avoids or simplifies a host of contingencies that are unique to the cohort of students who attend community colleges.[1] As the research we have reviewed so far suggests, measuring success at community colleges must be regarded as a very complex endeavor requiring great care and thoughtfulness.

For many years now there has appeared to be a dark and troubling mystery at the heart of the community college enterprise that was famously formulated by Burton Clark in 1960 ("The 'Cooling-Out' Function in Higher Education") and has since been taken up again in more recent work by a variety of scholars (Brint and Karabel 1989; Rouse 1995; Dougherty 2001; Beach 2011; Scherer and Anson 2014; Bailey et al. 2015; Kahlenberg 2015). To articulate the nature of this problem as plainly, fairly, and unequivocally as possible, let us turn to a key passage from a report by the United States Department of Education National Center for Education Statistics entitled *Profiles of Undergraduates in US Post-secondary Education Institutions: 2003–04, With an Analysis of Community College Students* (2006):

> Student persistence is of concern to educators and policymakers because large numbers of students who begin their college education in community colleges never complete it. For example, among a cohort of first-time freshmen who enrolled in community colleges in 1995–96, some 48 percent had either completed a credential (36 percent) or transferred to a 4-year institution (12 percent) 6 years after first enrolling (Hoachlander, Sikora, and Horn 2003). In contrast, among students who first enrolled in 4-year colleges or universities, 63 percent had completed a bachelor's degree, and another 18 percent were still enrolled or had completed an associate's degree or certificate (Berkner, He, and Cataldi 2003). (iii; see also Tinto)

There is other scholarship to which we might turn for evidence of this concern, including Thomas Bailey, Shanna Smith Jaggers, and Davis Jenkins's *Redesigning America's Community Colleges* (2015):

> The vast majority of students who enroll for credit in community colleges state that they want to complete a credential or transfer to complete a degree at a four-year school. Indeed, over 80 percent of entering community college students indicate that they intend to earn a bachelor's degree or higher. Yet six years after initial enrollment, only 15 percent have done so. This number would rise if we considered a longer time window, but it still represents a large gap between students' stated goals and their actual outcomes. (6; 200)

Richard D. Kahlenberg voices a similar concern in "How Higher Education Funding Shortchanges Community Colleges" (2015):

Community Colleges are pivotal institutions in American society—crucial to our economic competiveness and our efforts to revive the American Dream. As open-access institutions located close to where students live and work, community colleges are uniquely situated to jumpstart social mobility for those who aspire to the middle class. That is why President Obama has called for making community college free and the first two years of college universal, just as primary and secondary education have been for decades.

Yet, the outcomes today at community colleges are often dismal. While 81 percent of first-time community college students say they wish to earn a bachelor's degree or more, after six years, only 12 percent do so; two-thirds fail to get even an associate's degree or certificate after six years. With 86 percent of high school graduates going on to college, the central challenge in higher education has shifted from access to college to something different: access to *high-quality* programs that have the support to ensure graduation.

This is a question, of course, that is never far removed from most discussions about student "success" at community colleges. It also frequently comes into play in more theoretical discussions about the value of community colleges in scholarship and political debate. Unfortunately, there continues to be a fundamental misunderstanding about the nature of the community college and the students who attend these institutions, and this becomes especially obvious when community colleges are compared to selective admissions institutions.

Unprepared Students

Community colleges offer all kinds of students—and especially nontraditional students and students from the most marginalized and financially disadvantaged sectors of our society—what no other college or university has ever offered them before: opportunity, hope, and the chance to build more prosperous and satisfying futures for themselves. This is an unprecedented development in the long history of higher education in America, and it is to our enduring credit that we have helped shape the substance and character of this system. Until very recently, of course, colleges in America have been, as Bowen, Kurzweil, and Tobin have noted, "bastions of privilege" and not "engines of opportunity" (135; Karabel; Lavin and Hyllegard; Center for Community College Student Engagement "Making Ends Meet"). Community colleges were established to help address this long-standing, deeply entrenched inequality. Community colleges have become such an integral part of the higher education landscape now that even some faculty and staff members who work at these institutions are unfamiliar with this rich and radical history. Ultimately, it may not be possible to adequately measure or quantify what this single innovation has meant to the citizens of our nation. The stories included in Part I of this book are meant, in part, to provide a small sense of what this gift of hope has meant to real individuals living real American lives.

Of course, open admissions policies generate challenges as well, and the single most long-standing and intractable of these challenges are students who come to community colleges unprepared to do college-level work. As John and Suanne Roueche noted almost 20 years ago in *High Stakes, High Performance* (1999),

> On average, almost 50 percent of all first-time community college students test as underprepared for the academic demands of college-level courses and programs and are advised to enroll in at least one remedial class. This percentage of underprepared students has not changed significantly across the United States in at least two decades, and there is no evidence that it will be reduced in the near future, although in individual states percentages have fluctuated. (5)

This proportion remains largely unchanged today. As Bailey, Jaggers, and Jenkins note, "approximately two-thirds of incoming community college students fail to meet their institution's standards for college readiness" (119; Bailey "Challenge"). Selective admissions institutions also enroll a handful of underprepared students, but community colleges have always shouldered the bulk of this important work. This is as we might expect, given the very different admissions policies and cohorts of students that attend these institutions.

Graduation Rates at Selective Institutions

For many reasons, some of which we have already discussed, we cannot measure success at open admissions institutions the same way that we measure success at traditional, selective admissions institutions—typically, by composite graduation rates. Yale University, for example, has a graduation rate of approximately 96 percent (Yale). Obviously, for such schools, as well as for state colleges and universities with selective admissions, it makes sense to use composite graduation rates, at least as one measure of institutional success. Even in this regard, however, different demographic populations have very different graduation rates, and the composite scores reported by universities often mask such differences. As Sophie Quinton noted in a recent essay on this subject, "When a 43% Graduation Rate Means Success," "nationally, just 59 percent of all first-time college students, attending full-time, graduate in six years, according to the National Center for Education Statistics. The rate for African-American students is significantly lower—just 39.5 percent." This is a 20-point difference. At Yale, the graduation rate for black students is 94 percent ("Black"). But at other institutions, the discrepancy is much larger. At the University of Michigan, for example, the graduation rate for white students is 91 percent but for black students it is 78 percent. At the University of California, Berkeley, the graduation rate for white students is 91 percent but for black students it is 74 percent. There are significant gaps at many other highly selective institutions as well ("Black"). A recent report by Andrew Nichols and Denzel Evans-Bell, *A Look at Black Student Success Identifying Top- and Bottom-Performing Institutions* (2017), maps the nature of this pattern nationwide.

Graduation rates also track very closely with an institution's degree of selectivity, as we can see in Fig. 29.1. In fact, there is a linear relationship between an institution's degree of selectivity and its graduation rates. The United States Department of Education National Center for Education Statistics (2015) has documented how significant this difference is:

> Six-year graduation rates for first-time, full-time students who began seeking a bachelor's degree in fall 2007 varied according to institutions' level of selectivity. In particular, graduation rates were highest at postsecondary degree-granting institutions that were the most selective (i.e., had the lowest admissions acceptance rates), and graduation rates were lowest at institutions that were the least selective (i.e., had open admissions policies). For example, at 4-year institutions with open admissions policies, 34 percent of students completed a bachelor's degree within 6 years. At 4-year institutions where the acceptance rate was less than 25 percent of applicants, the 6-year graduation rate was 89 percent. (United "Institutional," 3)

Selective and highly selective institutions are typically very expensive, and this may be another hidden sorting mechanism that actually reflects class position and family income rather than the effectiveness of an institution. With more family resources to devote to a college education—which crucially translates into family resources that can be devoted to helping children prepare for college and then providing four years of uninterrupted time on campus to earn a degree—success rates climb. As it turns out, it appears that large numbers of high-achieving,

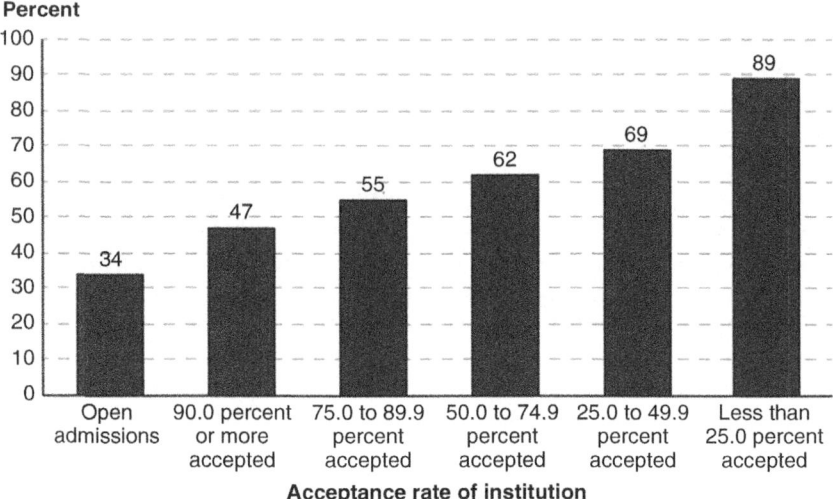

Fig. 29.1 Graduation rate (within six years) from first institution attended for first-time, full-time bachelor's degree-seeking students at four-year postsecondary institutions, by acceptance rate of institution: Cohort entry year 2007
(*Source*: United States Department of Education National Center for Education Statistics. *The Condition of Education 2015*, Chapter: 4/Postsecondary Education, "Institutional Retention and Graduation Rates for Undergraduate Students." https://nces.ed.gov/programs/coe/pdf/Indicator_CTR/coe_ctr_2015_05.pdf)

low-income students do not even bother applying to such institutions. Caroline Hoxby and Christopher Avery's Brookings Institute report on this subject, "The Missing 'One-Offs': The Hidden Supply of High-Achieving, Low-Income Students," documents how this aspect of income stratification continues to plague the American higher education system.

None of this should surprise us, of course, given what we know about the many variables at play in any kind of long-term endeavor like earning a college degree. We should also keep in mind the many, often invisible variables that can affect the academic performance of low-income and first-generation students that we discussed in Part II of this book. Should open admissions institutions be asked to compare themselves with selective admissions institutions when it comes to using graduation rates to measure success? The evidence strongly suggests that they should not.

"Unsureness"

We are currently working from a model of "success" established by selective admissions institutions built around conditions that require significant economic resources from students and their families and an investment of these resources over the course of at least four years. This model of success has been created by selective admissions institutions over many decades and is perhaps predicated now on an outmoded understanding of how students in America attend college—spending four years living on campus and focusing exclusively on earning a degree. Now that attending college is no longer the prerogative of a privileged minority (Bowen, Kurzweil, and Tobin; Karabel), and now that students attend colleges in all sorts of nontraditional ways, we may have to rethink some of our most basic understandings about how we measure success in college. As we know, this traditional model has changed dramatically in practice in recent years, although research and scholarship has been slow to accept the implications of this change. President Obama's original proposal for his College Scorecard was built around similar, outmoded assumptions about how the majority of students in America attend college (Toth, Sullivan, Calhoon-Dillahunt). The "average" college student is now no longer a "traditional" student. As far back as 2002, for example, the US Department of Education issued an important report acknowledging this fact:

> Today's undergraduate population is different than it was a generation ago. In addition to being 72 percent larger in 1999 than in 1970 (with fall enrollment growing from 7.4 to 12.7 million), proportionately more students are enrolled part time (39 versus 28 percent) and at 2-year colleges (44 versus 31 percent), and women have replaced men as the majority (representing 56 percent of the total instead of 42 percent) (indicator 5, US Department of Education 2002a). There are proportionately more older students on campus as well: 39 percent of all postsecondary students were 25 years or older in 1999, compared with 28 percent in 1970 (US Department of Education 2002b).
>
> The "traditional" undergraduate—characterized here as one who earns a high school diploma, enrolls full time immediately after finishing high school, depends on parents for financial support, and either does not work during the school year or works part time—is the exception rather than the rule. (*Nontraditional* 1)

How we judge the value of community colleges will depend in some very important ways on what kinds of benchmarks we establish to measure success, who sets these benchmarks, and what these benchmarks assume about students attending college. Using the traditional national benchmark established by selective admissions institutions, it therefore might appear, as Bailey, Jaggars, and Jenkins note in their recent book *Redesigning America's Community Colleges* (2015), that community colleges are "poorly designed to facilitate completion of high quality college programs" (13). This is emphatically not the case, as we will see.

Using composite graduation rates to measure success for students at open admissions institutions is a bad idea for a number of reasons. First of all, a significant percentage of students who enroll at open admissions institutions specifically indicate that they are *not* attending college in order to earn an associate's degree or to transfer to a four-year institution. For example, the 2014 Community College Survey of Student Engagement (CCSSE) Report Supplement and Methodology document accompanying their national report, "Engagement Rising: A Decade of CCSSE Data Shows Improvements Across the Board," documents the various goals students have who are attending our nation's community colleges:

Students' Primary Goals

Note: Students could select from among three choices: "primary goal," "secondary goal," and "not a goal." In reporting out these data researchers collapsed the "primary goal" and "secondary goal" together so the responses reported in this report are "goal" and "not a goal." If a student indicated that the item was a primary goal or secondary goal, the response was considered a "goal." The data regarding the goals cited here represent responses from over 1,800,000 community college students nationwide.
  Complete a certificate program: 52%
  Obtain an associate degree: 83%
  Transfer to a four-year college or university: 75%
  Obtain or update job-related skills: 74%
  Take one or more courses for self-improvement: 75%
  Change careers: 43% (120–5)

It is important to note that 25 percent of respondents to this survey specifically indicated that they were *not* interested in transferring to a four-year college or university. That number was almost half a million students (n = 484,188) (121). 16 percent of respondents to this survey specifically indicated that they were *not* interested in obtaining an Associate's degree. That number was also large (n = 340,805) (120).

Furthermore, even when community college students indicate—either informally or formally on surveys such as the CCSSE—that they want to graduate and "transfer" to a four-year institution and earn a bachelor's degree, they often have only the vaguest sense of what this actually means. Many are first-generation college students who have no firsthand or family experience with college, and many have only an emerging sense of what it might take to earn a bachelor's degree. For many Americans, saying that they hope to earn a bachelor's degree has become an almost automatic, involuntary, and reflexive response to queries about future plans, regardless of how prepared they may be academically and financially to pursue such a goal. Furthermore, when the typical community college student says that she wants to "obtain a bachelor's degree"—a key marker in the body of research devoted to this question—that student is often saying something very different than when the typical student attending a selective admissions institution says exactly the same thing.

This became clear to me recently as I talked with my children's high school friends about their plans for college. When I spoke with these young men and women about their goals, almost all of them talked about college without any trace of doubt or equivocation. Many of them had at least one college-educated parent, most of them had worked very hard in high school to prepare for college, and most of them had an absolute sense of clarity and certainty that they were going on to earn a bachelor's degree. For many of them, it was just a matter of deciding what college they would attend. Although each of these students would answer yes to a survey question that asked if they planned to attend college after high school and pursue a bachelor's degree, there is no way to account in such a survey for the absolute sense of sureness with which they would answer that question. Of course, as educators who believe in the transformative power of education, most of us would like to see this attitude more widely held.

There is considerably less sureness, however, among many of the students that I work with at my community college, especially among my basic writing students. This sense of unsureness is something that many students who attend community college share, whether they are basic writers or not. Although many community college students answer "yes" to survey questions about planning to get some kind of degree, a large number of these students often have only a very limited understanding of what this means, how they might go about earning such a degree, and how much is required in all areas of their lives to achieve such an ambitious goal.

The "Negative Function"

This is why claims by scholars that enrollment at a community college "reduces" students' "degree aspirations" are misleading and misguided—and the result of an unfortunate unfamiliarity with community colleges and community college students, even though some of these researchers clearly value the work that community colleges do. The idea is that community colleges might be in the business of "cooling out" student aspirations, drawing on Burton Clark's still powerfully present notion (180), which we will be discussing in more detail in the next chapter. This is a perspective that has been remarkably long-lived in community college scholarship (Pascarella and Terenzini 374–82), resistant to evidence and new ways of thinking, and has become a kind of entrenched wisdom about open admissions institutions that appears to need to be reiterated and restated every five years or so, as we will see. Especially when such researchers talk about "educational attainment and persistence," for example, they can seem almost dismissive of community colleges. Park and Pascarella characterize this as the "negative function of attending a community college" (701–2).

For the record, reducing anyone's aspirations—about college, about life, or about anything else—is the last thing most community college teachers, counselors, administrators, staff members, or college presidents want to do. The phrasing here, and the incomplete understanding of students who attend open admission institutions that this formulation reflects, is quite unfortunate. Scholars continue to be puzzled by this data set, and many have attempted to find some way to explain it (see Pascarella "New"; Pascarella and Terenzini 429–33; Beach; Scherer and Anson). Unfortunately, this pernicious idea related to community colleges continues to have wide social currency and considerable political influence in state legislatures.

Researchers have continued to wonder why students who enroll at four-year colleges with selective admissions persist and complete work for bachelor's degrees at a statistically higher rate than those who begin their academic careers at community colleges with what appear to be roughly comparable qualifications and family backgrounds. What is particularly puzzling about these data is that students who appear to have identical educational aspirations (as well as other similarities in terms of academic skills, family income, and parental educational achievement) obtain bachelor's degrees at very different rates.

As I have reviewed this research and reflected on the many students that I have encountered in my decades of teaching at a community college, I believe that this difference can be explained in ways that will be satisfactory to scholars and researchers. Perhaps the most important difference is that students who enroll at these different institutions *appear* to have expressed to researchers and survey takers that their goals are identical—that is, that they plan to "obtain a bachelor of arts degree," the key benchmark in this research (see, for example, Pascarella, Edison, Nora, Hagedorn, and Terenzini 181). In fact, however, in all sorts of subtle and not so subtle ways, *their goals are not by any means identical.*

The very act of applying to a selective admissions institution suggests—and, in fact, *requires*—a much more significant level of commitment to one's educational future. It is, in itself, an important marker for predicting persistence toward "obtaining a bachelor's degree." Students who pursue this educational option often have very different attitudes about college—even though both students might answer a survey question related to their academic goals in exactly the same way.

First of all, we know that applying to a selective admissions institution requires careful, long-term planning, virtually throughout a student's entire academic career. To have a chance of being admitted to a selective admissions institution, one must have earned strong grades throughout high school, which typically requires sustained focus, hard work, goal-setting, self-discipline, grit, creativity, and other skills and dispositions essential to academic success. Many of these skills and dispositions, in fact, are those identified by Arthur L. Costa and Bena Kallick as essential "habits of mind"—foundational intellectual behaviors that lead to "productive actions" (16) and to success in school, work, and life. Costa and Kallick have identified 16 "habits of mind" that they regard as essential for students. Earning strong grades in junior and senior high school in order to attend a selective admissions institutions will probably require students to develop most of them, at least to some degree:

- Persisting
- Managing Impulsivity
- Listening With Understanding and Empathy
- Thinking Flexibly
- Thinking About Thinking (Metacognition)
- Striving For Accuracy
- Questioning and Posing Problems
- Applying Past Knowledge to New Situations
- Thinking and Communicating with Clarity and Precision
- Gathering Data through All Senses
- Creating, Imagining, Innovating
- Responding with Wonderment and Awe
- Taking Responsible Risks
- Finding Humor
- Thinking Interdependently
- Remaining Open to Continuous Learning (xx–38)

Costa and Kallick suggest that these habits of mind are broad, enduring intellectual and dispositional skills that can be nurtured in classrooms and then used across a student's lifespan (xvii), equipping them for adult challenges and uncertainties.

Once students have demonstrated their ability to earn strong grades in high school over the course of many years, they must then complete a formal application to college, which often is itself a rigorous and time-consuming process. To apply to a selective admissions institution, one must prepare for and take high-stakes standardized tests or construct an online application portfolio (Jaschik), arrange to have letters of recommendation submitted, and complete an application and often a variety of accompanying essays. When students apply to such schools, they also know that they will be involved in a competitive process and that admission is not guaranteed.

These schools are also significantly more expensive than community colleges, and they require from admitted students a significant financial commitment. Most students must be ready to assume some level of debt in order to attend such schools. Some must be willing to assume very large debt burdens.

Students who attend these institutions must also embrace dramatic lifestyle changes as well. The vast majority of students attending selective admissions institutions move away from home for the first time, happily or reluctantly (often it's a little of both, of course), and they must forsake the comforts of familiar homes, neighborhoods, and communities. At these institutions, students typically live in dorms, where they encounter many new people and experience a new local culture, new daily rhythms, and new challenges related to food, friendships, social interaction, and workload. Attending a selective four-year institution requires a very significant level of commitment from students—financially, emotionally, and psychologically—as the parents of such students know very well.

Attending a community college, on the other hand, requires a much less significant personal commitment. Applying to an open admissions institution is much easier—and this is by design, of course. Standardized test scores, an application portfolio, or letters of recommendation are usually not required, and one's grades in high school are also not a factor. When students apply to such schools, they also know that, if they meet the basic general admissions requirements (usually a high school diploma or a GED), their admission is guaranteed. Long-term planning in high school is not necessary, and students can decide even a day or two before a semester begins, for example, to attend a community college and know that they will be admitted, regardless of what their grades in high school may have been. Community colleges are also significantly less expensive than selective admissions institutions, and they also do not require of students such a complete change of locale and lifestyle. The vast majority of students attending community colleges live at home with their parents or in their own apartments or homes. They can attend college while continuing to live in their home town, maintaining current friendships, jobs, and their network of community relationships.

Attending a community college requires a much different level of commitment from students in almost every area of their lives. This difference can help explain the graduation data that continues to puzzle researchers. It seems clear that even among those who self-identify in similar ways to data collectors about their degree aspirations, there is a very real qualitative difference between the level of commitment that students bring to the enterprise of completing a bachelor's degree indicated simply by where they choose to attend college. This difference explains a great deal in terms of the commitment and persistence differences between these two cohorts of students.

To put this idea in its simplest form, let us consider this question: If all things are equal in terms of a student's economic status, academic preparation, level of family educational attainment, and so on (to the best of our ability to measure these variables), which of the following students has demonstrated the greater commitment to "obtaining a bachelor's degree"?

- Student #1, who applies to, is accepted at, and then chooses to attend an institution that *offers* a bachelor's degree.

or

- Student #2, who attends an institution that *does not offer* a bachelor's degree [i.e., a community college].

I think the answer is obvious. Is it any wonder that community college students persist at a significantly lower rate in "obtaining a bachelor of arts degree" than those who attend selective admissions institutions? I do not mean to suggest that every student who attends a community college with the goal of "obtaining a bachelor's degree" fits this profile, but a considerable number of students do. This may well account for some of the difference we see in graduation rates. In fact, many students who attend a community college and indicate a desire to eventually earn a bachelor's degree have an inherently "cooler" commitment to that goal than those who attend selective admissions institutions that offer bachelor's degrees. We just don't have the mechanism yet to measure this difference accurately. Our institutions aren't "cooling them out." These students come to us with "cooler" expectations and commitment to begin with, even though both types of students may answer simple questions on surveys about their goals in exactly the same way.

"Six Distinct Populations"

Recent research has begun to make more careful and finely nuanced distinctions among the many different types of students who attend community colleges, and this work provides us with a better picture of what community colleges actually do and how we might better measure success for the students who attend them. We also now appear to be able to measure students' intentions and motivation more accurately.

For example, the United States Department of Education (National Center for Education Statistics) report, *Profiles of Undergraduates in US Post-secondary Education Institutions: 2003–04, With an Analysis of Community College Students* (2006), which we cited at the beginning of this chapter, offers us a much more sophisticated profile of community college students. The editors of this report identify "six distinct populations" of students attending these institutions:

> In a recent report, Adelman (2005) used data from the postsecondary transcripts of 1992 high school graduates to develop "portraits" of six distinct populations who attend community colleges. These portraits were based on the credits earned by traditional college-age students (23 or younger) in various degree programs. The first two portraits described students likely to persist and included students in (1) traditional academic paths leading to a transfer and bachelor's degree, and (2) occupational credential paths leading to vocational credentials or associate's degrees awarded by community colleges. The remaining four groups of students were much less successful in earning credits and completing credentials. These groups included (3) students with relatively weak high school academic preparation who struggled to acquire community college credits and then stopped; (4) students who withdrew almost immediately after enrollment with few if any credits earned; (5) those who were based in other institutions (i.e., taking most courses in another institution, primarily in 4-year colleges); and (6) a small population of "reverse transfers" with "declining momentum toward credentials at any level." (19)

For those who teach at community colleges, this will probably sound about right. Furthermore, when disaggregated like this, the numbers related to graduation and "success" look very different, as the editors make clear. The "cooling out" function, in effect, disappears:

> The results of this study suggest that students who enroll in community colleges with a strong commitment toward completing a program of study, whether to transfer to a 4-year college or obtain a degree or certificate,

maintain their enrollment for 1 year at relatively high rates. Yet such students made up just 49 percent of those enrolled in community colleges in 2003–04. They also tend to be younger and more traditional than students in less committed or nondegree tracks. Among the less committed students, about three-fourths of those enrolled in formal AA degree programs did not express an interest in completing a degree, while a clear majority reported personal interest as an important reason for enrolling. Despite their tentative commitment to obtaining a degree, however, these students showed strong enrollment continuity at higher rates than those who were not in a formal degree program.

The findings from this study help explain why community college students complete associate's degrees or certificates at relatively low rates. That is, graduation rates are typically based on all students enrolled in degree programs, yet findings from this study indicate that a substantial proportion of students enrolled in formal degree programs do not necessarily intend to complete a degree. (37)

As welcome as this news is, it probably won't surprise anyone who works at a community college. Community colleges certainly attract their share of "highly motivated" and well-prepared students who are capable of distinguishing themselves at any college in the nation. Many of them, in fact, transfer and do just that, earning bachelor's degrees, master's degrees, and PhDs, as many of my former students have done. Highly motivated students choose to begin their academic careers at a community college for a wide variety of reasons. Sometimes, it's just simple economics. Students from middle-class families are often less likely to choose certain types of selective admissions institutions because their families make too much money to qualify for financial aid but too little for the students to attend without financial assistance. Sometimes, it's convenience and ease of access or even a question of an important relationship that they are unable or unwilling to leave. Sometimes, it's a variable that would simply be impossible to imagine or invent.

But community colleges also attract other kinds of students as well. Some, for example, attend community colleges as "experimenters," as Manski (1989) and Grubb (1991) have noted. These students attend low-cost, low-risk open admissions institutions to give college "a try." Like many who attend open admissions institutions, Bethany Silver, who we met in Part I, began her college career as one of these experimenters ("It was a place where people went when they didn't know what they were doing or where they were going") and ended up finding direction and inspiration there. Success for this cohort of students might best be measured in terms of finding an answer to the question, "Is college for me?" Helping students find an answer to this question probably should be considered a kind of success as well. Students typically turn to community colleges, rather than to four-year institutions, to seek answers to this question.

Different Kinds of Material Conditions

Finally, students who attend open admissions institutions typically live very different kinds of lives than those who attend traditional selective admissions institutions, as we have seen. When we talk about persistence and success at open admissions institutions, we must always keep this key variable in mind: students who attend community colleges typically live very complex lives. Many are handling adult challenges that undergraduates at residential four-year institutions simply do not have to concern themselves with, and this, of course, puts them more at risk relative to long-term endeavors like earning a college degree. For the 2015 cohort of students who participated in the CCSSE, for example, 30 percent of community college students surveyed worked more than 30 hours per week; 18 percent worked between 21 and 30 hours a week; and 13 percent worked between 11 and 20 hours a week (CCSSE 8). Twenty percent spent more than 30 hours a week providing care for dependents living with them (parents, children, spouse, etc.). More than half overall (56 percent) devoted considerable time to providing this care (between 1 and 30 hours per week). Twenty-four percent spent over six hours a week commuting to and from classes (CCSSE 8). Also, as we have seen in the Center for Community College Student Engagement report *Making Ends Meet*, and as Sara Goldrick-Rab, Jed Richardson, and Anthony Hernandez document in *Hungry and Homeless in College: Results from a National Study of Basic Needs Insecurity in Higher Education*, many community college students are attempting to pursue academic careers while also contending with deep levels of basic needs insecurity. We now know more clearly than ever that "food and housing insecurity among the nation's community college students threatens their health and wellbeing, along with their academic achievements" (Goldrick-Rab, Richardson, and Hernandez 1). These additional stress factors related to scarcity obviously imperil any kind of long-term endeavor like earning a college credential, and these material conditions help explain the difference in graduation rates between open admissions community colleges and selective admissions four-year institutions.

Students who attend selective admissions institutions typically have dramatically fewer responsibilities outside of the classroom. It seems clear that these two cohorts of students are very different populations of students meeting different kinds of challenges.

Furthermore, for students who attend college part time—a large segment of the student body at most community colleges and an increasing demographic nationwide (United States, *Condition*)—the long-term goal of earning a college degree can pose almost impossible challenges. Students routinely speak to me about this problem—and often in the most heartbreaking of terms. One such student, who did excellent work all semester in one of my composition classes, recently spoke to me tearfully about her long-term prospects for a degree: "At this rate, I'm never going to finish. I'll be 40 years old before I complete my associate's degree, and I just can't bear that." Working toward a degree by taking one or two courses per semester requires extraordinary determination, resourcefulness, and perseverance. This is another risk factor that complicates chances for "success" for students at community colleges.

Conclusion

We began this discussion with "a dark and troubling mystery": "Student persistence is of concern to educators and policymakers because large numbers of students who begin their college education in community colleges never complete it." The research we have reviewed in this chapter, and in this book, should deepen our understanding of the complex social, psychological, and economic dynamics at play on campuses at open admissions institutions. We may finally be able to put to rest Burton Clark's ideas about the "cooling out function" of the junior college. Unfortunately, Clark's essay continues to be among the most widely cited works in the scholarly literature devoted to community colleges, and his ideas continue to inform the general understanding of the community college even today.

Note

1. A note about terminology: The vast majority of public two-year colleges are open admissions institutions. Most of these public two-year institutions refer to themselves as "community colleges." "Open admissions institution" and "community college" have come to be used interchangeably.

CHAPTER 30

Diverted Dreams, Cruel Hoaxes, and Institutional Ineffectiveness: The Community College "Failure" Narrative

"Deficit Thinking"

Narratives shape the way that we perceive and understand the world. They frame for us what we regard as possible, and they often help us make sense of complex conditions and experiences. In some ways, politics itself is most fundamentally a narrative art and elections a competition between competing story lines, each vying for supremacy for the hearts and minds of voters. Edward Said has suggested that "the power to narrate, or to block other narratives from forming and emerging" constitutes an essential component of political power (*Culture* xiii). In an ideal world governed only by reason, the marketplace of ideas in a democratic society envisioned by thinkers like John Milton in *Areopagitica* and John Stuart Mill in *On Liberty* would operate independently of power, wealth, and politics. In this theoretical model, good ideas naturally become self-evident and widely embraced, and public debate serves as a kind of crucible which tests and, in effect, certifies the value of competing ideas. As Fredrick Siebert notes about this theoretical model, the idea is that "the true and sound will survive; the false and unsound will be vanquished" (45). Unfortunately, as we know, the democratic process and the "search for truth" is always a much more complex process, complicated and sometimes compromised by many factors, including competing interests, political power, and wealth (F. Mayer *Narrative*). There are also processing complexities in human cognition and psychology which complicate this process still further. As Stiglitz and Greenwald have noted, these involve mindsets, societal rigidities, collective beliefs, the power of prior beliefs to shape the understanding of new information, confirmatory bias, the fact that cognitive frames which shape perceptions are largely socially determined, that such perceptions affect *collective* actions, and that socially dysfunctional beliefs and policies can persist and reproduce (*Creating* 457–472).

As a consequence of a profound misunderstanding related to graduation rates at open admissions institutions, a "failure" narrative has developed regarding community colleges that has been remarkably long-lived and persistent. Much of this scholarship supports deficit-model constructions of community college students and open admissions higher education. As Richard Valencia notes in his introduction to *The Evolution of Deficit Thinking*:

> Although there are several explanatory variants of this model, the deficit thinking paradigm, as a whole, posits that students who fail in school do so because of alleged internal deficiencies (such as cognitive and/or motivational limitations) or shortcomings socially linked to the youngster—such as familial deficits and dysfunctions. Given the endogenous nature of deficit thinking, systemic factors (for example, school segregation; inequalities in school financing; curriculum differentiation) are held blameless in explaining why some students fail in school. (xi)

The endogenous nature of this model suggests that deficits are without external cause and are produced, as it were, "inside the organism or system." Much past and current thinking about the community college draws on this model. It is important to acknowledge as well that much like figures of speech, narratives "are not mere frills. They think for us" (McCloskey xvii). The failure narrative about community colleges has become so entrenched, in fact, that in many ways it has come to do our thinking for us, even in the face of evidence that should complicate this view significantly. This narrative can also be examined as a kind of case study for how mindsets, societal rigidities, collective beliefs, the power of prior beliefs to shape the understanding of new information, confirmatory bias, and the fact that cognitive frames which shape perceptions are largely socially determined can all limit understanding.

"Soft" Failure

The community college "failure" narrative begins with Burton Clark's famous essay from 1960, "The 'Cooling-Out' Function in Higher Education." In this essay, Clark suggests that the primary social function of the American junior college is to "cool-out" ambitions and aspirations of students and to provide structural "soft failures" for a large population of ambitious young Americans. "A major problem of democratic society," Clark claims, "is inconsistency between encouragement to achieve and the realities of limited opportunity" (569). Because all aspirations cannot be realized, even though they are actively encouraged by an "ideology of equal opportunity" (570), a democratic society must develop mechanisms and institutions that can help manage this kind of failure in productive ways. Clark suggests that community colleges perform this function with admirable skill and non-transparency—opaqueness being a virtue for this kind of social sorting process. He postulates a fixed cohort of students who he labels "latent terminal" students (572)—individuals who enroll in junior colleges but who will never graduate or earn a credential because they are incapable of doing so. Rather than provide a "hard" denial of "unequivocal dismissal" (571), the public junior college provides a variety of "soft" failures that "cool-out" a student's ambition and prospects and usher such students gently out of the higher education system.

Clark identifies a number of features of this "cooling out function" (574), including "alternative achievement" (helping students embrace more modest goals and ambitions) (574–5), "gradual disengagement" (stalling progress toward goals that encourage students to "give up peacefully") (575), "objective denial" ("a record of poor performance helps to detach the organization and its agents from the emotional aspects of the cooling-out work" [575]), "agents of consolation" ("counselors are available who are patient with the overambitious and who work to change their intentions" [575]), and "avoidance of standards" (575). Clark also discusses "the importance of concealment":

> If high school seniors and their families were to define the junior college as a place which diverts college-bound students, a probable consequence would be a turning away from the junior college and increased pressure for admission to the four-year colleges and universities that are otherwise protected to some degree. (575)

Clark notes that "for an organization and its agents one dilemma of a cooling-out role is that it must be kept reasonably away from public scrutiny and not clearly perceived or understood by prospective clientele" (575). For Clark, the junior college is the institution in America's system of higher education "that specializes in handling students who will soon be leaving" (571–2). Although it markets itself as "a place where everyone is admitted and everyone succeeds" (576), the junior college is, in fact, an institution for Clark that promotes "wishful unawareness" in students (576) and provides a way for large cohorts of students to save "insult to their self-image" (576).

Readers may find it interesting to note that even in 1960, retention and graduation rates for college students were important concerns. In one of his footnotes, Clark cites data from Robert E. Iffert's *Retention and Withdrawal of College Students* (1958):

> One national report showed that one out of eight entering students (12.5 per cent) in publically controlled colleges does not remain beyond the first term or semester; one out of three (31 percent) is out by the end of the first year; and about one out of two (46.6 per cent) leaves within the first two years. (571)

These data are a half a century old.

Reading Clark's essay today, it is hard not to be impressed with its comprehensive cynicism about the junior college and its function in our democracy. Rather than liberate and ennoble, the function of the junior college in this view is focused primarily on promoting a covert kind of defeat and dismissal. Clark was writing at a time before the dramatic expansion of open admissions institutions across the US was fully underway. In fact, Clark's essay in some very obvious ways *predates* the modern community college. 750 community colleges were established after his essay was written (American "CC"). It is hard to know how one might apply Clark's ideas—written from another, earlier age in American higher education—to the community college system we have today. Nonetheless, scholars and legislators do apply them, and Clark's essay continues to be one of the most frequently cited in the literature devoted to community colleges.

Clark's postulation of the "latent terminal" student is especially grievous and unfortunate, suggesting a deficit model of insuperable internal deficiencies and shortcomings. As the research we have reviewed here by Carol Dweck, neuroscientists, and others has shown, there is no such thing as a "latent terminal student," except those with serious learning disabilities that impede their ability to learn and grow.

THE DIVERTED DREAM

Nonetheless, Clark's ideas have been hugely influential, and they have had a significant impact on framing the thinking about community colleges over the last 65 years. In fact, it seems like Clark's essay gets rewritten for a new cohort of readers every five years or so. I would construct a representative list of these iterations of Clark's essay this way:

1960: Clark, Burton. "The 'Cooling-Out' Function in Higher Education." *American Journal of Sociology* 65.6 (1960): 569–76.
1972. Karabel, Jerome. "Community Colleges and Social Stratification." *Harvard Educational Review* 42.4 (1972): 521–62.
1976. Zwerling, L. Steven. *Second Best: The Crisis of the Community College*. New York, McGraw-Hill, 1976.
1986. Zwerling, L. Steven, ed. *The Community College and Its Critics*. San Francisco: Jossey-Bass, 1986.
1989: Brint, Steven, and Jerome Karabel. *The Diverted Dream: Community Colleges and the Promise of Educational Opportunity in America, 1900–1985*. New York: Oxford UP, 1989.
1991. Dougherty, Kevin. "The Community College at the Crossroads: The Need for Structural Reform." *Harvard Educational Review* 61.3 (1991): 311–37.
1994. Traub, James. *City on a Hill: Testing the American Dream at City College*. New York: Da Capo, 1994.
1995: Rouse, Cecilia Elena. "Democratization or Diversion? The Effect of Community Colleges on Educational Attainment." *Journal of Business & Economic Statistics* 13.2 (1995): 217–224.
2001: Dougherty, Kevin J. *The Contradictory College: The Conflicting Origins, Impacts, and Futures of the Community College*. Albany, SUNY Press, 2001.
2011: Beach, J. M. *Gateway to Opportunity? A History of the Community College in the United States*. Sterling: Stylus, 2011.
2011. Flores, Roy. "False Hope" *Inside Higher Ed*, February 17, 2011.
2012. Complete College America. *Remediation: Higher Education's Bridge to Nowhere*. Washington: Complete College America.

2014: Scherer, Juliet Lilledahl, and Mirra Leigh Anson. *Community Colleges and the Access Effect: Why Open Admissions Suppresses Achievement.* New York: Palgrave Macmillan, 2014.

2015: Bailey, Thomas R., Shanna Smith Jaggers, and Davis Jenkins. *Redesigning America's Community Colleges: A Clearer Path to Student Success.* Cambridge: Harvard University Press, 2015.

Even a brief review of selected highlights from this foundational community college "failure" narrative over the last half century illustrates how appealing and enduring Clark's ideas have been. Again, what we may be seeing here is evidence of Stiglitz and Greenwald's claims about societal rigidities, collective beliefs, mindsets, the power of prior beliefs to shape the understanding of new information, confirmatory bias, the fact that cognitive frames which shape perceptions are largely socially determined, that such perceptions affect *collective* actions, and that socially dysfunctional beliefs and policies can persist and reproduce.

Steven Brint and Jerome Karabel's *The Diverted Dream: Community Colleges and the Promise of Educational Opportunity in America, 1900–1985,* for example, draws directly on Clark's work and reaches a similar conclusion. As the title of their book suggests, Brint and Karabel see the community college implicated in a system designed to divert dreams and ambition:

> As an institution centrally involved in what we have called the *management of ambition*, the community college—however firm its ideological commitment to democratization—has had little choice but to participate actively in the "cooling-out" process. The role of the public junior college as a place where a large number of students will be channeled away from four-year institutions and the professional and managerial occupations to which these institutions have historically provided access is thus not a matter of administrative preference but, rather, is built into the nature of the institution.[48] (225).

In the footnote here, Brint and Karabel note that "in *The Open-Door College,* Burton Clark also emphasized the centrality of diversion to the mission of the community college, referring to 'the specific operation of transforming transfer students into terminal students' as its 'most important feature' (Clark 1960, p. 146)" (269). This is the language and the theoretical framework that informs Brint and Karabel's understanding of the community college and from which they draw the title of their book.

Brint and Karabel also suggest that the community college has actively reproduced economic inequality and functioned overall as an antidemocratic institution:

> The very real contribution that the community college has made to the expansion of opportunities for some individuals does not, however, mean that its *aggregate* effect has been a democratizing one. On the contrary, the two-year institution has accentuated rather than reduced existing patterns of social inequality. Indeed, in both the social origins and the occupational destinations of its students, the community college clearly constitutes the bottom tier of a class-linked tracking system in higher education. As a growing body of evidence accumulated over more than two decades demonstrates, the very fact of attending a two-year rather than a four-year institution lowers the likelihood that a student will obtain a bachelor's degree. Similarly, entering a two-year as opposed to a four-year college has a negative effect on adult occupational status, even controlling for individual differences in socioeconomic background, measured mental ability, and other variables. (226)

We see here the focus again on "obtaining a bachelor's degree" as a key marker of success, along with a variety of conclusions drawn from that single puzzling data point.

Until very recently, as we have already observed, colleges in America were "bastions of privilege" and not "engines of opportunity" (Bowen, Kurzweil, and Tobin 135; Lavin and Hyllegard). In some ways, selective and highly selective institutions still function this way, and community colleges may make it easier for them to do so. We certainly have a stratified system of higher education in America, and in some very real ways, our educational system reproduces that stratification. Even Bourdieu and Passeron refer to the cooling-out function as a mechanism for "legitimating the 'social order'" (183–184). But they are careful to point out that many sociologists "are inclined to isolate dispositions and predispositions toward education—'hopes,' 'aspirations,' 'motivations,' 'will-power'—from their social conditions of production: forgetting that objective conditions determine both aspirations and the degree to which they can be satisfied" (207).

THE CONTRADICTORY COLLEGE

Of the scholars who have followed Clark and Brint and Karabel, Kevin J. Dougherty has been perhaps the most prolific and may be among the most important. Doughterty's book-length treatment of this subject, *The Contradictory College*, seeks to assess the nature of the cooling-out function. The key problem for Dougherty, which he comes back to again and again in his work, is this troubling concern about baccalaureate degree attainment. What he finds especially problematic is that students who appear to be identical in prematriculation characteristics earn bachelor's degrees at very different rates depending on whether they enroll at a community college or not. He devotes an entire chapter to this question in *The Contradictory College*, tellingly entitled "How Does the Community College Hinder Baccalaureate Attainment?" (83–111). For Dougherty, "the first years in the community college are lethal to the hopes of many baccalaureate aspirants" (85). To his credit, Dougherty works through this problem and engages the evidence very carefully, examining a wide variety of "institutional features" (106), including lower social integration of students (the lack of residential dormitories on campus contribute substantially to this), lower selectivity and prestige, the focus on vocational training, and a variety of problems related to transfer (106). Dougherty also suggests that "the greater dropout rate of community college students is not due just to their more modest backgrounds and academic aptitudes" (86). The key dilemma for Dougherty is one that Clark addresses as well: "Why does an institution that professes such a strong commitment to equality of opportunity so significantly hinder the academic progress of its baccalaureate aspirants? Is this effect intentional?" (186). Dougherty concludes that this effect—that many community college students "suffer academic death in the middle passage" (187) between community college and a four-year transfer institution—is incidental and not intentional. A large number of factors, he suggests, collude to have "unintended consequences" (187) for baccalaureate aspirants at community colleges, including (in addition to those we have already mentioned) a strong vocational focus ("Because it is strongly committed to vocational education, many baccalaureate aspirants are seduced away from their initial ambitions" [186–7]) and the many complexities involved with transferring to a new institution ("one that may be far away, deny many of their credits, refuse to give them as much student aid as they need, and fail to integrate them into the new institution" [187]).

Dougherty breaks with Clark in that his research suggests that the community college does not function intentionally as an institution devoted to cooling-out the ambitions of students:

> The wide range and malignant effectiveness of the hurdles community college entrants face in pursuing a baccalaureate can easily lead one to assume that these obstacles are deliberate. It seems plausible that because the community college's *effect* is to hinder baccalaureate attainment that this has been its *intent*. However, this assumption of a symmetry between effects and intents is mistaken. As we will see in Sections III and IV, the features of the community college that impede baccalaureate attainment are almost wholly not the result of a desire by private interest groups and government

officials to block students' life chances. Rather, these hindrances emerge from the community college's attempt to reconcile many different and often antithetical goals. It has contradictory effects because it has contradictory goals. (106; italics in original)

This is an important moment in our long history of scholarly engagement with the community college—and a rare positive assessment among many that are much less flattering.

GATEWAY TO OPPORTUNITY?

Since the publication of Dougherty's book in 2001, the community college "failure" narrative has continued to manifest itself repeatedly in academic scholarship and in reports from private foundations like Complete College America. This work has been unrelenting—and very effective in undermining confidence in the community college and confidence in the expertise of professionals who teach and work at these institutions. For example, in *Gateway to Opportunity? A History of the Community College in the United States,* J.M. Beach concludes that the community college has provided only "limited opportunity" to students (125–30) and has been a failure in providing a "gateway to opportunity." Following Burton Clark, Beach finds the cooling out function still very much at work:

> What is the legacy of community colleges? The junior college turned community college was designed to be a socioeconomic institution for sorting students and limited opportunity. It had two major objectives: transfer a select group of prepared undergraduates to the university, guiding them to a professional career, and cool out the majority of junior college students, delaying their entry into the labor market, and redirect them to the mid- to low-skilled labor market. On the one hand, community colleges allowed the universities, such as the University of California, to become more restrictive institutions of higher education. On the other hand, they also offered what appeared to be the democratization of higher education by giving a broad range of students who would have never been able to attend college the opportunity to at least gain some measure of higher education. However, while community colleges offered more students the opportunity for higher education, they also structured the failure of many students by not also providing the necessary support services, financial aid, and trained teachers that would ensure their success (not to mention the needed state programs to address segregated housing and labor markets). (125)

Beach suggests that if one looks "holistically at the history, missions, and performance of community colleges to date, it is not much of an opportunity and not easily obtained by the majority of community college students" (125–6). Beach also suggests that "the community college is a structurally limited opportunity that has been used to blame the victims of America's lingering class-based and race-based society for failure" (126). Like Clark, Beach finds mostly disappointment and failure at the heart of the modern community college experience.

A Cruel Hoax

Much of the focus of recent iterations of this "failure" narrative has been on the cohort of students that make the community college an open admissions institution in the first place—students who test into developmental courses. Complete College America's report, "Remediation: Higher Education's Bridge to Nowhere," essentially declares the entire enterprise of developmental education a grand experiment that has failed:

> The intentions were noble. It was hoped that remediation programs would be an academic bridge from poor high school preparation to college readiness—a grand idea inspired by our commitment to expand access to all who seek a college degree.
>
> Sadly, remediation has become instead higher education's "Bridge to Nowhere." This broken remedial bridge is travelled by some 1.7 million beginning students each year, most of whom will not reach their destination—graduation. It is estimated that states and students spent more than $3 billion on remedial courses last year with very little student success to show for it. (2)

Juliet Lilledahl Scherer and Mirra Leigh Anson, in their book *Community Colleges and the Access Effect: Why Open Admissions Suppresses Achievement*, make a similar claim, although they are certainly not fans of Complete College America or the Community College Resource Center (CCRC)—both funded by the activist and interventionist Gates Foundation (Mangan "How"). Scherer and Anson propose that we rethink the very idea of "open access" itself. Their reasoning, I'm afraid, often reflects deficit-model thinking about what students can and cannot do. They suggest that "allowing everyone to access a pathway that leads to great opportunities, but is too difficult for many to traverse, is not really granting access at all, but perpetrating a cruel hoax" (2). Scherer and Anson also come very close to making an essentialist claim about students in developmental programs:

"Developmental educators at open door community colleges who teach the lowest level courses will confirm that students regularly enroll who have virtually *zero* chance to exit the developmental sequence, qualify for college-level courses, and earn a two-year degree, due to intellectual ability" (14–15; italics in the original). Scherer and Anson recommend that we base access decisions not on potential or ambition but on "probability" (3). Like Ray Flores, who we met in an earlier chapter, Scherer and Anson ask if it is "fair and just to afford to each of those students the opportunity to fail when it is known in advance that nine out of ten of them would not succeed?" (3). The "only players in this open access game unaware of the high probability that the students will never complete a two- or four-year degree are the students themselves (and sometimes their parents or guardians)" (3). The authors suggest, furthermore, that "overenrolling low-income students beyond their financial and/or academic abilities actually *perpetuates* inequity" (167; italics in the original) by saddling them with debt incurred in pursuit of degrees they have virtually no chance of completing. Scherer and Anson recommend, instead, establishing performance incentives using a "momentum points" model for students who complete milestones toward degree or program completion (56–58). They also recommend applying Federal Student Aid regulations more rigorously for developmental students and strengthening alternative vocational pathways (135–63).

Scherer and Anson also suggest that open admissions policies are complicit in the failure of America's primary and secondary schools as well. "The complete absence of any admissions standard to a nationwide network of open-door institutes of higher education, coupled with easy access to FSA," they note, "is *driving* mass underperformance in the K-12 system" (4; italics in the original). The "word in the hallways," they suggest, is that "it really doesn't matter how you do; you can always get into the community college and get it paid for" (4). They summarize the current situation this way:

> Few recognize or are willing to discuss the central role that open door policy plays in tamping down secondary student engagement and achievement, which subsequently leads to poor postsecondary performance and a great deal of unfulfilled potential. Far from only or even mostly producing positive effects, open admissions policy negatively affects academic achievement and completion; many capable citizens are, in effect, unquestionably harmed by the utter lack of entry standards at a collection of community colleges blanketing the country. Open access policy provides such a cartoonishly large safety valve that it *contributes* to low post-secondary

completion by discouraging many from preparing meaningfully. (105; italics in the original)

So not only are community colleges failing their own students, they are also failing students in primary and secondary school systems as well. Scherer and Anson also include a harrowing analysis of the powerful effect private money has had on public higher education, most of which promotes neoliberal economic theory and the adoption of business models and methodology. These ideas, which have been thoroughly discredited in the public school system, include performance funding and economic rewards for improved completion rates (Ravitch *Reign*; Ripley; Rizga; Schneider; Tucker).

Widespread Failure, Disappointment, Frustration, and Thwarted Potential

Finally, we have Bailey, Jaggars, and Jenkins who categorically conclude in *Redesigning America's Community Colleges* (2015) that community colleges are "poorly designed to facilitate completion of high quality college programs" (13). This assessment is based, again, on graduation and completion rates: "Most students who enter these colleges never finish: fewer than four of every ten complete any type of degree of certificate within six years" (1). These low completion rates, the authors suggest, "reflect widespread failure, disappointment, frustration, and thwarted potential among the millions of students who do not achieve their educational goals" (1).

Bailey, Jaggars, and Jenkins use this "widespread failure" narrative to support a variety of proposals—some good, some dangerous and misguided. Their discussion of developmental education reform, for example, drawing on disciplinary knowledge through the work of Adams and Hern, is thoughtful and helpful. As is their idea for establishing a "guided pathways" approach to organizing community college programs, providing more advising, meta-majors, required orientation, and some form of directed self-placement or student advocacy in placement decisions. Their vision for a more student-centered, advisement-saturated community college experience for students is an appealing one that will likely gain many supporters. But as the authors note, this will require increased funding at a time of fiscal austerity. The focus on active learning and replacing the knowledge *transmission model* of learning (with a teacher spending most of her time lecturing and focused primarily on content acquisition) with a *learning facilitation* approach pioneered by scholars like Maryellen Weimer is also appealing and sensible (and also widely known and practiced on community college campuses, although perhaps not as widely practiced as it should be). The learning facilitation approach privileges active learning and class discussion, a focus on big questions, and limited use of lectures (Bailey, Jaggars, and Jenkins 81–118). The learning facilitation approach "explicitly addresses conceptual understanding, metacognition, and student motivation" and employs "more collaborative, discussion-based, and activity-based teaching methods" (87).

To fund these innovations, Bailey, Jaggars, and Jenkins recommend that states adopt a performance funding model similar to that used to such disastrous effect in the public school sector that has led to cheating scandals, over-testing, and poor learning outcomes reported in books like Marc Tucker's *Surpassing Shanghai: An Agenda for American Education Built on the World's Leading Systems*, Amanda Ripley's *The Smartest Kids in the World: And How They Got That Way*, Linda Darling-Hammond's *The Flat World and Education: How America's Commitment to Equity Will Determine Our Future*, Dana Russakoff's *The Prize: Who's In Charge of America's Schools?*, Peter Sacks's *Standardized Minds: The High Price Of America's Testing Culture And What We Can Do To Change It*, Richard Rothstein, Rebecca Jacobsen, and Tamara Wilder's *Grading Education: Getting Accountability Right*, Diane Ravitch's *Reign of Error: The Hoax of the Privatization Movement and the Danger to America's Public Schools*, and articles like Rachel Aviv's "Wrong Answer," which documents widespread cheating in the Atlanta public school system—driven by the idea that the values of the marketplace can save public education. This high-stakes testing environment created conditions in Atlanta that led a large number of educators to make "a shocking choice," doctoring answer sheets to standardized tests in order to meet performance goals:

> After more than two thousand interviews, the investigators concluded that forty-four schools had cheated and that a "culture of fear, intimidation and retaliation has infested the district, allowing cheating—at all levels—to go unchecked for years."

Aviv suggests that infatuation with certain kinds of data make this kind of behavior almost predictable. Such "accountability" schemes also frame the rich, deep, complex process of learning in very reductive and dangerous ways:

John Ewing, who served as the executive director of the American Mathematical Society for fifteen years, told me that he is perplexed by educators' "infatuation with data," their faith that it is more authoritative than using their own judgment. He explains the problem in terms of Campbell's law, a principle that describes the risks of using a single indicator to measure complex social phenomena: the greater the value placed on a quantitative measure, like test scores, the more likely it is that the people using it and the process it measures will be corrupted. "The end goal of education isn't to get students to answer the right number of questions," he said. "The goal is to have curious and creative students who can function in life." In a 2011 paper in *Notices of the American Mathematical Society*, he warned that policymakers were using mathematics "to intimidate—to preëmpt debate about the goals of education and measures of success."

That last sentence is crucially important for our purposes here: policymakers using mathematics "to intimidate—to preëmpt debate about the goals of education and measures of success." Performance funding would apply the same economic model to community colleges that was used for No Child Left Behind and, in the private sector, at businesses like car dealerships, where individuals work on commission, earning financial rewards for the number of vehicles sold. Community colleges would be put in the same position, earning bonuses in some proposals and baseline funding in others for meeting completion goals measured in degree and certificate attainment—the number of degrees and certificates awarded. Such a proposal assumes that community college professionals need additional motivation to help students succeed—and that with the right financial incentives, we can finally get this long-standing problem turned around. Such a proposal also suggests that faculty and staff at community colleges aren't already deeply invested in nurturing student success and haven't already worked with great dedication and resourcefulness to help students succeed. When we look at community colleges—with their learning centers, writing centers, counseling centers, advisement programs, basic writing and basic math curriculum, computer labs, peer tutors, reference librarian staffs, summer bridge programs, Brother to Brother and Sister to Sister programs—don't we see institutions doing everything they possibly can to help students succeed? For the student who needs it and has the desire to find it, help is almost always available. Such an incentivized funding model would destabilize a vitally important American institution, pitting individual institutions against sister institutions in the same state in a competition for vital resources and forcing community colleges to live hand-to-mouth each year depending on completion goals.

Performance funding appears to be a consistent feature in most higher education initiatives supported by the Gates Foundation (Scherer and Anson 31–37). One might read the entire book by Bailey, Jaggars, and Jenkins, in fact, as a justification (and perhaps also a legislative guidebook) for promoting neoliberal ideas and more widespread adaptation of the performance funding model for our nation's community colleges—a very popular idea among business leaders and philanthropists that would serve to advance the encroachment of neoliberal business ideas further into higher education. Although it sounds benign enough when formulated in the opaque economic language of neoliberalism, deliberately modeled on Milton Friedman's formulation—shifting "the basis of funding from *educational inputs* to *outputs that reflect policy priorities*" (Bailey, Jaggars, and Jenkins 185 [italics in original]; Friedman "Why" 2)—the results would weaken a great and noble American institution. This entire edifice is built on unsound evidence and a profound misunderstanding of the modern community college, produced in large measure by deficit model thinking and the inappropriate use of a neoliberal economic business model to assess an educational institution designed to promote the public good.

CHAPTER 31

The Developmental Education Crisis

Literacy in American Lives

No nation has ever attempted to prepare all of its citizens for college before, and for all the reasons we have documented in this book, this has been important and rewarding—and also challenging—work. The discipline of basic writing was founded only a few decades ago with the advent of open admissions policies nationwide. Unlike disciplines like math, history, and literary studies, which have long histories spanning centuries, the teaching of basic writing as a formal discipline began with open admissions. The first significant scholarship and theory only began appearing in the late 1960s (Otte and Mlynarczyk). There has been much we have needed to learn about literacy acquisition, best practices for preparing students for the deep intellectual work of college, and teaching reading, writing, and thinking. This work is still ongoing. We have attempted, in effect, to create, theorize, and field-test a brand new discipline—basic reading and writing—*as we have been teaching it*, with all the challenges and missteps inherent in that process.

There has been a great deal of important scholarship published on this subject since the 1960s, of course, including work featured in *The Journal of Basic Writing*, an important scholarly journal that has been advancing disciplinary knowledge about basic writing since 1975. *The Journal of Basic Writing* was founded by Mina Shaughnessy, a developmental education pioneer and author of the landmark book, *Errors and Expectations: A Guide for the Teacher of Basic Writing* (1977). Shaughnessy is renowned for her compassion and inclusiveness and for championing students who find themselves to be "strangers in academia" (3). Shaughnessy was especially interested in developing strategies for helping students who "had been left so far behind the others in their formal education that they appeared to have little chance of catching up" (2). Knowledge in this field is still developing and maturing, of course, as scholars respond to new discoveries and research from within the discipline of writing studies as well as from a variety of disciplines outside the field of reading and composition, including neuroscience, social science, and psychology (Ambrose, Bridges, Lovett, DiPietro, and Norman; Bean). There is always room to improve, there are always new things to learn, and there are always better best practices to develop. Thousands of teachers and scholars have worked in good faith over many decades to help move this process forward in order to bring literacy and opportunity to those who are seeking it at America's community colleges.

Citizens, philanthropists, and legislators critical of developmental course success rates often regard developmental courses as exactly the same as any other class that might be offered on a college campus. Students enroll, they either do well or they struggle, and then they get final grades and either pass or fail. This formulation is missing a key difference in the structural role that developmental courses play in the lives of students at open admissions institutions. Gatekeeper courses like basic reading, writing, and math classes are generally among the few courses on community college campuses open to underprepared students. These are the courses that underprepared "experimenters" (Manski; Grubb) are required to take when they come to our campuses. Many students who test into these courses are simply giving college a try and attempting to determine if college can work for them. This is a unique and vitally important function of these courses. So in addition to being identified as, say, English 93: Introduction to College Reading and Writing, as one of the developmental courses is at my home institution, for many students, this course could easily also be cross-listed as College Success 100: Am I Ready for College? or Study Skills 100: Success Strategies for College or even The Reckoning 101: Am I Even Interested In Attending College? There is a great deal that "being ready for college" requires, and when I discuss this with my developmental students by sharing an open letter I wrote for high school students about this subject ("Open"), they are often astonished by how much will be required of them. Obviously, the burden of this work is not shared equally across disciplines or departments. Just as a chemistry or biology class may be a good test for students who are considering health care as a profession, on a larger, more high-stakes scale, developmental courses help students identify strengths and weaknesses, assess their own dispositions and habits of mind (Costa and Kallick), and come to terms with their own level of college readiness in all the ways this needs to be measured and assessed. So it's not just disciplinary content that is being taught here. Something much grander and probably more important is going on as well. Most other courses on college campuses do not have this additional responsibility or this particular cohort of students, and they can therefore be evaluated using traditional metrics. Adding this additional set of complex variables into the mix—preparation, motivation, interest—makes assessment of these programs by traditional success rates very tricky. Some of the students who test into these courses simply need a refresher course and some fine-tuning. Many, though, never did well in English or math, and many never really liked school at all. They are attending college because they understand that this is the only option available to them at the moment if they hope to earn a living wage, start a family, and live independently.

Listening to some of the critics of developmental education today, one might think that underprepared students hadn't learned a single thing during the last 50 years in basic reading and writing classes in America. Yes, our goal must always be to graduate as many students as we can from developmental education programs and community colleges, but there are many complex cultural, economic, historical, social, and psychological reasons why the numbers are where they are.

Evidence suggests, in fact, that developmental education at America's community colleges has been very successful—and has been a very important part of what the community college has offered to its communities. There is a documented record of achievement in this regard. We also can't expect to assess developmental course offerings the same way that we might assess a credit-bearing course at a community college or a class offered at a selective four-year institution enrolling students who have already demonstrated in a variety of ways their ability to produce strong college-level work. Developmental classes are places where students learn to read, write, calculate, and study and also come to embrace important habits of mind and academic dispositions. They are also places where students who are unsure about their futures and their interests come to discover if college is for them. Developmental classes are also locations where students with all different kinds of motivations and levels of preparation and interest converge. There are profound questions being engaged for students in these classes that sometimes have nothing to do with subject matter and often cannot be accurately reflected in completion data: Do you have the discipline to be successful in college? Do you have the time and the financial, emotional, psychological, and family resources to devote to a long-term endeavor like earning a college degree? Do you like to read? Are you interested in challenging yourself in new ways? Are you interested in growing as an individual and as a citizen of the world? Do you like academic work? Are you attending college only because there are no other feasible options for a career that pays a living wage?

Pathways to a Degree or Professional Credential

In an attempt to discover if developmental education contributed in any structural way to degree attainment at my home institution in Connecticut, I worked with our Office of Planning, Research and Assessment to examine the past three years of students who earned an MCC degree, had started at MCC as new college students, and took a developmental class in either math or English or both. We excluded those for whom we had no placement information (approximately 10 percent of the total). What we found surprised us: *60 percent of our completers over these years were initially assigned to a developmental class in math or English* (see Fig. 31.1). Developmental education contributed in a profoundly positive way to degree attainment at our institution.

The percentage of students who place into developmental classes on our campus has remained relatively constant for many years—about 40 percent arrive college-ready and 60 percent arrive needing developmental work.

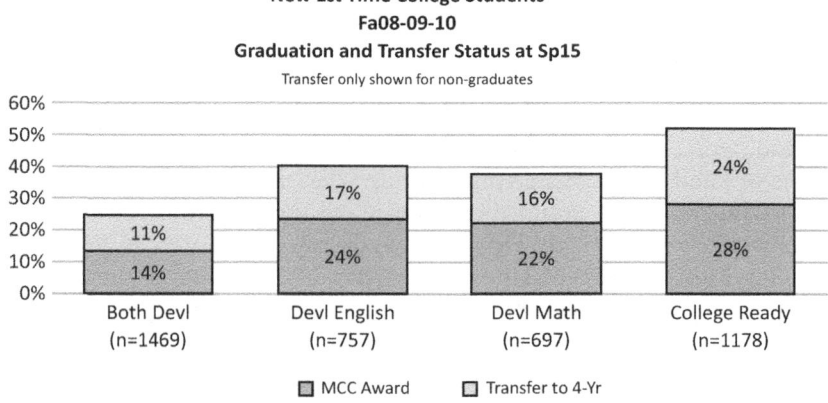

Fig. 31.1 New first-time MCC students: Graduation and transfer status

With the new PA 12-40 legislation in the state of Connecticut affecting placement, along with active outreach efforts we are conducting with area high schools, we now have 50 percent of entering students arriving ready for college. The graduating group reported in Fig. 31.1 is similar to new entering groups in terms of developmental placement. Furthermore, our high percentage of successful remediation holds if we look at all graduates, not just those who started their college careers at MCC. After excluding 34 percent who didn't have any placement info, we found 58 percent of this cohort of graduating students needed a developmental class at MCC.

These numbers agree with national figures provided by Bailey, Jaggars, and Jenkins (119–43) and Bailey and Cho in a paper they prepared for The White House Summit on Community Colleges in 2010, "Developmental Education in Community Colleges": "Less than one quarter of community college students who enroll in developmental education complete a degree or certificate within eight years of enrollment in college" (46). This is just a different way to present these data, one in which the glass is half full rather than half empty.

Similar success stories regarding developmental education are being realized across the nation. To give just one example, in California, disaggregated graduation data are available on the Student Success Scorecards pages, with reports on each of California's 113 colleges and on a composite statewide report (see the "completion outcomes" "degree/transfer" tab). These pages provide data about outcomes for students placed into developmental courses and tracks them longitudinally. Statewide, 39.6 percent of community college students in California who start in developmental courses (English, math, or both) go on to complete a degree or transfer outcome within six years (n = 153,479), compared to 70 percent of students who began "college prepared" (California). These numbers provide us with the "percentage of degree, certificate and/or transfer-seeking students starting first time in 2009–10 tracked for six years through 2014–15 who completed a degree, certificate or transfer-related outcomes" (California).

Our understanding of this, of course, is dependent on what proportion of the total student population is placed into developmental education overall. In California, approximately 75 percent of students are required to start in developmental courses. Nationally, the number is closer to 50 percent. At MCC, our number is now close to the national average. These data suggest the need to reframe our perception of the "crisis" in developmental education at community colleges. For approximately 60 percent of our completers at MCC and 39 percent of community college students in California, developmental education provided a pathway to a degree or professional credential.

"A Powerful Gravitational Pull"

Sensational public stories like the community college "failure" narrative can often "exert a powerful gravitational pull that winds up bending facts in its direction," to borrow a memorable phrase from investigative journalist Jonathan Mahler (45). This image from astronomy of a massive star or black hole with a gravitational pull so strong that it can bend and even trap light appears to be quite appropriate. Diane Ravitch has documented a similar dynamic at work in the public school sector, where the narrative of school "crisis" has effectively preempted alternative narratives and managed to protect such narratives against research and data that would discredit them. Narrative is something that F.A. Hayek cared very deeply about, of course, because he understood its power.

This appears to be the case for developmental education as well, which has lately become nearly synonymous with community college failure. A paradigmatic example of this narrative-building activity perniciously at work is Complete College America's report, *Remediation: Higher Education's Bridge to Nowhere*. As we have seen, their assessment is unsparing: Remediation has become higher education's "bridge to nowhere" (2). I'm afraid this is demonstrably not the case.

The cover of this report depicts a "bridge to nowhere," suggesting failure, incompetence, and potential violent loss of life (see Fig. 31.2). A more accurate visual metaphor for developmental education nationwide would be a graduation ceremony at a community college (see Figs. 31.3, 31.4, 31.5, 31.6, 31.7, and 31.8). At my college this spring (2016), 896 students graduated with degrees and certificates. Graduates came from 101 towns across Connecticut as well as from ten other states. A significant proportion of the students in graduating classes at American community colleges benefit in important ways from developmental education. In Figs. 31.3, 31.4, 31.5, and 31.6, for example, approximately 60 percent of these graduating classes from 2015 to 2016 completed a developmental English or math course before earning a credential or degree. In Figs. 31.7 and 31.8, approximately 39 percent of these graduating classes from 2015 completed a developmental English or math course before earning a credential or degree. For purposes of comparison, and to put this success into historical perspective, see Fig. 31.9, a photo of MCC's first graduating class from 1965.

The *Bridge to Nowhere* report is part of a systematic misrepresentation of the nature and achievement of developmental education at our nation's

Fig. 31.2 The cover of Complete College America's report, *Remediation: Higher Education's Bridge to Nowhere*. 2012 (*Source*: Complete College America. http://www.completecollege.org/docs/CCA-Remediation-final.pdf)

community colleges. This report may well be an example of the kind of "educational jeremiad" that Richard Hofstadter has identified as a permanent part of our educational tradition in America, stretching back hundreds of years. Hofstadter suggests that this "educational jeremiad" is as much a feature of our educational literature as "the jeremiad in Puritan sermons" (301). But it also participates in a very new tradition of crisis narrative that seeks to promote neoliberal economic ideas that privilege privatization, market metrics, and school "reform." Such jeremiads are dangerous, of course, because they often misrepresent, simplify, or selectively employ evidence, and they often use hyperbole as a rhetorical and political strategy. Recently, a number of developmental educators have begun to challenge the validity of the research studies used to support this "failure" narrative, many of which have issued from the CCRC. Hunter R. Boylan, who is the Director of the National Center for Developmental Education, and Alexandros M. Goudas surveyed the research studies used to support claims about the failure of developmental education and have found inconsistencies, inaccuracies, and overstatement. Their findings are significant:

Fig. 31.3 Graduation ceremony at Manchester Community College, May 2016. Approximately 60 percent of the students in this graduating class owe their success to developmental English or math courses. In 2016, 896 students graduated with degrees and certificates
(*Source*: Manchester Community College archives. Photo credit: Ann Montgomery)

> If we look at all the major studies of remediation, we find conflicting findings and inconclusive results. Given these findings, it is difficult to understand how any credible scholar familiar with the available evidence can decisively conclude that remediation has failed. (Boylan and Goudas; see also Goudas and Boylan)

A number of additional studies support these claims and provide a much more positive assessment about the effectiveness of developmental education (Bahr; Attewell, Lavin, Domina, and Levey; see also Bailey, Jaggars, and Scott-Clayton "Characterizing").

Democracy as a Way of Life

Given all the good news available about community colleges across a wide range of indicators, it is perhaps surprising that editorials, reports, and scholarship continue to suggest that our grand national experiment

Fig. 31.4 Photo from graduation ceremony at Manchester Community College, May 2015. Approximately 60 percent of the students in this graduating class owe their success to developmental English or math courses (*Source*: Manchester Community College archives. Photo credit: Ann Montgomery)

in equity and social justice at America's community colleges has been anything but an incomparable success. This is especially puzzling, given the many significant challenges inherent in the community college mission and mandate. Public commentary has focused relentlessly in recent years on the "failure" of developmental education at community colleges, and this appears to have bled over into a general sense that community colleges simply do not work and perhaps never had (Bailey, Jaggars, and Jenkins; Beach; Scherer and Anson). Perhaps this is a matter of confirmatory bias, lack of personal familiarity with these institutions, or the power of prior beliefs to shape understanding of new information. But it may even be simpler and more fundamental than that. It may be a problem that F.A. Hayek identified many years ago in the opening pages of *The Constitution of Liberty*, his book about personal freedom in a democracy:

> If old truths are to retain their hold on men's minds, they must be restated in the language and concepts of successive generations. What at one time are their most effective expressions gradually become so worn with use that

Fig. 31.5 Photo from graduation ceremony at Manchester Community College, May 2015. Approximately 60 percent of the students in this graduating class owe their success to developmental English or math courses
(*Source*: Manchester Community College archives. Photo credit: Ann Montgomery)

Fig. 31.6 Photo from the graduation ceremony at Manchester Community College, May 2016. Approximately 60 percent of the students in this graduating class owe their success to developmental English or math courses
(*Source*: Manchester Community College archives. Photo credit: Ann Montgomery)

Fig. 31.7 Recent graduates from Pierce College in Woodland Hills, California—one of California's 113 community colleges, May 2015. Approximately 39 percent of the students in this graduating class owe their success to developmental English or math courses
(*Source*: California Community Colleges Chancellor's Office. "Welcome to the California Community Colleges Chancellor's Office." 2015. Web. 12 Dec. 2015)

Fig. 31.8 Graduation ceremony at Southwestern College in Chula Vista, California—one of California's 113 community colleges, May 2015. Approximately 39 percent of the students in this graduating class owe their success to developmental English or math courses
(*Source*: Southwestern College. "Photos from the 2015 Commencement Ceremony" https://www.flickr.com/photos/88810833@N06/sets/72157654248797642)

Fig. 31.9 MCC's first graduating class in 1965 (*Source*: Manchester Community College archives)

> they cease to carry a definite meaning. The underlying ideas may be as valid as ever, but the words, even when they refer to problems that are still with us, no longer convey the same conviction; the arguments do not move in a context familiar to us; and they rarely give us direct answers to the questions we are asking. (47)

If Hayek is right, then perhaps some of our traditional language about "democracy's college"—language that was once rhetorically very effective—has now, through familiarity and constant use, lost its ability to inspire and convince. Perhaps some of these "old truths" have become so worn that they cease to convey the same conviction. Perhaps our case has to be remade in a new language for a new generation with direct answers to the new questions Americans are asking today. Those who believe in open admissions and the community college mission may also need to rediscover what Hayek has called the "courage to be Utopian" ("Intellectuals" 237). Certainly, the community college movement is a stirring example of this noble human impulse. Perhaps we do ourselves and our students a disservice by concerning ourselves exclusively with what seems "practicable in the existing state of opinion" ("Intellectuals" 237). Perhaps we need to "make the philosophic foundations of a free society once more a living intellectual issue, and its implementation a task which challenges the ingenuity and imagination of our liveliest minds" ("Intellectuals" 237). To do this, we will need to regain for ourselves and for our fellow countrymen "that belief in the power of ideas which was the mark of liberalism at its greatest" ("Intellectuals" 237).

At the end of *The Constitution of Liberty*, Hayek includes a postscript entitled, "Why I am Not a Conservative." In this brief essay, Hayek suggests that conservatism, by its very nature,

> cannot offer an alternative to the direction in which we are moving. It may succeed by its resistance to current tendencies in slowing down undesirable developments, but, since it does not indicate another direction, it cannot prevent their continuance. It has, for this reason, invariably been the fate of conservatism to be dragged along a path not of its own choosing. (520)

Hayek indicates that he "personally cannot be content with simply helping to apply the brake" (520). The liberal, for Hayek, serves a very different social and public function: "What the liberal must ask, first of all, is not how fast or how far we should move, but where we should move" (520). That is an important question, indeed: In what direction should we seek to move as a nation and as a democracy? Although definitions of these key terms have shifted in the years since Hayek wrote this, the differences in approach he outlines here remain enlightening and valuable.

Hayek reminds readers that "in the United States it is still possible to defend individual liberty by defending long-established institutions" (521). To the liberal, these institutions "are valuable not mainly because they are long established or because they are American but because they correspond to the ideals which he cherishes" (521). For Hayek and other neoliberals, these ideals are perhaps most essentially related to personal freedom and a "thorough sweeping-away of the obstacles to free growth" (521). For others, like Thomas Piketty, Amartya Sen, Walter McMahon, Joseph Stiglitz, Bruce Greenwald, Mina Shaughnessy, Nell Ann Pickett, Marilyn Sternglass, and Linda Darling-Hammond, these ideals are focused on equity and social justice.

I am not sure if F.A. Hayek would recognize how some of his ideas about resisting "central control" of a national economy have been put to use in contemporary America today. He is a very careful thinker, and he actively resisted simplistic theoretical formulations and inflammatory political rhetoric. I'm not sure we can say the same for some others who have taken up the neoliberal cause. As Daniel Stedman Jones documents in his book, *Masters of the Universe: Hayek, Friedman, and the Birth of Neoliberal Politics*, "the theory from Chicago and Virginia became cruder and the pens of Friedman, Stigler, and Buchanan grew stronger in their valorization of the market after 1950" (9). Stedman suggests that part of the strategy of neoliberal public rhetoric has been a deliberate "simplification" of their message that has helped neoliberal ideas "gain significant purchase in the public debates that accompanied the varying crises of liberalism and social democracy of the 1960s and 1970s" (9). As things have turned out, many neoliberal think tanks have been funded by powerful corporations and foundations to promote the interests of deregulation, privatization, and business. The original idealism, academic integrity, and philosophical independence of the MPS has, alas, been largely lost as neoliberalism has now become closely linked with the rich and powerful (J. Mayer; Reich).

Unfortunately, those who theorize a broader, more humanistic role for higher education in contributing to the public good have not been nearly as well-organized, well-funded, or as effective in the realm of public debate. Neoliberals have been championing their cause since the founding of the MPS in 1947. They have worked diligently for almost three-quarters of a century, and they have done an excellent job shaping public opinion and influencing public intellectuals. Those who care about community colleges and providing access to higher education to all Americans will need to make a similarly concerted, well-funded, long-term effort to champion the community college, social justice, and the public good. As David Cole has noted in his book about recent constitutional change in America, *Engines of Liberty: The Power of Citizen Activists to Make Constitutional Law*, change can be realized by groups who are willing to engage in "protracted, intensive, and incremental campaigns" (5). Much of this work involves helping to shape public opinion and "molding public sentiment" (221).

In his essay, "Creative Democracy—The Task Before Us," John Dewey characterized democracy as "a way of life" in a way that speaks directly to the practical idealism embodied in the community college:

> Democracy is a way of life controlled by a working faith in the possibilities of human nature. Belief in the Common Man is a familiar article in the democratic creed. That belief is without basis and significance save as it means faith in the potentialities of human nature as that nature is exhibited in every

human being irrespective of race, color, sex, birth and family, of material or cultural wealth. This faith may be enacted in statutes, but it is only on paper unless it is put in force in the attitudes which human beings display to one another in all the incidents and relations of daily life. To denounce Naziism for intolerance, cruelty and stimulation of hatred amounts to fostering insincerity if, in our personal relations to other persons, if, in our daily walk and conversation, we are moved by racial, color or other class prejudice; indeed, by anything save a generous belief in their possibilities as human beings, a belief which brings with it the need for providing conditions which will enable these capacities to reach fulfillment. The democratic faith in human equality is belief that every human being, independent of the quantity or range of his personal endowment, has the right to equal opportunity with every other person for development of whatever gifts he has. (341)

Dewey's celebration of the "potentialities of human nature" and his call to embrace a "generous belief" in the "possibilities" inherent in us all, "a belief which brings with it the need for providing conditions which will enable these capacities to reach fulfillment," are reminiscent of the language used by the Truman Commission. Dewy formulates here an approach to building a democracy that is deeply committed to opportunity, social justice, and the public good.

Unfortunately, the community college "failure" narrative may ultimately function to help distract attention from the real problems in America today, which we have documented in considerable detail in this book. Economic inequality and race have been key inhibitory factors in educational attainment since institutions of higher learning were established in America (Hutcheson; Karabel *Chosen*; Massey, Charles, Lundy, Fischer). We have known about these problems at least since James Coleman issued his devastating report in 1966. The current community college "failure" narrative may play an important role in cooling out interest in doing the very difficult work of engaging this unfinished work in our democracy. Instead, we have found it easier to simply blame the public school system and community colleges for not doing their jobs. Schools can help address social problems, of course, as we have seen, but they cannot solve them. As Diane Ravitch has urged, "if we mean to conquer educational inequity, we must recognize that the root causes of poor academic performance are segregation and poverty, along with inequitably resourced schools" (*Reign* 9). As my English 9000 students demonstrated, we must liberate ourselves from the idea that some students are "undeserving," incapable, or in Burton Clark's unfortunate phrase, "latent terminal." Many of my students were simply too consumed with earning a living and with the challenges of daily life to have much extra time or energy to devote to the very lengthy process of earning a college degree or credential. In so many ways, community college students are, to borrow a phrase from James Baldwin, what time, circumstance, history, have made of them, certainly, but they are also much more than that. So are we all ("Introduction," 810). The community college is dedicated to precisely this noble proposition.

PART IV

Conclusion

CHAPTER 32

Conclusion: "To Do" List

I am going to refer to some of the fundamentals that antedate parties, and antedate republics and empires, fundamentals that are as old as mankind itself. They are fundamentals that have been expressed in philosophies, for I don't know how many thousands of years, in every part of the world. Today, in our boasted modern civilization, we are facing just exactly the same problem, just exactly the same conflict between two schools of philosophy that they faced in the earliest days of America, and indeed of the world. One of them—one of these old philosophies—is the philosophy of those who would "let things alone." The other is the philosophy that strives for something new—something that the human race has never attained yet, but something which I believe the human race can and will attain—social justice, through social action.—Franklin D. Roosevelt, Campaign Address, Detroit, Michigan, October 2, 1932

It always seems impossible until it's done.—Nelson Mandela

Liberation

The modern community college's revolutionary open admissions policy is at the heart of its unique and irreplaceable contribution to American life. The community college embodies our most noble ideas about democracy and human potential, and it stands as a living, daily expression of our ideals as a nation. The modern community college's open door policy is among the most radical ideas ever formulated in the entire history of higher education, and much of what is transformative and indispensable about the community college proceeds from this foundational innovation. Our efforts to democratize higher education in America have also been supported by landmark federal legislation designed to promote the public good and address economic inequality, including the Higher Education Act in 1965 and the Federal Financial Aid program that resulted from this legislation. This is an unprecedented development in the long history of higher education, and it is to our enduring credit as a nation that we developed this system to distribute educational opportunity more fairly and equitably.

The community college's commitment to diversity, equity, and social justice can only be regarded as revolutionary. Community colleges now enroll approximately half of all undergraduates in America, including 57 percent of all Hispanic college students, 52 percent of all African American college students, 62 percent of all Native American college students, and 43 percent of all Asian/Pacific Island college students (AACC "Fast"; Mullin "Why"). Thirty-six percent of all community college students are first-generation college students, and 17 percent are single parents (AACC "Fast").

More than 65 years into this grand experiment, we continue to work toward realizing the enormous promise inherent in this open door policy. Open admission policies have brought triumph and success to many, but they have also brought their share of problems and challenges, too, foremost among these, of course, is the large number of academically underprepared students who enroll at our colleges. As we seek to address this complex issue, let us keep in mind educational theorist Jerome Bruner's wise counsel about "helping each student achieve his optimum intellectual development" (1960, 9). As Bruner suggests, even in a meritocracy, we must be careful not to forestall opportunities for students who do not excel early in school. Bruner suggests that a meritocracy is especially adept at identifying and providing benefits to able, motivated, early-blooming students. But there are perils for those who do not fit this profile. A meritocracy, he suggests,

> implies a system of competition in which students are moved ahead and given further opportunities on the basis of their achievement, with position in later life increasingly and irreversibly determined by earlier school records. Not only later educational opportunities but subsequent job opportunities become increasingly fixed by earlier school performance. The late bloomer, the early rebel, the child from an educationally indifferent home—all of them, in a full-scale meritocracy, become victims of an often senseless irreversibility of decision. (1960, 77)

Community colleges were designed, at least in part, to help offset this senseless irreversibility for the student who is not the "fast, early, and steady producer" (80).

Much of what we now regard as problematic with developmental education arises from dramatic changes in American culture and the American workplace in the last 100 years. A few generations ago, only a very small percentage of adults went to college after high school. Now, virtually every adult seeks to do so. We have come to view college education as an essential prerequisite for adult life and national economic growth, and we have embarked on the unprecedented national experiment of preparing all of our citizens to be "college ready." Two or three generations ago, of course, this would have been unthinkable. As Deborah Brandt has demonstrated in *Literacy in American Lives*, the last 100 years have been noteworthy for "the sheer acceleration of economic and technological change that courses through American lives" (187; Gordon). As Brandt notes, discussing the family history of one of the subjects of her book,

> In the opening decades of the twentieth century, Vopat's father, a man with a fourth-grade education, hammered out horseshoes and made his own tools on an anvil in a shop that he owned in a small crossroads town in the rural Midwest. By the 1920s, his shop was a franchise for Model T's, then Whippets, then Chryslers, and, by the 1950s, Vopat's father would be dealing television antennas. Turbulent economic and technological changes force changes in the nature of work, rearrangements in systems of communication and social relations, and fluctuation in the value of human skills. With the unique kinds of economic and technological changes of the twentieth century, those fluctuations came especially to affect the value of literacy. Demands on reading and writing rose sharply. (187)

America has embarked on an ambitious literacy project, with the goal of sending virtually every American adult to college. We are in the process of testing whether this is even possible. The "problems" we are experiencing with developmental education are a perhaps predictable product of this grand, ambitious, and historically unprecedented national literacy experiment. Four-year institutions certainly contribute to this endeavor, but the majority of this important work is being conducted right now on campuses at American community colleges. In this light, there is no crisis at all—just a grand and ambitious goal to spread literacy and learning as widely as possible.

As is often the case with acts of bold political idealism, there are often hidden costs and unforeseen complications. This has certainly been the case with open admissions and developmental education. We are just beginning to understand the full complexity of preparing all of our citizens to be "ready for college." We have seen impatience expressed by state legislatures that has resulted in unprecedented public legislation designed to "fix" developmental education. In retrospect, we perhaps should have expected that such an ambitious, forward-looking investment in our citizens, our workforce, and our democracy would entail substantial, long-term costs. It may be, in fact, that consideration of such costs must always come later in a radical, progressive process like this when very old, culturally inscribed patterns are challenged and displaced.

The positive, personal, human benefits that the modern community college has provided to our citizens and to our nation—measured in terms of opportunity, hope, and quality of life—are simply incalculable. Millions of students have attended our colleges, and millions more have graduated. There is no viable way to accurately measure what this opportunity has meant to people in a way that would fit a formula related to "value added" or "return on investment." How does one put a price on the kinds of futures, careers, and "selves" that our students have found for themselves at open admissions community colleges? As Mike Rose has observed, "One of the defining characteristics of the United States is its promise of a second chance; this promise is central to our vision of ourselves and to our economic and civic dynamism. When we are at our best as a society, our citizens are not trapped by their histories" (*Back* xiii). Open admissions two-year colleges are dedicated to the proposition that it is unacceptable for any American to be trapped by her history, by class or race, or by a higher educational system designed to perpetuate privilege and wealth. Given the research we have reviewed in this book, one conclusion about community colleges is perfectly clear: When we strengthen the community college, we strengthen democracy in America.

"Trapped by Categories"

In "Understandings of Community Colleges In Need of Resuscitation," John S. Levin suggests that our ongoing assessment of the community college has reached a kind of impasse: "The current state of both the literature on the community college and contemporary understandings of the institution suggests a hiatus—research and scholarly literature of the past four decades have run their course" (233). I would humbly and respectfully agree. In some ways, following Ellen Langer's work on mindfulness, we have become "trapped by categories" (12–14) and victims of "acting from a single perspective" (18–19). In some essential ways, we have become trapped by the traditional residential, competitive admissions, four-year model of success. Our reliance on a statistical model developed by these kinds of residential, competitive admissions institutions—measuring success by graduation and program completion rates—perpetuates a profound misunderstanding of the nature of the community college and its place in the American system of higher education. It also requires that we make community college students into something that many of them are not—fully knowledgeable about the many challenges that await them on our campuses as they seek to balance work responsibilities, family obligations, and coursework. Langer suggests that acting from a single perspective often produces what she call "premature cognitive commitment"—that is, accepting "an impression or piece of information at face value, with no reason to think critically about it" (24). Drawing on the large body of work devoted to attribution theory and following Jones and Nisbett's work on perception, we have attempted to examine in this book what we might have to gain from adopting an "actor's perspective" of the community college, rather than an "observer's perspective." In so doing, we have sought to move beyond a purely statistical model and sought to theorize a more qualitative perspective of this great institution. We have paid special attention to examining what we might learn from listening to students themselves as they discuss their goals and family histories and ideas about education. In doing this, we are seeking to enact Amartya Sen's ideas about the need for "an accomplishment-based understanding of justice" (*Idea* 18). This understanding of justice, which Sen positions in some important ways in opposition to John Rawls, is "linked with the argument that justice cannot be indifferent to the lives that people can actually live" (*Idea* 18). This book may be said to be dedicated to precisely this idea. Community college students live very complex lives, and this book seeks to acknowledge and celebrate that complexity.

Levin calls in his essay "for the next generation of scholars to inform practitioners and policy-makers about the actual behaviors and conditions of community colleges" (250). This book, and the Community College Success Stories Project which I am helping to initiate, seeks to answer this call. If, as Levin suggests, "what is missing generally" from the conceptual understanding of the community college is "an in-depth understanding of the institution, through its members and students" (246), this book seeks to help address this urgent need.

Forward

Given the research we have surveyed together in this book, it seems clear that it is time to set a new national agenda for the community college in America. There is significant evidence to suggest that, at the moment, the community college may be in danger of becoming the "neo-liberal college" (Levin 2007; Levin 2013, 233). A new national agenda is required to strengthen this important American institution, which has done so much to promote equity, opportunity, and social justice in our nation.

Here is what the research and scholarship we have reviewed together suggest in terms of a new action plan for the community college and higher education in America today:

1. Establish A New Mont Pelerin Society. The evidence we have reviewed in this book appears to require a radical change of direction in terms of how we think about democracy, American higher education, and the public good. The MPS has done some important work over the years for democracy, but its ideas appear to have run their course. Certainly, neoliberal thinking warned us against the considerable dangers of central control over a national economy, and these warnings helped us make thoughtful choices about how best to move forward after World War II. As we have noted, however, when neoliberal ideas are applied to areas of public policy not related to the central control of a national economy, the results have been much less benign. Inequality is at historic levels in America. Trust in the power of public policy to improve lives has dangerously eroded. And privatization and deregulation have turned out to amass power in the hands of the already rich and powerful. It is time to draw inspiration and guidance from a new generation of economists and higher education scholars. We must theorize a new, more progressive MPS built on the work of Piketty, Bourdieu, Acemoglu and Robinson, Sen, Stiglitz and Greenwald, McMahon, Darling-Hammond, Tucker, Martha Nussbaum, the Truman Commission, Martin Luther King, and educators like Mina Shaughnessy, Nell Ann Pickett, and Marilyn Sternglass, who devoted their professional lives to open admissions institutions and helping to build a better understanding of the students who attend them. This is an approach to development and public policy that would actively seek to make thoughtful, research-based decisions about the use of tax revenue to promote the public good. It is an approach that would define development as freedom, inequality as anti-democratic and dangerous to our safety and sovereignty, and higher learning as the key driver of economic prosperity, national security, and social justice. Understanding that in the long run, nothing will improve the security and vitality of our democracy more than spreading access to higher education as broadly as possible, community colleges must play a key role in this new approach to building a strong and vibrant democracy.

2. Restate Old Truths in New Ways for a New Generation of Americans. As F.A. Hayek suggests in the opening lines of *The Constitution of Liberty*, sometimes even great ideas need to be revivified and rediscovered for succeeding generations. We must engage this important work:

> If old truths are to retain their hold on men's minds, they must be restated in the language and concepts of successive generations. What at one time are their most effective expressions gradually become so worn with use that they cease to carry a definite meaning. The underlying ideas may be as valid as ever, but the words, even when they refer to problems that are still with us, no longer convey the same conviction; the arguments do not move in a context familiar to us; and they rarely give us direct answers to the questions we are asking. (47)

There is much that we can do that will help reconnect Americans to the inspiring ideas that created the community college. If Hayek is right, then perhaps some of our traditional language about "the open door" and "democracy's college"—which were once rhetorically very effective—has now through familiarity and constant use lost the ability to inspire and convince. Perhaps some of these "old truths" have become so worn that they cease to carry a definite meaning or convey the same conviction. Our case has to be remade in new language for a new generation with direct answers to the new challenges Americans are confronting today.

3. Rediscover the "Courage to be Utopian." Supporters of the community college also need to revitalize and rediscover what Hayek called the "courage to be Utopian" ("Intellectuals" 237). Certainly the community college movement is a stirring example of this noble human impulse. Perhaps we do ourselves and our students a disservice by concerning ourselves exclusively with what seems "practicable in the existing state of opinion" ("Intellectuals" 237). Perhaps we need to "make the philosophic foundations of a free society once more a living intellectual issue, and its implementation a task which challenges the ingenuity and imagination of our liveliest minds" ("Intellectuals" 237). To do this, we will need to regain for ourselves and for our fellow countrymen "that belief in the power of ideas which was the mark of liberalism at its greatest" ("Intellectuals" 237).

The community college was built on "the courage to be Utopian." We must recapture our faith in this luminous human capacity.

4. Understand That We Will Often Find Ourselves Working Against Entrenched Ideas That Leave Fundamental Questions and Assumptions Unexamined. Entrenched ideas often privilege long-held assumptions and protect them from critical examination. As theories become rigid, the ideas they contain become self-evident truths that are perpetuated across generations. We have seen this at work as it relates to community colleges in powerfully regressive ways. We have certainly seen evidence of Stiglitz and Greenwald's claims about societal rigidities, collective beliefs, mindsets, the power of prior beliefs to shape the understanding of new information, confirmatory bias, the fact that cognitive frames which shape perceptions are largely socially determined, that such perceptions affect *collective* actions, and that socially dysfunctional beliefs and policies can persist and reproduce. As times change and data sets are updated, we must seek to periodically and systematically reassess cherished beliefs and long-held views and submit them to careful scrutiny. We must persuasively demonstrate how we might conduct this important work—and how such work promotes a strong democracy. We live at an important historical moment for our democracy. It is vitally important to rethink how we apply theory—and which theories we apply—to the study of higher education. We must actively engage in this kind of regenerative and reconstructive scholarly activity, especially as it relates to neoliberal economic theory and current thinking about higher education and the public good.

5. Establish a New Model for Intellectual Public Discourse. Milton Friedman popularized a dangerous style of radically simplified rhetorical discourse in the public domain, translating complex disciplinary ideas for the public using rhetorical strategies based on bold sweeping statements, self-assurance, and stirring anecdotal examples. This has become the model for one sort of approach to public policy debate in recent years. This is a dangerous practice because it erodes confidence in the important role of evidence and logical reasoning, and it subverts the necessity for providing the "burden of proof" that is the basis for all legitimate argumentation. Such an approach to public policy degrades and problematizes the role of evidence and reasoned discourse in governance and policy debate. We must actively resist this kind of discourse wherever we find it, challenging its validity and documenting the many ways it does not promote a healthy democratic society. We must develop a new model of public discourse that translates for a general audience the many complexities and subtleties of research and scholarship without simplifying or distorting them.

6. Embrace the Inescapably Political Nature of Our Work. Here, we will be following both Hayek and Keynes in embracing the power of ideas to frame public perception and therefore to shape public policy. In "The Intellectuals and Socialism," Hayek counseled his neoliberal colleagues to engage in coordinated, focused, long-term efforts to shape public opinion about the free market and about neoliberal approaches to public policy. Hayek outlined a strategy that targeted intellectuals (journalists, teachers, ministers, lecturers, publicists, radio commentators, writers of fiction, cartoonists, and artists) as a way to effectively transmit ideas to a wider audience. Hayek was writing at a time when democracy and freedom itself appeared to be imperiled. The same might also be said for us now, although in very different ways. These intellectuals, Hayek suggested, "are the organs which modern society has developed for spreading knowledge and ideas, and it is their convictions and opinions which operate as the sieve through which all new conceptions must pass before they can reach the masses" (225). Joseph Stiglitz recently made much the same point, in effect updating Hayek's recommendations for engaging in this kind of public advocacy work.

A great deal depends, as Stiglitz suggests, on ideas "emanating from academia and from public intellectuals" (*Price* 161). Individuals who care about social justice, civil rights, and economic equality must engage this political work in ways that are systematic, methodical, and long-term. A first step, following the neoliberal model, would be to establish a nationwide system of well-funded think tanks and advocacy groups. This activism is likely to also require front-line, in-your-face political work as we seek to create positive change in our communities and on our campuses. We must also establish our own version of the American Legislative Exchange Council, which drafts model neoliberal legislation for local, state, and national governing bodies (Center for Media; Parti). We must also be willing to think longitudinally about our political work—in terms of decades and generations—just as the MPS did.

7. Resist the Oligarchy. Neoliberalism has been complicit in the dramatic recent redistribution of wealth in America to the very top earners. Deregulation, privatization, and attacks on government programs and the public good have served to enrich the already wealthy and powerful. The data on this is overwhelming and alarming. Stiglitz summarizes the current state of affairs this way: "it has increasingly been noted that America is becoming a plutocracy—not the land of opportunity that it perhaps once was, and that it likes to think of itself as still being" ("Reforming" 23; Reich). As Piketty's important work demonstrates, there couldn't be more at stake:

> The overall conclusion of this study is that a market economy based on private property, if left to itself, contains powerful forces of convergence, associated in particular with the diffusion of knowledge and skills; but it also contains powerful forces of divergence, which are potentially threatening to democratic societies and to the value of social justice on which they are based.
>
> The principal destabilizing force has to do with the fact that the private rate of return on capital, r, can be significantly higher for long periods of time than the rate of growth of income and output, g.
>
> The inequality $r > g$ implies that wealth accumulated in the past grows more rapidly than output and wages. This inequality expresses a fundamental logical contradiction. The entrepreneur inevitably tends to become a rentier, more and more dominant over those who own nothing but their labor. Once constituted, capital reproduces itself faster than output increases. The past devours the future.
>
> The consequences for the long-term dynamics of the wealth distribution are potentially terrifying, especially when one adds that the return on capital varies directly with the size of the initial stake and that the divergence in the wealth distribution is occurring on a global scale. (571)

Many of the scholars we have discussed in this book highlight the crucial importance of higher education and disseminating knowledge and skills as essential for promoting economic growth and equality. Most of these thinkers, following Piketty, see higher education playing a key role in helping "to achieve a just social order" (31).

8. Help Develop Alternate Pathways To Careers That Pay a Living Wage and Provide Worthwhile, Rewarding Lives For Those Who Do Not Wish To Go To College.

Until recently, individuals who did not wish to attend college could often find careers that paid a living wage and offered job security. With globalization and outsourcing, this has become increasingly difficult. Now that manufacturing work and blue-collar jobs have largely "disappeared" in America, to use William Julius Wilson's phrase, we find ourselves struggling with a new form of economic hardship. Even with a college education, employment in the US has become increasingly polarized and precarious (Kalleberg; Shipler; Greenhouse). Job prospects for Americans without at least some college education can only be described as bleak.

We must think carefully about this question: **Is college for everyone?** For many students, college will always be a viable path toward a better future and a living wage. But for some students, who have always disliked school, it won't be. We see this reflected in retention rates for students in developmental courses at community colleges, as students discover that they simply dislike or are uninterested in further schooling. The questions that naturally follow this one are crucial for our nation: How will students who don't want to go to college support themselves and raise their families? How will they live? What will they do? Right now, the answer appears to be: "We have no idea." There is a critical need to find viable, appealing answers to these questions. Developing a robust, practical, and educationally integrated occupational, vocational track for students not interested in a traditional college education is one potential solution. Such an option would also ideally provide, as Mike Rose suggests, "a strong education in the literacy and mathematics, the history and economics, the science and ethics that can emerge from the world of work" (*Back* 61; 57–65; Ton).

9. Make the Living Wage and Job Creation National Priorities. It is unacceptable that many Americans work full time and still qualify for public assistance (Greenhouse; Shipler; Ton). Following Arne L. Kalleberg, we must implement "a new social contract" that turns back the polarized and precarious employment systems driven by neoliberal theory that have dominated business practices in the US in recent decades (195–215; see also Meek *Private*; Meek "Somerdale"). To do this, we can follow Zeynep Ton's "good jobs strategy" which will help build a strong economy and a strong democracy.

10. Make Tuition at Community Colleges Affordable Again. Skyrocketing tuition rates have become burdensome at every level of higher education. They have also become problematic for community college students. Unfortunately, we may be reaching the economic threshold where the idea of open access has become fatally compromised by high tuition costs, increases in the cost of living, and by student aid being operationally defined as loans and debt (Goldrick-Rab, Richardson, and Hernandez; Sullivan, "What" Part I; Sullivan, "What" Part II). As Perna and Titus note, higher education enrollment patterns continue to be stratified by socioeconomic status:

> Even after controlling for student-level predictors of college and choice and state contextual variables, low-SES [socioeconomic status] high school graduates are less likely than other high school graduates to enroll in any type of college or university in the fall after graduating from high school. (518)

If only middle-class families can afford to send their children to community colleges, as appears to be increasingly the case, is the community college fulfilling its historic mandate? As Goldrick-Rab, Richardson, and Hernandez note in their report, *Hungry and Homeless in College: Results from a National Study of Basic Needs Insecurity in Higher Education* (2017),

> Community colleges are the most accessible, affordable points of entry to higher education in the United States and they exist in nearly every corner of the nation. They serve nearly one in two undergraduates and enroll by far the most economically and racially diverse students. While their tuition rates and administrative fees are significantly lower on average than those of other sectors, prices relative to the family incomes of their students have grown quite substantially, presenting barriers to degree completion. After all grant aid is accounted for, a dependent student from a family in the lowest annual income quartile, earning $21,000 per year, would have to pay $8,300, or 40 percent of her family's total income, for a year of community college. (4)

The Tennessee Promise initiative, a new program that provides free college tuition for students, is designed to address precisely this problem. Tennessee Promise began in the fall of 2015, offering free tuition for residents that can be used to enroll at the state's community and technical colleges and also at in-state independent and four-year public universities that offer an associate's degree (Drive "About"; Smith "Responding"). Tennessee Promise is a "last-dollar scholarship," meaning it will cover college costs not met from Pell, HOPE, or TSAA (Drive "Tennessee"). This program became one of the models for President Obama's America's College Promise, which proposes to offer the first two years of college free to students across America (White House "Fact Sheet: White House Unveils"; Fain "Free"). A key design feature of Tennessee Promise is its funding model, which seeks to keep the program insulated from fluctuating state budget conditions. As Paul Fain reports in an interview with Tennessee governor, Bill Haslam, program designers "estimated an initial annual price tag to the state of $34 million. To cover that cost, and do so in a way that would be protected from future budget cuts, Haslam called for the creation of a self-sustaining $300 million endowment ("Aggressive")."

This initiative is part of Tennessee's Drive to 55 program, which has set the ambitious goal of "increasing the number of Tennesseans who hold a college degree or certificate to 55 percent by 2025 (about one-third do now)" (Fain "Aggressive"). The program also requires students to complete a number of hours of community service and establish close working relationships with academic mentors. Although this program is designed for high school students only and does not offer the same free tuition to nontraditional students, this is nonetheless an excellent example of forward-looking public policy that seeks to promote the public good.

11. Theorize, Articulate, and Champion a Larger Purpose for the Community College Than Simply "Job Preparation." The community college is increasingly being cast by legislators primarily as a job-training site. Following Mike Rose, we must envision a much larger role for the community college in the lives of students than simply an institution that provides occupational training:

> While acknowledging the importance of the economic motive for schooling, our philosophy of education—our guiding rationale for creating schools—has to include the intellectual, social, civic, moral, and aesthetic motives as well. If these further motives are not articulated, they fade from public policy, from institutional mission, from curriculum development. Without this richer philosophy, those seeking a second chance will likely receive a bare-bones, strictly functional education, one that does not honor the many reasons they return to school and, for that matter, one not suitable for a democratic society. (*Back* 185–6).

A purely vocational focus diminishes the nature of the community college mission and impoverishes the idea of higher education for those who attend these institutions.

12. Address the Problem of "Disposable Teachers"
Systematic state and federal disinvestment in higher education has created a marginalized, low-wage labor force teaching the majority of college classes nationwide. This reliance on low-wage adjunct faculty has built up incrementally and invisibly over the years, blossoming into a national epidemic. This development is driven by neoliberal economic models that devalue human labor in the pursuit of efficiency, profit, and return on investment. As Marc Bousquet has noted, this has resulted in "the perma-temping of the labor force" at colleges, creating what he calls "the problem of 'tenured bosses and disposable teachers'" (158; Donoghue; Kroll). At my own institution, like most community colleges nationwide, we rely heavily on adjunct faculty. My own English department, for example, has numbers that are comparable to those nationwide at community colleges:

Fall 2015 semester

—135 sections of ENG classes—54 sections taught by FT;
  81 sections taught by PT. **40% of sections taught by FT;
  60% of sections taught by PT**

—73 faculty members—18 FT; 55 PT. **25% of faculty members FT; 75% of faculty members PT**

Nationally, the American Association of University Professors (AAUP) reports that 70 percent of all college faculty are contingent faculty—part-time and full-time non-tenure-track appointments (AAUP "Trends"). For our purposes here, it is important to note, as Adrianna Kezar and Daniel Maxey report, that

> Community colleges were the first institutions to increase their reliance on NTTFs [non-tenure track faculty], as a response to surges in enrollments in the 1960s and 1970s, and they still employ the largest percentage of NTTFs among non-profit institutions. According to the most recent provisional data available from the National Center for Education Statistics' (NCES 2012) Integrated Postsecondary Education Data Survey (IPEDS) from Fall 2011, part-time faculty now constitute approximately 69.2 percent of instructors at these institutions. And, they are responsible for teaching between half and two-thirds of all course sections (CCSSE 2009). (5)

The Center for Community College Student Engagement reports that "part-time faculty teach approximately 58% of US community college classes and thus manage learning experiences for more than half (53%) of students enrolled in community colleges (JBL Associates, 2008)" ("Contingent" 2). Unfortunately, as a recent report from the Center for Community College Student Engagement notes,

> For many part-time faculty, contingent employment goes hand-in-hand with being marginalized within the faculty. It is not uncommon for part-time faculty to learn which, if any, classes they are teaching just weeks or days before a semester begins. Their access to orientation, professional development, administrative and technology support, office space, and accommodations for meeting with students typically is limited, unclear, or inconsistent.
>
> Moreover, part-time faculty have infrequent opportunities to interact with peers about teaching and learning. Perhaps most concerning, they rarely are included in important campus discussions about the kinds of change needed to improve student learning, academic progress, and college completion.
>
> Thus, institutions' interactions with part-time faculty result in a profound incongruity: Colleges depend on part-time faculty to educate more than half of their students, yet they do not fully embrace these faculty members. Because of this disconnect, contingency can have consequences that negatively affect student engagement and learning. ("Contingent" 3)

The University of California at Berkeley's Center for Labor Research and Education has reported startling figures about the nature of this problem:

> 25 percent of "part-time college faculty" and their families now receive some sort public assistance, such as Medicaid, the Children's Health Insurance Program, food stamps, cash welfare, or the Earned Income Tax Credit. For what it's worth, that's not quite so bad as the situation faced by fast-food employees and home health care aids, roughly half of whom get government help. But, in case there were any doubt, an awful lot of Ph.D.s and master's degree holders are basically working poor. (Weissmann; Jacobs, Perry, and MacGillvary)

Part-time college faculty are grouped with fast-food workers, child care workers, and home care workers as among the cohorts of American workers most likely to rely on some form of public assistance (Jacobs, Perry, and MacGillvary 2). Many community college faculty, like adjuncts across the higher education sector, are "working in increasingly unprofessional circumstances"—teaching "too many students in too many classes too quickly, without security, status, or an office, working from standardized syllabi; using outsourced tutorial, remedial, and even grading services; providing no time for research or professional development" (Bousquet 4).

Obviously, there are strategic, political reasons for transitioning to an impoverished, transient, and powerless professoriate (Bousquet; Donoghue; Nelson and Watt). Furthermore, as Marc Bousquet notes, "The system of cheap teaching doesn't sort for the best teachers; it sorts for persons who are in a financial position to accept compensation below the living wage" (3). This is part of a national trend in what Arne L. Kalleberg calls the "rise of polarized and precarious employment systems in the United States" driven by neoliberal economic theory (1–18). Jacobs, Perry, and MacGillvary estimate that poverty-level wages cost US taxpayers 152.8 billion each year in public assistance support.

Unfortunately, this approach to devaluing teaching as a profession and devaluing college teachers as vital resources in the classroom is at odds with best practices internationally among the world's leading educational systems. Marc S. Tucker's book, *Surpassing Shanghai*, takes a close look at successful educational strategies from around the world (Finland, Japan, Canada, Shanghai, and Singapore) using data from a variety of sources including The Program for International Student Assessment (PISA). As we know, America's leading position in academic achievement internationally has eroded considerably in recent years. We now are only average in reading and science and below average in math (6). Among the world's leaders in education, teachers—and teacher compensation—play a foundational role in the success of these educational systems. In fact, overall, the Organisation for Economic Co-operation and Development (OECD), which sponsors PISA, concludes that "the only resource that correlates with student performance is teachers' salaries" (11).

When the OECD "looked at teachers' compensation in terms of how teachers are paid compared to other professions requiring the same level of education, only three OECD countries pay their teachers less than we do in the United States" (11). All the successful educational systems profiled in Tucker's book have built a tradition of respect and admiration for the profession of teaching—and all compensate their teachers accordingly. Teaching consequently attracts some of the best and brightest individuals in these countries to the profession of teaching. In Finland, for example, one of the world's leaders in education (Sahlberg), "teaching is now the most popular profession among Finnish young people, attracting the top quartile of high school graduates into its highly competitive teacher training programs" (Schwartz and Mehta 52). Robert B. Schwartz and Jal D. Mehta's chapter in Tucker's book, "Finland: Superb Teachers—How to Get Them, How To Use Them," provides a fascinating glimpse into why this might be the case. Ongoing professional development, an active community of practice, support and mentoring, and what Linda Darling-Hammond has described as professional problem-solving groups in schools that collaboratively "engage in a cycle of planning, action, and reflection/evaluation" that is based on "research and inquiry" are part of the daily life of teachers in Finland (qtd. in Schwartz and Mehta 65). In fact, as Darling-Hammond notes, "the entire system is intended to improve through continual reflection, evaluation, and problem-solving" (qtd. in Schwartz and Mehta 65). This investment in teaching and teachers is certainly very far removed from the model we see employed nationwide at America's community colleges. Unlike the Finnish model which is profoundly collaborative and team-focused, contingent faculty at community colleges also have only infrequent opportunities to interact with peers about teaching and learning (Toth and Sullivan). They also play a very limited role in important campus discussions about the kinds of change needed to improve student learning, academic progress, and college completion.

Teaching at America's community colleges has become a casualty of "a deified market" model, to borrow a phrase from Pope Francis (Carroll), which typically regards labor costs as an impediment to productivity. OECD data suggest precisely the opposite is true when it comes to education and teaching. We may take a measure of guidance and inspiration from the full quotation from which this phrase from Pope Francis is drawn: "In this system, which tends to devour everything which stands in the way of increased profits, whatever is fragile, like the environment, is defenseless before the interests of a deified market, which becomes the only rule" (Carroll). Many students who attend community colleges might be said to be "fragile" in exactly the way Pope Francis suggests here. They are at risk of being devoured and consumed by a system that does not understand or value them.

In addition to strengthening institutions with more full-time, tenure-track professors, we must also develop practices for more effectively engaging and integrating our adjunct faculty into our academic communities. As we move forward with this important work, we can follow Adrianna Kezar, a national leader on the subject of adjunct faculty, and Daniel Maxey and their report, "Dispelling the Myths: Locating the Resources Needed to Support Non-Tenure-Track Faculty." This report provides pragmatic advice for how institutions can begin integrating adjunct faculty more effectively into the life of the college. As Kezar and Maxey note, it is possible to produce

> a set of strategies for developing services and resources to support the whole faculty, not just full-time or tenured and tenure-track faculty members. But, it is important for leaders on campuses to begin to dispel the myth that constrained resources are the primary reason they do not provide what would often be considered to be even basic forms of support or opportunities for the involvement of non-tenure-track faculty. By exercising leadership and being attentive to aligning decisions about how to support faculty with their institutions' values and goals, administrators, faculty, and staff can identify opportunities to make improvements—often with little additional cost—that will yield benefits for faculty, as well as the students they teach. (1)

Kezar and Maxey recommend the following strategies:

- Enhance existing data collection efforts about non-tenure-track faculty (NTTF): "Engaging NTTFs in this way can also help faculty members to feel that their concerns and ideas are being heard by leaders" (2).
- Ensure or clarify protections for academic freedom.
- Provide access to instructional materials, resources, and support services.
- Provide access to on- and off-campus professional development opportunities.

- Extend the opportunity to participate in departmental meetings, curriculum design, and campus life.
- Extend the opportunity to participate in college governance.
- Facilitate opportunities for faculty mentoring.
- Ensure access to orientation for new hires.
- Provide access to administrative staff for support.
- Reconsider or change hiring practices: "At most institutions, NTTFs are hired—and rehired—through fairly casual or informal processes, as compared to tenure-track faculty. Institutions and departments should consider how they might improve the search and recruitment process for vacant NTTF positions or the timeline for hiring NTTFs, particularly if it is found that NTTFs are hired within only a few days or weeks of the beginning of the term, which allows them very little time to prepare" (9).
- Extend employment contracts to multiyear terms.
- Acknowledge and compensate NTTFs for time spent meeting with students in office hours and providing benefits.

13. Embrace the Crucial Need to Diversify Faculty and Staff

As John S. Levin has noted, one significant assumption frequently made about community colleges is that "faculty can be conceived of as a homogeneous group, instead of as two or more prominent groups—full-time and part-time; majority (or White) and minority" (233). Levin notes that this assumption "has been touched upon but only briefly by scholarship (Grubb et al. 1999; Levin et al. 2011), with the exception of minority faculty" (233). Given what we know about the diversity of the student body at community colleges and the power of a diverse faculty and staff to affect student learning among underrepresented groups, diversity becomes a vitally important concern for anyone interested in strengthening student retention and success at community colleges. The work of Claude M. Steele along with that of Douglas S. Massey, Camille Z. Charles, Garvey F. Lundy, and Mary J. Fischer has shown us the many complex dynamics at work for minorities attending college. As Steele notes, "poor college performance has many causes, and the Massey team concluded that black and Latino students face more such 'causes' than their white and Asian counterparts" (158). Disadvantages tied to "race, class, and ethnicity—contingencies of identify, if you will—outside of college, extract a toll on performance in college" (158). As Steele notes, the Massey team "did find something that alleviated this effect—black professors" (159).

Taiyon J. Coleman, Renee DeLong, Kathleen Sheerin DeVore, Shannon Gibney, and Michael C. Kuhne's essay, "The Risky Business of Engaging Racial Equity in Writing Instruction: A Tragedy in Five Acts," documents the explosive, dangerous work left remaining for us as we seek to address the issue of race and diversity within departments and institutions. As we do this work, we will be disrupting dominant racial narratives that inform stubbornly persistent beliefs about race in our country (Coleman, DeLong, DeVore, Gibney, and Kuhne 347; Delgado and Stefancic).

14. Use a More Reciprocal, Progressive Model to Theorize "Accountability." Here, we can follow Linda Darling-Hammond's advice about designing a "reciprocal, intelligent accountability" model that she outlines in her Foreword to *Surpassing Shanghai: An Agenda for American Education Built on the World's Leading Systems* (Tucker xi; see also Darling-Hammond *Flat*). Among the leading educational systems from around the world, none focus on "narrow test results, market-based reforms, a deskilled teaching force presumably motivated by threats of firing, or a competitive approach that sets up some schools, teachers, and, consequently, students as winners, while setting up others as losers" (ix). Instead, high-performing educational systems around the world do the following:

- Fund schools equitably, with additional resources for those serving needy students.
- Pay teachers competitively and comparably.
- Invest in high-quality preparation, mentoring, and professional development for teachers and leaders, completely at government expense.
- Provide time in the school schedule for collaborative planning and ongoing professional learning to continually improve instruction (typically 15–25 hours a week).
- Organize a curriculum around problem-solving and critical thinking skills.
- Test students rarely but carefully—with measures that require analysis, communication, and defense of ideas (Foreword ix–x).

Darling-Hammond also recommends creating an education governance structure that is "less politically vulnerable and more strongly steered by professional knowledge and research" (xi).

15. Continue to Innovate. Most of the state-mandated legislative initiatives for developmental education nationwide have derived from work pioneered at community colleges. Beth Bye, the Connecticut legislator perhaps most responsible for PA 12–40, acknowledged this fact when I spoke with her about the research that drove her committee's decision-making. She mentioned Katie Hern's work at Chabot College and Peter Adams's work at the Community College of Baltimore County. Most of what is good about PA 12–40 is built around innovations drawn from disciplinary knowledge produced recently in the field of English. Acceleration, embedded support, narrowing the developmental "pipeline," and using multiple measures for assessment are all key components of this legislation. For inspiration, we can follow a strategy that Argyris and Schon call "double-loop learning"—a deep form of self-examination that involves critique of even sacred assumptions and governing principles. This is a learning strategy, as Sweeney and Godfield note, that "requires self-awareness to recognize deeply held assumptions, brutal honesty to assess what is and isn't working, and accountability to action on what is learned" (xl).

16. Devote Greater Professional Attention to Work Being Done at Community Colleges. To borrow a phrase from Holly Hassel and Joanne Baird Giordano's essay, "Occupy Writing Studies," community college teachers "need a more effective and extensive body of scholarship that offers research-based best practices that are relevant to the daily work they do" (119). This will involve challenging misconceptions about students and instructors at community college and open admissions campuses and redefining the nature of knowledge-making on these campuses (117; Lewiecki-Wilson and Sommers).

17. Engage the Long-Overdue, Undone Work Related to Articulation and Alignment with Area High Schools. Community college personnel need to be more systematically and purposefully engaged with their local high schools and high school colleagues, forging working partnerships with these institutions and colleagues. This work will benefit students in all sorts of ways. Every community college should have a high school partnership, outreach, and articulation program (Barnett and Hughes; Hansen).

18. Engage Real Social Complexity. We can follow Charles Hale's suggestion in *Engaging Contradictions: Theory, Politics, and Methods of Activist Scholarship* that "research and political engagement can be mutually enriching" (2). In engaging such work, however, we must resist the impulse to accept "reductive, politically instrumental truths" at the expense of engaging real "social complexity" (Hale 2). In doing so, we can follow Edward Said's important caveat about "doubt" and intellectual work:

> However much intellectuals pretend that their representations are of higher things or ultimate values, morality begins with their activity in this secular world of ours—where it takes place, whose interests it serves, how it jibes with a consistent and universalist ethic, how it discriminates between power and justice, what it reveals of one's choices and priorities. Those gods that always fail demand from the intellectual in the end a kind of absolute certainty and a total, seamless view of reality that recognizes only disciples or enemies.
> What strikes me as much more interesting is how to keep a space in the mind open for doubt and for the play of an alert, skeptical irony (preferably also self-irony). (120)

We would be engaging this work in the service of a great American institution and students like Scott, Julie, Eddie, Sarah, Ashley, Chhan, Bethany, Michelle, Mikey, Sabina, Jenn, Tanya, Anton, Abby, Ashley, and Yanira, who we met in Part I of this book.

19. Become Activists. There are a number of ways that we might theorize such activism in relation to community colleges. Perhaps the most useful for our purposes here may be Dana Cloud's formulation in "The Only Conceivable Thing To Do: Reflections on Academics and Activism" from *Activism and Rhetoric: Theories and Contexts for Political Engagement*:

> Criticism of prevailing ideologies and consciousness is part of intellectual work, *but critique must happen in conjunction with practical political activity if it is to be relevant at all to the democratic project.* (15; Sudbury and Okazawa-Rey 3; Nelson and Watt 2)

Edward Said makes a similar point in *Representations of the Intellectual*. His comments here are particularly relevant for community college professionals at this moment in our ongoing national dialog about college readiness, open admissions institutions, and developmental education:

> The major choice faced by the intellectual is whether to be allied with the stability of the victors and rulers or—the more difficult path—to consider that stability as a state of emergency threatening the less fortunate with the danger of compete extinction, and take into account the experience of subordination itself, as well as the memory of forgotten voices and persons. (35)

There were a number of times during our many public, state-wide discussions of developmental education reform and Public Act 12–40 in Connecticut where it felt to me like we had, indeed, arrived at "a state of emergency threatening the less fortunate with the danger of compete extinction." One very unsavory element in the PA 12–40 movement, as we have discussed, seemed to be intended to close the open door at community colleges in Connecticut, remanding students deemed unfit and "undeserving" for college to regional remediation centers. Following Said, community colleges and developmental education itself may be said to "take into account the experience of subordination," seeking ways through literacy education to resist such diminishment and marginalization in our communities. Community colleges and developmental education may also be said to draw ideological power from the memory of forgotten voices and persons, citizens in our communities who have historically had no voices or futures and who were trapped by their histories and their economic conditions. As we have seen, "the victors and rulers" are actively consolidating economic and political power in America in ways that are alarming and perhaps, ultimately, undemocratic. Powerful regressive forces are at work in America today, threatening much of what was built during the early, idealistic years of open admissions institutions. We have many challenges ahead and much important work left to do.

Our goal, of course, is ultimately to "risk change" in order to awaken students to "their own self-determination, power, and collective agency" (Watson 10). We can join in common cause with our colleagues at four-year institutions, who are actively engaged in this work as well and have contributed in untold ways to forwarding progressive political action as well as policies and legislation that benefit students. This orientation toward our work at the community college can help us build bridges with colleagues across disciplines and across institutional boundaries.

20. Access Isn't Enough. As we have seen in the Center for Community College Student Engagement report *Making Ends Meet*, and as Sara Goldrick-Rab, Jed Richardson, and Anthony Hernandez document in *Hungry and Homeless in College: Results from a National Study of Basic Needs Insecurity in Higher Education*, many community college students are attempting to pursue academic careers while also contending with deep levels of basic needs insecurity. We now know more clearly than ever that "food and housing insecurity among the nation's community college students threatens their health and wellbeing, along with their academic achievements" (Goldrick-Rab, Richardson, and Hernandez 1). These additional stress factors related to scarcity obviously imperil any kind of long-term endeavor like earning a college credential. As Goldrick-Rab, Richardson, and Hernandez note, "addressing these basic needs is critical to ensuring that more students not only start college, but also have the opportunity to complete degrees" (1). Goldrick-Rab, Richardson, and Hernandez suggest, furthermore, that "investments in food and housing assistance programs to help community college students complete degrees will yield dividends, helping individuals improve their employment prospects and reducing their need for future support. Such strategies must become priorities of leaders in higher education" (2).

21. Understand, Following George C. Marshall, that the Real Enemies of Democracy Are Hunger, Poverty, Desperation, and Chaos.

*****

The Truman Commission Report, which helped invent the modern community college, is one of the most historically significant documents ever produced in America. It is a foundational American document because it speaks with unprecedented candor and eloquence about the nature of democracy and the ideals of equity and social justice. The Truman Commission Report articulates an ambitious vision for American democracy in ways that few other documents in our long history have ever done. The community college is at the heart of this noble new American idea. As we move forward with the important work of building a strong nation—and a strong democracy—let us keep this Commission's inspiring words and example clearly in mind. This is a vision of America that calls on all that is best in our history and all that is best in our character. Let us be equal to this challenge.

Let us go forward, then, as teacher-scholar-activists, inspired by our history and by a renewed commitment to furthering these democratic ideals. Let us continue the vitally important work of making the practical idealism of opportunity, economic equality, and social justice a living reality for students at our nation's community colleges.

Bibliography

Abrams, M.H. 1971. *The Mirror and the Lamp: Romantic Theory and the Literary Tradition*. New York: Oxford University Press. Print.
Acemoglu, Daron, and James Robinson. 2012. *Why Nations Fail: The Origins of Power, Prosperity, and Poverty*. New York: Crown. Print.
Adams, Peter, Sarah Gearhart, Robert Miller, and Anne Roberts. 2009. The Accelerated Learning Program: Throwing Open the Gates. *Journal of Basic Writing* 28(2): 50–69. Print.
Adichie, Chimamanda Ngozi. 2009. The Danger of a Single Story. *TED Talk*. Ted Conferences, July. Web.
Adler-Kassler, Linda. 2008. *The Activist WPA: Changing Stories about Writing and Writers*. Logan: Utah State University Press. Print.
Adler-Kassner, Linda, and Susanmarie Harrington. 2010. Responsibility and Composition's Future in the Twenty-First Century: Reframing 'Accountability'. *College Composition and Communication* 62(1): 73–99. Print.
Aeschylus. 1969. *The Oresteian Trilogy*, Trans. Philip Vellacott. New York: Penguin. Print.
Air Pollution in China Is Killing 4,000 People Every Day, A New Study Finds. 2015. *The Guardian*, August 13. Web. 7 Dec 2015.
Alexander, Michelle. 2012. *The New Jim Crow: Mass Incarceration in the Age of Colorblindness*, Rev. ed. New York: The New Press. Print.
Alexievich, Svetlana. 2006. *Voices from Chernobyl: The Oral History of a Nuclear Disaster*, Trans. Keith Gessen. Rpt. ed. New York: Picador. Print.
———. n.d. *Voices from Big Utopia*. Web. 31 Dec 2015.
American Association of Community Colleges [AACC]. 2000a. *CC Growth over Past 100 Years*. Web. 8 May 2016.
———. 2000b. *Community Colleges Past to Present*. Web. 21 Mar 2016.

———. 2016. *Fast Facts*. February. Web. 21 Mar 2106.
American Association of University Professors [AAUP]. 2013. *Trends in Faculty Employment Status, 1975–2011*. March 21. Web. 11 Dec 2015.
American College Testing Program [ACT]. 2006. *Reading between the Lines What the ACT Reveals about College Readiness in Reading*. Iowa City: ACT. Web. 21 June 2010.
———. 2010. *The Condition of College and Career Readiness 2010*. Web. 27 Nov 2010.
———. 2013. *The Reality of College Readiness 2013*. Web. 31 Dec 2015.
Angelou, Maya. 1988. *I Know Why the Caged Bird Sings*. New York: Bantam. Print.
Appelbaum, Eileen, and Rosemary Batt. 2014. *Private Equity at Work: When Wall Street Manages Main Street*. New York: Russell Sage Foundation. Print.
Arendale, David. 2010. *Access at the Crossroads: Learning Assistance in Higher Education*, ASHE Higher Education Report 35.6. San Francisco: Jossey-Bass. Print.
Argyris, Christopher, and Donald Schön. 1978. *Organizational Learning: A Theory of Action Perspective*. Reading: AddisonWesley. Print.
Armstrong, Elizabeth A., and Laura T. Hamilton. 2013. *Paying for the Party: How College Maintains Inequality*. Boston: Harvard University Press. Print.
Artz, Lee. 2011. Speaking Truth to Power. In *Activism and Rhetoric: Theories and Contexts for Political Engagement*, ed. Seth Kahn and Jong Hwa Lee, 47–55. New York: Routledge. Print.
Atkinson, Anthony B. 2015. *Inequality: What Can Be Done?* Cambridge: Harvard University Press. Print.
Attewell, Paul, and David E. Lavin. 2007. *Passing the Torch: Does Higher Education for the Disadvantaged Pay Off Across the Generations?* New York: Russell Sage. Print.
Attewell, Paul A., David E. Lavin, Thurston Domina, and Tania Levey. 2006. New Evidence on College Remediation. *The Journal of Higher Education* 77(5): 886–924. Print.
Atwell, Nancie. 1998. *In the Middle*, 2nd ed. Portsmouth: Boynton/Cook. Print.
———. 2007. *The Reading Zone*. New York: Scholastic. Print.
Aviv, Rachel. 2014. Wrong Answer. *The New Yorker* 21: 54–65. Print.
Bahr, Peter Riley. 2008. Does Mathematics Remediation Work? A Comparative Analysis of Academic Attainment among Community College Students. *Research in Higher Education* 49(5): 420–450. Print.
Bailey, Ronald. 1994. The Other Side of Slavery: Black Labor, Cotton, and Textile Industrialization in Great Britain and the United States. *Special Issue of Agricultural History* 68(2): 35–50. Print.

Bailey, Thomas. 2009. Challenge and Opportunity: Rethinking the Role and Function of Developmental Education in Community College. *New Directions for Community Colleges* 145: 11–30. Print.
Bailey, Thomas, and Vanessa Smith Morest (eds.). 2006. *Defending the Community College Equity Agenda*. Baltimore: Johns Hopkins University Press. Print.
Bailey, Thomas, Dong Wook Jeong, and Sung-Woo Cho. 2010. Referral, Enrollment, and Completion in Developmental Education Sequences in Community Colleges. *Economics of Education Review* 29(2): 255–270. Print.
Bailey, Thomas, Katherine Hughes, and Shanna Smith Jaggars. 2012. Law Hamstrings College Remedial Programs. *Hartford Courant*, May 19. Web. 14 Aug 2015.
Bailey, Thomas, Shanna Smith Jaggars, and Judith Scott-Clayton. 2013. *Characterizing the Effectiveness of Developmental Education: A Response to Recent Criticism*. Teachers College, Columbia University, Community College Research Center, February. Web. 26 Nov 2015.
Bailey, Thomas R., Shanna Smith Jaggers, and Davis Jenkins. 2015. *Redesigning America's Community Colleges: A Clearer Path to Student Success*. Cambridge: Harvard University Press. Print.
Baldwin, James. 1998. Introduction to *Notes of a Native Son*, 1984. In *Collected Essays*, ed. Toni Morrison, 808–813. New York: Library of America. Print.
Bandura, Albert. 1997. *Self-Efficacy: The Exercise of Control*. New York: W. H. Freeman. Print.
Baptist, Edward E. 2014. *The Half Has Never Been Told: Slavery and the Making of American Capitalism*. New York: Basic. Print.
Bargh, John. 1997. The Automaticity of Everyday Life. In *The Automaticity of Everyday Life: Advances in Social Cognition*, vol. 10, ed. R. S. Wyer, Jr. 1–61. Print.
Barnett, Elisabeth A., and Katherine L. Hughes. 2012. *Community College and High School Partnerships*. New York: Columbia University, Teachers College, Community College Research Center, October. Web. 24 Aug 2014.
Bates, Kevin. 2012. *Disposable People: New Slavery in the Global Economy*, 3rd ed. Berkeley: University of California Press. Print.
Batstone, David. 2010. *Not for Sale: The Return of the Global Slave Trade—and How We Can Fight It*. New York: Harper. Print.
Baxter Magolda, Marcia B. 2004. *Making Their Own Way: Narratives for Transforming Higher Education to Promote Self-Development*. Stylus: Sterling. Print.
Beach, J.M. 2011. *Gateway to Opportunity?: A History of the Community College in the United States*. Stylus: Sterling. Print.
Becker, Wesley C. 1977. Teaching Reading and Language to the Disadvantaged: What We Have Learned from Field Research. *Harvard Educational Review* 47(4): 518–543. Print.

Becker, Gary S. 1993. *Human Capital: A Theoretical and Empirical Analysis with Special Reference to Education*, 3rd ed. Chicago: University of Chicago Press. Print.

Becker, Aaron. 2013. *Journey*. Somerville: Candlewick. Print.

Beckert, Sven. 2014. *Empire of Cotton: A Global History*. New York: Knopf. Print.

Bell, Nathan E. 2012. Data Sources: The Role of Community Colleges on the Pathway to Graduate Degree Attainment. *GradEdge*, February 1. http://cgsnet.org/data-sources-role-community-colleges-pathway-graduate-degree-attainment-0. Web. 11 December 2015.

Bettinger, Eric, and Bridget Terry Long. 2009. Addressing the Needs of Underprepared Students in Higher Education: Does College Remediation Work? *Journal of Human Resources* 44(3): 736–771. Print.

Birnbaum, Pierre. 2015. *Léon Blum: Prime Minister, Socialist, Zionist*, Trans. Arthur Goldhammer. New Haven: Yale University Press. Print.

Bishop, Wendy. 1993. Students' Stories and the Variable Gaze of Composition Research. In *Writing Ourselves into the Story: Unheard Voices from Composition Studies*, ed. Sheryl Fontaine and Susan Hunter, 197–214. Carbondale: Southern Illinois University Press. Print.

Black Student Graduation Rates at High-Ranking Colleges and Universities. 2013. *The Journal of Blacks in Higher Education*, November 4. Web. 30 Apr 2016. https://www.jbhe.com/2013/11/black-student-graduation-rates-at-high-ranking-colleges-and-universities/

Blackburn, Robin. 2010. *The Making of New World Slavery: From the Baroque to the Modern, 1492–1800*, 2nd ed. Brooklyn: Verso. Print.

Blackwell, Lisa, Kali Trzesniewski, and Carol Sorich Dweck. 2007. Implicit Theories of Intelligence Predict Achievement Across an Adolescent Transition: A Longitudinal Study and an Intervention. *Child Development* 78(1): 246–263. Print.

Boggs, George R. 2010. Democracy's College: The Evolution of the Community College in America. Washington, DC: American Association of Community Colleges. August 19. Web. 2 Sept 2015. Print.

Bourdieu, Pierre. 1984. *Distinction: A Social Critique of the Judgement of Taste*, Trans. Richard Nice. Cambridge: Harvard University Press. Print.

———. 2010. The Forms of Capital. In *Cultural Theory: An Anthology*, Trans. Richard Nice, ed. Imre Szeman and Timothy Kaposy, 81–93. Malden: Wiley-Blackwell. Print.

Bourdieu, Pierre, and Jean-Claude Passeron. 2000. *Reproduction in Education, Society and Culture*, 2nd ed. Trans. Richard Nice. Thousand Oaks: Sage. Print.

Bowen, Betsy, and Kathryn Nantz. 2014. What Is the Value of the GED? *College English* 77(1): 32–54. Print.

Bowen, William, Martin Kurzweil, and Eugene Tobin. 2005. *Equity and Excellence in American Higher Education*. Charlottesville: University of Virginia Press. Print.

Boylan, Hunter R., and Alexandros Goudas. 2012. Knee-Jerk Reforms on Remediation. *Inside Higher Ed*, June 20. Web. 8 May 2015.

Brandt, Deborah. 2001. *Literacy in American Lives*. Cambridge: Cambridge UP. Print.

Bransford, John D., James W. Pellegrino, and M. Suzanne Donovan (eds.). 2000. *How People Learn: Brain, Mind, Experience, and School: Expanded Edition*. Washington, DC: National Academies Press. Print.

Brint, Steven, and Jerome Karabel. 1989. *The Diverted Dream: Community Colleges and the Promise of Educational Opportunity in America, 1900–1985*. New York: Oxford University Press. Print.

Brown, Dee. 2010. *Bury My Heart at Wounded Knee: An Indian History of the American West*. New York: Picador. Print.

Brown, Wendy. 2015. *Undoing the Demos: Neoliberalism's Stealth Revolution*. Brooklyn: Zone Books. Print.

Bruner, Jerome. 1977 [1960]. *The Process of Education*. Cambridge: Harvard University Press. Print.

Cahalan, Margaret, Laura Perna, Mika Yamashita, Roman Ruiz, and Khadish Franklin. 2016. *Indicators of Higher Education Equity in the United States: 2016 Historical Trend Report*. Washington, DC: Pell Institute for the Study of Opportunity in Higher Education, Council for Opportunity in Education (COE) and Alliance for Higher Education and Democracy of the University of Pennsylvania (PennAHEAD). Print.

Caldwell, Bruce. 2007. Introduction. In *The Road to Serfdom: Text and Documents*, By F. A. Hayek. 1944. The Definitive Edition, ed. Bruce Caldwell, 1–33. Chicago: University of Chicago Press. Print.

Calhoon-Dillahunt, Carolyn, Darin L. Jensen, Sarah Z. Johnson, Howard Tinberg, and Christie Toth. 2016. TYCA Guidelines for Preparing Teachers of English in the Two-Year College. NCTE/Two-Year College English Association. April 9, 2016. Web. 23 Mar 2017.

California Community Colleges. 2016. *Student Success Scorecard*. http://scorecard.cccco.edu/scorecardrates.aspx?CollegeID=000#home. Web. 5 June 2016.

Carnes, Jim. 1999. *Us and Them: A History of Intolerance in America*. New York: Oxford University Press. Print.

Carnes, Mark C. (ed.). 2007. *The Columbia History of Post-World War II America*. New York: Columbia University Press. Print.

Carroll, James. 2013. Who Am I to Judge? A Radical Pope's First Year. *The New Yorker*, December 23. Web. 11 Dec. 2015.

Carter, Deborah. 2001. *A Dream Deferred? Examining the Degree Aspirations of African American and White College Students.* New York: Routledge Falmer. Print.

Center for Community College Student Engagement. 2014. *Contingent Commitment: Bringing Part-Time Faculty into Focus.* Austin: The University of Texas at Austin, Program in Higher Education Leadership. Print.

Center for Community College Student Engagement. 2017. *Making Ends Meet: The Role of Community Colleges in Student Financial Health.* Austin: The University of Texas at Austin, College of Education, Department of Educational Administration, Program in Higher Education Leadership. Web.

Center for Media and Democracy. 2015. *Alec Exposed*, July 24. Web. 12 Dec 2015.

Center, Carole. 2004. Explaining My Opinion by My Own Words': Considerations for Teaching Linguistically Different Basic Writers. *Teaching English in the Two-Year College* 31(1): 297–310. Print.

Chambers, Tony, and Bryan Gopaul. 2008. Decoding the Public Good of Higher Education. *Journal of Higher Education Outreach and Engagement* 12(4): 59–91. Print.

Chambliss, Daniel F., and Christopher G. Takacs. 2014. *How College Works.* Cambridge: Harvard University Press. Print.

Chen, Xianglei, and C. Dennis Carroll. 2005. *First-Generation Students in Postsecondary Education: A Look at Their College Transcripts.* Washington, DC: National Center for Education Statistics, July. Web. 26 Nov 2015.

Cho, Sung-Woo, Elizabeth Kopko, Davis Jenkins, and Shanna Smith Jaggars. 2012 December. *New Evidence of Success for Community College Remedial English Students: Tracking the Outcomes of Students in the Accelerated Learning Program (ALP)*, CCRC Working Paper No. 53. New York: Columbia University. Web.

Choy, Susan P. 2001. *Students Whose Parents Did Not Go to College: Postsecondary Access, Persistence, and Attainment.* Washington, DC: National Center for Education Statistics. Web. 26 Nov 2015.

Clark, Burton. 1960. The 'Cooling-Out' Function in Higher Education. *American Journal of Sociology* 65: 569–576.

Cloud, Dana L. 2011. The Only Conceivable Thing to Do: Reflections on Academics and Activism. In *Activism and Rhetoric; Theories and Contexts for Political Engagement*, ed. Seth Kahn and JongHwa Lee, 11–24. New York: Routledge. Print.

Coates, Ta-Nehisi. 2015. *Between the World and Me.* New York: Spiegel and Grau. Print.

Cohen, Arthur M., and Florence B. Brawer. 2008. *The American Community College*, 5th ed. San Francisco: Jossey-Bass Publishers. Print.

Cohen, Arthur M., Florence B. Brawer, and Carrie B. Kisker. 2014. *The American Community College*, 6th ed. San Francisco: John Wiley & Sons. Print.
Coleman, James S. 1966. *Equality of Educational Opportunity* [The Coleman Report]. Washington, DC: U.S. Government Printing Office. Print.
Coleman, Taiyon J., Renee DeLong, Kathleen Sheerin DeVore, Shannon Gibnet, and Michael C. Kuhne. 2016. The Risky Business of Engaging Racial Equity in Writing Instruction: A Tragedy in Five Acts. *Teaching English in the Two-Year College* 43(4): 347–370. Print.
Community College Research Center. n.d. *Community College FAQs: What Percentage of Low-Income, Minority, and First-Time College Students Attend Community Colleges?* Teachers College, Columbia University. http://ccrc.tc.columbia.edu/Community-College-FAQs.html. Web. 4 Apr 2016.
Community College Survey of Student Engagement. *2015 Frequency Distributions Main Survey*. Austin: The University of Texas, Community College Leadership Program. Web. 18 Nov 2015, 8–12.
Complete College America. 2012. *Remediation: Higher Education's Bridge to Nowhere*. Washington, DC: Complete College America. Web.
———. n.d. *Essential Steps for States: Overview*. Web. 10 Dec 2015.
Connell, Raewyn. 2007. *Southern Theory: The Global Dynamics of Knowledge in Social Science*. Cambridge: Polity. Print.
Coolidge, Calvin. 1926. Address at the College of William and Mary in Williamsburg, Virginia. May 15. *The American Presidency Project*, ed. Gerhard Peters and John T. Woolley. Web. 7 Dec 2015.
Cook, Bryan, and Jacqueline E. King. 2004. *Low Income Adults in Profile: Improving Lives through Higher Education*. The American Council on Education (ACE). Web 12 Dec 2015.
Costa, Arthur L., and Bena Kallick (eds.). 2008. *Learning and Leading with Habits of Mind*. Alexandria: Association for Supervision and Curriculum Development. Print.
Crandall, Jennifer R., and Louis Soares. 2015. *The Architecture of Innovation: System-Level Course Redesign in Tennessee*. Washington, DC: American Council on Education. Web. 6 Dec 2015.
Darling-Hammond, Linda. 2010. *The Flat World and Education: How America's Commitment to Equity Will Determine Our Future*. New York: Teachers College Press. Print.
———. 2011. Foreword. In *Surpassing Shanghai: An Agenda for American Education Built on the World's Leading Systems*, ed. Marc S. Tucker, ix–xii. Cambridge: Harvard Education Press. Print.
Darling-Hammond, Linda, and Frank Adamson (eds.). 2014. *Beyond the Bubble Test: How Performance Assessments Support 21st Century Learning*. San Francisco: Jossey-Bass. Print.

de las Casas, Bartholomé. 2004. *A Short History of the Destruction of the Indies*, ed. and trans. Nigel Griffin. New York: Penguin. Print.

Delbanco, Andrew. 2015. Our Universities: The Outrageous Reality. *The New York Review of Books*, July 9. Web. 24 July 2015.

Delgado, Richard, and Jean Stefancic. 2012. *Critical Race Theory: An Introduction*, 2nd ed. New York: New York University Press. Print.

Deresiewicz, William. 2015. The Neoliberal Arts: How College Sold Its Soul to the Market. *Harper's*, September, 25–32. Print.

Desmond, Matthew. 2016. *Evicted: Poverty and Profit in the American City*. New York: Crown. Print.

Dewey, John. 1998. Creative Democracy—The Task Before Us. In *The Essential Dewey, Volume 1: Pragmatism, Education, Democracy*, ed. Larry Hickman and Thomas M. Alexander, 340–343. Bloomington: Indiana University Press. Print.

Doidge, Norman. 2007. *The Brain That Changes Itself*. New York: Penguin. Print.

Donoghue, Frank. 2008. *The Last Professors: The Corporate University and the Fate of the Humanities*. New York: Fordham University Press. Print.

Dougherty, Kevin J. 1991. The Community College at the Crossroads: The Need for Structural Reform. *Harvard Educational Review* 61(3): 311–336. Print.

———. 2001. *The Contradictory College: The Conflicting Origins, Impacts, and Futures of the Community College*. Albany: Suny Press. Print.

Drive to 55 Alliance. Web. 8 Dec 2015.

———. 2014 *Tennessee Promise*. Web. 8 Dec 2015.

———. n.d. *About Tennessee Promise*. Web. 8 Dec 2015.

Duncan, Greg J., and Richard J. Murnane. 2011a. Introduction: The American Dream, Then and Now. In *Whither Opportunity?: Rising Inequality, Schools, and Children's Life Chances*, ed. Greg J. Duncan and Richard J. Murnane, 3–23. New York: Russell Sage. Print.

——— (eds.). 2011b. *Whither Opportunity?: Rising Inequality, Schools, and Children's Life Chances*. New York: Russell Sage. Print.

Duncan-Andrade, Jeffrey M. 2009. Note to Educators: Hope Required When Growing Roses in Concrete. *Harvard Educational Review* 79(2): 181–194. Print.

Dweck, Carol. 2007. *Mindset: The New Psychology of Success*. New York: Ballantine.

———. 2008. Brainology: Transforming Students' Motivation to Learn. *Independent School Magazine*, Winter. Web. 26 Dec 2014.

Edin, Kathryn, and Maria Kefalas. 2005. *Promises I Can Keep: Why Poor Women Put Motherhood before Marriage*. Berkeley: University of California Press. Print.

Eichstedt, Jennifer L., and Stephen Small. 2002. *Representations of Slavery: Race and Ideology in Southern Plantation Museums*. Washington: Smithsonian. Print.

Elliott, Jane. 2006. *Jane Elliott's Blue Eyes Brown Eyes Exercise*. Web. 2 Oct 2015.

Ellwood, David T., and Thomas J. Kane. 2000. Who Is Getting a College Education? Family Background and the Growing Gaps in Enrollment. In

Securing the Future: Investing in Children from Birth to College, ed. Sheldon Danziger and Jane Waldfogel, 283–324. New York: Russell Sage. Print.
Evans, Richard J. 2009. *The Third Reich at War*. New York: Penguin. Print.
Evans, Gary W., and Michelle A. Schamber. 2009. Childhood Poverty, Chronic Stress, and Adult Working Memory. *Proceedings of the National Academy of Sciences*. 106(16): 6545–6449. Print.
Fain, Paul. 2012a. Graduate, Transfer, Graduate. *Inside Higher Ed*, November 8. Web. 26 Nov 2015.
———. 2012b. Overkill on Remediation. *Inside Higher Ed*, June 19. Web. 21 June 2015.
———. 2014. Aggressive Pragmatism. *Inside Higher Ed*, August 26. Web. 12 Dec 2015.
———. 2015a. Free Community College Catches On. *Inside Higher Ed*, July 9. Web. 12 Dec 2015.
———. 2015b. Two Years of Free Community College. *Inside Higher Ed*, January 8. Web. 14 Aug 2015.
Federal Deposit Insurance Corporation. 2014. *Who Is the FDIC?* October 30. https://www.fdic.gov/about/learn/symbol/. Web. 7 Dec 2015.
Flores, Roy. 2011. False Hope. *Inside Higher Ed*, February 17. Web. 8 May 2011.
Fontaine, Sheryl, and Susan Hunter. 1993. *Writing Ourselves into the Story: Unheard Voices from Composition Studies*. Carbondale: Southern Illinois University Press. Print.
Friedman, Milton. 1955. The Role of Government in Education. In *Economics and the Public Interest*, ed. Robert Alexander Solo, 123–144. New Brusnwick: Rutgers University Press. Print.
———. 1993. *Why Government Is the Problem*, Hoover Lecture. Stranford: Hoover Institution on War, Revolution, and Peace. Print.
———. 2002. *Capitalism and Freedom*, Fortieth Anniversary Ed. Chicago: University of Chicago Press. Print.
———. 2012. Neo-Liberalism and Its Prospects. In *The Indispensible Milton Friedman: Essays on Politics and Economics*, ed. Lanny Ebenstein, 3–10. New York: Perseus. Print.
Friedman, Milton, and Rose Friedman. 1990. *Free to Choose: A Personal Statement*. New York: Harvest. Print.
Gale, Trevor. 2012. Towards a Southern Theory of Student Equity in Australian Higher Education: Enlarging the Rationale for Expansion. *International Journal of Sociology of Education* 1(3): 238–262. Print.
Gale, Trevor, and Stephen Parker. 2014. Navigating Change: A Typology of Student Transition in Higher Education. *Studies in Higher Education* 39(5): 734–753. Print.
Gallagher, Kelly. 2009. *Readicide: How Schools Are Killing Reading and What You Can Do about It*. Portland: Stenhouse. Print.

Gates, Bill. 2015. We Need an Energy Miracle. Interview by James Benner. *Atlantic*, November: 56–64.
Genovese, Eugene. 1976. *Roll, Jordan, Roll.* New York: Vintage. Print.
Gilbert, Daniel T., and Patrick S. Malone. 1995. The Correspondence Bias. *Psychological Bulletin* 117(1): 21–38. Print.
Goldrick-Rab, Sara. 2016. *Paying the Price: College Costs, Financial Aid, and the Betrayal of the American Dream.* Chicago: University of Chicago Press. Print.
Goldrick-Rab, Sara, Jed Richardson, and Anthony Hernandez. 2017. *Hungry and Homeless in College: Results from a National Study of Basic Needs Insecurity in Higher Education.* Madison: Wisconsin Hope Lab and the Association of Community College Trustees. March 2017. Web.
Goldin, Claudia, and Lawrence F. Katz. 2010. *The Race between Education and Technology.* Boston: Belknap Press. Print.
Gordon, Robert J. 2016. *The Rise and Fall of American Growth: The U.S. Standard of Living since the Civil War.* Princeton: Princeton University Press. Print.
Goudas, Alexandros, and Hunter R. Boylan. 2012. Addressing Flawed Research in Developmental Education. *Journal of Developmental Education* 36(1): 2–13. Print.
Grandin, Greg. 2015a. Capitalism and Slavery. *The Nation*, May 1. Web. 15 Sept 2015.
———. 2015b. *The Empire of Necessity: Slavery, Freedom, and Deception in the New World.* New York: Picador. Print.
Greenhouse, Steven. 2008. *The Big Squeeze: Tough Times for the American Worker.* New York: Knopf. Print.
Grubb, W. Norton. 1991. The Decline of Community College Transfer Rates: Evidence from National Longitudinal Surveys. *Journal of Higher Education* 62(2): 194–222. Print.
Grubb, W. Norton, and Associates. 1999. *Honored But Invisible: An Inside Look at Teaching in Community Colleges.* New York: Routledge. Print.
Grubb, W. Norton, with Robert Gabriner. 2013. *Basic Skills Education in Community Colleges; Inside and Outside Classrooms.* New York: Routledge. Print.
Hackman, Daniel A., and Martha J. Farah. 2009. Socioeconomic Status and the Developing Brain. *Trends in Cognitive Science* 13(2): 65–73. Print.
Hale, Charles. 2008. Introduction. In *Engaging Contradictions: Theory, Politics, and Methods of Activist Scholarship*, ed. Charles Hale, 1–29. Berkeley: University of California Press. Print.
Hamowy, Ronald. 2011. Introduction. In *The Constitution of Liberty: The Definitive Edition*, ed. Ronald Hamowy, 1–22. Chicago: University of Chicago Press. Print.
Hansen, Kristine, and Christine R. Farris. 2010. *College Credit for Writing in High School: The "Taking Care of" Business.* Urbana: NCTE. Print.

Hanson, James L., Amitabh Chandra, Barbara L. Wolfe, and Seth D. Pollak. 2011. Association between Income and the Hippocampus. *PLOS ONE* 6(5), May 4. doi:10.1371/journal.pone.0018712. Web. 9 Apr 2016.

Harrington, Susanmarie. 1999. The Representation of Basic Writers in Basic Writing Scholarship, or Who Is Quentin Pierce? *Journal of Basic Writing* 18(2): 91–107. Print.

Hart, Betty, and Todd R. Risley. 1995. *Meaningful Differences in the Everyday Experience of Young American Children*. Baltimore: Paul H. Brookes. Print.

Harvey, David. 2005. *A Brief History of Neoliberalism*. New York: Oxford University Press. Print.

Haskins, Ron, and Isabel Sawhill. 2009. *Creating an Opportunity Society*. Washington, DC: Brookings Institution Press. Print.

Hassel, Holly, and Joanne Baird Giordano. 2011. First-Year Composition Placement at Open-Admission, Two-Year Campuses: Changing Campus Culture, Institutional Practice, and Student Success. *Open Words: Access and English Studies* 5(2): 29–59. Web.

———. 2013. Occupy Writing Studies: Rethinking College Composition for the Needs of the Teaching Majority. *College Composition and Communication* 65(1): 117–139. Print.

———. 2015. The Blurry Borders of College Writing: Remediation and the Assessment of Student Readiness. *College English* 78(1): 56–80. Print.

Hassel, Holly, Jeff Klausman, Joanne Baird Giordano, Margaret O'Rourke, Leslie Roberts, Patrick Sullivan, and Christie Toth. 2015. TYCA White Paper on Developmental Education Reform. *Teaching English in the Two-Year College* 42(3): 227–243. Print.

Hayek, F.A. 1980. 'Free' Enterprise and Competitive Order. In *Individualism and Economic Order*, 107–118. Chicago: University of Chicago Press. Print.

———. 1997. The Intellectuals and Socialism. In *Socialism and War: Essays, Documents, Reviews*, ed. Bruce Caldwell, 221–237. Indianapolis: Liberty Fund. Print.

———. 2007. *The Road to Serfdom: Text and Documents*, The Definitive Edition, ed. Bruce Caldwell. Chicago: University of Chicago Press. Print.

———. 2011. *The Constitution of Liberty*, The Definitive Edition, ed. Ronald Hamowy. Chicago: University of Chicago Press. Print.

Hegewisch, Ariane, and Heidi Hartmann. 2015. *The Gender Wage Gap: 2014*. Institute for Women's Policy Research, September. Web. 16 Nov 2015.

Heider, Fritz. 1958. *The Psychology of Interpersonal Relations*. Hillsdale: Lawrence Erlbaum. Print.

Herbert, Bob. 2007. Righting Reagan's Wrongs? *The New York Times*, November 13. Web. 10 Dec 2015.

Here Is Good News on Black Student College Graduation Rates But a Huge Racial Gap Persists. *The Journal of Blacks in Higher Education*, 8 June 2010. Web. 25 Apr 2016.

Hern, Katie. 2011a. *Unleashing Students Capacity through Acceleration: Reflections from an Integrated Reading and Writing Classroom.* English Council of Two-Year Colleges in California, October 20. Web. 15 Sept 2015.
———. 2011b. *Window into an Accelerated Classroom.* California Acceleration Project. Web.
———. 2012. Acceleration Across California: Shorter Pathways in Developmental English and Math. *Change,* May/June: 60–68. Print.
Hillocks, George. 2002. *The Testing Trap: How State Writing Assessments Control Learning.* New York: Teachers College Press. Print.
Hiltzik, Michael. 2011. *The New Deal: A Modern History.* New York: Free Press. Print.
Hochschild, Arlie Russell. 2016. *Strangers in Their Own Land: Anger and Mourning on the American Right.* New York: Perseus. Print.
Hodara, Michelle, Shanna Smith Jaggars, and Melinda Mechur Karp. 2012. *Improving Developmental Education Assessment and Placement: Lessons from Community Colleges Across the Country.* Community College Research Center Working Paper No. 51. New York: Columbia University, Teachers College, Community College Research Center, November. Web. 26 Nov 2012.
Hofstadter, Richard. 1963. *Anti-Intellectualism in American Life.* New York: Vintage. Print.
Holt, Tony. 1995. *Thinking Historically: Narrative, Imagination, and Understanding.* New York: College Board. Print.
Hoxby, Caroline. 2000. *Peer Effects in the Classroom: Learning from Gender and Race Variation,* NBER Working Paper No. 7867. Washington, DC: National Bureau of Economic Research, August. Web. 8 May 2015.
Hoxby, Caroline, and Christopher Avery. 2012. *The Missing 'One-Offs': The Hidden Supply of High-Achieving, Low Income Students,* NBER Working Paper No. 18586. Washington, DC: National Bureau of Economic Research, December. Web. 25 Apr 2016.
Hutcheson, Philo A. 2007. The Truman Commission's Vision of the Future. *Thought and Action,* 107–115. Print. http://www.nea.org/assets/img/PubThoughtAndAction/TAA_07_11.pdf.
Ichheiser, Gustav. 1949. Misunderstandings in Human Relations: A Study in False Social Perception. *American Journal of Sociology* 55(2.2): 1–70. Print.
Iffert, Robert E. 1958. *Retention and Withdrawal of College Students.* Washington, DC: U.S. Department of Health, Education and Welfare. Print.
Ignatieff, Michael. 2001. *The Needs of Strangers.* New York: Picador. Print.
Issues. 2015. National Organization for Women. http://now.org/issues/. Web. 16 Nov 2015

Jacobs, Ken, Ian Perry, and Jenifer MacGillvary. 2015. *The High Public Cost of Low Wages*. Berkeley: UC Berkeley Center for Labor Research and Education, April. Web. 10 Dec 2015.

Jaschik, Scott. 2015. Admissions Revolution. *Inside Higher Ed*, September 29. Web. 12 Nov 2015.

Jefferson, Thomas. 1903–04. Thomas Jefferson to William C. Jarvis, 1820. *ME* 15:278. The Writings of Thomas Jefferson [Memorial Edition], ed. Andrew A Lipscomb and Albert Ellery Bergh. Washington, DC. Print.

Jing, Chai. 2015. *Under the Dome*. [柴静雾霾调查:穹顶之下.] Documentary. 28 February. Web. 20 Dec 2015.

Johnson, Walter. 2013. *River of Dark Dreams: Slavery and Empire in the Cotton Kingdom*. Cambridge: Belknap Press. Print.

Johnstone, Rob. 2017. Foreword. *Making Ends Meet: The Role of Community Colleges in Student Financial Health*. Center for Community College Student Engagement. Austin: The University of Texas at Austin, College of Education, Department of Educational Administration, Program in Higher Education Leadership. Web.

Jolliffe, David A. 2007. Review Essay: Learning to Read as Continuing Education. Rev. of *Personally Speaking: Experience as Evidence in Academic Discourse* by Candace Spigelman; *Rhetorical Education in America* by Cheryl Glenn, Margaret M. Lyday, and Wendy B. Sharer; *Online Education: Global Questions, Local Answers* by Kelli Cargile Cook, and Keith Grant-Davie, eds. *CCC* 58(3): 470–494. Print.

Jones, Daniel Steadman. 2012. *Masters of the Universe: Hayek, Friedman, and the Birth of Neoliberal Politics*. Princeton: Princeton University Press. Print.

Jones, Edward E., and Richard E. Nisbett. 1972. The Actor and the Observer: Divergent Perceptions of the Causes of Behavior. In *Attribution: Perceiving the Causes of Behavior*, ed. Edward E. Jones, David E. Kanhouse, Harold H. Kelley, Richard E. Nisbett, Stuart Valins, and Bernard Weiner, 79–94. Morristown: General Learning Press. Print.

Jun, Ma. 2015. Chai Jing: Green Fighter. Time's 100 Most Influential People. *Time*, April 16. Web. 20 Dec 2015.

Kahn, Seth, and JongHwa Lee (eds.). 2011. *Activism and Rhetoric: Theories and Contexts for Political Engagement*. New York: Routledge. Print.

Kahlenberg, Richard D. 2015. How Higher Education Funding Shortchanges Community Colleges. *Century Foundation*, May 28. Web. 8 Dec 2015.

Kaling, Mindy. 2011. *Is Everyone Hanging Out Without Me?* New York: Crown. Print.

Kalleberg, Arne L. 2011. *Good Jobs, Bad Jobs: The Rise of Polarized and Precarious Employment Systems in the United States, 1970s to 2000s*. New York: Russell Sage. Print.

Kandel, Eric R., James H. Schwartz, Thomas M. Jessell, Steven A. Siegelbaum, and A.J. Hudspeth. 2012. *Principles of Neural Science*, 5th ed. New York: McGraw-Hill. Print.

Karabel, Jerome. 1971. Community Colleges and Social Stratification. *Harvard Educational Review* 42: 521–562. Print.

———. 2005. *The Chosen: The Hidden History of Admission and Exclusion at Harvard, Yale, and Princeton*. Boston: Houghton Mifflin. Print.

Katsnelson, Alla. 2015. News Feature: The Neuroscience of Poverty. *Proceedings of the National Academy of Sciences* 112(51): 15530–15532. Print.

Kennedy, David. 1999. *Freedom from Fear: The American People in Depression and War, 1929–1945*. New York: Oxford University Press. Print.

Keynes, John Maynard. 1936 [1976]. *The General Theory of Employment, Interest, and Money. The Collected Writings of John Maynard Keynes*, vol. 7, ed. Austin Robinson and Donald Moggridge. London: Macmillan and the Royal Economic Society. Print.

Kezar, Adrianna J. 2005. Challenges for Higher Education in Serving the Public Good. In *Higher Education for the Public Good: Emerging Voices from a National Movement*, ed. Adrianna J. Kezar, Tony Chambers, and John Burkhardt, 23–42. San Francisco: Jossey-Bass. Print.

Kezar, Adrianna, and Daniel Maxey. 2014. *An Examination of the Changing Faculty: Ensuring Institutional Quality and Achieving Desired Student Learning Outcomes*. Council for Higher Education Accreditation Occasional Paper, January. Web. 10 Dec 2015.

———. *Dispelling the Myths: Locating the Resources Needed to Support Non-Tenure-Track Faculty*. The Delphi Project on the Changing Faculty and Student Success, Pullias Center for Higher Education, University of Southern California. Web. 2014. 16 Dec. 2015.

Kezar, Adrianna J., Tony Chambers, and John Burkhardt (ed.). 2005. *Higher Education for the Public Good: Emerging Voices from a National Movement*. San Francisco: Jossey-Bass. Print.

Kiernan, V.G. 1978. *America: The New Imperialism: From White Settlement to World Hegemony*. London: Zed. Print.

King, Martin Luther Jr. 1986 [1963]. I Have a Dream. In *A Testament of Hope: The Essential Writings and Speeches of Martin Luther King, Jr.*, ed. James M. Washington, 217–220. New York: HarperCollins. Print.

King, Martin Luther, Jr. 2014. Nobel Lecture. *Nobelprize.org*, September 15. Web. 11 Dec 1964.

———. *Letter from Birmingham Jail*, The Martin Luther King, Jr. Research and Education Institute. Stanford: Stanford University. Web. 7 Dec 2015.

Kishiyama, Mark M., W. Thoms Boyce, Amy M. Jimenez, Lee M. Perry, and Robert T. Knight. 2009. Socioeconomic Disparities Affect Prefrontal Function in Children. *Journal of Cognitive Neuroscience* 21(6): 1106–1115. Print.

Klausman, Jeff, Leslie Roberts, Holly Hassel, Joanne Baird Giordano, Margaret O'Rourke, Patrick Sullivan, and Christie Toth. 2016. TYCA White Paper on Placement Practices. *Teaching English in the Two-Year College* 44(1): 1–23. Print.
Klingberg, Torkel. 2012. Working Memory and School Performance. *Psychology Today*, November 23. Web. 9 Apr 2016.
Korn, Melissa. 2015. Big Gap in College Graduation Rates for Rich and Poor, Study Finds. *Wall Street Journal*, February 3. Web. 12 Sept 2015.
Kristof, Nicholas D., and Sheryl WuDunn. 2009. *Half the Sky: Turning Oppression into Opportunity for Women Worldwide*. New York: Knopf. Print.
Lambert, Matthew T. 2014. *Privatization and the Public Good: Public Universities in the Balance*. Cambridge: Harvard Education Press. Print.
Langer, Ellen J. 1989. *Mindfulness*. Cambridge: Perseus. Print.
Lareau, Annette. 2011. *Unequal Childhoods: Class, Race, and Family Life*, 2nd ed. Berkeley: University of California Press. Print.
Lavin, David E., and David Hyllegard. 1996. *Changing the Odds: Open Admissions and the Life Chances of the Disadvantaged*. New Haven: Yale University Press. Print.
Levin, John S. 2006. Faculty Work: Tensions between Educational and Economic Values. *The Journal of Higher Education* 77(1): 62–82. Print.
———. 2013. Understandings of Community Colleges in Need of Resuscitation: The Case of Community College Faculty. In *Understanding Community Colleges*, ed. John Levin and Susan T. Kater, 233–253. New York: Routledge. Print.
———. 2014. *Nontraditional Students and Community Colleges: The Conflict of Justice and Neoliberalism*, Reprint ed. New York: Palgrave Macmillan. Print.
Levin, John S., and Susan T. Kater (eds.). 2013. *Understanding Community Colleges*. New York: Routledge. Print.
Levin, John S., Genevieve Shaker, and Richard Wagoner. 2011. Post Neoliberalism: The Professional Identity of Faculty off the Tenure-track. In *Universities and the Public Sphere: Knowledge Creation and State Building in the Era of Globalization*, ed. Brian Pusser, Ken Kempner, Simon Marginson, and Imanol Ordorika, 197–217. New York: Routledge. Print.
Lewiecki-Wilson, Cynthia, and Jeff Sommers. 1999. Professing at the Fault Lines: Composition at Open Admissions Institutions. *College Composition and Communication* 50(3): 438–62. Print.
Lipka, Sara. 2014. Some Colleges Try to Catch Students Up Before They're Behind. *Chronicle of Higher Education*, April 8. Web. 24 Aug 2014.
López Turley, Ruth N. 2009. College Proximity: Mapping Access to Opportunity. *Sociology of Education* 82(2): 126–146. Print.

Madison, James. 2008 [1787]. The Federalist Papers: No. 10. *The Avalon Project* [Yale Law School Lillian Goldman Law Library]. Web. 22 Apr 2016.

———. 2008 [1788]. The Federalist Papers: No. 51. *The Avalon Project* [Yale Law School Lillian Goldman Law Library]. Web. 24 Mar 2017.

Mahle-Grisez, Lisa. 2014. For Whom Does It Profit? Rev. of *Paying for the Party: How College Maintains Inequality* by Elizabeth A. Armstrong and Laura T. Hamilton, *Inside the College Gates: How Class and Culture Matter in Higher Education* by Jenny M. Stuber, *Going North, Thinking West: The Intersections of Social Class, Critical Thinking, and Politicized Writing Instruction* by Irvin Peckham, and *Back to School: Why Everyone Deserves a Second Chance at Education* by Mike Rose. *College Composition and Communication* 65(3): 478–85. Print.

Mahler, Jonathan. 2015. The Mysteries of Abbottabad. *The New York Times Magazine*, October 18: 42–7+. Print.

Mallon, Thomas. 2009. Possessed: Did Ayn Rand's Cult Outstrip Her Canon? *The New Yorker*, November 9. Web. 24 Aug 2014.

Mangan, Katherine. 2013. How Gates Shapes State Higher-Education Policy. *Chronicle of Higher Education*, July 14. http://www.chronicle.com/article/How-Gates-Shapes-State/140303/. Web.

———. 2014. Push to Reform Remedial Education Raises Difficult Questions for Colleges. *Chronicle of Higher Education*, April 8. Web. 24 Aug 2014.

———. 2015. Remedial Educators Warn of Misconceptions Fueling a Reform Movement. *Chronicle of Higher Education*, July 28. Web. 12 Dec 2015.

Manski, Charles F. 1989. Schooling as Experimentation: A Reappraisal of the College Dropout Phenomenon. *Economics of Education Review* 8(4): 305–312. Print.

Marginson, Simon. 2011. Higher Education and Public Good. *Higher Education Quarterly* 65(4): 411–433. Print.

Marshall, George C. n.d. The Marshall Plan Speech [Harvard University, 5 June 1947]. *The George C. Marshall Foundation*. Web. 19 Dec 2015.

Massey, Douglas S. 2007. *Categorically Unequal: The American Stratification System*. New York: Russell Sage. Print.

Massey, Douglas S., and Nancy A. Denton. 1993. *American Apartheid: Segregation and the Making of the Underclass*. Cambridge: Harvard University Press. Print.

Massey, Douglas S., Camille Z. Charles, Garvey F. Lundy, and Mary J. Fischer. 2003. *The Source of the River: The Social Origins of Freshmen at America's Selective Colleges and Universities*. Princeton: Princeton University Press. Print.

Mayer, Frederick W. 2014. *Narrative Politics: Stories and Collective Action*. New York: Oxford University Press. Print.

Mayer, Jane. 2016. *Dark Money: The Hidden History of the Billionaires Behind the Rise of the Radical Right*. New York: Doubleday. Print.

McCloskey, Donald N. 1985. *The Rhetoric of Economics*. Madison: University of Wisconsin Press. Print.

McDonough, Patricia M. 2004. *The School-to-College Transition: Challenges and Prospects*. Washington, DC: American Council on Education. Print.

McMahon, Walter W. 2009. *Higher Learning, Greater Good: The Private and Social Benefits of Higher Education*. Baltimore: Johns Hopkins University Press. Print.

———. 2015. Financing Education for the Public Good: A New Strategy. *Journal of Education Finance* 40(4): 414–437. Print.

Meek, James. 2015. *Private Island: Why Britain Now Belongs to Someone Else*. London: Verso. Print.

———. 2017. Somerdale to Skarbimierz. *London Review of Books*, April 20: 3–15. Print.

Meier, Ken. 2013. Community College Mission in Historical Perspective. *Understanding Community Colleges*, ed. John Levin and Susan T. Kater. New York: Routledge, 3–18. Print.

Mettler, Suzanne. 2014. *Degrees of Inequality: How the Politics of Higher Education Sabotaged the American Dream*. New York: Basic Books. Print.

Mill, John Stuart. 1996. On Liberty. *Mill: The Spirit of the Age, On Liberty, The Subjection of Women*. New York: W.W. Norton. Print.

Miller, Donalyn. 2009. *The Book Whisperer: Awakening the Inner Reader in Every Child*. San Francisco: Jossey-Bass. Print.

Milton, John. 2016 [1644]. *Areopagitica and Other Writings*. New York: Penguin. Print.

Mitchell, Karrie D. 2008. *Finding Their Way: Cultural Capital Facilitators and First-Generation Community College Students*. Saarbrücken: Verlag. Print.

Mont Pelerin Society. 1947. *Statement of Aims*. April 8. Web. 9 Sept 2015.

Morgan, Edmund S. 2003. *American Slavery, American Freedom*, Reissue ed. New York: W. W. Norton. Print.

Mosteller, Frederick, and Daniel P. Moynihan. 1972. A Pathbreaking Report: Further Studies of the Coleman Report. In *On Equality of Educational Opportunity: Papers Deriving from the Harvard University Faculty Seminar on the Coleman Report*, ed. Frederick Mosteller and Daniel P. Moynihan, 3–66. New York: Vintage. Print.

Mullainathan, Sendhil, and Eldar Shafir. 2014. *Scarcity: The New Science of Having Less and How It Defines Our Lives*. New York: Picador. Print.

Mullin, Christopher. 2012a. *Why Access Matters: The Community College Student Body*, American Association of Community Colleges Policy Brief 2012-01PBL, February. Web. 11 Dec 2015.

———. 2012b. Student Success: Institutional and Individual Perspectives. *Community College Review* 40(2): 126–144. Print.

———. 2012c. *Transfer: An Indispensable Part of the Community College Mission.* American Association of Community Colleges Policy Brief 2012-03PBL, October. Web. 11 Dec 2015.

Nation, Kate. 2005. Children's Reading Comprehension Difficulties. In *The Science of Reading: A Handbook*, ed. Margaret Snowling and Charles Hulme, 248–265. Malden: Blackwell. Print.

National Endowment for the Arts. 2004. *Reading at Risk*, Research Division Report 46. Washington, DC: National Endowment for the Arts. Print.

———. 2007. *To Read or Not to Read: A Question of National Consequence.* Research Division Report 47. Washington, DC: National Endowment for the Arts. November. Web. 30 Dec 2014.

National Student Clearinghouse Research Center. 2012. *Degree Attainment. Outcomes of Students Who Transferred from Two-Year to Four-Year Institutions.* http://www.studentclearinghouse.info/snapshot/docs/SnapshotReport8-GradRates2-4Transfers.pdf. Web. 19 Nov 2015.

———. 2015. *Contribution of Two-Year Institutions to Four-Year Completions.* March 24. http://nscresearchcenter.org/snapshotreport-twoyearcontribution fouryearcompletions17/. Web. 26 Nov 2015.

Nelson, Cary, and Stephen Watt. 2004. *Office Hours: Activism and Change in the Academy.* New York: Routledge. Print.

Newfield, Christopher. 2008. *Unmaking the Public University: The Forty-Year Assault on the Middle Class.* Cambridge: Harvard University Press. Print.

Newkirk, Thomas. 2012. *Holding On to Good Ideas in a Time of Bad Ones.* Portsmouth: Heinemann. Print.

Nichols, Andrew, and Denzel Evans-Bell. 2017. *A Look at Black Student Success Identifying Top- and Bottom-Performing Institutions.* Washington, DC: The Education Trust. March 2017. Web.

Nisbett, Richard E., Joshua Aronson, Clancy Blair, William Dickens, James Flynn, Diane F. Halpern, and Eric Turkheimer. 2012. Intelligence: New Findings and Theoretical Developments. *American Psychologist* 67(2): 130–159. Print.

Nisbett, Richard E., Craig Caputo, Patricia Legant, and Jeanne Marecek. 1973. Behavior As Seen By the Actor and As Seen By the Observer. *Journal of Personality and Social Psychology* 27(2): 154–164. Print.

Nixon, Jon. 2011. *Higher Education and the Public Good: Imagining the University.* New York: Continuum. Print.

Nussbaum, Martha. 2010. *Not for Profit: Why Democracy Needs the Humanities.* Princeton: Princeton University Press. Print.

Otte, George, and Rebecca Williams Mlynarczyk. 2010. *Basic Writing.* West Lafayette: Parlor Press. Print.

Packer, George. 2013. *The Unwinding: An Inner History of the New America.* New York: Farrar, Straus, and Giroux. Print.

Park, Sueuk, and Ernest T. Pascarella. 2010. Community College Attendance and Socioeconomic Plans. *Community College Journal of Research and Practice* 34(9): 700–716. Print.

Parti, Tarini. 2015. 'Dark Money': ALEC Wants Image Makeover. *Politico*, June 30. Web. 12 Dec 2015.

Pascarella, Ernest T. 1999. New Studies Track Community College Effects on Students. *Community College Journal* 69(6): 8–14. Print.

Pascarella, Ernest T., and Patrick T. Terenzini. 2005. *How College Affects Students. Volume 2: A Third Decade of Research*. San Francisco: Jossey-Bass.

Pascarella, Ernest T., Marcia Edison, Amaury Nora, Patrick T. Terenzini, and Linda Serra Hagedorn. 1998. Does Community College Versus Four-Year College Attendance Influence Students' Educational Plans? *Journal of College Student Development* 39(2): 179–193. Print.

Pascarella, Ernest T., Gregory C. Wolniak, and Christopher T. Pierson. 2003. Influences on Community College Students' Educational Plans. *Research in Higher Education* 44(3): 301–314. Print.

Patterson, James T. 1996. *Grand Expectations: The United States, 1945–1974*. New York: Oxford University Press. Print.

———. 2000. *America's Struggle Against Poverty in the Twentieth Century*, 4th ed. Cambridge: Harvard University Press. Print.

———. 2001. *Brown v. Board of Education: A Civil Rights Milestone and Its Trouble Legacy*. New York: Oxford University Press. Print.

Paul, Annie Murphy. 2010. *Origins: How the Nine Months Before Birth Shape the Rest of Our Lives*. New York: Free Press. Print.

Pay Equity and Distribution. n.d. Institute for Women's Policy Research. http://www.iwpr.org/initiatives/pay-equity-and-discrimination. Web. 16 Nov 2015.

Perfetti, Charles A., Nicole Landi, and Jane Oakhill. 2005. The Acquisition of Reading Comprehension Skill. In *The Science of Reading: A Handbook*, ed. Margaret Snowling and Charles Hulme, 227–247. Malden: Blackwell. Print.

Perna, Laura, and Marvin Titus. 2004. Understanding Differences in the Choice of College Attended: The Role of State Public Policies. *Review of Higher Education* 27(4): 501–525. Print.

Pickett, Nell Ann. 1998. The Two-Year College as Democracy in Action. *College Composition and Communication* 49(1): 90–98. Print.

Piketty, Thomas. 2014. *Capital in the Twenty-First Century*. Boston: Belknap Press. Print.

Polanyi, Karl. 2001. *The Great Transformation: The Political and Economic Origins of Our Time*, 2nd ed. Boston: Beacon. Print.

Porfilio, Brad, Julie Gorlewski, Paul R. Carr, and P.L. Thomas. 2014. Introduction: Social Context Reform—A Pedagogy of Equity and Opportunity. In *Social Context Reform—A Pedagogy of Equity and Opportunity*, ed. P.L. Thomas, Brad Porfilio, Julie Gorlewski, and Paul R. Carr. New York: Routledge. Print.

President's Commission on Higher Education. 1947. *Higher Education for Democracy: A Report of the President's Commission on Higher Education*, Establishing the Goals, vol 1, 5–103. New York: Harper & Brothers. Print.

Principles of Social Psychology. Chapter 6.2: Inferring Dispositions Using Causal Attribution. Creative Commons Attribution-NonCommercial-ShareAlike. University of Minnesota Libraries Publishing, 2010. Open Source.

Pronin, Emily, Daniel Y. Lin, and Lee Ross. 2002. The Bias Blind Spot: Perceptions of Bias in Self Versus Others. *Personality and Social Psychology Bulletin* 28(3): 369–381. Print.

Putnam, Robert. 2015. *Our Kids: The American Dream in Crisis*. New York: Simon and Schuster. Print.

Quinn, Jocey. 2010. Rethinking "Failed Transitions" to Higher Education. In *Transitions and Learning Through the Lifecourse*, ed. Kathryn Ecclestone, Gert Biesta, and Martin Hughes, 118–129. London: Routledge.

Quinton, Sophie. 2014. When a 43% Graduation Rate Means Success. *Atlantic*, April 15. http://www.theatlantic.com/education/archive/2014/04/when-a-43-graduation-rate-means-success/360672/. Web. 20 Nov 2015.

Raby, K. Lee, Glenn I. Roisman, R. Chris Fraley, and Jeffry A. Simpson. 2015. The Enduring Predictive Significance of Early Maternal Sensitivity: Social and Academic Competence through Age 32 Years. *Child Development* 86(3): 695–708. Print.

Rand, Ayn. 1967. *Capitalism: The Unknown Ideal*. New York: Signet. Print.

Ravitch, Diane. 2013. *Reign of Error: The Hoax of the Privatization Movement and the Danger to America's Public Schools*. New York: Knopf. Print.

Rawls, John. 1999. *A Theory of Justice*, Rev. ed. Cambridge: Belknap. Print.

Reardon, Sean F. 2011. The Widening Academic Achievement Gap Between the Rich and the Poor: New Evidence and Possible Explanations. In *Whither Opportunity?: Rising Inequality, Schools, and Children's Life Chances*, ed. Greg J. Duncan and Richard J. Murnane, 91–115. New York: Russell Sage. Print.

Reich, Robert B. 2015. *Saving Capitalism: For the Many, Not the Few*. New York: Knopf. Print.

Richards, Sam. 2010. *A Radical Experiment in Empathy: At TEDxPSU*. October 10. https://www.youtube.com/watch?v=kUEGHdQO7WA. Web. 24 Aug 2015.

Ripley, Amanda. 2013. *The Smartest Kids in the World: And How They Got That Way*. New York: Simon and Schuster. Print.

Rizga, Kristina. 2015. *Mission High: One School, How Experts Tried to Fail It, and the Students and Teachers Who Made It Triumph*. New York: Nation Books. Print.

Robinson, Ken. 2011. *Out of Our Minds: Learning to Be Creative*, 2nd ed. Westford: Capstone. Print.

Rodriquez, Richard. 1983. *The Hunger of Memory: The Education of Richard Rodriguez*. New York: Bantam. Print.

Rohde, Robert A., and Richard A. Muller. 2015. Air Pollution in China: Mapping of Concentrations and Sources. *PLOS/ONE*, August 20. Web. 7 Dec 2015.

Roosevelt, Franklin. n.d. Address at Oglethorpe University in Atlanta, Georgia May 22, 1932. *The American Presidency Project: Franklin D. Roosevelt*, ed. Gerhard Peters and John T. Woolley. Web. 7 Dec 2015.

———. n.d. Campaign Address at Detroit, Michigan October 2, 1932. *The American Presidency Project: Franklin D. Roosevelt*, ed.Gerhard Peters and John T. Woolley. Web. 20 Dec 2015.

———. 1937. Second Inaugural Address. 20 January. *The American Presidency Project: Franklin D. Roosevelt*, ed. Gerhard Peters and John T. Woolley. n.d. Web. 7 Dec 2015.

———. 1938. *The Public Papers and Addresses of Franklin D. Roosevelt*. Vol. V. New York: Random House. Web.

Rose, Mike. 1989. *Lives on the Boundary: A Moving Account of the Struggles and Achievements of America's Educationally Underprepared*. New York: Free Press. Print.

———. 1996. *Possible Lives: The Promise of Public Education in America*. New York: Penguin. Print.

———. 2009. *Why School? Reclaiming Education for All of Us*. New York: New Press. Print.

———. 2011. Remediation at a Crossroads. *Inside Higher Ed*, April 21. Web. 8 May 2011.

———. 2012. *Back to School: Why Everyone Deserves a Second Chance at Education*. New York: New Press. Print.

Rothstein, Richard. 2004. *Class and Schools: Using Social, Economic, and Educational Reform to Close the Black-White Achievement Gap*. Washington, DC: Economic Policy Institute. Print.

———. 2014a. *The Making of Ferguson: Public Policies at the Root of Its Troubles*. Washington, DC: Economic Policy Institute. October 15. Web. 19 Oct 2015.

———. 2014b. *The Racial Achievement Gap, Segregated Schools, and Segregated Neighborhoods—A Constitutional Insult*. Washington, DC: Economic Policy Institute. November 12. Web. 6 Oct 2015.

Rothstein, Richard, Rebecca Jacobsen, and Tamara Wilder. 2008. *Grading Education: Getting Accountability Right*. Washington, DC: Economic Policy Institute. Print.

Roueche, John E., and Suanne D. Roueche. 1999. *High Stakes, High Performance: Making Remedial Education Work*. Washington, DC: Community College Press.

Rouse, Cecilia Elena. 1995. Democratization or Diversion? The Effect of Community Colleges on Educational Attainment. *Journal of Business & Economic Statistics* 13(2): 217–224. Print.

Russakoff, Dale. 2015. *The Prize: Who's in Charge of America's Schools?* New York: Houghton Mifflin. Print.

Rustick, Margaret Tomlinson. 2007. Grammar Games in the Age of Anti-Remediation. *Journal of Basic Writing* 26(2): 43–62. Print.

Saenz, V.B., S. Hurtado, D. Barrera, D. Wolf, and F. Yeung. 2007. *First in My Family: A Profile of First-Generation College Students at Four-Year Institutions Since 1971.* Los Angeles: Higher Education Research Institute. Print.

Sahadi, Jeanne. 2014. Slave Labor in America Today. *CNN Money*, October 21. Web. 2 Dec 2015.

Sahlberg, Pasi. 2011. *Finnish Lessons: What Can the World Learn from Educational Change in Finland?* New York: Teachers College Press. Print.

Said, Edward. 1993. *Culture and Imperialism.* New York: Vintage. Print.

———. 1996. *Representations of the Intellectual: The 1993 Reith Lectures.* Reprint ed. New York: Vintage. Print.

———. 2004. *Humanism and Democratic Criticism.* New York: Columbia University Press. Print.

Satell, Greg. 2013. 4 Government Programs That Drive Innovation. *Forbes*, July 2. Web. 26 Oct 2015.

Scherer, Juliet Lilledahl, and Mirra Leigh Anson. 2014. *Community Colleges and the Access Effect: Why Open Admissions Suppresses Achievement.* New York: Palgrave Macmillan. Print.

Schneider, Mercedes K. 2014. *A Chronicle of Echoes: Who's Who in the Implosion of American Public Education.* Charlotte: Information Age Publishing. Print.

Schumpeter, Joseph A. 2008 [1941]. *Capitalism, Socialism, and Democracy.* New York: Harper. Print.

Schwartz, Robert B., and Jal D. Mehta. 2011. Finland: Superb Teachers—How to Get Them, How to Use Them. In *Surpassing Shanghai: An Agenda for American Education Built on the World's Leading Systems*, ed. Marc S. Tucker, 51–77. Cambridge: Harvard Education Press. Print.

Scott-Clayton, Judith, and Georgia West Stacey. 2015. *Improving the Accuracy of Remedial Placement.* New York: Community College Research Center. Web. 8 Aug 2015.

Sen, Amartya. 1999. *Development as Freedom.* New York: Anchor. Print.

———. 2009. *The Idea of Justice.* Belknap: Cambridge. Print.

Shapiro, Doug, Afet Dundar, Mary Ziskin, Yi-Chen Chiang, Jin Chen, Autumn Harrell, and Vasti Torres. 2013. *Baccalaureate Attainment: A National View of the Postsecondary Outcomes of Students Who Transfer from Two-Year to Four-Year Institutions*, Signature Report No. 5. Herndon, VA: National Student Clearinghouse Research Center. Web. 20 Nov 2015.

Shaughnessy, Mina P. 1979. *Errors and Expectations: A Guide for the Teacher of Basic Writing.* New York: Oxford University Press. Print.

Shipler, David K. 2004. *The Working Poor: Invisible in America.* New York: Knopf. Print.

Shonkoff, Jack P., and Deborah A. Phillips. 2000. *From Neurons to Neighborhoods: The Science of Early Childhood Development.* Washington, DC: National Academy Press. Print.

Siebert, Fredrick. 1984 [1956]. The Libertarian Theory. *Four Theories of the Press: The Authoritarian, Libertarian, Social Responsibility, and Soviet Communist Concepts of What the Press Should Be and Do.* Fred S. Siebert, Theodore Peterson, and Wilbur Schramm. Urbana: University of Illinois Press. Print.

Skinner, E. Benjamin. 2009. *A Crime So Monstrous: Face-to-Face with Modern-Day Slavery.* New York: Free Press. Print.

Skitka, Linda J., Elizabeth Mullen, Thomas Griffin, Susan Hutchinson, and Brian Chamberlin, B. 2002. Dispositions, Scripts, or Motivated Correction? Understanding Ideological Differences in Explanations for Social Problems. *Journal of Personality and Social Psychology* 83(2): 470–487. Print.

Slaughter, Sheila, and Gary Rhoades. 2004. *Academic Capitalism and the New Economy: Markets, States, and Higher Education.* Baltimore: Johns Hopkins University Press. Print.

Smith, Robert C. 2010. *Conservatism and Racism, and Why in America They Are the Same*, Suny Series in African American Studies. Albany: Suny Press. Print.

Smith, Cheryl Hogue. 2012. Interrogating Texts: From Deferent to Efferent and Aesthetic Reading Practices. *Journal of Basic Writing* 31(1): 59–79. Print.

Smith, Ashley. 2015a. Addressing the Inequality Gap. *Inside Higher Ed*, May 28. Web. 11 Dec 2015.

———. 2015b. Community College to Bachelor's. *Inside Higher Ed*, March 26. Web. 20 Nov 2015.

———. 2015c. Responding to Free. *Inside Higher Ed*, August 26. Web. 26 Nov 2015.

———. 2017. Money Woes Extend Beyond Tuition. *Inside Higher Ed*, 21 Feb 2017. https://www.insidehighered.com/news/2017/02/21/financial-insecurity-could-keep-some-community-college-students-completing. Web.

Smith, Jonathan, and Kevin Stange. 2015. *A New Measure of College Quality to Study the Effects of College Sector and Peers on Degree Attainment*, NBER Working Paper No. 21605. National Bureau of Economic Research. October. Web. 26 Nov 2015.

Smith, Michael W., and Jeffery D. Wilhelm. 2002. *Reading Don't Fix No Chevys: Literacy in the Lives of Young Men.* Portsmouth: Heinemann. Print.

Smith, Michael W., Jeffery D. Wilhelm, with Sharon Fransen. 2013. *Reading Unbound.* New York: Scholastic. Print.

Snow, Catherine E., and Connie Juel. 2005. Teaching Children to Read: What Do We Know about How to Do It? In *The Science of Reading: A Handbook*, ed. Margaret Snowling and Charles Hulme, 501–520. Malden: Blackwell. Print.

Snowling, Margaret J., and Charles Hulme. 2005. *The Science of Reading: A Handbook.* Malden: Blackwell. Print.

Social Security, Press Office. 2015. *Social Security Basic Facts.* October 23. https://www.ssa.gov/news/press/basicfact.html. Web. 7 Dec 2015.

Solnit, Rebecca. 2015. The Mother of All Questions. *Harper's*, October: 5–7. Print.

Sroufe, L. Alan, Byron Egeland, Elizabeth A. Carlson, and W. Andrew Collins. 2009. *The Development of the Person: The Minnesota Study of Risk and Adaptation from Birth to Adulthood*. New York: Guildford Press. Print.

St. John, Edward, Shouping Hu, and Amy S. Fisher. 2010. *Breaking through the Access Barrier: How Academic Capital Formation Can Improve Policy in Higher Education*. New York: Routledge. Print.

State of Connecticut. 2012. *Public Act 12–40*. May 31. Web. 8 July 2015.

Steele, Claude M., and Joshua Aronson. 1995. Stereotype Threat and the Intellectual Test Performance of African Americans. *Journal of Personality and Social Psychology* 69(5): 797–811. Print.

Steele, Claude M. 2010. *Whistling Vivaldi: How Stereotypes Affect Us and What We Can Do*, 16–43. New York: W.W. Norton. Print.

Sternglass, Marilyn. 1997. *Time to Know Them: A Longitudinal Study of Writing and Learning at the College Level*. Mahwah: Lawrence Erlbaum Associates. Print.

———. 1999. Students Deserve Enough Time to Prove that They Can Succeed. *Journal of Basic Writing* 18(1): 3–20. Print.

Stiglitz, Joseph E. 2012. *The Price of Inequality: How Today's Divided Society Endangers Our Future*. New York: W. W. Norton. Print.

———. *Reforming Taxation to Promote Growth and Equity*. White Paper. Web. 28 May 2014. New York: Roosevelt Institute. [Adapted and condensed: Phony Capitalism. *Harper's* September 2014: 14–16. Print].

Stiglitz, Joseph E., and Bruce C. Greenwald. 2014. *Creating a Learning Society: A New Approach to Growth, Development, and Social Progress*. New York: Columbia University Press. Print.

Stuber, Jenny M. 2011. *Inside the College Gates: How Class and Culture Matter in Higher Education*. Lanham: Rowman and Littlefield. Print.

Sudbury, Julia, and Margo Okazawa-Rey (eds.). 2009. *Activist Scholarship: Antiracism, Feminism, and Social Change*. Boulder: Paradigm. Print.

Sullivan, Patrick. 2005. Cultural Narratives about Success and the Material Conditions of Class at the Community College. *Teaching English in the Two-Year College* 33(2): 142–160. Print.

———. 2009. An Open Letter to Ninth Graders. *Academe*, January/February: 6–10. Print.

———. 2010a. What Can We Learn about "College-Level" Writing From Basic Writing Students?: The Importance of Reading. In *What Is "College-Level" Writing? Volume 2: Assignments, Readings, and Student Writing Samples*, ed. Patrick Sullivan, Howard Tinberg, and Sheridan Blau, 233–253. Urbana: NCTE. Print.

———. 2010b. What Is 'Affordable' Community College Tuition? Part I. *Community College Journal of Research and Practice* 34(8): 645–661. Print.

———. 2010c. What Is 'Affordable' Community College Tuition? Part II. *Community College Journal of Research and Practice* 34(9): 687–699. Print.

———. 2014. *A New Writing Classroom: Listening, Motivation, and Habits of Mind*. Logan: Utah State University Press. Print.

Sullivan, Alice, and Matt Brown. 2013. *Social Inequalities in Cognitive Scores at Age 16: The Role of Reading*, Center for Longitudinal Studies Working Paper 2013/10. London: Institute of Education, University of London. September. Web. 10 Aug 2015.

Sullivan, Patrick, and David Nielsen. 2013. 'Ability to Benefit': Making Forward-Looking Decisions about Our Most Underprepared Students. *College English* 75(3): 319–343. Print.

Sweeney, Camille, and Josh Gosfield. 2013. *The Art of Doing: How Superachievers Do What They Do and How They Do It So Well*. New York: Plume. Print.

The Declaration of Independence: A Transcription. *The Charters of Freedom: A New World Is at Hand*. National Archives [USA.gov]. n.d. Web. 20 Apr 2016.

Thelin, John R. 2004. *A History of American Higher Education*. Baltimore: The Johns Hopkins University Press. Print.

Tinberg, Howard. 1993. Seeing Ourselves Differently: Remaking Research and Scholarship at the Community College. *Teaching English in the Two-Year College* 20(1): 12–17. Print.

Tinberg, Howard, and Jean-Paul Nadeau. 2010. *The Community College Writer: Exceeding Expectations*. Carbondale: Southern Illinois University Press. Print.

Tinto, Vincent. 1993. *Leaving College: Rethinking the Causes and Cures of Student Attrition*, 2nd ed. Chicago: University of Chicago Press.

Ton, Zeynep. 2014. *The Good Jobs Strategy: How the Smartest Companies Invest in Employees to Lower Costs and Boost Profits*. New York: Houghton Mifflin. Print.

Torney-Purta, Judith, Rainer Lehman, Hans Oswald, and Wolfram Schulz. 2001. *Citizenship and Education in Twenty-Eight Countries: Civic Knowledge and Engagement at Age Fourteen*. Amsterdam: International Association for the Evaluation of Educaitonal Achievement. Print.

Toth, Christie, and Sullivan Patrick. 2016. Toward Local Teacher-Scholar Communities of Practice: Findings from a National TYCA Survey. *Teaching English in the Two-Year College* 43(3): 247–273. Print.

Toth, Christie, Patrick Sullivan, and Carolyn Calhoon-Dillahunt. 2016. A Dubious Method of Improving Educational Outcomes: Accountability and the Two-Year College. *Teaching English in the Two-Year College* 43(4): 391–410. Print.

Tough, Paul. 2006. What It Takes to Make a Student. *The New York Times Magazine*, November 26: 44–51+. Print.

———. 2012. *How Children Succeed: Grit, Curiosity, and the Hidden Power of Character*. Boston: Houghton Mifflin Harcourt. Print.

———. 2016a. *Helping Children Succeed: What Works and Why*. New York: Houghton Mifflin Harcourt. Print.

———. 2016b. How Kids Really Succeed. *Atlantic*, July, 56–66.

———. 2014. Who Gets to Graduate? *The New York Times Magazine*, May 18, 26–30+.

Traub, James. 1995. *City on a Hill: Testing the American Dream at City College*. New York: Perseus. Print.

Tucker, Marc S. (ed.). 2011. *Surpassing Shanghai: An Agenda for American Education Built on the World's Leading Systems*. Cambridge: Harvard Education Press. Print.

Turk, Jonathan M. Christopher J. Nellum, and Louis Soares. 2015. *State Policy as a Tool for Postsecondary Developmental Education Reform: A Case Study of Connecticut*. Washington, DC: American Council on Education. Web. 6 Dec 2015.

Turner, Cory. 2015. President Obama Signs Education Law, Leaving 'No Child' Behind. *NPR*, December 10. Web. 11 Dec 2015.

Tzanakis, Michael. 2011. Critical Review. Bourdieu's Social Reproduction Thesis and the Role of Cultural Capital in Educational Attainment: A Critical Review of Key Empirical Studies. *Educate* 11(1): 76–90. Print.

United States, Department of Education, National Center for Education Statistics. 2002. *Nontraditional Undergraduates*, NCES 2002-012. Web. 11 Dec 2015.

———. 2006. *Profiles of Undergraduates in U.S. Post-Secondary Education Institutions: 2003–04, With an Analysis of Community College Students*. http://nces.ed.gov/pubs2006/2006184_rev.pdf. Web. 11 Dec 2015.

———. 2009. *Achievement Gaps: How Black and White Students in Public Schools Perform in Mathematics and Reading on the National Assessment of Educational Progress*. Washington, DC: Institute of Education Sciences. July 14. Web. 8 Apr 2016.

———. 2011. *Achievement Gaps: How Hispanic and White Students Perform in Public Schools Perform in Mathematics and Reading on the National Assessment of Educational Progress*. Washington, DC: Institute of Education Sciences. June. Web. 8 Apr 2016.

———. 2015. *The Condition of Education 2015*. Chapter: 4/Postsecondary Education, "Institutional Retention and Graduation Rates for Undergraduate Students." https://nces.ed.gov/programs/coe/pdf/Indicator_CTR/coe_ctr_2015_05.pdf. Web. 24 March 2017.

United States, Department of State. n.d. *What Is Modern Slavery?* http://www.state.gov/j/tip/what/. Web. 2 Dec 2015.

United States, Department of Veterans Affairs. *Education and Training: History and Timeline*. http://www.benefits.va.gov/gibill/history.asp. Web. 7 Dec 2015.

United States, Environmental Protection Agency. 2016. Clean Air Act Overview: Progress Cleaning the Air and Improving People's Health. *EPA: United States Environmental Protection Agency*, March 29. https://www.epa.gov/clean-air-act-overview/progress-cleaning-air-and-improving-peoples-health#pollution. Web. 22 Aprl 2016.

Vance, J.D. 2016. *Hillbilly Elegy: A Memoir of a Family and Culture in Crisis*. New York: Harper. Print.

Valencia, Richard R. 2014. Introduction. In *The Evolution of De cit Thinking: Educational Thought and Practice*. Reprint edn, ix–xvii. Ed. Richard R. Valencia. London: RoutledgeFalmer. Print.

Vaughan, George. 1984. Forging the Community College Mission. *Educational Record* 65(3): 24–29. Print.

Wallace, David Foster. 2009. *This Is Water: Some Thoughts, Delivered on a Significant Occasion, about Living a Compassionate Life*. New York: Little, Brown. Print.

Walton, Gregory M., and Geoffrey L. Cohen. 2011. Outcomes of Minority Students: A Brief Social-Belonging Intervention Improves Academic and Health. *Science* 331: 1447–1451. Print.

Wardle, Elizabeth. 2012. Creative Repurposing for Expansive Learning: Considering 'Problem-Exploring' and 'Answer-Getting' Dispositions in Individuals and Fields. *Composition Forum*, 26. Web. 24 Aug 2014.

Watson, Vajra. 2011. *Learning to Liberate: Community-Based Solutions to the Crisis in Urban Education*. New York: Routledge. Print.

Weil, David. 2014. *The Fissured Workplace: Why Work Became So Bad for So Many and What Can Be Done to Improve It*. Cambridge: Harvard University Press. Print.

Weissmann, Jordan. 2015. Someone Calculated How Many Adjunct Professors Are on Public Assistance, and the Number Is Startling. *Slate*, April 13. Web. 21 June 2015.

White House, Office of the Press Secretary. 2015a. *Fact Sheet: Congress Acts to Fix No Child Left Behind*. December 2. Web. 11 Dec. 2015.

———. 2015b. *Fact Sheet: White House Unveils America's College Promise Proposal: Tuition-Free Community College for Responsible Students*. January 9. Web. 12 Dec. 2015.

Williams, Eric. 1994. *Capitalism and Slavery*. Chapel Hill: University of North Carolina Press. Print.

Wilson, Smokey. 1994. What Happened to Darleen? Reconstructing the Life and Schooling of an Underprepared Learner. In *Two-Year College English: Essays for a New Century*. Urbana: NCTE, 37–53. Print.

Wilson, William Julius. 1996. *When Work Disappears: The World of the New Urban Poor*. New York: Vintage. Print.

Winston, Gordon C., and David J. Zimmerman. 2004. Peer Effects in Higher Education. *College Choices: The Economics of Where to Go, When to Go, and How to Pay For It*. Washington, DC: National Bureau of Economic Research, 395–424. Print.

Wolf, Maryanne. 2008. *Proust and the Squid: The Story and Science of the Reading Brain*. New York: Harper. Print.

Worthen, Helena. 2001. The Problem of the Majority Contingent Faculty in the Community Colleges. In *Politics and Writing Instruction at the Two-Year*

Campus, ed. Keith Kroll and Barry Alford, 42–60. Portsmouth: Heinemann/ Boynton- Cook. Print.

Yates, Tuppett M., Byron L. Egeland, and Alan Sroufe. 2003. Rethinking Resilience: A Developmental Process Perspective. In *Resilience and Vulnerability: Adaptation in the Context of Childhood Adversities*, ed. Suniya S. Luthar, 243–266. Cambridge: Cambridge University Press. Print.

Yeager, David S., and Gregory M. Walton. 2011. Social-Psychological Interventions in Education: They're Not Magic. *Review of Educational Research* 81(2): 267–301. Print.

Zamani-Gallaher, Eboni M., Jaime Lester, Debra D. Bragg, and Linda Hagerdorn (eds.). 2014. *ASHE Reader on Community Colleges*, 4th ed. New York: Pearson. Print.

Zook, George F. (ed.). 1947. *Higher Education for American Democracy: A Report of the President's Commission on Higher Education*, Vols I–VI. New York: Harper and Brothers. Print.

Zwerling, L. Steven (ed.). 1976. *Second Best: The Crisis of the Junior College*. New York: McGraw-Hill. Print.

——— (ed.). 1986. *The Community College and Its Critics*. San Francisco: Jossey-Bass. Print.

Index[1]

A
accountability, 181, 191, 312, 353, 393, 394
Acemoglu, Daron, 154, 155, 320, 380
achievement gap, 142, 157, 158, 234, 235
the actor and observer, 134–7
"actor's perspective," 2, 226, 379
adjunct faculty, 192, 387, 391
Alexievich, Svetlana, 4
American Association of Community Colleges (AACC), 153, 192, 233, 243, 376
"average" college student, 329

B
Baldwin, James, 372
Baptist, Edward, 185–7
Beckert, Sven, 187, 188, 190
Bourdieu, Pierre, 9, 10, 12, 161, 196–201, 203, 206, 212, 213, 215, 234, 258, 261, 320, 347, 380

C
capital, 9, 10, 41, 123, 161–3, 181, 197, 200–3, 205, 238, 292, 308, 384
"chance" and "choice," 178, 179, 237
child care, 389
choice, 35, 36, 48, 50, 61, 85, 90, 91, 96, 113, 129, 140, 147, 154, 170–2, 178–80, 190, 192, 203, 206, 207, 220, 227, 237, 239, 243, 256, 261, 268, 270, 284, 287, 300, 305, 312, 313, 320, 330, 346, 353, 380, 385, 395
Clark, Burton, 324, 332, 340, 343, 344, 346–50, 371
class, 9, 10, 20, 35, 39, 67, 69, 72, 81, 105, 106, 112, 119, 127, 128, 157, 159, 200, 211–20, 244–8, 254–9, 265, 266, 327, 358–60
Coleman Commission/Coleman Commission Report, 148, 158, 196, 206, 234, 235
collective beliefs, 318, 342, 346, 382
collectivism, 178

[1] Note: Page numbers followed by "n" denote endnotes.

college readiness, 212, 264, 269, 326, 350, 359
"the common good' is a meaningless concept," 288–90
community colleges, 1–13, 15–18, 33, 35–8, 57, 63, 67, 70–3, 91, 97–9, 101, 106, 107, 109, 115, 116, 121, 122, 132–42, 148, 149, 151, 153–6, 159, 162–4, 169, 173, 177, 185, 191–3, 197–9, 201, 206–11, 214, 220, 223–5, 228, 229, 232–4, 239–48, 262–4, 271n1, 286–8, 298, 302, 303, 312, 314–21, 323–6, 330–55, 358–72, 375–82, 385–92, 394–7
The Community College Success Stories Project, 3, 17, 199, 247, 379
Community College Survey of Student Engagement (CCSSE), 330, 331, 339, 388
Connecticut's Public Act 12–40, 214, 241–71
Coolidge, Calvin, 278
"cooling out function," 7, 324, 337, 343, 345, 347, 349
"cooling out" function of junior colleges, 7, 323, 340
"the country-clubization of the American university," 161
"courage to be utopian," 11, 321, 368, 381, 382
"cultural capital," 161, 196, 198–200, 258

D

deficit model, 3, 342, 344, 350, 355
deficit thinking, 341–2
defining student success, 17, 99, 131–42
"a deified market model," 168, 295–310, 390, 391

democracy, 1, 2, 6, 9–12, 18, 138, 145–8, 150, 151, 153–5, 162, 164–6, 168, 169, 173, 179, 184, 190, 201–3, 205, 206, 238, 248, 263, 270, 271, 276–8, 282, 284, 288, 289, 293, 295–7, 303, 306, 314–16, 318–21, 344, 375, 378, 380–3, 385, 397
democracy as a way of life, 364–72
democracy's college, 6, 248, 368, 381
democracy's unfinished business, 147, 206, 239, 242, 271
the Depression, 278–81, 283, 284
"deserving" students, 192, 243
developmental education, 5, 7, 10, 139, 163, 179, 197, 211, 214, 215, 224, 225, 241–71, 287, 288, 350, 352, 357–72, 377, 378, 394–6
development as freedom, 311–21, 380
Dewey, John, 370, 371
"the disposable student," 192
"the disposable worker," 192
Dweck, Carol, 224, 244–7, 265, 344

E

economic inequality, 6, 147, 172, 178, 192, 206, 207, 211, 219, 221, 223, 231, 242, 256, 277, 280, 282, 284, 298, 321, 346, 371, 376
economic inequality and higher education, 153–64
egalitarianism, 161, 162
Elliott, Jane, 226, 227
Empire of Cotton, 187, 188
equity, 5, 6, 9, 12, 13, 134, 145, 158, 232, 258, 263, 267, 298, 299, 303, 306, 314, 319, 321, 365, 369, 376, 380, 397
"experimenters," 338, 358
extractive economic institutions, 154

F

"failure" narrative about community colleges, 6, 342
family income and academic success, 148, 158, 159
family resources and academic success, 234–6
figures of speech, 236–40, 342
first-generation college students, 63, 67, 69, 217, 229, 232–4, 239, 331, 376
freedom, 11, 55, 125, 138–40, 150, 155, 166–73, 178–82, 184, 185, 191, 192, 195, 196, 216, 227, 236, 284, 285, 288, 289, 305, 308, 311–21, 365, 369, 380, 383, 391
Free To Choose, 178, 179, 181, 184, 185, 195, 203
Friedman, Milton, 150, 166, 168, 169, 177–88, 190, 191, 195, 196, 203, 205, 236–8, 291, 296, 313, 355, 370, 382

G

Gale, Trevor, 132, 133, 248
gatekeeper courses, 358
government, 16, 40, 42–5, 47, 51, 53, 76, 83, 84, 107, 146, 154, 166, 167, 169–71, 173, 177–82, 188, 190–2, 195, 202, 205, 229–32, 236, 276–8, 282–92, 297, 300, 302, 303, 316–18, 348, 383, 389, 393
"government is the problem," 190
graduation gap, 157
graduation rates, 4, 134, 137, 199, 239, 242, 256, 323, 326–8, 330, 336, 338, 339, 342, 344
"a great nation is a compassionate nation," 174, 265–7
The Great Transformation, 169, 190

H

The Half Has Never Been Told: Slavery and the Making of American Capitalism, 185
Harvey, David, 168, 181, 191, 192, 263
Hayek, F. A., 10, 11, 166–75, 177–9, 181, 184, 188, 190, 191, 205, 236–8, 284–8, 292, 296, 297, 300, 313, 318, 362, 365, 368–70, 381, 383
history, 4, 9, 47, 62, 75, 119, 121, 123, 136, 145, 146, 148–50, 153, 160, 162, 168, 182–5, 187, 188, 190, 199–202, 224, 225, 232, 235, 237, 241, 242, 245–8, 270, 275–93, 300–2, 325, 326, 349, 350, 357, 372, 375–8, 385, 397
Holmes, Oliver Wendell, Sr., 4
hope, 3, 4, 16–18, 31, 43, 47, 49, 53–6, 67, 73, 76, 96, 98, 99, 102, 104, 105, 127, 129, 147, 149, 154, 156, 167, 169, 231, 232, 243, 246, 261–4, 282, 325, 326, 331, 347, 348, 359, 378
"Hope Required When Growing Roses in Concrete," 261–4
the human brain, 221, 245, 246

I

"ideas of economists and political philosophers," 167
identity contingencies, 225–9
ideology(ies), 184, 218, 289, 300, 303, 315, 343, 395
I Know Why the Caged Bird Sings (Angelou, Maya), 279
"this imaginary universe of perfect competition," 9–11, 200, 237, 238
inclusive economic institutions, 153–6
"individual responsibility," 179, 286
"The Intellectuals and Socialism," 10, 168, 318, 383
intersubjectivity, 225

J

Jones, Edward E., 2, 135, 136, 226, 379

K

King, Martin Luther, Jr., 145, 151, 173, 267, 293, 320, 380

L

a learning society, 316–19
luck and chance, 205, 236–8

M

material conditions, 339
measuring student success, 9, 199, 255, 256, 330, 339, 349, 354
mindsets, 125, 207, 210, 224, 244, 245, 318, 342, 346, 382
The Minnesota Longitudinal Study of Risk and Adaptation, 223
Mont Pelerin Society (MPS), 166, 320, 370, 380, 383
"The Mother of All Questions" (Solnit, Rebecca), 140–2

N

narrative(s), 4, 6, 7, 10, 132, 133, 137, 140–2, 153, 183–7, 199, 241, 254, 262, 293, 311, 319, 341–55, 362, 363, 371, 393
negative function, 332
neoliberalism, 5, 10, 164–6, 169, 181, 191–3, 202, 237, 241–71, 296, 303, 304, 320, 355, 370, 383
neuroscience, 221–3, 244–6, 358
The New Deal, 170, 282
Nisbett, Richard E., 2, 135, 136, 226, 244, 379
"a nobler, cleaner capitalism," 187–91
non-traditional students, 325, 387

O

"observer's perspective," 2, 137, 226, 268, 379
old poverty, 275–84
open admissions institutions, 3, 4, 6, 7, 15, 16, 142, 159, 163, 197, 238, 240, 242, 244, 258, 288, 323–40, 342, 344, 350, 358, 380, 395, 396
open door, 2, 154, 241, 242, 246, 287, 351, 375, 376, 381, 396
opportunity differentials, 10, 172, 178, 195–203, 284, 289
opportunity gap, 235

P

parenting styles, 215–20
Parker, Stephen, 132, 133, 248
personal responsibility, 179, 191, 192, 199, 206, 227, 254, 287
Piketty, Thomas, 6, 151, 162, 163, 165, 168, 200–3, 231, 237, 320, 369, 380, 384
Polanyi, Karl, 169, 190
poor children, 217, 221, 223, 236
poor information, 304–10
the power of ideas, 11, 167, 168, 297, 300, 321, 369, 381, 383
"the power to narrate," 183, 341
privatization, 295, 296, 300, 306, 308, 311, 312, 320, 363, 370, 380, 383
the public good, 5–7, 9–12, 17, 140, 148, 149, 151, 154, 163, 164, 168, 169, 173, 175, 190–2, 263, 275–93, 295–9, 301–4, 307, 308, 310, 313, 314, 317, 318, 320, 321, 323, 355, 370, 371, 376, 380, 382, 383, 387

public policy(ies), 6, 11, 137, 151, 163–5, 167–71, 173–5, 177, 180, 184, 190, 193, 202, 214, 231, 238, 239, 260, 262, 267, 275, 277, 284–6, 295–7, 299–303, 305, 306, 313–18, 320, 321, 323, 380, 382, 383, 387
public purpose for higher education, 150

Q
"*The Quest for Peace and Justice*", 173

R
readicide, 260, 261
The Road To Serfdom, 166, 169, 170, 173, 181, 185, 284
Robinson, James, 154, 155, 320, 380
Roosevelt, Franklin, 170, 271, 280, 282, 375

S
Said, Edward, 6, 182, 183, 293, 341, 395, 396
scarcity, 206–11, 255–8, 260, 339, 397
school segregation, 342
"security against severe physical privation," 171–5
Sen, Amartya, 2, 134, 168, 271, 313–15, 320, 369, 379, 380
"a single story line," 140–2
slavery, 95, 150, 165–75, 181–8, 190, 315
social inequalities, 10, 107, 108, 161, 188, 222, 347
socialism, 165–75, 177, 188, 292, 293
"socialism means slavery," 165–75, 188

social justice, 2, 5, 6, 9, 11–13, 17, 134, 145, 148, 151, 154, 159, 162–4, 173, 175, 232, 267, 285–7, 295, 299, 303, 313, 319–21, 365, 369–71, 375, 376, 380, 383, 384, 397
social mobility, 156, 325
societal rigidities, 318, 342, 346, 382
socioeconomic status, 213, 222, 385
The Source of the River, 228, 229
state and federal housing policies, 229–32
state legislatures, 267–9, 332, 378
Steele, Claude M., 135–7, 225–8, 392
stereotype threat, 135, 225–9
Stiglitz, Joseph E., 6, 155, 156, 165, 168, 202, 297, 316–20, 342, 346, 369, 380, 382, 383
"student-present" research, 3–5
success, 2, 3, 8–11, 17, 27, 28, 31, 40, 56, 72, 73, 84, 97–9, 101, 104, 107, 118, 125, 126, 131–42, 148, 157–9, 161, 172, 196, 197, 199–201, 206, 208, 212, 214, 218, 223, 224, 229, 234–6, 238, 239, 247, 255, 256, 262, 264, 265, 268, 287, 288, 296, 316, 318, 321, 323–40, 347, 349, 350, 354, 358, 359, 361, 362, 364–7, 376, 379, 390, 392

T
transition "as becoming," 131–4
"trapped by categories," 2, 134, 378–9
Truman Commission, 138, 139, 146–9, 151, 154, 155, 158, 164, 168, 201, 239, 242, 243, 271, 315, 320, 371, 380

Truman Commission Report, 145–51, 154, 155, 163, 166, 236, 278, 316, 397
tyranny(ies), 167, 182, 183, 275, 288, 315

U
umpire, 178, 179
unfreedom, 146, 177–93, 236, 292, 313, 315
unprepared college students, 268, 325–6
unsureness, 329–32

V
vocabulary acquisition, 197, 211, 214, 258

W
"war capitalism," 188
wishful thinking, 268
working class children, 157, 211, 212, 214–17, 219–21
World War II, 75, 76, 145–7, 150, 151, 153, 156, 166, 202, 302, 320, 380